EISENHOWER CENTER STUDIES ON WAR AND PEACE

Stephen E. Ambrose *and* Günter Bischof, *editors*

EISENHOWER

EISENHOWER
A Centenary Assessment

EDITED BY

GÜNTER BISCHOF *and* STEPHEN E. AMBROSE

LOUISIANA STATE UNIVERSITY PRESS
Baton Rouge and London

Designer: Amanda McDonald Key
Typeface: Bembo
Typesetter: Moran Printing, Inc.
Printer and binder: Thomson-Shore, Inc.

Library of Congress Cataloging-in-Publication Data
Eisenhower: a centenary assessment/edited by Günter Bischof and
    Stephen E. Ambrose.
        p. cm.—(Eisenhower Center studies on war and peace)
    Includes bibliographical references (p.   ) and index.
    ISBN 0-8071-1942-3 (cl   :   alk. paper)
    1. Eisenhower, Dwight D. (Dwight David), 1890–1969.   2. World War,
    1939–1945—United States.   3. United States—Politics and
    government—1953–1961. I. Bischof, Günter, 1953– . II. Ambrose,
    Stephen E. III. Series.
    E836.E397 1995
    973.921'092—dc20   94-27045
                                                                      CIP

The paper in this book meets the guidelines for permanence and durability of the Committee on Production Guidelines for Book Longevity of the Council on Library Resources. ∞

To Dick Boebel and Ollie Brown

CONTENTS

ILLUSTRATIONS

following page 108

ACKNOWLEDGMENTS

The Eisenhower Center at the University of New Orleans is dedicated to the study of the life and times of General and President Dwight D. Eisenhower. We could not let the occasion of the centenary of Eisenhower's birthday pass without recognizing the achievements of a great American military and political figure. We decided to space the 1990 celebration out over the entire year and invited a number of distinguished Eisenhower scholars—old and young, American and European—to come to the University of New Orleans and give public lectures on important and interesting aspects of Eisenhower's distinguished career. No attempt was made to remember this towering figure in twentieth-century American history in only a laudatory fashion. In fact, some of the presentations were critical of Eisenhower, as the essays in this volume show. For the benefit of a broader audience, the lectures were updated and are presented here as an assessment of Eisenhower's life achievements.

The Eisenhower Center is fortunate to have a very generous and active board of directors. Ollie Brown (founding chair emeritus), Arthur Davis, Richard Stephens, Mary Mohs, Richard Holtz, John Dunlap, Donald Hoffman, Lee Schlesinger, and William Hines not only made the lecture series possible with their continuous support but also attended the lectures and social events around the lectures. Freeport-McMoRan, great corporate benefactor of the New Orleans area, as always contributed generously to our activities. The Louisiana Endowment for the Humanities supported the lecture series with a grant. We are grateful to Michael Sartisky and Kathryn Mettelka for their help in administering the grant, as well as Mary Louise Trammel of UNO's Research Division for helping us through the intimidating paper trail.

Our chairmen in the History Department, Gerald Bodet and Arnold Hirsch, were the most enthusiastic of supporters for this project, and our colleague Joseph Logsdon has guided us with a sympathetic critical eye. UNO's Metropolitan College and the Eisenhower Center staff worked together with their usual efficiency to make it all happen. Dean Robert Dupont has blessed the Eisenhower Center daily with his hands-on guidance; Gloria Alvarez and Barry Fosberg were instrumental on the publicity side; and Kathi Jones, Carolyn

Smith, Marissa Ahmed, Tracy Hernandez, and Maria Andara have been the superb Eisenhower Center staff who tirelessly attended to the innumerable details of the project. We are deeply indebted to two Eisenhower Center junior fellows: Olga Ivanova, who left Moscow right at the time of the summer 1991 coup attempt for graduate studies at UNO, compiled the bibliography; Gunther Breaux was very helpful with last-minute details for the completion of the manuscript and in the selection of the photos.

The Eisenhower Library's (Abilene, Kansas) audiovisual archivist Kathleen A. Struss was most generous as always in meeting our requests for almost instant reproduction of photo material.

At Louisiana State University Press, Les Phillabaum, Margaret Dalrymple, our production editor, Julie Schorfheide, and our copy editor, Jane Taylor, and their devoted staffs made the process of editing and production the pleasure we have come to take for granted from this first-rate academic press.

Linda Webster compiled the index with her usual thoroughness and dispatch. It has been a distinct pleasure working with these first-rate professionals on this project.

Our wives, Melanie Boulet (who gave birth to three vivacious children while this book was produced) and Moira Ambrose, have kept our spirits high with their loving support during this project. This book is dedicated to two great New Orleans pioneers in the oil patch who have a keen interest in history, especially military history. They are the kind of intense history buffs whose vast reading and impressive insights constantly astound the professional historian. Their unflagging support has been a constant inspiration to the success of the Eisenhower Center and our personal careers. We have appreciated Ollie Brown and Richard Boebel's encouragement and generosity for a long time.

FOREWORD
GENERAL ANDREW J. GOODPASTER, CHAIRMAN,
THE ATLANTIC COUNCIL

During the Eisenhower Centennial Year, which started with the anniversary of his birth on October 14, 1990, two things seemed to me particularly noteworthy:

First, there was a lift to the spirit and a sense of well-being, recaptured through sharing a moment with Dwight Eisenhower, even if only in memory. It was clear that for many millions of Americans, "I Like Ike" still held true.

Second, there was the experience of looking back once again to his presidency across the decades, to see more clearly what was done, and how and why, that bore his stamp and may hold lessons for us today. There were opportunities and impetus for further scholarly study, well reflected in these essays, both of the Eisenhower administration and of his own leadership.

It is of particular importance, in my view, to assess the goals he set for himself and for our country, the methods he chose for pursuing them, and the results that were achieved, within the United States and around the world. To what extent were the goals appropriate, the methods effective, and the results adequate when measured against the needs and issues of the time? How can our conclusions help us in understanding and acting on the problems of today and the future?

Change has come to be so sweeping in these times, both at home and abroad, that each decade takes on its own distinctive character. The 1950s, when Eisenhower was president, were no exception. As we look back, we see that decade as a period different in many ways from the tempestuous times that had gone before, and from those that followed. In retrospect, it was significant not so much for apocalyptic events such as marked the decades earlier and later—wars and domestic upheavals—as for their absence.

That absence distinguishes the Eisenhower years. For in his presidency there was no Bay of Pigs; no Cuban Missile Crisis; no prolonged U.S. fighting in Vietnam without the prerequisite hard top-level decisions; no Watergate; no Iran hostages; no abortive rescue attempt in the desert; no "Iran-gate" diversion of arms sales funds; no double-digit inflation; no multibillion budget deficit; no multibillion foreign trade deficit; no S&L financial scandal costing the taxpayer hundreds of billions; and no gridlock between the executive branch and Congress, denying the people of our country fiscally responsible handling of their government's financial affairs. We cannot know with certainty or in specific terms how Eisenhower would have handled such issues and events, or avoided them, but we do know that there was nothing comparable in his administration. Their absence should not go unnoticed.

It was not that tough problems were lacking, for in every area of the world the United States was faced with the unfinished business of World War II—tough, complicated issues, many involving harsh confrontation with the Soviet Union—in Trieste, Austria, West Germany and Berlin, Japan, and elsewhere. To those difficulties the postwar years soon added not only the military clash in Korea but new problems in the Middle East shaped by the Arab-Israeli conflict; the emergence of new, strife-torn states in Asia and Africa; and a wave of demands from the less-developed world for economic assistance and advancement. Difficult adjustments were required as a result of the death of Stalin, the accession of Khrushchev, the creation of thermonuclear arsenals, and the development of intercontinental missiles.

Problems were not lacking; what seems to have distinguished the period is the way they were dealt with. The characteristic response was to dampen and deflate them, rather than dramatizing or inflaming the issues, to check them and move them toward peaceable resolution, to confine and reduce their emotional impact on our people. President Eisenhower had a guiding, often determining hand in that process. One result was an interval sufficiently calm and quiet as to be disappointing at the time to those who looked for controversy and excitement, but an interval appreciated more and more during subsequent periods of excess.

Some scholars at the time thought they saw in Eisenhower a passivity that those of us who worked closely with him well knew was not the case. Their reaction may have resulted, at least in part, from a paucity of available documentary materials to support serious exploration. Compared to other administrations, there seems to have been less unauthorized "leaking" and disclosure of confidential, insider information by staff members or others with purposes of their own. Over time, the problem was materially eased as the papers at the Eisenhower Library were opened to the public. Scholars have often been surprised at what they learned—some of them frankly stating to me, "This is not the Eisenhower I thought I knew." The resulting reappraisal of his presidency has elevated him to the level shared by a handful of our most effective leaders.

He had come to the office with a background of unusual executive experience and responsibility. There was in him a deep awareness of the need to see that the great and dangerous challenges that confronted him, and affected our country for good or ill, were dealt with steadily, comprehensively, and continuously—with moderation and a wise sense of limits. Others in the legislative and political arenas might select particular issues on which to concentrate their attention and make their mark, picking and choosing the matters with which they would personally deal; but his was a wider concept of responsibility, reflected in the term *balance*, which he came to use more and more in his last year in office as he weighed conflicting needs and conflicting goals.

Shaping his *modus operandi* were the methods and mechanisms he set up to control and conduct executive branch action: the carefully delimited role and operating style of his White House staff; the kinds of people he called to serve as his chief assistants—his immediate advisers and his major cabinet officers; and the kinds of operating responsibilities he delegated to those who had the task of leading the government's principal executive departments and agencies in its day-to-day operations.

Eisenhower's characteristic method for conducting security affairs put heavy emphasis on orderly organization and systematic process. While he often emphasized that "organization cannot make a genius out of a dunce, nor make decisions for its head," he added that national security issues are so broad and complex that the president's principal role must take the form of directing and guiding the operating departments and agencies. One example, in the area of national security, may suggest the nature of the Eisenhower thought process behind the organizational forms he adopted. His National Security Council and its supporting committee and staff structure were primarily concerned with policy and long-range plans, which he used as the basic tools to guide his administration.

Operations, in contrast, were charged to the cabinet departments and executive agencies, along with coordinating committees. Issue-specific meetings were held in his own office, often off-the-record, to deal with such matters as intervention in Lebanon or the handling of the Suez in 1956. He kept the policy-planning function separate from his day-to-day operating decisions, recognizing that when policy and planning are combined with operations, the latter will always tend to dominate, to the detriment of perspective and long-range goals.

Beyond organization and process lay the issues themselves that he as president had to shape and confront, whether by offering guidance and setting goals and priorities or by taking personal charge through presidential action.

With the end of the Korean War came the need to reshape and restructure the armed forces. Out of his own experience, he set a budget level and laid down key guiding principles covering such things as the role of nuclear weapons, the need to plan for the long pull, and the need to plan from a unified national perspective rather than as separate military services. Looking ahead, he formally assigned "highest national priority" to the development of intercontinental ballistic missiles, which were to become a mainstay of strategic nuclear deterrence.

But later he repeatedly rejected proposals and public pressures—military, industrial, and congressional—to convert this effort into "crash programs" to fill a "missile gap" he knew was never there. While supporting NATO, he pressed for European moves toward integration and toward assumption of greater responsibilities for Europe's own defense.

A second task he set for himself was to establish the policy orientation of U.S. international relations, including in particular the policy we would follow toward the Soviet Union. Early in his administration he initiated a careful study, the Solarium project, to define a basic line of policy reflecting examination of three major possibilities: containment, rollback, and drawing a line. The outcome was a policy of containment accompanied by efforts to keep alive the hopes for freedom behind the Iron Curtain, but only by nonmilitary means, and it served as a basic guideline throughout his term of office.

The peaceful liberation of Eastern Europe that we have now seen would be to Eisenhower the fulfillment of his hopes. The fate of the people there was a deep and enduring concern throughout his presidency. His goals, as I saw them, were twofold. First, that these countries and their people should become free and, second, that this be accomplished in peace. To achieve those goals, several things in his view would be required, in which our country could and should be of help: that these people, in his words, should keep alive the burning desire to live in freedom, a freedom that we here have come almost to take for granted. Our hearts go out to them, he said, and we trust that they at last may have the opportunity to live under governments of their own choosing. A second requirement as he saw it was that the Soviet Union should with the passing years become willing to let these countries go. Again, in his words, "The day of liberation may be postponed where armed forces for a time make protest suicidal. But all history testifies that the memory of freedom is not arrested by the fear of guns, and the love of freedom is more enduring than the power of tyrants."

Strongly in favor of efforts to project abroad in a peaceful way the values of freedom and democracy central to our own society, he repeatedly rejected the proposals of "brushfire war" advocates, while finding ways to avoid being drawn into such conflicts. A basic aim with the Soviet Union was to shift away from military confrontation, and the summit meeting at Geneva in 1955, where he presented his Open Skies and exchange of blueprints proposal, was an important step in this new direction.

Deeply concerned over the world's growing thermonuclear arsenals, he established the office of Special Assistant for Disarmament—the first in U.S. history—and entered into serious dialogue with the Soviets on this issue. Throughout the Berlin crisis in 1958, he sought to act through diplomacy while holding fast to our support for West Berlin, finally obtaining Khrushchev's agreement at Camp David to lift the ultimatum he had earlier imposed.

As clearly as anyone else I have ever known, he saw the fundamental change that the introduction of thermonuclear weapons imposed. It affected the overall role and place of warfare in human affairs—and the need to find ways to maintain the security of our people, of our territory, and of our way of life and its values without the disaster of actual nuclear war.

Both at home and abroad, the working objectives President Eisenhower set for his administration and for the country were in my view worthy and sensible—true to America's traditions, interests, and values. And they were achieved to a creditable degree and in a creditable fashion. This was in no small measure due to his own leadership and direction. Frequently, he set the stage for discussion and debate with the deceptively simple question, "What's best for America?"

Knowing what he stood for, the American people held him in special regard. In his famous Guildhall speech to the British people after the end of World War II, he said something that was true in more ways than he probably realized at the moment: "I come from the heart of America."

Deeply imbedded in his makeup were his sense of duty and the deliberately reasoned decision process with which he had earlier exercised the responsibilities of high military leadership. Where other administrations might focus on presidential power, he put his emphasis on presidential responsibility. His farewell address opens with the words: "My fellow Americans: Three days from now, after half a century in the service of our country, I shall lay down the responsibilities of office."

To him, a crucial part of his duty as president was the obligation to promote among his fellow citizens some of the same sense of responsibility, seriousness, and restraint that he himself observed in dealing with the great and divisive issues that faced us at the time—particularly those issues where strong differences of interest or opinion existed.

He abhorred—in his phrase, "as the devil hates holy water"—the idea of inflaming or inciting passion and violence, particularly emotion that would set one person against another. He knew how quickly antagonism could turn into the destructive rage of the mob. Though we saw this anxiety most often in his concern about the domestic scene, he often cited it in the world arena as well, pointing out how easy it is to take countries down the road of deepening mutual hatred, how slow and painful is the course of reconciliation. The great admiration he expressed for Monnet, Schumann, de Gaulle, and Adenauer was a tribute to what he felt they had done to end the enmity of France and Germany after World War II.

The Eisenhower criteria—accentuation of the positive and constructive; accent on harmony and joint effort; good preparation and thorough deliberation; and confidence and optimism founded on realism and restraint—were well reflected in the shaping of events and conditions during his administration, both at home and abroad. Disappointments and setbacks there were, but overall, the international order had been strengthened, and the health of the American body politic was good.

How adequate were his criteria to the needs of our country? Here Dwight Eisenhower would have suggested, I believe, that in reaching our judgment, the proper standard is not perfection but practical possibility—in the words of our first president, "A standard to which the good and the wise may repair." In thought, word, and deed, he did much to show how that standard should be applied.

EISENHOWER

INTRODUCTION

For two decades, from 1942 to 1961, Dwight D. Eisenhower was a major world figure whose judgments and actions affected the lives of people everywhere, not to mention the fates of great nations. Because he played a central role for so long a period, his impact, contributions, successes, and failures will be subject to reinterpretation and debate so long as Western civilization lasts. His reputation has already undergone ups and downs and will continue to do so as new documentation becomes available and as scholars of the twenty-first century look on his career with the fresh eyes of those who were born since his death (1969) and grew up with the consequences of his decisions. This is the inevitable cycle of scholarship; along the lines of the adage "all history is contemporary history," the ever-changing contemporary scene allows fresh perspectives.[1] For example, Eisenhower's decision to stop at the Elbe River and avoid Berlin in 1945, leaving the city to the Red Army, looks much different in 1992 than it did only a decade earlier; so too his decision in 1956 to stay out of Central Europe during the Hungarian uprising, or to force a British-French retreat from Suez that same year. It is the essence of scholarship to look at old problems with new perspectives and, using new documentation or innovative methods, to arrive at new conclusions.

The one hundredth anniversary of Eisenhower's birth, October 14, 1990, set off an intense year-long reexamination of his place in history. The Eisenhower centennial provided the occasion for conferences on the general-president on his home turf in Abilene and Lawrence, Kansas, at Gettysburg College,[2] in Washington, D.C., as far away as Moscow, and elsewhere around the world. There were a number of commemorative publications.[3] The Eisenhower Center at the

1. For a valuable and complete annotated bibliography see R. Alton Lee, ed., *Dwight D. Eisenhower: A Bibliography of His Times and Presidency* (Wilmington, Del., 1991).

2. The conference papers are published in Shirley Anne Warshaw, *The Eisenhower Presidency* (Westport, Conn., 1992).

3. Michael Beschloss, *Eisenhower: A Centennial Life* (New York, 1990); Chester J. Pach, Jr., revised and expanded Elmo Richardson's *The Presidency of Dwight D. Eisenhower* (Lawrence, Kans., 1991); Stephen E. Ambrose, *Eisenhower: Soldier and President* (New York, 1990). See also the Eisenhower Centennial issues of *Kansas History*, XIII (1990); *Presidential Studies Quarterly*, XX (1990);

University of New Orleans, founded in 1983, sponsored a year-long series of lectures by established and younger scholars on the man and his times; these lectures are presented here as the Center's contribution to the ongoing process of assessing and revising Eisenhower's place in history.

Current reassessment of Eisenhower concentrates on his eight-year presidency, but it does not neglect his thirty-seven years as a professional soldier, or his youth.[4] The Eisenhower Library in Abilene, Kansas, regularly collects and opens new documentation, the most notable recently being his West Point letters to his high-school girlfriend Ruby Norman and the diary he kept in the Philippines in the late 1930s.

His performance in World War II is less subject to dramatic revisions than his presidential performance, mainly because most of the basic sources have been open for three decades. Still, scholars and armchair strategists will never cease reevaluating and arguing about his generalship. Controversy over such subjects as the Darlan Deal, the broad versus narrow front approach to the invasion of Hitler's Germany, Market-Garden, Berlin, and others will never end. More recently, his treatment of German prisoners of war at the end of World War II has come under heavy attack and has led to a lively scholarly debate.[5] As Supreme Commander, Allied Expeditionary Force, for Operation Overlord and in the ensuing campaign in Northwest Europe, Eisenhower commanded more firepower

---

Military Review, LXX (1990). See also Stephen E. Ambrose, ed., *The Wisdom of Eisenhower* (New Orleans, 1990).

4. Daniel F. Holt, on the basis of special access to Eisenhower's Philippines diaries, points to Mark W. Clark's crucial role in bringing Eisenhower back to the United States and to the attention of men like Marshall. See Holt, "An Unlikely Partnership and Service: Dwight D. Eisenhower, Mark Clark and the Philippines," *Kansas History,* XIII (1990), 149–65. Cole C. Kingseed stresses that Eisenhower was already recognized as one of the army's most brilliant staff officers prior to his meteoric rise during World War II. See Kingseed, "Eisenhower's Prewar Anonymity: Myth or Reality?" *Parameters,* XXI (Autumn, 1991), 87–98.

5. The Canadian novelist James Bacque blamed Eisenhower personally for orders that resulted in the death of some 700,000 German POWs. See Bacque, *Other Losses* (Los Angeles, 1991). For scholarly critiques of Bacque's principal charges against Eisenhower and the U.S. Army, as well as a close scrutiny of his methodology, see Günter Bischof and Stephen E. Ambrose, eds., *Eisenhower and the German P.O.Ws: Facts Against Falsehood* (Baton Rouge, 1992), and Arthur L. Smith, *Die 'vermisste Million': Zum Schicksal deutscher Kriegsgefangener nach dem Zweiten Weltkrieg* (Munich, 1992). For further critiques of Bacque's theses, see also Edward N. Peterson, *The Many Faces of Defeat: The German People's Experience in 1945* (New York, 1990); Wolfgang Benz and Angelika Schardt, eds., *Kriegsgefangenschaft* (Munich, 1991), 7–15.

with greater success than any other general in war. If Chief of Staff George C. Marshall was the "organizer of victory," Eisenhower may be considered "implementer of victory." Military historians and their readers being what they are, however, we can take it for granted that the already huge outpouring of books on General Eisenhower will continue and grow even further.[6]

Eisenhower's postwar period, although hardly as spectacular as when he was supreme commander, is more in need of further exploration. There is no monograph as yet on his crucial performance as the first U.S. military commander in occupied Germany in 1945, none on his service as Chief of Staff during the demobilization of the army, 1946–1947, nor on his Columbia University presidency. There is surprisingly little scholarship on his central role in the setting up of the NATO structure and shaping European and German rearmament as the SHAPE (Supreme Headquarters, Allied Powers Europe) commander.[7] The sources for these monographs are readily available, in the Eisenhower Library and in the magnificent volumes of *Eisenhower Papers* edited under the direction of Louis Galambos at Johns Hopkins University.[8]

By way of contrast, Eisenhower's 1952 campaign and his eight years as president have been extensively studied and written about. In the process, his reputation has undergone some startling shifts. Every president and his administration go through cycles of reevaluation, especially those who serve two full terms. This is a reflection of fuller access to the documentary record and shifting political perceptions.[9]

With Eisenhower, evaluation began immediately after he retired. The initial judgment, from journalists, professional pundits, and intellectuals, generally was

6. See, for example, Stephen E. Ambrose, *Eisenhower: Soldier, General of the Army, President-Elect, 1890–1952* (New York, 1983); David Eisenhower, *Eisenhower* (New York, 1986); Geoffrey Perret, *There's a War to Be Won: The United States Army in World War II* (New York, 1991); Eric F. Larrabee's "Eisenhower" in his magisterial *Commander in Chief: Franklin Delano Roosevelt, His Lieutenants, and their War* (New York, 1987), 412–508; Martin Blumenson, "Eisenhower Then and Now: Fireside Reflections," *Parameters*, XXI (Summer, 1991), 22–34. See also the recent biography by Robert F. Burke, *Dwight D. Eisenhower: Hero and Politician* (Boston, 1986).

7. For an ambitious new study on the genesis of NATO strategy through most of Eisenhower's stewardship in Paris and Washington, see Robert A. Wampler, "Ambiguous Legacy: The United States, Great Britain, and the Foundations of NATO Strategy, 1948–1957" (Ph.D. dissertation, Harvard University, 1991), and Timothy J. Botti, *The Long Wait: The Forging of the Anglo-American Nuclear Alliance, 1945–1958* (New York, 1987). See also the chapter by Thomas M. Sisk in this volume.

8. Louis Galambos *et al.*, eds., *The Papers of Dwight D. Eisenhower* (Baltimore, Md., 1975–89), Vols. VI–XIII.

9. The reevaluation of the Eisenhower presidency has already produced a number of rich scholarly collections of essays. See Richard M. Melanson and David Mayers, eds., *Reevaluating Eisenhower:*

overwhelmingly negative. By the mid-1980s, when Eisenhower's scholarship had become dominated by political scientists and historians, broadly labeled as revisionists, the judgment was overwhelmingly positive. By the early 1990s, a younger set of scholars, coming under the rubric of postrevisionists, concluded that, while Eisenhower was not nearly so bad as his first critics had said, neither was he quite so good as the revisionists had presented him. In short, this is the familiar cycle of thesis, antithesis, synthesis—except that there can never be a final judgment, so the process will continue.[10]

By now the typical historiographical sketch of the Eisenhower presidency is a familiar one.[11] In the view of contemporary pundits and writers, Eisenhower was an ineffective, do-nothing president. In their opinion, the fifties was a decade of "the bland leading the bland." The contrast between the activist presidencies of Franklin D. Roosevelt and Harry S Truman and Eisenhower's apparent refusal to lead struck not only journalists and Democratic politicians but historians as well. A national poll of academic historians, taken shortly after Eisenhower left office, placed him nearly at the bottom of the list of all presidents. (The popular judgment was entirely different; the American people in 1961, according to Gallup polls, rated Eisenhower consistently first or second among American presidents.)[12] Representative of the intellectuals' condescending views of Eisenhower was Norman Mailer's preposterous statement that the 1950s was "one of the worst decades in the history of man."[13] Mailer said that about a decade in which—for the last time—both gross national product and real wages went up while inflation stayed below 2 percent and the federal budget was either

---

American Foreign Policy in the Fifties (Urbana, Ill., 1987); Joann P. Krieg, ed., *Dwight D. Eisenhower: Soldier, President, Statesman* (Westport, Conn., 1987); Richard H. Immerman, ed., *John Foster Dulles and the Diplomacy of the Cold War* (Princeton, N.J., 1990).

10. An insightful analysis of this familiar cycle of scholarship is John Lewis Gaddis' famous essay, "The Emerging Post-Revisionist Synthesis on the Origins of the Cold War," *Diplomatic History,* VII (1983), 171-90.

11. For good recent syntheses of the historiographical cycle of Eisenhower scholarship, see Stephen G. Rabe, "Eisenhower Revisionism: A Decade of Scholarship," *Diplomatic History,* XVII (1993), 97-115; Richard H. Immerman, "Confessions of an Eisenhower Revisionist: An Agonizing Reappraisal," *Diplomatic History,* XIV (1990), 319-40; Immerman, ed., *Dulles and the Diplomacy of the Cold War,* 3-20; Alan Brinkley, "A President for Certain Seasons," *Wilson Quarterly,* XIV (1990), 110-19; Melanson and Mayers, eds., *Reevaluating Eisenhower,* 1-10; William Howard Moore, "Do We 'Like Ike'?" *Kansas History,* XIII (1991), 190-97; Joachim Arenth, "Das Phänomen des Eisenhower-Dulles-Revisionismus, 1953-1993." For a useful bibliographical summary, see Pach and Richardson, *Eisenhower,* 263-72.

12. Beschloss, *Eisenhower: A Centennial Life,* 215.

13. Mailer quoted in Lance Morrow, "Dreaming of the Eisenhower Years," *Time,* July 28, 1980, p. 33.

balanced (three of the eight years) or nearly so; a decade in which the nation fought no wars, lost no territory, and contained the Communists in Europe and Southeast Asia; a decade that saw the building of the St. Lawrence Seaway and the Interstate highway system, and began the process of desegregation in American schools and public life, and otherwise moved forward. For a majority of Americans, the 1950s was the best decade of the century.[14]

After living with Eisenhower's successors, even intellectuals and partisan Democrats began to realize that simple truth. The upheavals of the sixties led Americans to look back on the Eisenhower years as a better age, even a "golden age." Contrasting Eisenhower with John F. Kennedy, Lyndon Johnson, and Richard M. Nixon, instead of with Roosevelt and Truman, made Eisenhower look much better. Beginning with Murray Kempton's influential article in *Esquire* in 1967, on the underestimation of Eisenhower, the pendulum started to swing.[15] seen from the perspective of foreign policy, as Robert Divine, one of the early revisionists, has observed, "In the aftermath of Vietnam, it can be argued that a President who avoids involvement in the internal affairs of other nations deserves praise rather than scorn."[16] Viewed from the domestic arena, as Richard Immerman, a leading revisionist, has written, "In contrast to the Kennedyesque ideal of the 1960's, in the post-Vietnam, post-stagflation era, Eisenhower's restraint and penny-pinching ways appeared more positive."[17]

Simultaneously, with the changed judgments based on seeing how well (or how badly) Eisenhower's successors handled the problems of a postindustrial society caught in a cold war, the Eisenhower Library began opening the documentary record (most especially the Ann Whitman Files of Eisenhower's personal papers, minutes of meetings with the cabinet and congressional leaders, memorandums of Oval Office conferences, Dulles' personal papers, and much more); a number of highly revealing collections of private Eisenhower diaries and letters appeared, as did memoirs and diaries from his family and associates.[18] This

14. David Halberstam, *The Fifties* (New York, 1993); William L. O'Neill, *American High: The Years of Confidence, 1945–1960* (New York, 1986); John Patrick Diggins, *The Proud Decades: America in War and Peace, 1941–1960* (New York, 1988). For a more critical view of the self-righteous 1950s and its oppressive domestic culture of anti-Communism, see Stephen J. Whitfield, *The Culture of the Cold War* (Baltimore, Md., 1991).

15. Murray Kempton, "The Underestimation of Dwight Eisenhower," *Esquire,* September, 1968, pp. 108–109, 156.

16. Robert A. Divine, *Eisenhower and the Cold War* (New York, 1981), 154.

17. Immerman, ed., *Dulles and the Diplomacy of the Cold War,* 6.

18. Robert H. Ferrell, ed., *The Eisenhower Diaries* (New York, 1981); Robert Griffith, ed., *Ike's Letters to a Friend, 1941-1958* (Lawrence, Kans.,1984); Robert H. Ferrell, ed., *The Diary of James C.*

led to a "boomlet of Eisenhower studies." [19] Some were negative, especially when it came to Eisenhower's handling of the problem of Senator Joseph R. McCarthy, the anti-Communist crusade, civil liberties, and sexual politics,[20] and on his civil rights policies,[21] but most were complimentary and sympathetic, especially on his defense and foreign policies.[22] Perhaps the most notable feature of the revisionist scholarship, however, was the universal conclusion that Eisenhower was very much in command. No one could spend even one day with the documents and deny it. He did not leave domestic policy to his chief of staff, Sherman Adams, or foreign policy to his secretary of state, John Foster Dulles, or defense policy to his secretary of defense, Charles Wilson.[23] Eisenhower ran the show. Whether the scholars approved of the policies of the Eisenhower administration or disapproved, they agreed that those policies were Eisenhower's.

The most influential of the revisionists was Fred I. Greenstein, political scientist at Princeton University and author of the 1982 book *The Hidden-Hand Presidency*. In Greenstein's view, Eisenhower was a dynamic, activist chief executive.[24] George H. Quester went as far as calling Eisenhower a "political genius"

Hagerty: Eisenhower in Mid-Course, 1954-1955 (Bloomington, Ind., 1983); Kenneth W. Thompson, ed., *The Eisenhower Presidency: Eleven Intimate Perspectives of Dwight D. Eisenhower* (Lanham, Md., 1984); John S. D. Eisenhower, *Strictly Personal* (Garden City, N.Y., 1974); Milton S. Eisenhower, *The President Is Calling* (Garden City, N.Y., 1974); Henry Cabot Lodge, *As It Was: An Inside View of Politics and Power in the '50s and '60s* (New York, 1976).

19. Moore, "Do We 'Like Ike'?" 193.

20. Jeff Broadwater, *Eisenhower and the Anti-Communist Crusade* (Chapel Hill, N.C., 1992), and Gary Reichard's review of it, "Seeing Red: Eisenhower, the Republicans, and the Anticommunist Consensus," *Reviews of American History*, XXI (1993), 482–87; Günter Bischof, "Before the Break: The Relationship Between Eisenhower and McCarthy, 1952–1953" (M.A. thesis, University of New Orleans, 1980); John D'Emilio, "The Homosexual Menace: The Politics of Sexuality in Cold War America," in *Passion and Power: Sexuality in History*, ed. Kathy Peiss and Christina Simmons (Philadelphia, 1989). More complimentary of Eisenhower's handling of McCarthy are Fred I. Greenstein, *The Hidden-Hand Presidency: Eisenhower as Leader* (New York, 1982), and William Bragg Ewald, Jr., *Who Killed Joe McCarthy?* (New York, 1984).

21. Robert F. Burke, *The Eisenhower Administration and Black Civil Rights* (Knoxville, Tenn. 1984), and Robert F. Burke, "Dwight D. Eisenhower and Civil Rights: Reflections on a Portrait in Caution," *Kansas History*, XIII (1990), 178–90.

22. Douglas Kinnard, *President Eisenhower and Strategy Management* (Lexington, Ky., 1977); Burton I. Kaufman, *Trade and Aid: Eisenhower's Foreign Economic Policy, 1953–1961* (Baltimore, Md., 1982); Stephen E. Ambrose, *Eisenhower: The President* (New York, 1984); Gary W. Reichard, *Politics as Usual: The Age of Truman and Eisenhower* (Arlington Heights, Ill., 1988).

23. For a different perspective, trying to resurrect Dulles' single-handed foreign policy leadership, see Frederick W. Marks III, *Power and Peace: The Diplomacy of John Foster Dulles* (Westport, Conn., 1993).

24. Fred I. Greenstein, "Eisenhower as an Activist President: A New Look at New Evi-

and argued that the "Eisenhower style of charade and deliberate obfuscation" was shrewd politics, which fooled contemporaries as to who was in charge, but not later scholars.[25]

William Howard Moore has recently argued in a fine historiographical review essay on the Eisenhower presidency that the zenith of Eisenhower revisionism may well have been reached with Robert Griffith's work on Eisenhower's "Corporate Commonwealth" and John Lewis Gaddis' fine synthesis of his containment policy.[26] One can agree with Moore's judgment and add that McGeorge Bundy's judicious and sympathetic analysis of Eisenhower's deep immersion and pained grappling with nuclear weapons and deterrence theory made him the first American president to define a successful national security policy and strategy in the nuclear age; Bundy's superb analysis may well constitute the monumental achievement of sophisticated Eisenhower revisionism.[27]

Partly in reaction to what may have been the excessive enthusiasm of the scholars of the late seventies and early eighties for Eisenhower, partly as a result of even more of the record becoming available, a new scholarship began to emerge in the late 1980s. Chester J. Pach, Jr., has summarized the arguments of this new "postrevisionist" scholarship: "The Eisenhower presidency was more complex and not as successful as many revisionists have maintained"; on the other hand, "It also accepts the argument that Eisenhower was a thoughtful and skillful leader."[28] Under this definition English author Piers Brendon, in his 1986 biography of Eisenhower, was not so much postrevisionist as a throwback.[29] He portrayed Eisenhower in much the same light as Eisenhower's intellectual contemporaries, in spite of the benefit of the full archival record.

More serious and important, but detached, was the work of younger scholars, born during Eisenhower's presidency or later, and thus uninvolved as partisan participants, yet in their intellectual development very much affected by

---

dence," *Political Science Quarterly,* LXXXIV (1979–80), 575–99; Greenstein, *The Hidden-Hand Presidency.*

25. George H. Quester, "Was Eisenhower a Genius?" *International Security,* III (1979), 159–79.

26. Robert Griffith, "Dwight D. Eisenhower and the Corporate Commonwealth," *American Historical Review,* LXXXVII (1982), 87–122; John Lewis Gaddis, *Strategies of Containment: A Crtical Appraisal of Postwar American National Security Policy* (New York, 1982), especially chapters 4, 5, and 11. For further refinement of Gaddis' theses, see also his *The Long Peace: Inquiries into the History of the Cold War* (New York, 1987). See Moore, "Do We 'Like Ike'?" 195–96.

27. McGeorge Bundy, *Danger and Survival: Choices About the Bomb in the First Fifty Years* (New York, 1988), chapters 6 and 7.

28. Pach and Richardson, *Eisenhower,* xiii.

29. Piers Brendon, *Ike: His Life and Times* (New York, 1986).

the upheavals of the sixties and seventies. They brought new strength to their studies; they had the revisionists' scholarship to build on and to react to; their view of the cold war, especially after the demise of the Soviet empire in 1989 and the Soviet Union in 1991, was less polarized by traditional cold war *mentalités* and more objective; some of them added a valuable non-U.S. perspective;[30] they had access to National Security Council files and to newly published volumes of *Foreign Relations of the United States* from State Department historians, especially for the first term. Out of this came postrevisionism, critical of Eisenhower not so much on the old issues, such as civil rights or McCarthyism, as on his foreign and defense policies.

The revisionists had praised Eisenhower for his calibrated New Look national security strategy and his restraint on the arms race, for example, resting their case on the way in which he had refused to cave in to contemporary hawks, both Democrat and Republican (as exemplified by Kennedy's 1960 campaign charge that Eisenhower had allowed a "missile gap" to develop because of his commitment to a balanced budget), and on the vast increase in defense spending under his successors. But H. W. Brands, in 1990, charged that Eisenhower's New Look policy was never fully implemented due to Pentagon resistance; his giving in to demands both for more conventional and nuclear weapons showed that he could not control the Pentagon, that he based "American security on possession of the latest scientific and military technology" and thereby "surrendered to the defense bureaucrats" and "promoted the growth of the military-industrial complex," and that he fueled the cold war with his "overblown rhetoric."[31] In a similar vein, David Alan Rosenberg had charged even before the coming of postrevisionism that Eisenhower was not able to contain the air force's "bootstrapping," the mul-

---

30. See, for example, Peter G. Boyle, ed., *The Churchill-Eisenhower Correspondence, 1953–1955* (Chapel Hill, N.C., 1990); the essays in Michael Dockrill and John W. Young, eds., *British Foreign Policy, 1945–56* (London, 1989); Rolf Steininger, *The German Question: The Stalin Note of 1952 and the Problem of Reunification* (New York, 1990); Günter Bischof, "The Western Powers and Austrian Neutrality," *Mitteilungen des Österreichischen Staatsarchivs,* XLII (1992), 368–93; Saki Dockrill, "Eisenhower's New Look: A Maximum Deterrent at a Bearable Cost: A Reappraisal," in *Economic and Nonrational Dimensions in Strategy,* ed. Michael Handel (Carlisle Barracks, Pa., forthcoming); Saki Dockrill, "The United States' Alliance Diplomacy for the Security of Western Europe, 1953–54," *Diplomacy and Statecraft,* V (1994), 138–82. See also Saki Dockrill, *Britain's Policy for West German Rearmament, 1950–1955* (New York, 1991). See also Martin Beglinger, *Containment im Wandel: Die amerikanische Aussen- und Sicherheitspolitik im Übergang von Truman zu Eisenhower* (Stuttgart, 1988).

31. H. W. Brands, Jr., "The Age of Vulnerability: Eisenhower and the National Insecurity State," *American Historical Review,* XCIV (1989), 963–89; Brands's views were challenged by R. Gordon Hoxie in "Dwight David Eisenhower: Bicentennial Considerations," *Presidential Studies Quarterly,* XX (1990), 253–64. As already mentioned, McGeorge Bundy gave Eisenhower high marks for his nuclear strategy and defense policies; see Bundy, *Danger and Survival,* 236–357.

tiplication of targets in the Soviet Union leading to a proliferation of nuclear weapons and thus an "overkill" nuclear capacity and a general acceleration of the arms race.[32] Steven Metz criticizes Eisenhower's New Look strategy for never preparing "for lesser military actions short of all-out war" and for "postponing difficult strategic decisions rather than confronting them."[33] Saki Dockrill has shown the manifold frustrations experienced by the Eisenhower administration in trying to achieve their goals in Europe—both in the German question and in applying the New Look strategy to the NATO area. Matthew Evangelista accused Eisenhower of ignoring unilateral Soviet conventional disarmament and using disarmament largely for propaganda purposes.[34]

There is much talk among postrevisionists about "lost opportunities"— Dulles being more often blamed for the rigidity of Eisenhower's policy vis-à-vis the Soviet Union than Eisenhower.[35] Postrevisionists are chiding Eisenhower for his refusal to listen to Winston Churchill's pleadings for entering into serious negotiations with Soviet leaders to ease tensions in the cold war, and perhaps even bringing on earlier German reunification.[36] In his review essay on the *Churchill-Eisenhower Correspondence,* John Lukacs has been most outspoken for blaming Eisenhower and a "sinister" Dulles for "potentially missed historic opportunities" to bring about an era of détente with the new Kremlin leadership after Stalin's death.[37]

It is something of a paradox that postrevisionists have concluded that Secretary of State Dulles was a more complex figure than commonly believed, that he

32. David Alan Rosenberg, "The Origins of Overkill: Nuclear Weapons and American Strategy, 1945–1960," *International Security,* VII (1983), 3–71.

33. Steven Metz, "Eisenhower and the Planning of American Grand Strategy," *Journal of Strategic Studies,* XIV (1991), 49–71 (esp. 54–66).

34. Matthew Evangelista, "Cooperation Theory and Disarmament Negotiations in the 1950s," *World Politics,* XLII (1990), 502–528; for an opposite view see Robert A. Strong, "Eisenhower and Arms Control," in *Reevaluating Eisenhower,* ed. Melanson and Mayers, 241–66.

35. Representative for this view is W. W. Rostow's statement, "Dulles is generally portrayed as the hard-hearted cold warrior, resisting and then diluting the decent and generous impulses of his chief, arguing against summitry" (Rostow, *Europe After Stalin: Eisenhower's Three Decisions of March 11, 1953* [Austin, Tex., 1982], 78).

36. Steininger, *The German Question,* 100–112; Günter Bischof, "Österreichische Neutralität, die deutsche Frage und europäische Sicherheit, 1953–1955," in *Die doppelte Eindämmung: Europäische Sicherheit und deutsche Frage in den Fünfzigern,* ed. Rolf Steininger et al. (Munich, 1993), 133–76. W. W. Rostow also makes a case for "lost opportunities" in *Europe after Stalin,* 69–83.

37. John Lukacs adds that the *Churchill-Eisenhower Correspondence,* edited by Peter Boyle, provides "ample evidence for the need to revise the lately fashionable academic approbation of Eisenhower's statesmanship." See his "Ike, Winston and the Russians," *New York Times Book Review,* February 10, 1991, pp. 3, 26–27.

was prepared to negotiate with the Russians, and that he was realistic about the limits of American power.[38] Nevertheless, as with recent critiques of the shortcomings of Truman's Third World policies,[39] the postrevisionists are critical of the Eisenhower administration for failing to understand or appreciate the power of nationalism in the emerging colonial world in Africa, the Middle East, and Asia, and for simple-minded confusing of nationalism and Communism.[40] "From a long-term perspective," charges Steven Metz, "Eisenhower's inability to understand revolution, nonalignment, and nationalism in the Third World was the most corrosive shortcoming of the New Look."[41]

Overall, however, the younger generation of scholars have done some of their best work on the involvement of the Eisenhower administration in the Third World, seeing the president and his secretary of state as sophisticated and realistic policy makers regarding Third World problems. Eisenhower and Dulles understood the dilemmas of decolonization but found it difficult to extricate themselves from the containment framework because of domestic pressures and the relentless engagement of Moscow and Peking, as the Communist leaders continued to meddle in the Third World, and because of the unrealistic expectations of Third World leaders in their requests (blackmail?) for military and economic aid to stop the Communists in their countries.

38. See especially the essay by John Lewis Gaddis, "The Unexpected John Foster Dulles: Nuclear Weapons, Communism, and the Russians," in *Dulles and the Diplomacy of the Cold War,* ed. Immerman, 63–74. Similarly, Ronald Pruessen paints a much more open and sophisticated approach by Eisenhower and Dulles to the Geneva Summit than has hitherto been maintained; see his "Beyond the Cold War—Again: 1955 and the 1990s," *Political Science Quarterly,* CVIII (1993), 59–84.

39. What Melvyn P. Leffler has written of the Truman administration and the Third World by and large is also an often heard critique of Eisenhower's handling of the Third World crises: "U.S. officials exaggerated the ability of the Soviet Union to capitalize on the rising tide of nationalism in the Third World and incorrectly assessed the relationships between most Third World Communists and Moscow . . . indiscriminate anticommunism that generally characterized U.S. policy everywhere in the Third World. . . . U.S. officials wanted to isolate, discredit, and eliminate Communist factions rather than maneuver to loosen their alleged ties to Moscow or to convince them of the openness of U.S. policy. . . . So obsessed were U.S. officials about the Communist threat in the Third World areas that they frequently confused nationalism and indigenous discontent with externally supported Communist movements. . . . Throughout the Third World, the United States established linkages with discredited elites who, in pursuit of their own ends, were willing to work with the Americans (as they had often done with the British and French)." See his magisterial, prizewinning *A Preponderance of Power: National Security, the Truman Administration, and the Cold War* (Stanford, Calif., 1992), 508–509.

40. Robert J. McMahon, "Eisenhower and Third World Nationalism: A Critique of the Revisionists," *Political Science Quarterly,* CI (1986), 453–73. For Latin America, see Stephen G. Rabe, *Eisenhower and Latin America* (Chapel Hill, N.C., 1988).

41. Metz, "Eisenhower and American Grand Strategy," 64.

India is an interesting test case for postrevisionist studies, as both Dennis Merrill and H. W. Brands demonstrate. Merrill has stressed that U.S. policy toward India "abounded with contradictions." The Eisenhower administration was skeptical of India's neutral posture in the cold war and gave preferential treatment in the dispersal of aid to authoritarian regimes such as South Korea, Formosa, and South Vietnam. The United States saw India as a model democratic nation in the Third World but resented Nehru's independent neutral course in the East-West confrontation. Merrill charges that United States foreign policy makers often failed to allow for greater flexibility in their aid programs "because of their exaggerated fear of communism, their tendency to underestimate the power of nationalism in India and other non-Western nations, and their serious misreading of regional politics"; he adds, "All too often American leaders lacked historical perspective needed to gauge the vast political, economic, and ideological gaps that separated India and the United States." As they downplayed "that country's history, its unique customs, and its rigid socioeconomic hierarchy, they usually encouraged the adoption of American-style capitalism in India." [42]

Among the postrevisionists, "neutralism" no longer is the dirty word that it had been among earlier critics of Eisenhower and Dulles. H. W. Brands contests the notion of contemporaries and traditionalist historians alike that Eisenhower and Dulles could not stomach neutralism. In a perceptive study that represents the best of postrevisionism, Brands demonstrates that despite their anti-neutralist rhetoric, Dulles and Eisenhower had considerable insights into and flexibility in their approach to Third World neutralism. In his case studies of U.S. policy toward Iran, Yugoslavia, and Egypt, Brands comes to the conclusion that "appearances deceived." U.S. policy makers in the Truman and Eisenhower administrations may often have "*spoken* in ideological terms," but they "tended to *act* in a remarkably non-ideological fashion." Brands concludes, "They commonly packaged their policies in the wrappings of ideology; but the product they sold reflected primarily a geopolitical interpretation of American strategic, military, diplomatic, and economic interests, and demonstrated a shrewd weighing of the effects on the international balance of power of the particular activities of specific nonaligned countries. . . . They bootlegged Bandung in Yalta bottles." [43]

42. Dennis Merrill, *Bread and the Ballot: The United States and India's Economic Development, 1947–1963* (Chapel Hill, 1989), 205–207.

43. H. W. Brands, Jr., *The Specter of Neutralism: The United States and the Emergence of the Third World, 1947–1960* (New York, 1989), 9. Brands had already argued the case for a more complex Dulles and a more sophisticated Eisenhower foreign policy process in his interesting prosopography of Ike's lieutenants in the making of foreign policy. See Brands, *Cold Warriors: Eisenhower's Generation and American Foreign Policy* (New York, 1988).

Postrevisionism is more critical of Eisenhower's policy toward Vietnam. David Anderson charges that "the Eisenhower Administration simply postponed the day of reckoning in Vietnam," and insists that support for South Vietnam after the 1954 Geneva Accords was "an example of flawed containment. U.S. strategy was negative. It sought to hold off defeat and wait for a better day with little regard for the internal dynamics of Vietnamese society." [44]

There is much more going on in the field of recent postrevisionist Eisenhower studies, including the work of Robert M. Spaulding on export controls, Diane Kunz on his economic diplomacy in the Suez crisis of 1956, Rosemary Foot on the Korean armistice negotiations, and Melanie Billings-Yun on the Dien Bien Phu crisis of 1954.[45] The study of Eisenhower's foreign policy is also benefiting from a number of fine bilateral studies critically analyzing Eisenhower's record from the perspective of foreign archival holdings. Isaac Alteras' monograph on U.S.-Israeli relations covers an important gap in the literaure; Oliver Rathkolb's study of U.S.-Austrian relations, as well as Hermann-Josef Rupieper and Detlef Felken's exhaustive books on U.S.-German relations in the 1950s and Joachim Arenth's study of the second Berlin crisis are contributions of a younger generation of foreign scholars in the best tradition of international history.[46] The study of nuclear crises such as the one over the Taiwan Strait in 1954 has received much critical attention, as has Eisenhower's use of the CIA in covert operations—a favorite of the revisionists also.[47] In fact, Richard Immerman and Blanche Wiesen Cook's pathbreaking works on Eisenhower and

44. David L. Anderson, *Trapped by Success: The Eisenhower Administration and Vietnam, 1953–61* (New York, 1991), xiii–xiv. See also the review article on Vietnam by Robert A. Divine, "Vietnam Reconsidered," *Diplomatic History*, XII (1988), 79–93.

45. Robert Mark Spaulding, Jr., "Eisenhower and Export Control Policy, 1953–1955," *Diplomatic History*, XVII (1993), 223–49; Diane B. Kunz, *The Economic Diplomacy of the Suez Crisis* (Chapel Hill, N.C., 1991); Rosemary Foot, *A Substitute for Victory: The Politics of Peacemaking at the Korean Armistice Talks* (Ithaca, N.Y., 1990); Melanie Billings-Yun, *Decision Against War: Eisenhower and Dien Bien Phu., 1954* (New York, 1988).

46. Isaac Alteras, *Eisenhower and Israel: U.S.-Israeli Relations, 1953–1960* (Gainesville, Fla., 1993); Oliver Rathkolb, "Grossmachtpolitik gegenüber Österreich 1952/63–1961/62 im U.S. Entscheidungsprozess" (Vienna, forthcoming). Hermann-Josef Rupieper's very thorough study of American-German relations, *Der besetzte Verbündete: Die amerikanische Deutschlandpolitik, 1949–1955* (Opladen, 1991); Detlef Felken, *Dulles und Deutschland: Die amerikanische Deutschlandpolitik, 1953–1959* (Bonn, 1993); Joachim Arenth, *'Der Western tut nichts!' Transatlantische Kooperation während der zweiten Berlin-Krise (1958–1962)* (Frankfurt am Main, 1993).

47. See, for example, H. W. Brands, Jr., "Testing Massive Retaliation: Credibility and Crisis Management in the Taiwan Strait," and Gordon H. Chang, "To the Nuclear War Brink: Eisenhower, Dulles, and the Quemoy-Matsu Crisis," *International Security*, XII (1988), 96–151.

the CIA, although they predated postrevisonism, were highly critical of his use of the agency for covert action in the Third World.[48]

A collective volume such as this is bound to be highly selective by nature. These essays do not pretend to cover every aspect of Eisenhower's remarkable career, nor are they designed to achieve balance in terms of domestic and foreign policy aspects of the Eisenhower presidency. In fact, crucial questions of domestic politics, such as Eisenhower's management of the economy and labor, his skills as a communicator in dealing with the press, and his handling of McCarthy, are not covered.[49] The collection aims to be representative, however, of the full sweep of Eisenhower scholarship, both revisionist and postrevisionist. The essays try to present an intimate approach to Eisenhower historiography and his role as military commander, particularly in the first section of the book, written by three giants in the field, complemented by a younger scholar.

In Section I on historiography, Forrest Pogue, the *éminence grise* in American military history on World War II, shows how Eisenhower was interested early on in seeing the history of the remarkable successes of Anglo-American alliance in Northwest Europe in the years 1944–1945 written from a scholarly perspective. Eisenhower gave the talented young Pogue all the help and contacts he needed to write *The Supreme Command,* a history that has withstood the tests of later scholarship uniquely well. Pogue's essay not only gives us an intimate perspective on the genesis of one of the great books on World War II military history but also is a highly revealing piece of a young historian's brushes with great men such as de Gaulle and Montgomery, and his self-discovery in the throes of Anglo-American warfare over constructing the pantheon of World War II military heroes.

If Pogue's essay is an eye-opener in the historiography on Eisenhower's World War II role, Fred I. Greenstein's essay traces a similar personal journey for Eisenhower's presidency. It is the tale of the genesis of Eisenhower "revisionism" as seen through the eyes of its foremost practitioner. M. R. D. Foot—the historian

48. Blanche Wiesen Cook, *The Declassified Eisenhower: A Divided Legacy* (Garden City, N.Y., 1981); Richard H. Immerman, *The CIA in Guatemala: The Foreign Policy of Intervention* (Austin, Tex., 1982); John Prados, *Presidents' Secret Wars: CIA and Pentagon Covert Operations Since World War II* (New York, 1986).

49. For solid recent studies of these issues, see John Sloan, *Eisenhower and the Management of Prosperity* (Lawrence, Kans., 1991); Raymond J. Saulnier, *Constructive Years: The U.S. Economy Under Eisenhower* (Lanham, Md., 1991); Martin J. Medhurst, *Dwight D. Eisenhower: Strategic Communicator* (Westport, Conn., 1992); R. Alton Lee, *Eisenhower and Landrum-Griffin: A Study in Labor-Management Politics* (Lexington, Ky., 1990); Broadwater, *Eisenhower and the Anti-Communist Crusade*.

of SOE, British counterintelligence operations during World War II—presents a British perspective on Eisenhower's crucial role in forging the Anglo-American military alliance during World War II. Thomas M. Sisk, who is beginning to close the research gap in Eisenhower scholarship on the general's central leadership role as the first NATO Supreme Allied Commander Europe, completes this pre-presidential section. Sisk concludes that although Eisenhower was highly successful as SACEUR in building an effective integrated allied military force and strengthening European morale in the response to the Soviet threat, he failed to bring American troops home within the time frame he set for himself.

Section II presents two assessments of Eisenhower's domestic policies. William O'Neill, a well-respected historian of the fifties and sixties, shows Eisenhower's successful economic and social policies in the era of what he calls the "American high." Stanley Kutler, one of America's foremost constitutional historians, reassesses the more mixed record of Eisenhower's civil rights policies and the positive effects of his judicial appointments.

Section III presents a medley of ongoing research into select areas of Eisenhower's foreign policy by a generation of younger scholars—both revisionist and postrevisionist. These essays indicate how the cottage industry of Eisenhower studies is still a growth field. They also demonstrate that the evaluation process of Eisenhower's handling of foreign affairs remains in ferment. These chapters deal with the unique challenges the Eisenhower administration faced in fashioning a globally applicable national security policy. These essays also show how demanding a job it was to effectively rule the disparate American interests around the world and survive as a superpower in the nuclear era.

Anna Kasten Nelson, the well-respected historian of the early National Security Council, shows Eisenhower's hands-on involvement in the process of reorganizing the NSC. The NSC reorganization allowed for an integrated national security policy and the supervision of myriad American interests around the globe—more recently defined as the "American Empire." With his initial overreliance on nuclear weapons in his New Look policy, Eisenhower created a number of nuclear crises (such as the Quemoy and Matsu crises) that brought the world close to the nuclear brink. Eisenhower's "procrastinating leadership style" produced a state of "national insecurity," charges the leading postrevisionist, H. W. Brands. In a similar vein, Günter Bischof agrees with the "missed opportunities" thesis. Eisenhower and Dulles failed to be responsive to and negotiate with the new Kremlin leadership after Stalin's death. Bischof's European perspective is a case study of a small power's successful maneuvering between the superpowers and their rigid cold war mindsets. Eisenhower and Dulles were reluctant to negotiate with the Soviets but were much more pragmatic when it came to neutrality than has been traditionally held.

Robert Wampler shows how crucial Eisenhower was in forging NATO and a nuclear strategy. In fact, Eisenhower's nuclear strategy foreshadowed Kennedy's "flexible response," as Wampler shows. Along the lines of Bundy's scholarship, Wampler shows how the "unexpected" Dulles and Eisenhower were less nuclear "brinksmen" than has often been charged. In the mid-fifties they increasingly tried to address and solve the paradoxes of an overreliance on nuclear weapons and fairness in alliance burden sharing. Even the stationing of battlefield tactical nuclear weapons in Europe never fully resolved the dilemma of pursuing options "between acquiescence and nuclear holocaust."

Eisenhower's China policy may have been intransigent in the Quemoy and Matsu crises, as Gordon Chang's essay explains, but it was more complex than has often been assumed. Eisenhower never liked Chiang Kai-shek and the Nationalists but had to support them to contain communism in Asia. For a while he even toyed with the idea of a "two-China policy" by seating the Chinese Communists in the United Nations; he was also considering the promotion of a deepening of the Sino-Soviet split. Chang closes his essays with a speculative yet fascinating comparison of two contemporaries, Eisenhower and Mao Tse-tung.

Eisenhower's views on the Germans during World War II reflected the general hatred of Hitler and the Nazis, as Thomas Schwartz explains. This did not blind him to the need after the war to quickly reconstruct Germany; along with most Americans he made a quick 180-degree turn. Eisenhower became one of the fathers of German rearmament and a "dual containment" strategy regarding the Federal Republic; this ingenious parallel containment of both the Soviet Union and Germany kept the Soviets out of Central Europe by rearming the Germans; it also kept the Germans within the Western military club and under tight control, as Schwartz points out.[50]

The only case study of Eisenhower's Third World policies in this volume is Steven Grover's essay on Cuba. Eisenhower gets a mixed review. While he was pragmatic in resisting the demands of the American sugar lobby to cut Cuban import sugar quotas, his ambassadorial appointments to Havana were disastrous and contributed considerably to the American misinterpretation of events in Cuba and Castro's political standing. More knowledgeable reporting from Cuba might have spared the United States the turmoil in years to come with Castro and Cuba.

Stephen E. Ambrose closes the volume off with a broad summary of Eisenhower's achievements and legacies.

50. On the theme of the "dual containment" of Germany, see also the recent collection of essays by an international group of scholars in Steininger *et al.*, eds., *Die doppelte Eindämmung.*

I Eisenhower, World War II, SACEUR, and Historiography

FORREST C. POGUE

The Genesis of *The Supreme Command:*
Personal Impressions of Eisenhower the General

About a year ago Steve Ambrose phoned me to describe a series of lectures he was arranging to be given at the University of New Orleans to celebrate the centennial of Dwight D. Eisenhower's birth. He proposed that I give the concluding lecture on my personal impressions of Eisenhower as a general. I proposed that I focus in particular on my experiences in writing the army's official volume on Eisenhower as supreme commander in Europe, 1944–1945. That volume was based on Eisenhower's personal files, pertinent files of SHAEF (Supreme Headquarters, Allied Expeditionary Force), the War Department, the Joint Chiefs of Staff, the Combined Chiefs of Staff, interviews with Eisenhower and with some one hundred American, British, and French political and military leaders. Steve agreed.

First, I have to discuss how I came to be selected for this work, my early impressions of the general, and some of my meetings with him and his contemporaries. Since this is to be a personal account, you will hear more of me personally than is justified by my role in the making of the Eisenhower story, but it may be of interest to illustrate what went into the writing of early accounts of this great commander in Europe from 1944 to 1945.

One day in mid-November, 1945, I was called into the office of the Theater Historian of Headquarters, U.S. Forces in the European Theater at Saint Germain-en-Laye just outside Paris. I had been working there and in Paris since May 12, 1945, on a battle narrative of the recently concluded Operation Overlord. At the moment I was editing one of the army's so-called pamphlet series on campaigns of the war, David Garth's *St. Lô*. After about forty-two months in the army as a soldier, I had taken a discharge earlier in October and was employed as a civilian historian for a year to write on phases of World War II. The theater historian, Colonel S. L. A. Marshall, named to that position near the end of the war in Europe, was a newsman famed for his combat historian experiences in the Pacific and Northwest Europe. He had a new assignment for me. When General Eisenhower went to Washington to succeed George C. Marshall as chief of staff, he had left instructions with Lieutenant General Walter Bedell Smith, his wartime chief of staff, to find a historian to write a short history of SHAEF. The British and American historians assigned to SHAEF had returned home at the end of the war, and the history of the command had not proceeded beyond D-Day. Would "Slam" Marshall send a replacement? The chief factor in my selection for this plum of an assignment was that I already had contracted to remain in the theater for a year to write army history and thus was on hand.

Some of my background helped. Before entering the army, I had taught European history at college level since 1933. In getting my Ph.D. (1939) in international relations and diplomatic history, I had studied at the University of Paris from 1937 to 1938 and traveled several weeks in France, Germany, Italy, Austria, and Czechoslovakia—countries that would see much fighting in the war. Drafted into the army in 1942, I had been assigned a year later to Headquarters, Second Army (Memphis, Tennessee), as assistant to the historian of that army. I assisted in writing its training history until I was transferred to the Historical Division, War Department, to be briefed as one of ten "combat historians" who were to be sent to London before D-Day. General George Marshall had decided that he wanted a series of pamphlets written on battles or campaigns of the war and distributed as soon as possible to participants in these actions and their families. The need for speed resulted in the use of combat historians to gather material from combat units to flesh out their after-action reports.

Our group had arrived in London by mid-April, and after general briefings on what we might find in the invasion period, some of us were assigned to First Army and then attached to VII or V Corps, which would land units on Utah and Omaha Beaches on D-Day. At this point, we were allowed to read the highly classified invasion plans.

On June 2, my partner, Lieutenant William Fox, and I went aboard an LST off the Cornish coast near Falmouth. We were attached to a company of the 29th Division headed for Omaha Beach, but we became much aware of Eisenhower's decisive role in the war when he postponed D-Day to June 6, hoping to get better weather. We crossed the Channel in the late evening of June 6, attached to fighting units that were to land that evening on Omaha, while we and twenty-eight other "parasites" were to stay on board until the beach was cleared. Almost at once, Fox and I began to interview lightly wounded men brought aboard for minor surgery.

Getting ashore on D-Day plus two, my duties for three months included interviewing men fighting in the hedgerows, and helping compile material for a combat history. In September I was sent to headquarters in Paris to assist a War Department officer from the Pentagon begin work on the Omaha Beach pamphlet. I worked in Paris for twelve weeks. Eisenhower was in his headquarters in

Versailles, and I glimpsed him once or twice in Paris. In late November I returned to combat interviewing with V Corps located in Belgium near the German border. In the remaining months of the war, to my campaign stars for Normandy and northern France, I added those for the Ardennes, the Rhineland, and central Germany, and I saw the linkup with the Russians at Torgau on the Elbe. The war ended while V Corps was in Pilzen, Czechoslovakia, and we knew the war was over in Europe on May 8 even before we heard the official announcement, when the lights all suddenly came on for the first time in years.

I was among those ordered back to Paris to begin work on a narrative history of the war and in October had accepted a discharge from the army and signed up for a year as a civilian historian to work on this history, when Colonel Marshall took me to Frankfurt to begin a history of the Eisenhower command.

In the short time I had before beginning my new assignment, I thought over what I knew about the supreme commander. As a student and teacher and prospective draftee, I had carefully followed newspaper accounts of the army after war began in Europe in 1939. I had not read much, if anything, about General Eisenhower until Hanson Baldwin devoted a special column to him in the New York *Times* and an article in *Life* after maneuvers in Louisiana in 1941. I learned a great deal more about this officer while writing of the 1941 maneuvers as a Second Army historian in 1943. Somewhere I learned that General Krueger had written General Marshall in June, 1941, to ask that Colonel Eisenhower be assigned as his chief of staff. He told Marshall that he wanted "a man possessing broad visions, progressive ideas, a thorough grasp of the magnitude of the problems of handling an army, and lots of initiative and resourcefulness." Marshall approved the assignment and, after Eisenhower's performance in the maneuvers, recommended him for his first star.

One week after Pearl Harbor, Marshall called him to Washington to fill the place in the War Plans Division left vacant by the death in a plane crash of the expert on the Philippines. Eisenhower, who had worked with General Douglas MacArthur while the latter was army chief of staff and had gone with him to the Philippines as a planner for the defense of the islands, was told by Marshall to concentrate on getting aid to our forces there. Soon, Eisenhower, the Far East expert, moved up to head the War Plans Division and began work on operations for invading France. This new job brought a second star. In June, Marshall sent him to Command Headquarters, European Theater of Operations, U.S. Army. That called in time for three stars. Marshall liked his plans for a cross-Channel operation, but in the face of British opposition had to accept instead plans for an invasion of North Africa in the fall. The British agreed that the Allied forces commander for this November operation should be Eisenhower. After the Al-

Ike was a public icon in both Europe & USA

lied conference at Casablanca, Marshall persuaded Roosevelt to give him a fourth star. By this time his smiling face as he moved easily among Allied leaders and troops had become familiar in the newspapers, and headline writers increasingly referred to him as "Ike."

Reading army releases on its key commanders, I found in 1943 that Ike had within a year become the chief American leader in Europe. By the summer of 1943, his forces were moving into Sicily. Soon, Italy was out of the war and Ike was leading the fight to drive the Germans from the country. Although wide speculation had Marshall as commander of the coming attack on Northwest Europe, near the end of the year, at the Cairo Conference, Roosevelt decided that he could not spare Marshall from Washington. Eisenhower became the Supreme Commander, Allied Expeditionary Forces.

My chief impressions of Eisenhower so far had come from the newspapers. But when I went to London in April, 1944, I felt somewhat closer to him because I was assigned to First Army commanded by General Omar Bradley, who had been with Ike in North Africa and Sicily. I was on an LST near Falmouth when word came that Ike had postponed D-Day because of the weather and reset the invasion for June 6. Clearly, this was a man who could make hard decisions. I carefully kept my copy of his D-Day message to the troops and placed it in the Marshall Museum when it was dedicated in 1964 by Eisenhower and President Johnson.

In Normandy I heard rumors of Eisenhower's problems with the overall ground commander, General Montgomery, and his efforts to stir that commander to action. I was glad in August that he did not let Patton fritter away time in Brittany but sent him eastward instead, across the Seine and south of Paris, and that he authorized Bradley to move a French division into Paris and, later, to parade an American division through the city on the way to the front. I recall the first, distant glimpse I got of the general in Paris early in September. In the fall of 1944, I heard something of the new trouble with Monty over his slowness in opening the way to Antwerp. As a soldier with the First Army in the Ardennes fighting, I shared the general unhappiness when First Army was placed for a time under Montgomery and cheered with others some weeks later when Eisenhower opposed Monty's plan for a narrow thrust to Berlin and favored the broad front advance proposed by Bradley and Patton, giving Bradley control of four armies for the final phase.

US general

In a German barracks near the Czech frontier, we read Eisenhower's brief announcement to his superiors that he had fulfilled his mission. All my impressions of Eisenhower, formed from reading, from rumor, and from discussions with other historians, and the controversies with Monty, and British complaints because Ike had stopped at the Elbe instead of going on to Prague and Berlin, were in my head as I prepared a general outline of what I thought should be in the study I was to write on SHAEF. Within days after arriving in Frankfurt, I sent this outline to General Smith, who said, "Very good indeed!" Smith's initial assignment for me was one that he said Eisenhower had given first priority. At SHAEF a small British section had supervised plans for cover and deception operations, but those records had gone back to Britain at the close of the war. Smith said I was to go to London and examine those files. I was to write an account of their contents, classify my account "Top Secret," and withdraw it from my manuscript. That Christmas season, doing research in a bitterly cold London office introduced me to aspects of SHAEF I had never known and hinted of other classified matters such as ULTRA, which I would not know fully for many months.

In the Frankfurt stage of my research, I worked in the cable logs and other SHAEF files still left in the European Theater, getting excellent background from a group of younger officers who had worked with Eisenhower and Smith at SHAEF during the war, and from a few ranking officers elsewhere in Germany. Among them was Lieutenant General Sir Frederick Morgan, who had headed the COSSAC staff for cross-Channel planning before Eisenhower was named supreme commander. A great admirer of Eisenhower, he greeted me by saying, "There was a man sent from God and his name was Ike." His American deputy at COSSAC and later fellow staff member at SHAEF, Major General Ray W. Barker, now commanding the Berlin sector, gave me great assistance then and later.

With all this help, I finished my short history by late spring of 1946. Months earlier, before General Smith left Frankfurt to be U.S. ambassador to the Soviet Union, I had explained to him that I could not write a complete history of the Supreme Command without access to the personal papers of General Eisenhower, which he had taken back to the States, and to other important army files in Washington. He passed these observations along to Eisenhower and notified me that when I had completed the short history, I should report to General Eisenhower in Washington for a new directive.

In Washington in July, 1946, I was hired as a War Department historian. Soon afterward, the chief of military history, War Department, took me to meet General Eisenhower. I was strongly impressed on this first meeting by General Eisenhower's clear grasp of the importance of carefully researched history. He mentioned that Douglas Freeman had urged him to publish a collection of World War II documents comparable to those issued on the Civil War. Ike replied that such a venture would run to five thousand volumes. He told me (and other of-

ficial historians) that he wanted us to write from the record and to footnote fully
our volumes so that scholars could find basic materials in the Archives. He
showed great interest in all of the volumes soon in progress on the war and com-
plied eagerly when the chief historian invited him to sit in on a review panel of
a volume on the War Plans Division covering the time Ike had been in it. He had
already taken action to make available to the Historical Division part of the
surplus army post-exchange funds, which met Historical Division budget requirements for months to come.

(Later, when he returned to Europe as commander of SHAPE, he promptly
appointed a historian and instructed his officers to make use of materials assembled for the short history of SHAEF.)

Soon after my meeting with General Eisenhower, he issued a directive that
named me as the historian of SHAEF. Technically, the Supreme Headquarters
no longer existed, but by agreement the original papers, except for British
ones I had seen, had passed into United States custody, and the files for the Allied Force Headquarters had earlier gone to Britain. Eisenhower suggested to the
head of the British Mission in Washington that a British historian be assigned to
work with me, but Field Marshal Sir Henry Maitland Wilson said I should represent both countries, and so I became the designated author of what the chief
historian had already titled *The Supreme Command*. General Eisenhower invited
me to use his personal papers, then stored in his other office in the Pentagon,
and to use all War Department and Joint Chiefs of Staff documents that he had
authority to open to me. SHAEF papers were so mixed with those of all the
services, plus some White House papers, British War Cabinet papers, and papers
from the State Department, that to open any large file to general access was
bound to violate security regulations of one agency or another. Soon afterward,
when I borrowed volumes of papers on some of the great conferences from
the secretary, general staff, of the War Department, I received a frantic message
that I was not permitted to see them. I asked General Eisenhower if he could get
me access. He directed his deputy, General Thomas T. Handy, to arrange the
matter. Handy passed on the task to Major General Harry J. Malony, chief of the
Historical Division, who took me to the building where the files of the Joint
Chiefs of Staff were kept. Malony was told that he could copy out parts of the
documents that pertained to army matters, but only those, since I was not
cleared to read other portions. Malony made careful notes for nearly an hour.
At the end of that time, he called in a lieutenant colonel and told him that he
had not spent a lifetime in the army to end up as an amanuensis. "Doctor Pogue
can take his own notes." He left to get coffee and I took up the copying where
he had left off.

After the files had been moved to the Pentagon, I called the new office to ask for certain papers. There was a pause, then an elderly clerk, soon to retire, said that she knew I had seen the documents because I had given her information from them, "but you are not on the cleared list." She suggested that I send my research assistant, who had been officially cleared, to take notes for me until my own name was put on the cleared list. I did so, but I had been back to Europe for several months before I was officially permitted to see material I had already used in writing a chapter.

In that summer of 1946, I sometimes sat at the desk of one of Eisenhower's senior aides, now on terminal leave, while taking notes from Eisenhower's personal files. I read letters to and from the general and Roosevelt, Truman, Churchill, Attlee, de Gaulle, Bradley, Patton, Montgomery, and many others —an experience invaluable in my later research. On a trip back to England, I talked with the marshal of the Royal Air Force, chief of the air staff, Sir Arthur Tedder, about his relations with Field Marshal Montgomery. He diplomatically parried my probings about his criticisms of Montgomery. Finally, I said, "I want to ask about your letter to Eisenhower in which you write, 'If you want to ask for Montgomery's removal from command, I am willing to cooperate.'" Tedder replied, "Did Ike show you that letter?" When my answer was affirmative, he said, "Then why am I evading your questions!" With that, he arranged for me to see a journal in which this and other matters were more candidly discussed. Only my access to Eisenhower's private papers could have gotten me this kind of cooperation.

As the summer wore on, my ideas about my subject deepened and expanded. Comments on experiences of working with Ike by members of his staff who had been with him in Europe and some of their reactions to the flood of visitors that came to the office often shed light on SHAEF. They would sometimes point out or give me names of individuals I should interview, and even helped arrange appointments. Since my project had the general's backing, they smoothed my way whenever they could. When the general happened to read an offending statement about World War II that he wanted to challenge or clarify, he sometimes asked that I be sent into his inner office. I recall his surges of anger, his bouncing up from his chair to pace restlessly as he castigated a piece of misinformation and asked if I wanted the whole story. He did not stop with denials. He knew that a historian needed hard facts, and he would name individuals or documents that would supply them. Helpful as his aides were to me, they made it clear that I must not let my search for facts interfere with the general's scheduled appointments. An aide would say as I started into the inner office, "Be sure you get out in fifteen minutes," and I would reply that I was not in the habit of walking out on five-star generals. Usually, his staff realized that discussing war episodes gave Ike a respite from current problems. One day, however, his chief aide said as he sent me in, "I bet you get out quickly this time. His next appointment is at the White House."

With the coming of fall, I prepared for extensive interviews that Eisenhower suggested I seek in Europe, and for which he promised to write letters of introduction. With his directive to interview widely, I asked the Historical Division to give me flexible orders that would permit me to visit battlefields. My resulting orders exceeded anything I had expected, inviting me to visit most of Europe's major capitals, and cities in North Africa. I was authorized to visit them in such order and as often as I should deem necessary. Mere display of these orders was usually enough to convince prospective interviewees that General Eisenhower was fully behind the project.

I flew to Paris in the fall of 1946 and went to the office of the American military mission there. The executive officer read my orders, nodded, and asked, "Do you want a jeep, sedan, command car, or ambulance?" When I expressed wonder about the ambulance, he explained that isolated areas I wanted to visit might not have accommodations, and I could sleep in an ambulance. Also, inexpensive gasoline would be scarce, and I could carry my own supply in an ambulance. I agreed that an ambulance or sedan might be more comfortable on a good highway, but I wanted to go over beaches and visit heavily bombed forts and cratered battlefields. The colonel agreed that a jeep was indicated, and arranged for a jeep with a trailer filled with jerricans of gasoline, plus a driver who had come to Europe at the war's end, telling him that this was a chance to see battle sites before he went home at the end of our trip.

We set off next day by way of Rouen to Caen, Bayeux, and the British invasion beaches. On the second evening, we stopped at a small American depot soon to be abandoned. I was warned not to stop overnight in the neighboring French town because strong anti-American feeling had been aroused by an accident on the previous day. An American truck driven by a German prisoner of war had killed a Frenchwoman, and the Americans had defended the driver. Preferring quarters in the local hotel to the cramped, overheated supply depot, I decided to brave the outraged citizenry. I left my driver to spend the night at the depot, telling him where to look for me the next morning, and registered at the one hotel available. Then I went into the small bar adjoining the dining room. My French was understood by the locals, nursing their drinks. When I identified myself as one who had crossed the Channel on D-Day, the chill I had first felt disappeared, and soon we were exchanging war stories and drinks.

The next few days included visits to Cherbourg, the base of the Cotentin,

Saint-Lô, Granville (the girls' school that had been one of Ike's first headquarters in France), Avranches, Mont-Saint-Michel, Saint-Malo and Brest. Recalling that Eisenhower had changed plans to send Patton's Third Army into Brittany and instead ordered most of it eastward, we followed Patton's route, which I had missed in 1944, back to a point south of Paris. After a weekend in Paris, we moved toward another area I had missed in 1944, Antwerp, which Eisenhower had pressed Monty to capture. Then on to Walcheren Island, Rotterdam, Arnhem, and back to more familiar territory in cities in the Rhineland, south along the Rhine to Strasbourg, then west toward Paris with a stop at the "little red schoolhouse" at Reims, Eisenhower's headquarters, where the armistice was signed with German representatives by Ike's chief of staff while the general waited in an adjoining room.

The two weeks spent in this travel had permitted me to review in my mind many phases of the campaign in Northwest Europe and would help me in dozens of interviews that lay ahead. In a few weeks I would discuss the ceremony at Reims with Tedder, Sir Kenneth Strong, and Morgan in England and with Eisenhower and Bedell Smith in Washington. Near the end of November, I left a chill and somber Paris for an equally somber and even colder London. The next few weeks brought Europe its severest winter of the century, and there was not enough food or fuel, from southern Italy northward. For the book on the Supreme Command I gained near-pneumonia and a personal understanding of the problems that were to result in the Marshall Plan, which would be used in a chapter of a much later volume.

In Washington in the summer of 1946, I had seen Eisenhower's former G-1 (the officer responsible for personnel) whom I had met earlier in Berlin. Hearing that I was going to London for interviews, he proposed that I suggest to General Eisenhower that he be sent along to guide my approach to old SHAEF hands. Ike had agreed, and I found General Barker awaiting me in London. He had already set up interviews for me with General Morgan, his former boss, and the two of them took me to see General Sir Hastings L. Ismay, former chief of staff to Churchill in his capacity as minister of defense. Ismay had met regularly with the British chiefs of staff, and he gave me several pages of names, with titles and addresses, of many of the people I needed to see. All three sketched in background on each individual and warned of possible problems. Ismay said that my hope of talking with Churchill was almost impossible to realize because he was working on his memoirs and had already turned down a member of the State Department and a couple of newsmen. Only if Eisenhower asked him was there a remote chance.

Off to Washington went a cable to Eisenhower, who then asked Churchill to grant me an appointment. Churchill later replied that "your man Pogue" had asked him more questions than he could answer in a year. I was upset lest Ike think that I was annoying his old friend. I had submitted a carefully selected list of possible questions to General Ismay, and he had marked those that he knew the former prime minister could answer without difficulty, since Ismay himself had supplied material on these points for the memoirs. Ismay consoled me by telling me that his boss had sold his memoirs for a very large sum and did not want to give someone else any of the cream of their contents. Fortified by this knowledge, I explained to Eisenhower that Churchill had not been exactly truthful in turning down an interview with me, and Ike was understanding because he had dealt with Churchill before. I knew I could never change the old man's mind, but I stubbornly wrote him that Ismay had approved the questions that I had sent him. The next day I received a telegram thanking me for my "interesting message." I also received a handwritten reply with a signature that looked like Churchill's, but I never put it with my autograph collection.

For four and a half strenuous months I shuttled, mainly by military transportation, from London to Paris, Rome, Caserta, and then to Cairo, hoping to see Montgomery's Second Army commander and Eisenhower's chief British planner at SHAEF, only to find they had gone to new British headquarters at Fayid, where after a drive across the desert I got a look at the Suez Canal.

I went to Berlin for a week of interviewing and also because Bedell Smith had said he would send his plane there to take me to Moscow if I could get a visa. I was unable to get a permit, and had to wait for several months to see our ambassador to the Soviet Union when he was back in Washington. The trip to Egypt had been a warm contrast to frostbitten northern Europe, and I had a second brief release from heavy snows when I flew to the Isle of Jersey to talk with Eisenhower's former chief of civil affairs, now lieutenant governor of the island, which was 25 degrees warmer than Britain or the Continent because of the Gulf Stream. For friends in London he entrusted me with a parcel of two or three dozen eggs, which his own hens had laid. I carried them back on my lap and doled out two or three at a time to the long list of grateful recipients that I had been told to see.

Lord Mountbatten was on my list, but I found him busy. Several others I interviewed asked me what he was up to and opined that something mysterious was in the works. Suddenly, a second reply came to my request for an interview, saying that Mountbatten could see me briefly that afternoon but not again for several months, since he was on the eve of leaving England. I went to his apartment, where, between instructions to his secretary and answering phone calls, he told me that many of my questions could be answered by reading some of his papers held by Alan Campbell-Johnson, his wartime aide, who also would soon be leaving the country. He called the aide to tell him I would come by, so I dropped by the man's house late that afternoon, and he made the material available. Next day I learned what all the stir and hurry were about. Mountbatten, accompanied by Alan Campbell-Johnson and others, was leaving for India the day after he saw me, where, as the last viceroy, he would pave the way for Indian independence.

By this time I had begun to send back to the Historical Division some of my crudely typed interviews. Some of these were passed on to General Eisenhower, who made occasional comments or added information. He showed particular interest in any information I received from de Gaulle, deeming it of special importance.

I had begun attempts to get an appointment with de Gaulle before the end of 1946, but he had recently resigned from the government and was giving no interviews. When I asked our military attaché in Paris for help, he said the affair was too big for him and sent me to Ambassador Caffery, who also gave a pessimistic reply but promised to put me in touch with one of de Gaulle's aides. I made a number of flights from London to Paris over the weeks, where I negotiated with the aide. It became clear that I had no chance of seeing the French leader if he thought I was a journalist. The head of the New York *Times* Paris bureau thought that I might succeed if I stressed that I was trying to portray de Gaulle's role in a crucial period of history. On my fourth trip to Paris, after I had submitted experimental lists of questions, the aide told me that the general had decided that I was "un historien avec esprit scientifique" and would see me, returning my amended list of questions with suggestions for several others that I might add.

When I made my next trip across the Channel to Paris, Ambassador Caffery sent me in one of the embassy's most impressive limousines to see the general. When I was driven to de Gaulle's home at Colombey-les-deux-Églises after lunch, a servant told me that the general was not at home. She explained that he and madame had gone to the railway station to say farewell to their son, who was on his way to Indochina by way of troopship from Marseilles.

The general returned in a short time, austere and commanding in appearance, as I had thought he would be. But he was also gracious and showed admirable control as I began the conversation in what I think was one of the most courageous acts of my life. A college minor in French, a year in school in Paris, and several months in France in the years 1944–1945, did not result in adequate French with which to chat with Charles de Gaulle. I struggled to keep in mind what I wanted to ask next, while striving to remember proper use of the past perfect tense and correct subjunctive forms. After about half an hour, in which the general had avoided wincing or showing discomfort, he said gently that he realized the problem of conducting an interview in a foreign language. He proposed that I speak in English and he in French.

We communicated in that fashion for nearly an hour. Then he came to the problems that had developed with President Roosevelt and the manner in which Eisenhower had handled them. He now explained that he wanted me to understand his exact meanings and asked if he could call in his aide, whose mother was American. The aide would not translate our conversation word for word, but would be present if either of us wanted to make certain of nuances that might appear in our talk. From time to time he would say to the aide, "Ask Doctor Pogue if this expression is completely clear." More often than not, he would hear my explanation of an issue as I understood it, and he would nod agreement. In that manner we proceeded through a most candid survey of his problems with President Roosevelt and the difficulties that had arisen over control of the troops in France. He made clear that any questions he had with Eisenhower were due only to orders coming from Washington. He spoke approvingly of the way they had worked together, especially praising Eisenhower's reversal of decision during the Ardennes campaign to withdraw Allied forces from Strasbourg when de Gaulle explained that a shortening of the Allied line might be sound military policy for Eisenhower but would be politically disastrous for the French, who would have to withdraw again from Alsace, regained only a few months before from the Germans. On this and other political issues, Ike had ultimately won Roosevelt's agreement to recognize de Gaulle as the one French figure likely to be accepted by a majority of the French. Eisenhower had clearly ameliorated the previous bad feeling between de Gaulle and Washington.

I reported to the Pentagon that my interview with the general had ended on a pleasant note, for at the close of our talk, he invited me to go into the salon, where he said madame wished to offer me an English tea. And so it proved to be, with the aide now translating most of the conversation. After a finger sandwich and a sip of tea, de Gaulle suggested that I might like to sample a glass of chartreuse from one of the few bottles that he had been able to hide from the Germans when they occupied this part of France. I would, indeed.

I followed the de Gaulle interview with talks with General de Lattre de Tassigny and Marshal Juin, now minister of defense. My talk with de Lattre was brief because he was leaving for Marseilles to say farewell to French troops leaving to fight in Indochina. We talked enough for me to understand the comments later made in interviews with General Jacob Devers, who had de Lattre's army in his Sixth Army group, and Senator Henry Cabot Lodge, who had been Devers' liaison officer to de Lattre, that finesse was needed to get his full cooperation.

I described Juin in my notes as a plainspoken soldier who had been a remarkable leader in the fighting in Italy. But when I mentioned problems with SHAEF in the south of France along the Italian border, he assured me that there had been no difficulty with the Americans and all had gone well. I might have believed him had not SHAEF messages told a different story. Bedell Smith had told me that Juin had spoken to him in such a way that he would have knocked him down had he been an American officer.

Later, when General Eisenhower had returned these notes to the Historical Division, I found that he had written opposite my notes on Juin, "He sure got his number."

On my return to London, I interviewed Sir Robert Bruce Lockhart, who had dealt with Special Operations concerning the French. He took me to lunch at the St. James Club, explaining over a dish of curried guinea that while British food was bad, the club still had an excellent wine cellar. He related in some detail Eisenhower's efforts to get de Gaulle to broadcast an appeal for support of Eisenhower on the eve of D-Day. The French leader had been balky because he had not been in on the planning of the invasion. He finally agreed to follow Eisenhower's broadcast to the French people. He had praised Churchill but said nothing about the Americans. He had directed French officials in the invasion areas of France not to accept for tax payments the special invasion money carried in by Allied troops, until Eisenhower's representatives had threatened to use American dollars that would drive down the value of the franc. De Gaulle had insisted that French armor enter Paris early, when Eisenhower preferred to bypass it. Once in the city, he delayed giving orders for the French division to leave the city until Eisenhower urged that it rejoin the battle. Once de Gaulle had entered the city and had widespread acceptance, he proved more amenable to SHAEF orders. Lockhart, like Eisenhower and other Allied leaders, warmly praised the assistance given by Resistance forces.

The wartime chiefs of staff were high on my interview list in Britain. Charles Portal, wartime chief of the air staff, talked of Eisenhower's struggle to get control of the air support for his ground battles. The former first sea lord, Andrew Brown Cunningham, had strongly supported Eisenhower in the Mediterranean and liked Ike's plan for the invasion of southern France, and spoke warmly of him.

Eisenhower had been greatly interested in what General Sir Alanbrooke, former chief of the Imperial General Staff, might have to say in my interview with him. The British army head had been Montgomery's greatest supporter in disputes with the supreme commander, but I found him conciliatory, inclined to stress points of agreement. He was gracious, agreeing to come to my hotel and retape parts of an initial interview that I, in my clumsiness, had partially erased. It was not until his diary was published, with postwar comments, that I saw that he had disguised his unhappiness at the prospect of losing the Supreme Command to Marshall and then of having to accept Ike. His outbursts of frustration, such as his observation that Ike was on the golf course at Reims during periods of difficult fighting, would cause him embarrassment later when I returned in 1961 to interview him in connection with my biography on General Marshall.

One of the most helpful persons I interviewed was General Sir Kenneth Strong, Eisenhower's chief of intelligence at SHAEF. Strong had been the British military attaché in Berlin before the war and was the translator of terms to German delegates in the armistice session at Reims at the war's end. He was especially helpful on G-2 matters, while being careful not to reveal any evidence of the ULTRA operation. He had been present at the meetings at Portsmouth leading to the postponement of D-Day by one day and then the final dramatic session. (He came to life in the first of Steve Ambrose's "D-Day to the Rhine" tours, thirty-six years after D-Day, in the restored briefing room of the Naval Headquarters in Portsmouth, where Eisenhower had made his decision. He arose and walked about the room, pointing out where each of Eisenhower's officers had sat, and painted a vivid picture of Ike marching up and down, pointing at each officer in turn to ask his opinion on whether to go ahead with the Normandy invasion on June 6. I was to find in Washington SHAEF files descriptions of this episode by two of the men present, but there was nothing of Strong's fire. When Steve Ambrose and I talked about what had happened, I said, "The ghosts came back.")

The interviews furnished a mass of descriptive materials of the way SHAEF worked and the problems faced by the supreme commander with generals, political leaders, governments, and local populations. From many sources I gathered impressions of Ike as a popular commander who liked people and made them like him, whose instincts favored understanding the problems of others and a bent for accommodation. His tendency to find solutions to conflicting ideas led some of his American subordinates to the cruel commentary that he was the best general the British had. Careful analysis of what I heard suggested that here was a man no one walked over.

An analysis of the quality of Eisenhower's leadership came from Alan Moorehead, an Australian correspondent who had been with Montgomery in the African desert, Sicily, Italy, and northern Europe. He gave me a powerful vision of Ike erupting. At the end of August, 1944, under pressure from Marshall, Ike had activated the U.S. Twelfth Army group and had taken direct control of ground operations. Montgomery was unhappy with his apparent demotion, and the British press protested to the extent that Churchill felt he had to announce Montgomery's elevation to field marshal. Events led Eisenhower to grant Monty's request for an attempt to capture a bridge over the Rhine at Arnhem. Despite a successful beginning, the Germans retook the bridge. When the drive later slowed, Montgomery suggested mistakes had been made, and there should be a return to the old command arrangement. He went too far. Eisenhower replied that if Montgomery persisted in this demand, the Combined Chiefs of Staff should make the decision. Bedell Smith talked with General de Guingand, Montgomery's chief of staff, to make clear that it was a showdown. Moorehead knew that de Guingand had a heart condition and said he had taken a stiff drink before going in to report to his superior. He informed Montgomery that the time for decision on the command matter had come. The matter would go to the British and American chiefs. "Somebody will go and it won't be Ike," said de Guingand. Montgomery asked de Guingand to help him with a reply. In it, the field marshal expressed regret that he had added to Eisenhower's heavy burdens. He closed by saying, "You have stated your views and I have stated mine and I will support your views." The letter was signed "Your most obedient servant."

The matter was reopened by the German breakthrough in mid-December. Within three days, the enemy bulge threatened to separate Bradley's southern army from the two American armies on Monty's side of the bulge. Eisenhower decided that the lack of communications between Bradley in Luxembourg and the Americans in the north made it necessary for him to give Montgomery temporary command north of the breakthrough. Moorehead described to me the scene of a press conference that Montgomery called a few days later to stop criticism among Americans of the SHAEF commander's action. Monty had come in with a jaunty air that, Moorehead thought, made matters infinitely worse. He praised American soldiers but hinted that they lacked a firm command. Reports of the press interview infuriated Bradley and Patton and led to such an uproar that the London press reported that a German radio station had broadcast a fake interview exaggerating what Montgomery had said. Eisenhower's reaction was such that Churchill hastily told the House of Commons that victory had been won by American soldiers and their leaders. Bradley soon regained the First Army, and the issue quieted down.

As preparations began for a resumption of the drive to the Rhine, the prime minister raised another issue. He told Eisenhower that his deputy, Air

Chief Marshal Tedder, was needed for a British air command and suggested that
a British ground force deputy be appointed in his place. Perhaps he meant this
spot for Montgomery. Eisenhower's reply settled that issue. He told Montgomery
that if Tedder had to go, perhaps they needed a British ground force commander
as deputy, in which case he would suggest Field Marshal Alexander. Montgomery
at once declared himself satisfied with matters as they were, and Tedder was allowed to stay.

Before I left England, I wanted to talk to Montgomery about his relations with
Eisenhower. His aide said he was sure his superior would see me. Next morning
the embarrassed aide explained that the field marshal had a policy of granting appointments only if he had a request from the principal involved. I passed the message back to Washington. Back came Eisenhower's reply, "Don't bother with subordinates."

On my return to Washington, I felt ready to concentrate on research in
SHAEF files. I was given office space in the Historical Division and file cabinets
full of records of the SHAEF period. Bedell Smith sent word that I could use
his files, then housed in the Army Library in the Pentagon. I asked General Eisenhower if he would get me access to the full text of the diary kept by his former
aide, Captain Butcher. (Portions of this "diary" had been published, but not all.)
Across my request when it came back to me, Ike had scribbled, "The so-called
'Butcher Diary' that was kept in my office is in my outer office and may be con-
sulted there."

When I examined the big, looseleaf "Butcher Diary," I found by happenstance
tucked in among its pages a smaller and shorter diary kept by Eisenhower himself
before Butcher became his aide, during the first six months of 1942. He had given
excerpts from it to one of the Historical Division's historians, but the original that
I found revealed Ike in his most frustrated moments. In addition to listing his
problems, he had added personal comments on people with whom he had to
deal. He did not have to speak softly when he wrote on these short pages, so he
let fly with opinions such as that the war would be finished sooner if we could
shoot Admiral King, or, General MacArthur is a prima donna.

When I told the general that I had found this diary of his, he said, "I thought
that it had been destroyed." But he kept it. (It went to Columbia with him, and
after his death, it turned up at the Eisenhower Library. There an enterprising
scholar found it listed under "Acquisitions," got access to it, and published the
parts that Eisenhower had not circulated, noting that Ray Cline and Forrest
Pogue had never seen this part of Ike's diary. I wrote a letter to the Washington
Star declaring that because a historian did not always publish everything he found
did not mean that he had not seen it.)

General Eisenhower's spare time was soon filled with his dictation of the text of *Crusade in Europe,* for which the publishers wanted careful footnotes and references to pertinent documents. They engaged two former members of Eisenhower's staff to get references to his official papers. One was an oldtime friend of Eisenhower's and a member of the SHAEF planning staff, who worked closely with the Historical Division. We were able to tell him where the papers were now located, and he could explain to me how Ike solved some of the problems of the war.

In Washington, I mixed file research with local interviews and occasional trips to retirement areas. In San Antonio, I interviewed Courtney Hodges, commander of First Army in the latter part of the war, and General Simpson, commander of Ninth Army, who had served under Montgomery and then under Bradley. Also in San Antonio I found T. J. Davis, who had served with Eisenhower in the Philippines, when Davis was aide to MacArthur and Eisenhower was a chief planner. Hodges spoke of Ike's support during the dark days of the Ardennes, and Simpson about the Rhine crossing and the encirclement of the Ruhr. Davis was cautious in his talks with me. The Republican convention of 1952 was about to begin. It was assumed that MacArthur would be used by Senator Taft's forces to block Eisenhower's nomination. Davis told me that he had refused several offers for his memoirs of his Philippine service under MacArthur and later during the war as Eisenhower's chief of press relations and as SHAEF adjutant general.

My interviews with General Bradley came when he was director of the Veterans Administration. Eisenhower was still chief of staff, and Bradley expected to succeed him. So he was careful to speak generally when I asked about problems in the Ardennes. Later, Bedell Smith told me that "Brad" was still smoldering about Monty assuming command of his forces north of the Bulge. But at that time, Bradley showed to me nothing of the strong feeling that his later biographer describes as characteristic of his last years. To me, he stressed the West Point years shared with Ike, their close relations in North Africa and in Normandy, and his satisfaction in the period after the Rhine was crossed when Eisenhower chose the broad front strategy that Bradley advocated.

My close contact with Eisenhower's office ended on February 7, 1948, when he retired as chief of staff. The SHAEF papers were still in the Pentagon and the so-called Bedell Smith papers did not go to the Eisenhower Library until years later.

It was not until after Eisenhower went to Europe as SHAPE commander late in 1950 that I found a means of getting the general's reaction to my manuscript. The army's Historical Division selected as SHAPE historian an old friend, Professor Roy Lamson, who had been a combat historian in Italy during the war. His office became the channel through which I could communicate with the general. I shall always remember Eisenhower's response after I had sent a draft chapter to Lamson for Ike's comment on it. Several days later, Lamson wrote back that the general had said, after reading my account, "I would like to think that I was smarter than that, but if that is the way Pogue found it, let it stand."

I recall only one instance of his suggesting a change. I had found a transcript of his first press conference in Normandy, in which he said that he didn't give a goddam about some criticism that had been made. When he saw the transcript in Normandy, he wrote, "Better take that out, think what the Bible would say." I retold this story in my manuscript sent to SHAPE and waited to see if there was a reaction from Eisenhower. Back it came: "Better change it, think what the Bible Belt would say." This was in 1951, and it seemed that only a prospective candidate would worry about the Bible Belt's reaction, so I restored the cleaned-up version of 1944.

Near the end of 1951, a paper that I gave at the American Historical Association in New York City on Eisenhower's decision to stop the Allied advance in the spring of 1945, at the Elbe, spurred a small controversy. The cold war was heating up. The program committee of the association early in 1951 asked two of us in the Historical Division to address a session on U.S.-Soviet military relations in World War II. Our front office approved the program, provided there were prior clearances of the papers. Well in advance of the meeting, I submitted my paper to authorities at the Department of State, the Department of Defense, and the Department of the Army. All of them gave favorable clearances. Just to be sure, I suggested that an information copy be sent to Eisenhower's headquarters. As time approached for the meeting, we assumed there was no objection. (Eisenhower's senior aide at SHAPE later told me that in view of the other clearances, he did not show it to his boss.)

When I read my paper, the likelihood of Eisenhower's presidential candidacy ensured a large audience and good coverage. Basing my paper on research for my manuscript, I explained that in the closing weeks of the war, Eisenhower had notified Stalin that to get a well-defined point of meeting, he would stop at the line of the Elbe River. Churchill did not want the Soviet forces to take Berlin and Prague and urged the supreme commander to continue his advance. Eisenhower radioed the Joint Chiefs of Staff that he was prepared to go forward for political reasons, but on military grounds he preferred to stop at the Elbe. The Joint Chiefs left the decision to Eisenhower. General Marshall, speaking as executive of the chiefs, said that he would be loath for purely political reasons to continue the advance. So Eisenhower's decision stood, and on a military basis, it was right.

Next day a Pentagon general bawled me out for speaking on such a sensitive subject without clearance. My exhibits of clearances settled that question, but editorials in the Chicago *Tribune* and the McCormick-owned Washington *Times-Herald* charged that "an alleged historian" had undertaken to whitewash the Democratic administration and Eisenhower. The *Tribune* then printed a letter from an Illinois representative citing a letter from Eisenhower's aide saying that his boss would not have made the decision except by direct order from Washington. A *Tribune* correspondent called to ask if I was prepared to retract my speech now that I had been repudiated by Eisenhower. I said my paper had been based on official documents, but if others existed that I had not seen, I would make the necessary changes. To Lamson, Eisenhower's historian, I wrote that I had quoted from Eisenhower's own files and from papers in the War Department, and that my account on this matter was ready to go to press and it would so appear unless I received different information. General Eisenhower sent me a lengthy response that upheld my interpretation. My final text cited his letter and a similar letter from Bedell Smith. Meanwhile, I had learned from Eisenhower's aide that his letter cited by the Illinois representative had been written several months before I read my paper in New York.

After Eisenhower returned to pursue the presidential nomination, the McCormick papers began to say that the general had not answered the "charges" of the historian.

During his fall campaign, Eisenhower decided to clarify the issue. When he went to Detroit, he asked Slam Marshall, back at his duty on the Detroit *News*, for suggestions. My former boss called me, and I reminded him that I had recently sent a copy of my completed manuscript for his comments. Apparently, he passed it on to Ike's office. In 1954, after I had presented my book to the president, an aide took me to lunch. He introduced me to one of Eisenhower's speech writers, who had written the part of Ike's Detroit speech dealing with the stop at the Elbe. The writer told me that the general had told him to follow my line on the matter.

Early in 1952 I had completed the manuscript of *The Supreme Command* and went to work for an operations research office that had several contracts with the U.S. Army. This office hired several historians from the Historical Division to work in U.S. Army Theater Headquarters in Heidelberg. After final revisions, I sent a copy to Lamson and asked for the general's final comments. I forwarded another copy to the British Historical Office for criticism and asked them to show it to Field Marshal Montgomery for his views. I also sought the comments of Montgomery's wartime chief of intelligence, E. T. Williams, a former Oxford don, whom I had interviewed when he was British military representative at the United Nations at Lake Success. He was now back at Oxford as warden of Rhodes House.

Realizing that I wanted the sort of careful reading that a tutor would give a student's paper, Williams gave me judicious and detailed comments, but did not go beyond saying that the British had another view on some matters, or that there might be sources I had not seen. The British official historians indicated some differences and gave me additional records. In return, they asked me if I could supply copies of Montgomery's correspondence with Eisenhower, which the field marshal had refused to give them.

A short time later, Lamson wrote from SHAPE that Montgomery had been told by his former Second Army commander that he had better read my manuscript, and had come by to suggest to Eisenhower that my book should not appear, lest it strain Anglo-American cooperation. Eisenhower had replied that I had sent the manuscript to many authorities for helpful suggestions and that a final version would be available to the field marshal. I wrote a letter for Lamson to show Ike, pointing out that I had written British historians for suggestions, and that in 1947 I had attempted to interview Monty with results that Ike would remember. Now I had sent a copy of the manuscript to Montgomery on the same basis as the one to Eisenhower: for corrections and helpful comments, not for censorship.

Ike returned home to run for the presidency, the British Historical Office accepted my final revision of the manuscript, and the book was published in 1954. I presented the first copy to President Eisenhower at the White House on the ninth anniversary of VE-Day, May 8, 1954.

Several years later, a British author wrote a popular volume dealing with the controversial period of Arnhem and the delays in clearing the Scheldt Estuary, heavily critical of Montgomery. He wrote that Monty had caused Eisenhower to suppress part of my initial manuscript.

The chief historian of the U.S. Army promptly protested this statement to the British writer, who promised to make a correction in his next edition (which never appeared). The incident stuck in Monty's mind. When I again asked to see him, in 1961, to get material for my biography of George C. Marshall, he agreed. He recalled that he had refused to see me and Corelli Barnett (who had criticized Montgomery in *The Desert Generals* some years ago), and that we both had written rude things of him.

Technically, my story of my experiences connected with writing about SHAEF ends here. But a better ending exists in General Marshall's letter of congratulations to General Eisenhower at the end of the war in Europe. Marshall wrote:

You have completed your mission with the greatest victory in the history of warfare.

You have commanded with outstanding success the most powerful military force that has ever been assembled.

You have met and successfully disposed of every conceivable difficulty incident to varied national interests and international political problems of unprecedented complications.

You have triumphed over inconceivable logistical problems and military obstacles and you have played a major role in the complete destruction of German military power.

Through all this, since the day of your arrival in England three years ago, you have been selfless in your actions, always sound and tolerant and altogether admirable in the courage and wisdom of your military decisions.

You have made history, great history for the good of mankind and you have stood for all that we hope for and admire in an officer of the United States Army. These are my tributes and personal thanks.

M. R. D. FOOT

Eisenhower and the British

It is an impertinence for anyone—particularly for someone who is not even an American citizen—to discuss any aspect of Dwight Eisenhower in the presence of Stephen Ambrose, who has forgotten more about him than most of us will ever know. At least I served under Eisenhower, willingly; and will do what I can.

Eisenhower did not encounter the British until he was past fifty years of age, but then—after a moment's initial chill—worked with them intimately through four strenuous years of world war during which they learned to trust him, and he them, utterly. From the closeness of their wartime cooperation with him, the British imagined, wrongly, that they would have a special hold on his attention when he became president; this is a story of enthusiasm that turned to disillusion.

Eisenhower first met the British, in any quantity, at the Arcadia Conference in Washington, D.C., at midwinter 1941–1942. He did not greatly care for what he saw. He thought them standoffish—most Americans think the British officer class standoffish, correctly; it is a class that lives behind its faces, brought up not to enthuse. Worse, he thought they despised the Americans as amateur soldiers, and may well have been right; worse still, he thought them militarily timid. There he may have been wrong: They were simply being practical. They knew that their own forces were still pitiably weak and inexperienced, after twenty years' neglect between the great wars, and that the United States, in spite of tremendous potential, was at that moment weak as water militarily; to make immediate plans to deploy American strength was a waste of time.

Besides, the British were caught in a strategic fix that the Admiralty had long been explaining would be unbearable: the necessity of trying to fight the Germans, the Italians, and the Japanese all at the same time. That task, theoretically plumb impossible, was made no more easy to attempt by the incompetence of the old colonial staff in Southeast Asia, which seemed to have infected many members of the fighting services as well, as was becoming daily more appallingly visible, both in Whitehall and on the spot.[1]

1. For a recent, telling statement of what this felt like at the sharp end, see Terence O'Brien's *Chasing After Danger* (London, 1990).

One benefit did arise for Eisenhower and for the British from Arcadia, thanks to his good manners and his common sense: Both Prime Minister Churchill and the British officers who had met him went back to London with the knowledge that he was polite and businesslike. Here, they realized, was a competent staff officer who was interested in fighting war, rather than in protecting his own position on the staff—a knowledgeable and affable man who was not out to make trouble.[2]

When Eisenhower paid his first visit to London, at the end of May, 1942, on a reconnaissance mission for Marshall, he found a small, isolated American army staff, working leisurely hours, trying to run the European Theater of Operations in plainclothes. This was not his idea of how wars ought to be fought, even by the staff, and he was outspoken to Marshall when he got back to Washington. He then discovered that Marshall had already decided to put him in charge of Operation Torch, and he went back to London for a longer stay.

He was at once received into the staff stratosphere. Churchill, who had encountered him in Washington and taken to him immediately, himself initiated him into the ultra-secret decipher system, which unraveled enough of the messages the Germans sent over the Enigma machines they thought indecipherable to give the Allied High Command priceless insights into German strength and intentions.[3] To this innermost strategic circle he now belonged. He was treated as an equal by the chiefs of staff and by the leading men in the secret services; he was received, quite informally, by the king. He now had by British standards a rich man's income: he lived in the Dorchester Hotel; he adopted Claridge's as a favorite evening watering hole; and he found a country hideaway, Telegraph Cottage, just outside London at Kingston.

This might be the moment to dismiss, as Ambrose does, any serious suggestion that Eisenhower had an affair with Kay Summersby, his London driver, a story that seems at the time to have impressed even Bill Casey, then a very junior officer in the United States Navy, but not one with which history need bother any longer.[4]

Eisenhower found a quiet church in South Audley Street where he could pray, and he had a main headquarters in Grosvenor Square, not far from where his statue now stands outside the American embassy. Under his authority, the Americans pressed on with Operation Bolero, the transfer across the Atlantic

2. Compare and contrast initial British impressions of General Stilwell, who earned his nickname of "Vinegar Joe."

3. The opening chapter in Stephen E. Ambrose's *Ike's Spies: Eisenhower and the Espionage Establishment* (Garden City, N.Y., 1981).

4. See Joseph E. Persico, *Casey* (New York, 1990), 92–93.

of men, arms, machines, and aircraft in colossal quantities. He did his operational planning out of Norfolk House, in the southeast corner of St. James's Square. I was one of a horde of British and American officers who were in and out of Norfolk House, for months on end, while Torch was planned and, later, while Overlord was being planned from the same building. As an army intelligence officer, I had to deal with his intelligence staff. The branch of it that dealt with the German forces that Overlord was to attack was headed by J. L. Austin, a philosopher from Magdalen College, Oxford, ill-disguised as a lieutenant colonel. He was said to have made Aristotle's books more intelligible than they had ever been since Aristotle died and carried his clarity into his unaccustomed new work. His weekly Martian reports, widely read among those of the staff who were classified "Bigot"—that is, who knew roughly when and where the next major landing was to be—became a vital tool for understanding the enemy.

Many of the British knew, but none of us were tactless enough to mention to any of our American friends, that Norfolk House was the site of the birthplace of King George III, whom every good American is brought up to abhor. There is no reason to suppose that Eisenhower was aware of the ill omen; in any case, he turned the omen around. For he built up first of all a genuinely international staff in Norfolk House, one in which Americans and Britons worked side by side for a common aim, quite irrespective of nationality. Eisenhower would have agreed with E. C. Bentley's clerihew:

> George III
> Ought never to have occurred.
> One can only wonder
> At so grotesque a blunder.

Certainly, his building up of this international staff was an important contribution to Anglo-American amity, then and later; the staff became, in the end, a formidable instrument in securing the defeat of the Axis.

Here is an example, perhaps unfamiliar, of his standing among the leading personalities in war direction who were in England at the time. The source for it, Brian Urquhart, later Sir Brian and a distinguished figure in the United Nations headquarters, was then a young major in the nascent British airborne forces, on the staff of General "Boy" Browning (Daphne du Maurier's husband, and reputed ever since he had been adjutant at Sandhurst the smartest officer in the army). Browning was in the process of welding airborne troops into a *corps d'élite* and wanted to show off what they could do. Urquhart, who did not much care for parachuting, found himself in charge of a party who were to give a demonstration drop on Salisbury Plain, on a blustery day, to Eisenhower among others:

Emerging from our aircraft, I could easily see that the situation was not promising. The line of seated VIPs, which was supposed to be at a safe distance, seemed rapidly to get nearer as I descended and the wind blew our little group off course. At about 300 feet I could sense the distinction of the lonely line, the prime minister, the air minister, Sir Archibald Sinclair, the sinister Lord Cherwell, [the] Chief of the Imperial General Staff [Sir Alan Brooke], and the American general, as well as our own General Browning. Shouting a warning and trying to side-slip, I landed with a sickening bump just in front of General Eisenhower. The wind then took my parachute and dragged me at 30 miles an hour straight through the VIP line. Detaching my parachute harness, I came to a halt, stood up and, for want of anything better to do, saluted.

The British, except for Browning, behaved badly, muttering "Disgraceful," "Damned poor show," and so on, and looking embarrassed. General Eisenhower, on the other hand, was perfectly charming. "Are you all right, son?" he asked. "You shouldn't be jumping in this wind anyway." He looked quizzically at the cylindrical cardboard container around my neck. I explained that it contained two carrier pigeons for communicating with Headquarters, and I extracted one, attached a message cylinder to its leg, and threw it into the air to launch it on its mission. The pigeon had evidently had enough nonsense for one day and flew to the top of a nearby bush, where it sat cooing and eyeing the company with an evil look. "I see we shall have to do something about your communications," Eisenhower said.[5]

Churchill agreed with Eisenhower that the closer the English and the Americans worked together, the better. While Torch was in the planning stage, he used to have a weekly meal with Eisenhower and Mark Clark, à trois; in his own phrase, "We talked all our affairs over, back and forth, as if we were of one country."[6] Once this friendship went rather far. At an informal meeting of potentates, at which several others were present also, Churchill deluged Clark with detailed advice for his ludicrous mission by submarine into Algeria a few weeks before the operation began, a mission so risky that it does little credit to the common sense of any of those who authorized it.

One of these potentates, then Lord Louis Mountbatten, became a particular friend of Eisenhower's in London, encouraged him to move around and make friends among the highest command—with whom Mountbatten lived in princely ease—and aroused his interest in special devices and special operations, with which he himself as chief of Combined Operations had plenty to do.

5. Brian Urquhart, *A Life in Peace and War* (London, 1989), 54–55.

6. W. S. Churchill, *The Hinge of Fate* (Boston, 1951), Vol. IV of *History of the Second World War;* Martin Blumenson, *Mark Clark* (London, 1984), 472.

At Combined Operations Headquarters he ran—against the grain of all three armed services—a combined services staff, of which, most suitably, the chief was a Royal Marines brigadier with pilot's wings. Under Mountbatten's powerful leadership, officers at COHQ learned to think in interservice terms, instead of concentrating on the outlook of their own service; and Mountbatten's example helped Eisenhower in his struggle to impose, by a different but also an intense kind of leadership, an international outlook on his staff at Allied Force Headquarters, both during the planning and during the conduct of Torch and of Overlord.

Eisenhower had political troubles enough with the French not to need any with the English as well. When he got to Gibraltar to take charge of Torch, shortly before the D-Day landings, he found himself confronted by General Giraud, who had just been spirited out of the south of France in comic-opera circumstances, in a British submarine that had a U.S. Navy captain on board for diplomatic cover.[7] Giraud believed he was to take charge of Torch himself, having done none of the planning and having, indeed, no idea of how to conduct an operation of such size and intricacy; he had spent most of the previous two years in a prisoner of war camp, not a life tending to sharpen strategic grasp. Eisenhower was able to subdue Giraud to his own stronger will, only to be confronted at once with the problem of Admiral Darlan, the senior French politico-military figure in Northwest Africa.

The Eisenhower-Darlan agreement saved a lot of trouble and anxiety in North Africa; yet it caused still more trouble and anxiety in England and in metropolitan France. There were unhappy repercussions on the English left and center; the entire staff of the French section of the BBC, for example, resigned in protest. In France itself, resistance work came to a practical standstill, for Darlan was Pétain's deputy, a leading figure in the Vichy regime, which almost all resisters sought to overturn. That the Americans should be on such friendly terms with him seemed deeply suspicious. When they moved on from Algeria to France, would there be an Eisenhower-Pétain agreement, under which leading resisters would be kept in jail? (Darlan did nothing to release those few held, often in noisome prisons, who had tried to oppose the Vichyste regime in Algeria or Tunis.)

From these embarrassments everybody was saved when on Christmas Eve, 1942, a young French royalist walked up to Darlan in his office and shot him dead. Giraud had the young man shot in his turn, two days later. Years afterward, it turned out that the young man, Fernand Bonnier de la Chapelle, was an officer in SOE's local training section, and was using an SOE pistol.[8] It also emerged

7. Marie-Madeleine Fourcade, *Noah's Ark* (London, 1973), 143–71.
8. Sir Douglas Dodds-Parker, *Setting Europe Ablaze* (Windlesham, Surrey, 1983), 115–16.

that he was acting on his own initiative—or so at any rate his superiors in SOE have always maintained; this is probably one of those questions into which historians will do well not to inquire too closely.

Eisenhower's own slate, at any rate, was perfectly clean in this affair, and he soon indicated to the Allied secret service heads in Algiers that he wanted them, as well as the rest of his staff, to act together rather than to act separately. Early in January, 1943, he sent for the heads of OSS and of SOE in Algiers and saw them in his office in the presence both of General Donovan, the head of OSS, and of General Gubbins, the mainspring of SOE. Eisenhower sat at his desk, his hands clasped in front of him, and besought OSS and SOE to work as closely with each other as his fingers were joined together. Everyone nodded in agreement. As the meeting broke up, Donovan took Dodds-Parker of SOE to one side and explained that Dodds-Parker was not to mind if, now and again, OSS agents went off and did something odd entirely by themselves, for Donovan needed to keep up a supply of interesting telegrams he could show to Roosevelt.

As an international—Anglo-American—staff, the staff of Allied Force Headquarters at Algiers worked well. Eisenhower soon had a chance to show how carefully he meant to hold the balance level between the two nationalities. After the setback in the Kasserine Pass in February, 1943, he sacked the American corps commander, Fredendall, and, to show fair play, also sacked his own chief of intelligence, the British brigadier Mockler-Ferryman, who returned to London and was understood to have gone back to work in the Boy Scout movement, of which he had been a supporter. In fact, Gubbins, who had served in Dublin with him at the end of the Troubles, 1921–1922, snapped him up for SOE, in which he became the coordinator of operations into northwestern Europe. Experts still dispute how much blame Mockler-Ferryman really ought to have carried for the Kasserine upset; whether or not he correctly interpreted the ultra-secret material he was sent before he laid it before Eisenhower is too technical a question to be embarked on here.

That spring, Eisenhower forged two significant friendships with senior British personages. The first was Harold Macmillan, the British minister-resident in Algiers. His post was political, rather than diplomatic; his job was to provide a link between Eisenhower and Churchill, and so to ensure that the British did have some say in the policies Eisenhower carried out. Care had been taken that the Torch landings were under the Stars and Stripes rather than the Union Jack, in order to spare the sensibilities of the French armed forces, still outraged by the necessary killings at Mers-el-Kebir in July, 1940, when the British fleet had had to shell a French one to keep it out of German hands. All the same, the British felt that, as they had provided for Torch part of the transport, much of the naval support, much of the air cover, most of the combined operations know-how, and a decent proportion of the fighting soldiers, they ought not to be left entirely in the political cold thereafter. Macmillan's initial reception by Eisenhower was chilly —someone had made a muddle about warning him in advance about what Macmillan's role was to be—but the newcomer disarmed the general at once by explaining that his mother had been born in a small town in Indiana, and thereafter they got on perfectly amicably.[9]

Eisenhower also soon established a perfect rapport with Field Marshal Alexander. Alexander was a modern *chevalier sans peur et sans reproche;* imperturbable from childhood, a Guards brigadier-general on the Western Front while still in his twenties, a survivor of the struggle for Latvian independence, of the retreats from Dunkirk and Burma, he had plenty of experience of battle, as well as ideal manners. Eisenhower was happy to leave to him the grand tactics (if we may borrow a phrase from General Koenig) of driving the Germans out of Tunisia, by combining the efforts of the First and the Eighth Armies in a campaign that remains a model of how to operate on exterior lines, while he himself looked after politics and relations with the Combined Chiefs of Staff.

The victory they achieved in May, 1943, secured more Axis prisoners than the much more trumpeted victory of the Red Army had done at Stalingrad in the previous February.

Eisenhower's next task was to supervise the planning of Husky, the invasion of Sicily, which, again, he left largely to the experts, while he exercised a broad supervision over what they did. In the course of preparing it, he had his first detailed insights into the work of the deception staffs, headed in Africa by the enigmatic Dudley Clarke. Their masterpiece there, operation Mincemeat, eventually became the subject of a world bestseller, Ewen Montagu's *The Man Who Never Was.*[10] It completely deceived the Germans, who reinforced Sardinia and the Peloponnese instead of reinforcing Sicily; experience here encouraged Eisenhower to make full use of deception in the next great combined operation he had to command.

Meanwhile, there were plenty of political troubles arising out of Husky's success. The invasion of Sicily precipitated Mussolini's fall from power, within three weeks, and Eisenhower had to handle the approaches to the Allies made by his successors, Badoglio and Victor Emmanuel III. His chief difficulty was how to find a secure line of communication to them while the conditions of Italy's unconditional surrender were worked through.[11]

9. Alastair Horne, *Macmillan* (London, 1988), I, 156.

10. Ewen Montagu, *The Man Who Never Was* (London, 1953).

11. On this still controversial phrase, see A. E. Campbell, "Franklin Roosevelt and Unconditional Surrender," in *Diplomacy and Intelligence During the Second World War,* ed. Richard Langhorne (Cambridge, 1985), 219–41, 312–15.

Unexpectedly, SOE turned out able to provide a sufficiently secret channel. Dick Mallaby, an agent of theirs dropped into Lake Maggiore in the spring and fished out promptly by the carabinieri, was in Italian, not German, hands in a prison in Rome, and Dodds-Parker was able to assure Eisenhower that messages could be passed through him without German awareness of their content. This story seemed so improbable when it was first printed in the early 1950s that for years historians treated it as one of the sensational legends that get attached to secret agents; it now turns out to be perfectly true.

The administrative complications that accompanied the Italian surrender in early September were almost too much for Eisenhower, or for anybody else, to master. Churchill observed sourly that his civil servants were trying to force on him four times as many officials to manage half Italy as the India Office needed to manage all India. The free French, observing from the sidelines, made a discovery that interested them; de Gaulle, after what he had seen being prepared for the Italians, set up his Missions Militaires de Liaison Administrative to make sure that it was he, and not Churchill or Roosevelt, who secured local political power in France when the Germans were evicted from it.

Evicting the Germans from France turned out to be Eisenhower's next great task. He was the obvious man to command Overlord, if Roosevelt would not release Marshall for the purpose; Marshall turned out to be indispensable in Washington. Alan Brooke would dearly have loved the Overlord command himself, but turned out to be indispensable in Whitehall; besides, the American share in the expedition was going in the end to be so large that it had to have an American commander. Brooke bore the disappointment, as he bore everything, calmly. He used to let off steam in his diary about how intolerable his master and his working conditions were, but this was only letting off steam—his real feelings were under control.

Eisenhower made sure that planning for Neptune, the assault phase of Overlord—the actual D-day landings in western Normandy on June 5–6, 1944—intertwined properly with planning for Bodyguard-Fortitude, the major deception plan. Again, all the details of Fortitude had—manifestly—to be left to the experts of MI-5, the Security Service, which ran back captured German spies, and the London Controlling Section, which handled deception; on the rare occasions when they needed very senior support, it was Eisenhower who provided it. In particular, it was he who prevailed over the foreign secretary, Eden, when Eden wanted to relax all the restrictions on diplomatic missions' message sending abroad as soon as it was clear that the Normandy landings were safe ashore. Eisenhower had to remind Eden that the whole point of Fortitude was to persuade the Germans that Normandy was a feint, preparatory to General Patton's major assault from Kent with his notional army on the beaches south of Boulogne, which German general staff doctrine had laid down was the proper spot for the Allies to make their *Schwerpunkt*. Eden gave way; the ban continued for some weeks.[12]

This thoroughly perilous undertaking bore out Eisenhower's view, stated as far back as 1939, that an opposed landing from the sea was the most difficult task a general could undertake; his attempt was crowned with success.

Under him, the principal land commander was Montgomery, who much improved the plan that had been drawn up in 1943 by the chief of staff to the (then still unknown) Supreme Allied Commander; in particular, he expanded the original landing force from five divisions to eight. But the extra divisions imposed extra delay, from early May to early June, while the Russians' patience wore thin. I can testify, from my own knowledge as a junior staff officer at Combined Operations Headquarters, to the absolutely critical nature of the shortage of landing craft; more landing craft had to be found to carry the extra troops on whom Montgomery insisted, and they simply were not available in time to meet the May dateline that Churchill had promised Stalin. Postwar critics who argue that there were plenty of landing craft in the Pacific forget that in those days they could not be transported almost instantaneously to another ocean: Moving them took months.

So complete, by the spring of 1944, was British trust in Eisenhower that even the Royal Navy, always conscious of its role as the world's oldest organized fighting force and always jealous of its independence of all other authority, was prepared to cede to him the absolutely critical decision: Exactly on what day was Neptune to take place? The decision depended on tide, on weather (not too windy for parachutists), and on the state of the moon (airborne troops do not enjoy night drops with no moonlight at all).

When it came to deciding, Eisenhower fell back on the advice of a civilian, disguised as a group captain RAF to give him adequate gold braid for standing in the presence of many very senior officers—J. M. Stagg of the Air Ministry, weather forecaster. Luckily, Stagg's long experience enabled him to give a forecast that was better than an educated guess. Bad though the weather was on June 4, the day before the proposed invasion, Stagg was able to predict that there would shortly be enough mild improvement to make the landings feasible on the night of June 5–6; Eisenhower decided, "Let's go," and the weather held.

So did the courage of the sailors, soldiers, and airmen involved: Neptune succeeded, and Overlord developed from it, slowly but surely. Eisenhower re-

12. Sir Michael Howard, *British Intelligence in the Second World War* (London, 1990), V, 124–25, 191–96.

mained, as he had done in North Africa, well above the melee, perhaps a little too far above it. Montgomery retained command of the battle till September 1. And when Eisenhower did move across the Channel, he settled his main headquarters at Granville on the west side of the Cherbourg Peninsula, where Montgomery at least thought he was too remote from the actual fighting to be able to give any coherent leadership to it.

It is odd that so much attention has been given by sensationalists—some of them journalists, some of them pretending to be historians—to the differences of opinion between Eisenhower and his land commanders during the execution of Overlord, and so little to their real achievements. It is true that Montgomery, an unusually conceited general, did not enjoy subordination; he was once saved by de Guingand, his chief of staff, from a really serious blunder, which might have cost him his job—and showed his gratitude by dismissing de Guingand, cavalierly enough, at the end of the war. But it is also true, and far more important, that the advance from the Seine to the Scheldt conducted under Eisenhower's overall command by American, British, Canadian, French, and Polish forces was exceptionally swift, and also fit to go into staff college textbooks as a shining example: Paris fell on August 25, Brussels on September 1. This was a lot faster than General Guderian's celebrated advance in the opposite direction in May and June, 1940. Brussels had fallen to the Germans on May 18, Paris on June 14.

Beside this feat, the quarrel about the broad front versus the sharp thrust begins to look a trifle petty. I will not comment on it further, beyond remarking that while Patton ran out of gas, Montgomery ran out of sense.

Wavell, the British army's greatest modern brain, used to say that the core of generalship lies in logistics, rather than in tactics; and over logistics both Montgomery and Eisenhower made a mistake in the autumn of 1944 that has not perhaps received the attention it deserves from historians. The port of Antwerp, sedulously prepared for demolition by the Germans, was by a resistance miracle secured for the Allies practically intact, at the beginning of September, 1944. It was not open for traffic before the end of November because the mouth of the Scheldt had to be cleared of Germans first. Part of the blame for failing to clear the Scheldt promptly rests on both generals, as does part of the responsibility for the lives lost in the dreary Canadian campaign to free its left bank, and in the expensive descent on Walcheren. Supply, meanwhile, had to continue to come from remote Norman or Breton ports and beaches.

Efforts might have been much more profitably directed to clearing that estuary than to the glorious failure of Market-Garden, the airborne descent on Eindhoven, Nijmegen, and Arnhem that went, in Browning's phrase, "a bridge too far." It is easy to say this in retrospect, less easy to remember the elation, euphoria even, that permeated the whole of the Allied High Command after the breakthrough into Belgium. It seemed to everyone that the war in the West was about to come to a splendid conclusion; everyone had underestimated the tenacity and the fighting will of the Germans. Hitler, Himmler, and Goebbels went on into their Götterdämmerung, sustained by a historical memory that roused no echoes west of the Rhine. They all recalled that when Frederick the Great's Prussia was at its last gasp, attacked from two sides and about to succumb, Frederick's military genius had, after all, pulled it through. Hitler kept a portrait of Frederick by him and was conceited enough to think himself the King of Prussia's equal.

The British were by now recognizably inferior to the Americans. Not till July, 1944, we are proud to remember, were there more American than British divisions in actual contact with the enemy; but thereafter the balance of manpower engaged tilted decisively. All the British High Command, both in Whitehall and in the field, had themselves fought as more junior officers through the bloodbaths of the Somme and Passchendaele; all knew that the nation could not afford another such bloodletting so soon and were therefore extra cautious about casualties. None of them noticed that the nation was in fact undergoing another critical set of losses—the 55,000 dead of Bomber Command, Royal Air Force, consisted of the cream of the nation's technologists, whose loss would be bitterly felt in the fifties and sixties, when their savoir-faire might have rescued British declining industries.

The Americans were not as careless of casualties as the Russians were, but they could afford them in a way that the British could not. Eisenhower led his combined, largely American, armies to a total victory; past the hiccup in the Ardennes, much inflated both by Nazi propaganda at the time and by subsequent commentators unwilling to admit that their own side might have been right. The Ardennes offensive did not get as far as its half-way mark, the Meuse; it came nowhere at all near seizing its goal, which was Antwerp. It gave Eisenhower personally an uncomfortable fortnight, as he had to put up with some intense bodyguarding to protect himself from a supposed threat by Otto Skorzeny, the German coup de main expert; but as military setbacks go, it was minor. He pursued his broad front strategy with success, and in May, 1945, received at Rheims the surrender of his opponents. By then, even the champagne was flat. The war had gone on too long; it had been necessary to squash that Nazi viper absolutely.

Eisenhower's relations with the British remained warm. The king, who liked him, created him a Grand Commander of the Order of the Bath, the highest

English military knighthood. The University of Oxford acclaimed him on St. Crispin's day, 1945—anniversary of Agincourt as well as Balaclava—in a degree ceremony in which he was honored alongside Winant, Clark, Freyberg VC, Tovey, Alanbrooke, Montgomery, and Tedder. The public orator, in his eulogy of Eisenhower, referred to Normandy D-Day as "Illum diem sempiternae hominum memories commendatum." Tedder had been a tremendous strength and stay to Eisenhower, all through the Overlord battle, and it was fitting that they should get their honorary degrees side by side.

A few weeks later Eisenhower received a yet more signal honor: He was made a freeman of the City of London. This was a distinction that he treasured, both because it reminded him of his august predecessors and because he liked London and Londoners. His acceptance speech gives a curious foretaste of Kennedy's more famous "Ich bin ein Berliner."

He then went back to the United States and to his own brief academic career, at Columbia, whence duty again called him away, this time into politics. For some years past he had been an obvious piece of presidential timber; no one in Europe felt sure whether he was a Republican or a Democrat. He turned out a Republican, and a reliable election winner in November, 1952.

As president, Eisenhower's relations with the British were entirely transformed from what they had been when he had been a wartime commander in chief. During the war, the British had stood in a more special relation toward the Americans than usual. It had been the British task to put up some sort of stand against a Nazi war machine that threatened to conquer the world, eventually. The British victory in the Battle of Britain in 1940 had snatched the possibility of ultimate victory from the ruins of the debacle in France, earlier in the year; the British had continued, doggedly, to stay at war with Germany while the Germans decided to fight Russia as well, and then joined their Japanese allies in declaring war on the hitherto neutral United States. Great Britain provided the base from which the U.S. Air Force and Army could mount the final attack on Germany, of which Eisenhower had been the supreme commander. Yet the war had exhausted the British, emotionally as well as financially; national bankruptcy had loomed uncomfortably close in the late 1940s, and British delegations to Washington appeared rather as suppliants than as knowledgeable equal partners. It was into this altered world scene that Eisenhower reemerged into prominence as president. The British were no longer strong enough to demand the greater part of his attention. He found this out for himself during his spell as Supreme Allied Commander, Europe, 1951–1952.

The aging Churchill, prime minister of England again since October, 1951, was enchanted at the general's election victory: There was his old friend and dinner companion of the wartime years holding the greatest office in the world, and their intimacy could surely be renewed. Churchill turned out to be wrong; the magic spells did not really work any more. His appointments of Alexander, first as defense secretary and then as governor-general of Canada, were useful but not critical. He sometimes himself spoke of Eisenhower, strictly in private, in terms of disappointment—an old man's remarks to which perhaps too much weight has been attached by historians who are hostile to Eisenhower.[13]

Eisenhower remained devoted to Churchill—"Personal trust based upon more than a dozen years of close association and valued friendship" was the president's phrase—but such devotion was not enough to outweigh the national interest of the United States or to override the constitutional brakes on presidential action.[14] While Eisenhower remained "personally restive if not irritable under the restriction of formal agenda," and enjoyed meeting his old friend now and again, he was able to insist that their Bermuda Conference, held December 4–7, 1953, include the French as well as the British prime minister, and was able to dissuade Churchill altogether from the older man's plan to engineer a prompt meeting with Stalin's successors after that ogre died on March 5, 1953.[15]

A minor difficulty was that Eisenhower got on well with Churchill's foreign secretary, Eden, whom he admired, while Churchill frankly disliked Eisenhower's secretary of state, John Foster Dulles. John Foster's brother, Allen Dulles, got on well with his wartime friends who had stayed on in the British secret services; but these secret matters still seem to have to remain secret. It was more important for Eisenhower that he could not conduct foreign policy independently of Congress, in some parts of which anticolonialism combined with savage Anglophobia. He himself knew the English too well, and liked them too much, to sympathize with such far-right Republicans as Senator Knowland of California, who detested them, or with the Irish-American clans of Boston or Chicago, who detested them rather on historical than on political grounds. Yet he had sympathy enough with the anticolonial feeling then endemic in the United States to press on Churchill an anticolonial theme for the prime minister's final political gesture: also in vain.[16]

The correspondence with Churchill demonstrates how well Eisenhower was

13. Martin Gilbert, *Never Despair, 1945–1965* (Boston, 1988), 868, 1251, Vol. VIII of Randolph S. Churchill and Martin Gilbert, *Winston S. Churchill.*

14. Dwight D. Eisenhower to Winston S. Churchill, July 8, 1954, in Peter G. Boyle, ed., *The Churchill-Eisenhower Correspondence, 1953–1955* (Chapel Hill, 1990), 156. I am grateful to Dr. Günter Bischof for drawing my attention to this text, not yet available in London.

15. Eisenhower to Churchill, May 22, 1953, *ibid.,* 58.

16. Eisenhower to Churchill, July 22, 1954, *ibid.,* 163–65.

equipped to be president, because of his three years' intense experience of high politics and strategy, from the summer of 1942 to that of 1945; and in it he sometimes reveals his political philosophy. This was not confined to mistrust of Russian and of Chinese Communists in office, profound though that mistrust had become by the time his presidency began. "I grow very weary of bad manners in international relationships," he wrote in 1954, adding, a few lines later, "The salvation of liberty rests upon the unremitting effort of all of us to establish a solidarity among ourselves that in major objectives and purposes will remain firm against any assault." [17]

That Churchill, indeed Great Britain, would support him and the United States firmly in any major anti-Communist crisis he knew; and he despised journalists' "chatter about an Anglo-American rift which can benefit no one but our common foes." [18] But he knew, too, that time was creeping up on Churchill, born almost sixteen years before himself, and several times smitten by strokes —including a severe one in the summer of 1953, which postponed the Bermuda meeting by months. This may have led him and his advisers to discount a curiously prophetic warning Churchill uttered on June 21, 1954, six weeks after the fall of Dien Bien Phu: "In no foreseeable circumstances, except possibly a local rescue, could British troops be used in Indo-China, and if we were asked our opinion, we should advise against United States local intervention except for rescue." [19]

Eden, who had never been as close to Eisenhower as either Churchill or Alexander had been, was less affectionately disposed toward him; this did Anglo-American relations no good at the time of the Suez catastrophe.

It is time to grasp the nettle of Suez, a traumatic experience for the British, because it brought home to everybody what the ruling class had known for ten years and suspected for twenty—that Great Britain was no longer a power quite in the first rank. Eden tried to apply the methods of the mid-1940s as if nothing had changed since, with an insistence on secrecy extreme enough sometimes to defeat its object.

The crisis could hardly have come at a less convenient moment for Eisenhower, who was busy getting reelected. By that rule, inflexible as the laws of the Medes and the Persians, dating back to 1787, the vote fell on the Tuesday after the first Monday in November, 1956. By that moment Eden's disaster was plain for all to see. It was based on a faulty grasp of history, a false analogy between the Nasser of 1956 and the Hitler of 1938, and on his own failing health. Eisenhower behaved throughout with his usual straightforwardness. The British, looking

17. Eisenhower to Churchill, February 9, 1954, *ibid.*, 120.

18. Eisenhower to Churchill, May 24, 1954, *ibid.*, 143.

19. Churchill to Eisenhower, June 21, 1954, *ibid.*, 147.

round (as people always do) for someone else to blame, for what was precisely their own fault, sought to blame "the Americans" for having let them down at the crisis, but, when pressed, they always specified John Foster Dulles rather than Eisenhower as the villain.

When in January, 1957, Macmillan succeeded Eden as prime minister, he sought at once to renew his Mediterranean friendship with the president—with limited success. He was able to rebuild a part of the special relationship that the English continue to feel binds them to their transatlantic cousins. This feeling fails to notice that power is shifting away from the white Anglo-Saxon Protestant old ruling class, a shift of which the very name of Eisenhower ought to have helped to make them aware.

After his experiences in Algiers, Macmillan had always been particularly sensitive to the weight of the intelligence dimension in strategy and politics; at least he was able to bind up some of the rifts that had opened between the British and the American secret services after the flight of Maclean, and to reestablish a quiet and extremely efficient worldwide cooperation on signals and electrical intelligence that has flourished unobtrusively down to the present day.

Yet in 1960 at the U-2 crisis, Macmillan, like Charles the Tall, had only a walk-on part. This was a straight confrontation between the two superpowers: There was neither time nor room for the lesser fry. If Eisenhower wanted a text from the sermons of his childhood, he could find one at 2 Samuel 1:27— "How are the mighty fallen, and the weapons of war perished!"

FRED GREENSTEIN

Eisenhower's Leadership Style

I n the mid-1970s, I decided to pursue my longstanding interest in the impact of personality on politics by studying the personal characteristics of modern American presidents and their effects on national and international affairs. It seemed to me that I might most usefully proceed by identifying the presidents who have been most deeply preoccupied with placing their stamp on their times and studying them with the best available evidence of their characteristics and actions— namely, the testimony of their former associates and the published and unpublished documents of their presidencies.

Therefore, when I received invitations to give talks on the study of presidential leadership at two California universities, I resolved to stop in transit to the West Coast to examine the papers of a president who signaled his commitment to decision making with a desk placard that read "The buck stops here"— Harry S. Truman. After spending a week at the Truman Library, in Independence, Missouri, I planned to drive a few hours farther west on my way to California and take a perfunctory look at the holdings in the Eisenhower Library, in Abilene, Kansas.

It would take little time, I reasoned, to confirm the well-established view that even to speak of Eisenhower and leadership in the same phrase was a contradiction in terms. This was the president who had been ranked twenty-first by a panel of distinguished historians in a 1961 poll of presidential greatness—a tie with Chester Arthur. The view that Eisenhower was ill-suited for presidential leadership was widely shared during his years in the White House. I myself could still remember his vague, syntactically tangled answers to reporters' questions in press conferences, and his assertions that he was not familiar with matters that had been discussed in the New York *Times*. I had joined the laughter at the 1950s joke that, while it would be bad if Ike died and Nixon became president, it would be worse if White House chief of staff Sherman Adams died and Eisenhower became president.

I stopped in Abilene, in part to get evidence of how the presidency operated when a passive figurehead occupied the Oval Office. I also had been told by a former Eisenhower aide, General Andrew J. Goodpaster, that his boss really had been a shrewd, informed leader, and that I should take seriously a clever but speculative article by journalist Murray Kempton that described Eisenhower as an underestimated political genius.[1] I dismissed Goodpaster's assertion as the well-meaning idealization of an Eisenhower loyalist, but I did recognize that it would be necessary to check out his claim.

The Truman archives proved to be disappointing. There was no reason to challenge Truman's reputation as an activist, but neither he nor his aides had kept much of a record of his thoughts and behind-the-scenes deliberations. The Eisenhower Library archivists told me that I would find Eisenhower well documented. They pointed me to a recently opened set of papers—the files kept by Eisenhower's personal secretary, Ann Whitman. Mrs. Whitman's files included Eisenhower's most confidential correspondence, his private diary, notes on his meetings and telephone conversations, and even transcripts of secret recordings of some of his one-to-one meetings.

I had barely begun examining this material when I realized that, if anything, Goodpaster had understated his case. The Eisenhower revealed to me was far from being the superannuated general who, in the phrase of the keynote speaker at the 1956 Democratic convention, whiled away his time on "the green fairways of indifference."[2] Instead, he was at the center of his administration's decision making. He ran the show in his White House, not Sherman Adams or Secretary of State John Foster Dulles. The Whitman files were full of direct evidence of Eisenhower engaging in persuasion, bargaining, and other, less direct, political maneuvers. Moreover, the files showed him to be well informed and politically sophisticated, with a capacity to convey his views both on the substance of policy and on political strategy in precise, literate prose that bore no resemblance to the scrambled verbiage of his press conferences or the platitudes of his public addresses.

After two days in Abilene, I had to leave in order to meet my speaking obligations. In my first presentation, I circulated photostats from the Whitman papers to illustrate the ways in which the interests of political scientists might be illuminated by the evidence available in historical archives. The contents of the documents elicited so much interest that I decided to devote all of my second colloquium to advancing the thesis that students of the presidency had misunderstood the real character of Eisenhower. My listeners could scarcely have been more skeptical, but for each of their objections I managed to produce a doc-

1. Murray Kempton, "The Underestimation of Dwight D. Eisenhower," *Esquire,* September, 1969, pp. 108 ff.

2. The speaker was Tennessee Governor Frank G. Clement. The passage quoted can be found in *Facts on File Yearbook, 1956* (New York, 1957), 269.

ument providing powerful evidence that they were misjudging Eisenhower's leadership. It was clear that I had come upon impressively counterintuitive evidence about a modern presidency.

By the time I returned to Princeton, I had made up my mind to embark on an extended study of Eisenhower's leadership—the study that eventually appeared a number of years later with the title *The Hidden-Hand Presidency: Eisenhower as Leader.*[3] I shall summarize and illustrate my conclusions from that work and then briefly present some afterthoughts.

At the core of my analysis is the proposition that Eisenhower was a presidential activist, but that his distinctive kind of activism accounted for the underestimation of him by his contemporaries. It was an activist style that resolved a contradiction inherent in the job specifications of the American presidency. In most democracies, executive power is shared by two individuals with fundamentally different responsibilities: those of *head of state* and of *political leader* of the government. In Britain, for example, the queen stands for the nation and commands broad respect. The prime minster has the intrinsically controversial political responsibility of leading the government. In the United States we ask a single chief executive to do both and are regularly disillusioned when the individual we expect to be above politics enters the fray, making deals and otherwise engaging in practices that are unedifying but necessary components of democratic leadership.

It is not surprising that virtually every post–World War II president has gone through substantial periods of public disapproval after an initial honeymoon. Eisenhower, who experienced the longest sustained approval of any president in the period, was a conspicuous exception. One cause of Eisenhower's popularity appears to have been the distinctive way he dealt with the dilemma posed by the tension between the expectations that the president be an uncontroversial head of state and that he nevertheless be successful as a political leader. What he did was play up his activities as head of state while simultaneously working hard at the politics of the presidency, but doing the latter largely without publicity. Because he did not take the credit for his off-the-record politicking, scholars and Washington professionals thought he was inept. They failed to observe that he avoided the blame that comes from taking sides in political controversies.

One Eisenhower operating rule for being a private prime minister and public chief of state—a rule that I now find being imputed to his behavior even in situations where it did not apply—was hidden-hand leadership. When there were messy political jobs, he farmed them out. This was strikingly so in the case

3. Fred I. Greenstein, *The Hidden-Hand Presidency: Eisenhower as Leader* (New York, 1982).

of his administration's successful campaign to neutralize Senator Joseph Mc-Carthy in 1954. Eisenhower denied that the McCarthy affair had anything to do with him—it was the Senate's business. In fact, he pulled strings extensively, working privately through intermediaries to undermine the Wisconsin senator, occasionally taking an obliquely worded public swipe at McCarthy. He acted indirectly out of the conviction that he would lose and McCarthy would gain if he tangled directly with a political gutter fighter.

Another of Eisenhower's rules was the instrumental use of language. Some presidents—for example, Jimmy Carter—appear to use language in much the same way in public and in private. Eisenhower's discourse varied with the purposes it served. He went to great lengths to make his speeches sound presidential, while at the same time simplifying their rhetoric so that they might reach a broad audience. In his memoranda to aides, however, he often advanced complex arguments, doing so with impressive lucidity and logical clarity. And the language of his press conferences was notoriously vague.

We now know that Eisenhower's use of language was deliberate. We know this because the declassified records show what he said in his briefing sessions with Press Secretary James Hagerty just before he met the press. And we have his own testimony in the account in his memoirs of an illuminating exchange he had with Hagerty during the off-shore islands crisis on an occasion when Hagerty conveyed to Ike a State Department request that he refuse to answer questions about whether the United States would reply with force to an attack from the mainland on Quemoy and Matsu.

"Don't worry, Jim," Eisenhower replied. "If that question comes up, I'll just confuse them." The question did come up and Eisenhower said this:

> I cannot answer that question in advance.
> The only things[s] I know about war are two things: the most changeable factor in war is human nature in its day-by-day manifestation; but the only unchangeable factor in war is human nature.
> And the next thing is that every war is going to astonish you in the way it occurred, and the way it is carried out.
> So for a man to predict, particularly if he has the responsibility for making the decision, to predict what he is going to use, how he is going to do it, would I think exhibit his ignorance of war; that is what I believe.
> So I think you just have to wait, and that is the kind of prayerful decision that may some day face a president.

If this exercise in what has come to be called stonewalling baffled the press, it advanced Eisenhower's purposes by confusing the Chinese Communists. Eisenhower probably would not have fought for the island outposts adjacent to

China. But in the context of the 1950s, it would have been politically costly to lose them. In leaving China uncertain about what price it would have to pay for taking Quemoy and Matsu, Eisenhower was not necessarily leaving the American people up in the air. Who better to make such prayerful decisions, in their view, than the former supreme commander?

Eisenhower's off-the-record, prime ministerial leadership was also marked by a highly contingent mode of delegating authority. He gave different aides different amounts of leeway to act on their own. He also sometimes delegated the responsibility of announcing controversial policies to subordinates, leaving it to them to take the heat. James Hagerty once reminisced that when Eisenhower asked him to make some controversial assertion to the press, he would reply, "If I go to that press conference and say what you want me to say, I would get hell. "With that," Hagerty reported, Eisenhower "would smile, get up and walk around the desk, pat me on the back and say, 'My boy, better you than me.'"

What of the other side of Eisenhower's leadership? How did he hold his broad popularity as a noncontroversial head of state? He did this in large part by preventing political catastrophes, while not showing himself as the active agent in the controversial politics of keeping them from occurring. But he also protected his popularity in more positive ways. The films of cheering crowds exhibiting their enthusiasm for the beaming, gesticulating Ike are vivid reminders of his capacity to exhilarate his audience.

Eisenhower's public manner was so genuinely appealing we take it for granted that he evoked public enthusiasm without effort. That was not the case. He revealed how hard he worked at being an exuberantly inspirational leader in a document he did not mean to see the light of day—a draft introduction to his World War II memoir, *Crusade in Europe,* which reveals more of his hopes and feelings than he chose to include in the published book. In it, he recollected the tense days he spent in November, 1942, in a dismal, damp headquarters deep within the fortress of Gibraltar, awaiting the intelligence he needed to decide whether to order the invasion of North Africa.

"During those anxious hours," he wrote, "I first realized . . . how inexorably and inescapably strain and tension wear away at the leader's endurance, his judgement and his confidence. The pressure becomes more acute because of the duty of a staff constantly to present to the commander the worst side of any eventuality." Realizing that the commander has the double burden of "preserving optimism in himself and in his command" and that "optimism and pessimism are infectious and they spread more rapidly from the head down than in any direction," he made a personal resolution: "I firmly determined that my mannerisms and speech in public would always reflect the cheerful certainty of victory—that any pessimism and discouragement I might ever feel would be reserved for my pillow. To translate this conviction into tangible results . . . I adopted a policy of circulating through the whole force to the full limit imposed by physical considerations. . . . I did my best to meet everyone from general to private with a smile, a pat on the back and a definite interest in his problems."

President Eisenhower was as committed to inspiring morale as General Eisenhower had been. He insisted in appearing in motorcades, even though he found them bruising and exhausting. His commitment to the inspirational side of political leadership was so strong that he made it his habit to preach his own practice of reaching out eagerly to the public. White House aide Bryce Harlow remembered that Eisenhower told the professional politicians with whom he appeared: "Now here's what you do. Get out there. Don't look so serious. Smile. When the people are waving at you wave your arms and move your lips, so you look like you're talking to them. It doesn't matter what you say. Let them see you're reacting to them."

Since publishing *The Hidden-Hand Presidency*, I conducted another study—reported in a book entitled *How Presidents Test Reality*—comparing Eisenhower's actions in the sequence of events that led to the decision not to intervene in Indochina in 1954 with Lyndon Johnson's decision making in the 1965 intervention in Vietnam.[4] My concern and that of my coauthor, University of Vermont political scientist John Burke, was not so much with whether intervention in Vietnam and the other Associated States was or was not desirable in the two episodes as with the caliber of the decision making in the two administrations. In particular, we asked whether it was grounded in the available information and whether it was marked by a rigorous examination of the available options.

That study bears on my remarks today in that it enabled me to examine records on Eisenhower's leadership that were still classified when I wrote *The Hidden-Hand Presidency*. It therefore permitted me to conduct an independent test of the validity of my characterization of Eisenhower in that work. My coauthor and I found the same patterns I had observed earlier—for example, hidden-hand leadership and instrumental use of language. We did not conclude, as one recent historical work does, that the failure of Eisenhower to intervene in Indochina in 1954 was the result of a sweeping exercise of hidden-hand leadership in which he fooled his closest aides into thinking that he was seriously considering intervention, while acting in ways that made such an outcome impossible.[5]

4. John P. Burke and Fred I. Greenstein, *How Presidents Test Reality: Decisions on Vietnam, 1954 and 1965* (New York, 1989).

5. Melanie Billings-Yun, *Decision Against War: Eisenhower and Dien Bien Phu, 1954* (New York,

But there were more specific manifestations of hidden-hand leadership—for example, in connection with a key meeting on April 3, 1954, the date of what has sometimes been misleadingly called "The Day We Didn't Go to War."

In that meeting, John Foster Dulles, the secretary of state, and Admiral Arthur Radford, chairman of the Joint Chiefs of Staff, met with key congressional leaders to feel them out about how far Congress would go in the direction of permitting the administration to threaten military intervention in support of the besieged French garrison at Dien Bien Phu. The aim was to strengthen the French hand in the peace negotiations under way. Any discussion of American military intervention in Asia was profoundly controversial that soon after the Korean War. So was any implication that the United States would be passive in the face of a Communist victory. The declassified record shows that Eisenhower carefully orchestrated the April 3 meeting with his aides, the previous day. Then he absented himself to Camp David for the weekend, remaining in telephonic contact with Dulles, and insulating himself from what proved to be a contentious discussion.

Eisenhower's instrumental use of language was as evident in the Indochina crisis as had been in the evidence available when I wrote *Hidden-Hand Presidency*. His few references to Indochina in speeches were general and did not commit him to a specific course of action. His statements in press conferences, while grammatical, were not highly specific. In the most famous of them, he compared the relationship of Indochina to its neighbors with that of the first domino in a row of dominoes ready to be toppled, a metaphor that left room for the use of American military force in Indochina. But a few weeks later, when it became clear there would be no intervention, he changed the metaphor to that of a row of dominoes that the United States wanted to bolster so that it could withstand the fall of one of its fellows.

Eisenhower's most striking language in the Indochina crisis was in his private deliberations with his aides, and his personal correspondence. He was magisterial in the weekly NSC meetings. Sometimes waiting for aides to air their views,

1988). For a critique of the author's thesis see Burke and Greenstein, *How Presidents Test Reality*, 111n. The Billings-Yun study is part of an extensive and instructive research literature on Eisenhower and his presidency that appeared in the decade following the publication of *The Hidden-Hand Presidency*, including some works by authors who bill themselves as "postrevisionists" to signal their intention of modifying the insights of the first authors, who sought to document a different Eishenhower from the passive, inept nonleader of 1950s stereotypes. In general, the postrevisionist works tend to accept the latter-day finding that Eisenhower was intelligent and politically sophisticated, but challenge the ends to which he turned his efforts and the tenacity with which he advanced those ends. See the valuable bibliographical review in Chester J. Pach, Jr., and Elmo Richardson, *The Presidency of Dwight D. Eisenhower* (Lawrence, Kans., 1991), 263–72.

sometimes jumping into debates early, he framed issues, stated options, gave orders, all with authority and clarity, yet without inhibiting discussion. He displayed a comprehensive vision of the politico-military issues of the incipient Communist victory in Vietnam, showing the breadth and depth of his thinking in a letter to his former friend and subordinate, NATO chief Alfred Gruenther, that delineated the factors, personalities, and issues in the Indochina situation and spelled out their policy implications.

Throughout the 1954 Indochina crisis, Eisenhower showed a remarkable capacity for reality testing. His strengths are particularly evident when compared with the performance of Lyndon Johnson and his aides in 1965. In 1965, decisions were made on Southeast Asia without reflection about their consequences; there was little sustained policy analysis, and the decision makers allowed themselves to slide into an open-ended conflict, without examining evidence their own administration had produced that showed they were not doing enough to achieve victory, and that even if they did, they probably could not win. In contrast, Eisenhower's thinking was hard-headed, rigorous, and informed, and he orchestrated an impressively complementary advisory process.

Eisenhower's decision making on Indochina was not flawless, however. Although he performed impressively in the Indochina crisis, he did not systematically address the implications of his administration's later actions with respect to Indochina. It was, after all, a more or less unexamined Eisenhower administration commitment to support South Vietnam that the Kennedy and Johnson administrations inherited.

Eisenhower's failure to take a rigorous long-range view of America's stakes in Indochina no doubt was partly a result of the tendency for immediate crises to prevent any president from considering the longer view. But it also seemed to be the case that he sometimes contented himself with clarifying his own views about a policy problem and then failed to do what was necessary to persuade others of his position. McGeorge Bundy, for example, has argued persuasively that Eisenhower had a uniquely sophisticated view of nuclear strategy and was correct in resisting demands that he rectify a nonexistent missile gap. Nevertheless, Bundy asserts, Eisenhower simply failed to do an effective job of communicating his position and persuading his adversaries.[6]

The discrepancy between Eisenhower's penetrating private analyses of strategic matters and his rather unpersuasive public pronouncements on the topic leads me to a concluding speculation about what made Eisenhower tick. In a curious way, Eisenhower suffered from two of his strengths—his self-confidence and

6. McGeorge Bundy, *Danger and Survival: Choices About the Bomb in the First Fifty Years* (New York, 1988).

his capacity for rational analysis. His confidence in the correctness of his own views could lead him to forget that what was self-evident to him might be obscure to others. His rationality was accompanied by a distrust of the emotionalism of others. This fed his predilection for hidden-hand leadership, even on occasions when it might have been more effective for him to sell his policies to the public.

Eisenhower's periodic lack of follow-through on his own policy views probably also resulted from his remarkable freedom from a motivation one expects to find in generous proportions in the psyches of presidents—the ambition to be remembered in the history book chapters on presidential greatness.

The presidency was a postlude of Eisenhower's career. He had made his mark by 1945. His brother and chief confidant, Milton Eisenhower, told me a story with which I will conclude. In 1955, when Milton was president of Pennsylvania State University, Ike agreed to be commencement speaker. As the time for the outdoor ceremony approached, storm clouds formed. It would be possible to move the ceremony to an indoor amphitheater that could accommodate only a fraction of the guests, but at the considerable cost of disappointing parents and alumni. Distraught, Milton turned for advice to Dwight, who with utter equanimity replied: "I haven't worried about the weather since June 6, 1944."

Thomas M. Sisk

Forging the Weapon: Eisenhower as NATO's Supreme Allied Commander, Europe, 1950–1952

Dwight David Eisenhower served as the first Supreme Allied Commander Europe (SACEUR) and played a pivotal role in shaping the relationship between NATO's constituent parts as the head of the organization's military arm. Eisenhower's was the decisive voice in all military aspects of NATO. His opinion was also the mitigating factor in interallied diplomacy and in the Allies' domestic policies related to the alliance. When Eisenhower left his position as the commander of the Supreme Headquarters Allied Powers Europe (SHAPE), NATO had been transformed from little more than a debating society into an effective and integrated combat force.

What price did America pay for this achievement? The downside to this accomplishment was the growing and long-term American troop commitment to European defense. The United States realized that it had to help safeguard European security as the fates of both areas were inseparable. But this long-term troop commitment was never the intention of either the Truman administration or of Eisenhower as SACEUR. It is my contention that Eisenhower played a crucial role in bringing this long-term American troop commitment for the defense of Western Europe to pass. The related areas of strategy, diplomacy, and Allied domestic politics will be examined for evidence of this. Due to limited space, nuclear issues within NATO will not be dealt with.

Despite the importance of Eisenhower's tenure as SACEUR, this remains among the least studied areas of his life.[1] The existing works are laudatory and primarily devoted to the administrative development of SHAPE. More surprisingly, they consist of little more than either chapters in works of greater scope or as parts of chapters on a wider subject.[2] The situation is similar for stud-

1. See the historiographical introduction, this volume.

2. Examples are Stephen E. Ambrose, *Eisenhower: Soldier, General of the Army, President-Elect, 1890-1952* (New York, 1983); Ambrose with Morris Honick, "Eisenhower: Rekindling the Spirit of the West," in Robert S. Jordan, ed., *Generals in International Politics: NATO's Supreme Allied Commander, Europe* (Lexington, Ky., 1987); and Blanche Wiesen Cook, *The Declassified Eisenhower: A Divided Legacy* (Garden City, N.Y., 1981).

ies of Eisenhower's effect on NATO's military strategy.[3] This essay looks to help fill this gap in the Eisenhower literature.

One must understand the events leading to the founding of NATO and its subsequent militarization to fully appreciate Eisenhower's actions while SACEUR. Europe lay prostrate and broken after the horror of the Second World War. No country, save Switzerland, remained untouched. The economic infrastructure of each was in shambles. The psychological state of Europeans fared no better. The United States stepped into this void on June 5, 1947, with the declaration of the European Recovery Program (or Marshall Plan), conceived by Secretary of State George C. Marshall's State Department. There were many motivations behind this American commitment to help Europe rebuild. Among them were American guilt over pre-war isolationism, the realization that the economies of the United States and Western Europe were closely linked, and the fear of either a proto-Nazi or Communist subversion or Soviet aggression arising in the power vacuum of Western and Central Europe. The Marshall Plan set the stage for the economic recovery of Europe.[4]

Nonetheless, Europe remained militarily weak when seen against the growing perception of a Soviet threat.[5] This was despite incipient efforts at collective security such as the 1948 Western European Union (WEU). The problem with the WEU and other fledgling attempts at collective security was the reemergence of old rivalries among the major European powers. Franco-German mistrust stifled bids for West German rearmament and military integration and thereby all efforts to close the Western force requirement gap vis-à-vis the massive Red Army. The British, for their part, were largely unwilling to permanently station troops on the Continent. As with the Marshall Plan, the United States stepped into the breach by responding to the British call for an Ameri-

3. For examples see Marc Trachtenberg, *History and Strategy* (Princeton, N.J., 1991); Walter S. Poole, *The Joint Chiefs of Staff and National Policy, 1950–1952* (Wilmington, Del., 1980), Vol. IV of *The History of the Joint Chiefs of Staff;* and Robert A. Wampler, "Ambiguous Legacy: The United States, Great Britain, and the Foundations of NATO Strategy, 1948–1957" (Ph.D. dissertation, Harvard University, 1991). The author would like to thank Dr. Wampler for his insightful comments and suggestions on earlier drafts of this paper. These and his dissertation have greatly impacted its shape and direction.

4. The best overall surveys of the Marshall Plan are Michael J. Hogan, *The Marshall Plan: America, Britain, and the Reconstruction of Western Europe, 1947–1952* (New York, 1987), and Charles S. Maier and Günter J. Bischof, eds., *The Marshall Plan and Germany* (New York, 1991).

5. For an overview of the world situation at this time see John Lewis Gaddis, *Strategies of Containment: A Critical Appraisal of Postwar American National Security Policy* (New York, 1982), 3–89. Gaddis bases his argument on the importance of threat perception to the formulation of strategy and geopolitical world view. Also see Melvyn P. Leffler, *A Preponderance of Power: National Security, the Truman Administration, and the Cold War* (Stanford, Calif., 1992).

can military alignment with Europe. This was done with the negotiation of the North Atlantic Treaty in mid-1949 and the establishment of the Mutual Defense Assistance Program (MDAP) in October of 1950. While the former increasingly tied the United States to European defense, the latter provided the European countries with assistance in purchasing weaponry to strengthen their defenses without harming their recovering economies.[6]

The North Atlantic Treaty (NAT) did two things. First, it declared Western Europe to be America's special sphere of influence, thereby warning the Soviet Union against interference in regional affairs. The second effect of the NAT was to assure Europeans that the United States would not revert to its traditional military isolationism[7] and leave their countries alone to face either the Soviets or a resurgent Germany. It intended to integrate Western Europe rather than uniting the United States with Europe.[8] Given the strong Western European desire for an American commitment on the continent, one cannot view this decision as a sign of American "imperialism."[9] The impetus for a more direct U.S. involvement in Europe clearly originated with the Europeans. Ernest Bevin, the British foreign secretary, initiated the North Atlantic Treaty negotiations.[10] This initiative's psychological foundation was the European bewilderment at facing another foe so soon after defeating the Nazis. Above all else, Europeans wanted an assurance of U.S. assistance in stiffening their resolve to avoid the mistakes made after the First World War.[11] Finally, the Americans wanted nothing to do with a permanent presence in Europe. As Marc Trachtenberg has argued, ex-

6. Douglas L. Bland, *The Military Committee of the North Atlantic Alliance: A Study of Structure and Strategy* (New York, 1991), 93–112. For an overview of the Mutual Defense Assistance Program see Lawrence S. Kaplan, *A Community of Interests: NATO and the Military Assistance Program, 1948–1951* (Washington, D.C., 1980); and Chester J. Pach, Jr., *Arming the Free World: The Origins of the United States Military Assistance Program, 1945–1950* (Chapel Hill, N.C., 1991).

7. This is to differentiate between an American wariness of military and political entanglements with Europe and, according to Walter LaFeber, the fact that the United States had been economically involved with Europe long before it won its independence. See Walter LaFeber, *The American Age: United States Foreign Policy at Home and Abroad Since 1750* (New York, 1989), especially pp. xiv–xx.

8. See Lawrence S. Kaplan, *NATO and the United States: The Enduring Alliance* (Boston, 1988), 16–21, 34; Dean G. Acheson, *Present at the Creation* (New York, 1969), 380–81. See also Leffler, *Preponderance of Power*, 231, 233, 279–86, 316, 320–22, 348–51, 387, 390, 411, 460.

9. Geir Lundestad, *The American "Empire" and Other Studies of U.S. Foreign Policy in a Comparative Perspective* (London, 1990). Lundestad argues the case for the existence of an informal American empire. For a more useful definition of imperialism see Michael W. Doyle, *Empires* (Ithaca, N.Y., 1986), 30–47.

10. Alan Bullock, *Ernest Bevin: Foreign Secretary, 1945-1951* (New York, 1983), 614–21.

11. Robert H. Ferrell, "The Formation of the Alliance, 1948–1949," in *American Historians and the Atlantic Alliance,* ed. Lawrence S. Kaplan (Kent, Ohio, 1991), 11, 21–23, 25, 27.

amples of the American desire for a deployment of limited duration fills the early formative period of NATO.[12]

All this affected the development of American strategic thought. Robert E. Osgood has observed the interplay between military strategy and political influence.[13] American military commanders and strategists were divided among themselves over a "peripheral" strategy and one of forward defense. On the one hand, the air force was the proponent of a peripheral strategy. It wanted to defend Europe by means of strategic bombardment. The priority here was on obtaining air bases in North Africa, the United Kingdom, and the United States from which to launch conventional and atomic air strikes against Soviet cities. On the other hand, the army and the navy countered this emphasis on the periphery. These adherents of the forward strategy wanted to defend a line as far to the east of France as possible. The emphasis was placed on ground troops, tactical air and naval support, and the strategic bombing of Soviet liquid fuel plants.[14]

Interservice rivalry played some part in the drafting of these strategies.[15] But this was not the sole reason why the army and navy advocated this approach. The forward strategy simply made more sense. Militarily, this approach did not necessitate a withdrawal from the Continent. Peripheral strategy called for another D-Day type landing, which was rendered impossible with the Soviet development of an atomic capability. Politically, the forward strategy assured the Europeans that the United States was not isolationist and would not abandon them in the event of war. The crucial psychological effect of such an American commitment must not be underestimated. With the United States holding a defensive line in Germany, Europeans knew that they could draw on the immense American reserves in men and matériel. It also reassured them that, if overrun, their cities would not be among the targets of American bombers. The debate between these two strategies raged on for approximately two years before the logic of the forward strategy prevailed.[16]

Domestic policy affected diplomacy and strategy further as the Americans

12. Trachtenberg, *History and Strategy*, 167. Robert H. Ferrell takes a slightly different approach. He states that the Europeans were not overly eager for a permanent American presence but would accept it if that was necessary. Ferrell, "Formation of the Alliance," 11.

13. Robert E. Osgood, *NATO: The Entangling Alliance* (Chicago, 1962), 349–50. Also see Wampler, "Ambiguous Legacy," xxiv–xxv.

14. Trachtenberg, *History and Strategy*, 156–57.

15. See Ernest R. May, "The American Commitment to Germany, 1949–1955," *Diplomatic History*, XIII (1989), 446–47.

16. Steven L. Rearden, *The Formative Years, 1947–1950*, and Doris M. Condit, *The Test of War, 1950–1953* (Washington, D.C., 1984 and 1988), Vols. I and II of Alfred Goldberg, *History of the Office of the Secretary of Defense*. These are the most comprehensive overviews of the subject.

and Europeans looked to keep defense spending down. Army-navy forward strategy called for additional troops to hold a defensive line on the Rhine. These forces would have to be approved by an economy-minded Congress and the various European parliaments. The driving force here was economic prosperity. The Americans were looking to protect their economy from continuing budget deficits, and ensuing inflationary pressures, while the Europeans wanted to protect their social welfare gains. The primary bone of contention was where the emphasis was to be placed. Going back to the Marshall Plan rationale, the Europeans felt that the more important goal was economic prosperity. This would guarantee political stability and prevent Communist subversion. Their argument was that their economies were too fragile to support heavy defense expenditures. Therefore, the wealthy Americans ought to confront Soviet expansion with heavy defense spending. Europeans, for their part, wanted to fight the war against subversion by growing their economies and providing for the happiness and well-being of their people with high social spending.

Americans envisioned the threat somewhere between covert and overt Soviet actions. Truman and his advisers felt that the European economies had recovered sufficiently to face the threat of Communist subversion. The more immediate threat lay in overt Soviet aggression. The American military advised the Truman administration that a "window of vulnerability" had opened with the detonation of the first Soviet atomic device in late 1949. This is reflected in National Security Council paper NSC-68, a major rethinking of American strategy.[17] NSC-68 has been viewed as a fleshing out of Secretary of State Dean Acheson's strategy of creating "situations of strength." These men wanted a stronger conventional defense built while the rapidly weakening American atomic deterrent still held.[18] The Truman administration yielded to these pressures and pushed the Europeans for greater efforts in the field of military manpower.

Rapid German rearmament provided a deus ex machina for the Western manpower requirements. The question of German participation in European affairs cut across diplomatic, strategic, and domestic political issues. Integration of western Germany into European affairs would provide enough troops to help

17. For more on NSC-68 and its effect on the Truman administration see Gaddis, *Strategies of Containment*, 89–126; Paul H. Nitze, *From Hiroshima to Glasnost: At the Center of Decision, a Memoir* (New York, 1989), 82–140; Leffler, *Preponderance of Power*, 346–60; and Ernest R. May, ed., *American Cold War Strategy: NSC-68* (Boston, 1993).

18. For the complete text of NSC-68 see U.S. Department of State, *Foreign Relations of the United States, 1950*, I, 235–92 (hereinafter cited as *FRUS, 1950*); also newly reprinted in May, ed., *NSC-68*, 23–82. This document also reflects Acheson's "total diplomacy" speech of February 16, 1950, *Department of State Bulletin*, March 20, 1950. Trachtenberg, *History and Strategy*, 100–107.

offset the imbalance between forward defense requirements and the universal un-willingness of the Allies to pay for the increases themselves. However, domestic politics in France would not permit this.[19]

It was in the context of such systemic complications that NATO faced the challenge of the North Korean attack on June 25, 1950. This watershed event gave the United States a pretext to massively rearm and alter NATO's structure. NATO was militarized and restructured to solve its systemic problems. Among the more important of these issues were the shortcomings of the Marshall Plan, the inadequacies of European conventional forces, and the German rear-mament question.[20]

The North Korean surprise attack shattered the myth of the U.S. atomic de-terrent. Truman initiated the conventional force buildup advocated under NSC-68. He also decided that American troops were needed to pressure the Europeans for greater efforts in this sphere. The president announced the approval of "sub-stantial increases" in U.S. forces in Western Europe during September, 1950. This increase was tied to evidence of matching efforts by other NATO countries. In November, the activation of the U.S. Seventh Army in Germany, accompanied by expanded military assistance, augmented the increase. The approved money was to offset the shortcomings of the Marshall Plan. Britain and France were fac-ing budget crises as a result of increased defense spending. Additionally, the French Indochina War drained much of their available military manpower and equipment. This remained a serious problem for NATO until the French defeat at Dien Bien Phu in 1954.[21] The appointment of an American as SACEUR was made dependent on the approval of a plan for German rearmament and integration into European defense. The acceptance of the French Pleven Plan on December 19, 1950, paved the way for this, and Truman announced Eisen-hower's appointment as SACEUR the same day. The path was now clear for the

19. See Saki Dockrill, *Britain's Policy for West German Rearmament, 1950–1955* (New York, 1991), 4–20, and Thomas A. Schwartz, *America's Germany: John J. McCloy and the Federal Republic of Germany* (Cambridge, Mass., 1991), 113–55.

20. Walter LaFeber, "NATO and the Korean War: A Context," in Kaplan, *Atlantic Alliance,* 33–51, puts forth the thesis that the changes made in NATO at the outbreak of the Korean War were not a drastic change of course in President Harry S. Truman's foreign policy. They were merely part of a policy rooted in the detonation of the first Soviet atomic device. The Korean War simply added an urgency to the necessity of these changes. Leffler takes a similar stance in *Preponderance of Power,* 18. He sees NSC-68 as part of the development of Truman's policy, not as a dramatic departure in his national security strategy. This contradicts Gaddis' argument in *Strategies of Containment,* 89–117, which sees NSC-68 as a major point of departure for the administration.

21. Kaplan, *Community of Interests,* 172; Brian R. Duchin, "The 'Agonizing Reappraisal': Eisenhower, Dulles, and the European Defense Community," *Diplomatic History,* XVI (1992), 208–15; and Dockrill, *Britain's Policy for West German Rearmament,* 9, 106, 120, 139.

Americans, primarily through Eisenhower, to exercise considerably more influence on the course of Western defense.[22]

It was through Eisenhower's decisive leadership, based on his fame from World War II, that many of NATO's systemic problems were either resolved or started in that direction. This was accomplished through the three pillars of Eisenhower's authority as SACEUR. These were his own personal prestige, the grant of power given him by Truman and the Allies, and the symbolic nature of his position.

Eisenhower's personal prestige gave him unprecedented authority in military matters. The West viewed him as its preeminent military authority because of his role in the liberation of Europe from the Nazi yoke during World War II. Eisenhower's prestige was such that his was the only name mentioned in connection with the appointment of a SACEUR. The foreign ministers of the NATO countries unanimously requested Truman to appoint Eisenhower as SACEUR on December 19, 1950.[23] This prestige was decisive in settling diplomatic, strategic, and domestic issues of a military nature.

The grant of authority given to Eisenhower by the Allies and Truman was extensive. He asked for and received "absolute authority to train the national forces assigned to his command and to organize them into an effective integrated defense force." Additionally, the SACEUR was charged with preparing the means for executing the missions given to him and ensuring that they were coordinated with NATO planning. He was delegated as the chief adviser to the Standing Group, a committee composed of the chiefs of staff of the NATO countries. This advisory role covered the deployment of troops and building of infrastructure. In keeping with SACEUR's stature, Eisenhower was given direct access to national ministers and heads of government when necessary. This was necessitated by the authority given to him by the alliance.[24] With this grant, Eisenhower was given full power to determine the strategy and look of NATO defense. His direct access to chiefs of staff and governments gave him the right and method to influence domestic policy in the various countries to further this end.

The third pillar of Eisenhower's authority as SACEUR was the symbolic na-

22. A more detailed explanation of this period in NATO's development can be found in Timothy P. Ireland, *Creating the Entangling Alliance: The Origins of the North Atlantic Treaty Organization* (Westport, Conn., 1971), 183–207, and Acheson, *Present at the Creation*, 435–45, 457–59, 478–88.

23. See U.S. Delegate Minutes of the First Meeting of the Sixth Session of the NAT Council with the Defense Minister, Annex B, December 18, 1950, in *FRUS*, 1950, III, 594–95 and the President to General of the Army Dwight D. Eisenower, December 19, 1950, *ibid.*, 605–606.

24. See Final Communiqué, 6th session, NAC, December 18–19, 1950, in Ismay, *NATO*, 186.

ture of the position. He was the embodiment of the U.S. commitment to Europe. As such, Eisenhower was an important sounding board for European statesmen. They sought out Eisenhower to gauge American response to matters of policy. They also tried to influence him to bring about sympathy for their various national positions.

The converse was true as well. Eisenhower was a major conduit for the transmission of the Truman administration's policies. Eisenhower wore two hats in Europe. One was that of the SACEUR. The other was that of the commander of American troops in Europe. Therefore, Eisenhower was responsible for implementing administration policy in Europe. But, as a NATO official he was also responsible for devising an alliance strategy that supported NATO's central purpose, securing its members from the Soviet threat.[25] Eisenhower's actions proved him to be more an agent of American policy than of European.

Eisenhower's strategic concept for NATO was based on the alliance's central purpose, collective security from the Soviet threat. This security rested on two principles. First was the preservation of the internal stability of member countries. The Marshall Plan and MDAP ensured this. The second principle was the creation of a plausible military deterrent to Soviet strength. The ultimate aim was the development of enough military strength to drive back an invader.[26]

The strategy for NATO defense was outlined for Truman on January 31, 1951. Eisenhower saw Europe as a bottle with its widest part in Russia, its neck in Western Europe, and the opening in Spain. On either side of the bottle were bodies of water controlled by the Western Allies, with land masses on the far side that were suitable for air bases. Eisenhower's concept was to use superior air and sea power on both flanks and rely on land forces in the center. Then, if the Soviets attacked in the center after sufficient forces were in place, he would "hit them awfully hard from both flanks. I think if we build up the kind of forces I want, the center will hold and they'll have to pull back." [27] Eisenhower's strategy exploited the advantages of the defender. He employed a numerically inferior but well-entrenched force and supported it with massive air and naval power. He refuted arguments that such a force on the Rhine might threaten Russia by explaining that such a force was merely defensive, and that the Soviets understood it as such. Eisenhower's reasoning was that fifty divisions could not attack Russia because much of its manpower would be consumed in protecting flanks and the zone of the interior for defense in depth.[28]

25. Wampler, "Ambiguous Legacy," xiii.
26. Kaplan, Community of Interests, 75.
27. Notes on a Meeting at the White House, January 31, 1951; U.S. Department of State, Foreign Relations of the United States, 1951, Vol. III, pt. 1, p. 454 (hereinafter cited as FRUS, 1951); see also p. 427.
28. Ibid., 455.

Eisenhower's strategy for NATO defense reflected the culmination of his experience to that point. It showed his commitment to the ground defense of Europe, the theory of collective security, and the concept of balanced forces. The first part of the equation was acquired during his time as the temporary chairman of the Joint Chiefs of Staff (TCJCS) during the years 1949–1950. This time also reinforced the balanced force and collective security ideas and experience he had gained from World War II.

Eisenhower accepted the need for a solid ground defense of Europe during the FY 1951 budget debate. Truman had appointed him as the TCJCS to help move the services toward agreement after the bitter fight over armed forces "unification" had all but killed interservice cooperation. Eisenhower was mandated to coerce the Joint Chiefs of Staff into compromises on force configurations that fell within tightening budget constraints and still provided for an acceptable national security posture. Eisenhower considered the president's budget ceiling of $13 billion unreasonable and unrealistic but agreed to work within its constraints, fully realizing the pressures on Truman from the Congress and Bureau of the Budget.[29]

Shortly after being appointed as the TCJCS, Eisenhower told Secretary of Defense James V. Forrestal which types of forces merited priority consideration. These were strategic air power; an effective submarine navy with at least one naval carrier task force; and an army capable of rapid mobilization for the defense of Alaska, the Suez region, and possibly limited operations in Western Europe.[30] He altered this approach as the budget debates intensified. The peripheral strategy remained the operative war plan for FY 1951, but Eisenhower directed the development of OFFTACKLE, a plan that called for greater ground and sea forces to hold defensive lines in Europe and the Middle East. He thereby came to accept the concept of a forward defense with this plan. This change came from diplomatic pressures from European Allies, the realization that a reentry into Europe would be difficult given Soviet troop strength and atomic capability, and the belief that this could help compose service differences by reassuring each that they had an important role to play.[31]

The budget process also reveals Eisenhower's commitment to balanced forces. He remained convinced of strategic bombing's efficacy, but privately realized

29. Rearden, *Formative Years,* 364–65; Robert H. Ferrell, ed., *The Eisenhower Diaries* (New York, 1981), 153; Townsend Hoopes and Douglas Brinkley, *Driven Patriot: The Life and Times of James Forrestal* (New York, 1992), 405–14.

30. Eisenhower to Secretary of Defense Forrestal, December 21, 1948, in Louis Galambos *et al.,* eds., *The Papers of Dwight David Eisenhower* (Baltimore, Md., 1984), X, 379–381 *passim,* 382 specifically.

31. Rearden, *Formative Years,* 365.

that during the first few months of a war, "a few big carriers might be our great-est asset." He personally believed that the United States needed an active fleet of ten carriers with six to eight of those in constant operation.[32] One of Eisen-hower's final actions before relinquishing his duties as TCJCS was to urge Louis Johnson, the new secretary of defense, to restore a cut made in air force allocations. The basis of this request was that the proposed funding for FY 1951 made a reliance on strategic air power unavoidable. This meshed with the stress U.S. strategists placed on the deterrent power of military preparedness. Fi-nally, Eisenhower emphasized the need to preserve and enhance America's ability to launch a sustained and vigorous long-range bombing offensive.[33] Eisen-hower proved his commitment to balanced forces by working to ensure that each service received funding according to its importance under his strategic concept.

Eisenhower's commitment to an American ground presence in Europe demonstrates his devotion to collective security. His request, as a condition of accepting the SACEUR position, for full authority to train troops and weld them into an effective and integrated defense force supports this as well. Col-lective security was something he had learned from working with the British and French during World War II. Eisenhower stressed NATO's importance to U.S. safety and its need for U.S. equipment, leadership, and patience to an informal joint congressional meeting on February 1, 1951.[34] He saw that the United States needed Western and Central Europe as a forward defensive perimeter. He also realized that the Europeans could not defend themselves without U.S. assistance in the short term. Eisenhower believed in collective security because the polit-ical and economic health of the United States and the individual European na-tions relied on the cooperation of the Western free world community.

Eisenhower accepted the American troop commitment to Europe as the best way to bring about collective security from the Soviets. He never believed that this commitment should be permanent, a sentiment he shared with the Truman administration. What Eisenhower did accept was the strategy for collective de-fense outlined in the NAT negotiations. This gave the United States the chief responsibility for strategic bombing, delegated the conduct of naval operations in the open sea to the United States and Great Britain, assigned the primary bur-den for tactical air warfare and raising the hard core of ground power to the con-tinental countries, and stipulated that the other NATO countries should not at-tempt to duplicate the naval and strategic air functions.[35] Eisenhower accepted

32. *Ibid.*, 157.
33. *Ibid.*, 373.
34. Condit, *Test of War*, 340.
35. Note by the Secretary of the North Atlantic Defense Committee (Donnelly) to the

that the European economic situation would not permit them to build large forces immediately. He concluded that the Americans needed to exert a dynamic leadership and provide troops until the Europeans could slowly rebuild their armies. This was necessitated by the growing Soviet threat. If the West did not strengthen its military might before the Soviets came to preponderant power, then the NATO allies would have no room to maneuver afterward.[36]

Eisenhower believed that the best way to exhibit American leadership in Europe was through an early and massive infusion of troops into Europe. But this troop commitment was to be of a limited duration. Before accepting the command position, he wrote that no period of time could be affixed to the length of U. S. involvement in NATO, but it could be one that might last for "ten, fifteen, or twenty years."[37] After returning from his initial tour of European capitals prior to establishing command, Eisenhower added a handwritten note to this entry in which he stated his opinion that "in the element of time, the *U.S. should establish clear limits* and should inform Europe of these estimates. This applies to the length of time we should maintain sizable American forces in Europe."[38]

Two letters that Eisenhower wrote afford a further glimpse of his thoughts on the duration of American troop commitment. Late in February, 1951, he wrote an informal report to President Truman. Eisenhower expressed his pleasure with the administration's decision to add four divisions to its troop strength in 1951 but cautioned that this commitment should not give anyone at home or abroad the impression that the number was a permanent solution to the West European dilemma. Furthermore, while he did not believe it possible to predict future force requirements, Eisenhower felt that if the NAT signatories could "by combined effort produce quickly the strength needed, it should be possible, *within some 4 to 8 years, to reduce the American ground forces stationed here at the same rate that European systems develop the trained reserves to replace American units.*"[39] In a more forceful statement of this position, he wrote: "*If in ten years all American troops stationed in Europe for national defense purposes have not been returned to the United States, then this whole project will have failed.*"[40] The reasoning for this

Committee, Enclosure, Strategic Concept for the Defense of the North Atlantic Area, December 19, 1949, in U.S. Department of State, *Foreign Relations of the United States,* 1949, IV, 353–58.

36. Leffler, *Preponderance of Power,* 383–85, 406–408, 411–16, 450–57; Trachtenberg, *History and Strategy,* 103–10.

37. Diary entry for October 28, 1950 (emphasis added), in Louis Galambos *et al.,* eds., *The Papers of Dwight David Eisenhower* (Baltimore, Md., 1984), XI, 1391 (hereinafter cited as *EP,* XI).

38. Handwritten note added on February 1, 1951, in *EP,* XI, 1392 n14.

39. Eisenhower to Edward John Bermingham, February 28, 1951 (emphasis added), in Galambos *et al.,* eds., *The Papers of Dwight David Eisenhower* (Baltimore, Md., 1989), XII, 69 (hereinafter cited as *EP,* XII).

40. *EP,* XII, 77 (emphasis added). In thirty years there would be 490,000 American troops stationed in different locations abroad. See *EP,* XII, 78n11.

conviction was his belief that the United States could not be a "modern Rome guarding the far frontiers with our legions if for no other reason than because these are *not,* politically, *our* frontiers. What we must do is to assist these people [to] regain their confidence and get on their own military feet." This was a sentiment he was to repeat.[41]

The political issue was not, however, the most important point for Eisenhower. Next to political psychology and European dependence on the United States, Eisenhower's foremost reason for not wanting to maintain an indefinite troop presence in Europe was the effect it would have on the American economy. Solvency and economic prosperity were the end all to his thinking on American security. In his eyes, large defense expenditures and ensuing budget deficits would lead to fiscal insolvency.[42] Eisenhower felt that "bankruptcy for us would be a tremendous, if not decisive, victory for the Kremlin," because of the disgraceful image communism painted of capitalism.[43]

The question then became one of how, and at what intervals, to achieve the desired withdrawal of troops. This became intertwined with how best to provide the second area of NATO's mission, integrated and effective collective security. Eisenhower believed that this required five elements. In the early phases of development it involved American troops, the American nuclear "umbrella," American leadership, and German rearmament. These elements would provide the protection necessary for the development of the most important part of Western European security, the political, economic, and military integration of the region. In a diary entry dated June 11, 1951, Eisenhower exclaimed, "I am coming to believe that Europe's security problem is never going to be solved satisfactorily until there exists a U.S. of Europe. . . . It seems scarcely necessary to enumerate the problems that arise out of or are exaggerated by the division of West Europe into so many sovereign nations." [44]

European integration also became Eisenhower's solution to the German question. Europe and the United States were on the horns of a dilemma from midsummer to fall of 1950. There was general disagreement on whether to rearm Germany, and if so, how and when that was to be accomplished. A temporary solution was reached at the December, 1950, meeting of the NAC in

41. Quote is from *EP,* XII, 77. For further evidence of this expression see letter to Robert A. Lovett, Secretary of Defense, dated September 25, 1951, *ibid.,* 566.

42. This was a major difference between his thinking and that of the administration in approving NSC-68. The document was based on Keynesian economics and its theory of deficit spending spurring economic growth. See *FRUS,* 1950, I, 235–93. For an expression of Eisenhower's belief see the letter to Martin Withington Clement on November 9, 1952, in *EP,* XII, 865–69.

43. *EP,* XII, 75.

44. *Ibid.,* 340. For other incidences of this view see *ibid.,* 398, 408, 457–63, 1102.

New York when the French tabled the Pleven Plan for an all-European army composed of regimental combat teams from France and Germany, primarily. These forces were to be grouped together to form divisions and placed under French command. This was eventually compromised with the Spofford Plan, which seemed to overcome some of the various objections of the Americans.[45] However, there remained doubts about the efficacy of the proposed European Defense Force (EDF). Eisenhower, as both SACEUR and the West's preeminent military authority, held the key to this problem. He was originally against the Pleven Plan because it seemed to include "every kind of obstacle, difficulty, and fantastic notion that misguided humans could put together in one package,"[46] but became convinced of its usefulness by at least July 18, 1951. Soon thereafter, Eisenhower cabled Secretary of Defense George C. Marshall, stating that he had become convinced that the time had come to push for the earliest possible implementation of the European Defense Community (EDC) concept. He added that he was prepared to do whatever he could to obtain these units, which were to include a German contribution.[47]

The evidence suggests that John J. McCloy, the U.S. high commissioner for Germany, and Jean Monnet, a longtime French internationalist, played a role in changing Eisenhower's mind about the EDF.[48] The apparent reasons for this change of mind were a growing frustration with the slow progress in European rearmament, a sense of a general political and economic weakness in Europe, and the difficulties he was experiencing in his dealings with twelve different countries. These all led him to believe that Europe needed some type of "spectacular accomplishment" to break its inertia. Paramount in all this was a fear that the Europeans expected to lean on American support indefinitely. The desire to discover a method of breaking down this dependency was what led Eisenhower to agree with the European-wide sense of internationalism that pervaded the period. He believed the EDF would lead to a politically united Europe, his idea of a United States of Europe.[49]

To further this goal, Eisenhower personally intervened in the Paris discussions on the EDF and affected them tremendously. By throwing his support

45. For an overview of this rather complicated issue see Dockrill, *Britain's Policy for West German Rearmament*, 21–58, and Schwartz, *America's Germany*, 113–55. Also see Konrad Adenauer, *Memoirs, 1945–1953* (Chicago, 1965), 344–59, 400–402, and Jean Monnet, *Memoirs* (Garden City, N.Y., 1978), 336–49.

46. Telegram from Eisenhower to George Catlett Marshall, August 3, 1951, *EP,* XII, 458.

47. *Ibid.*

48. Robert McGeehan, *The German Rearmament Question: American Diplomacy and European Defense After World War II* (Chicago, 1971), 129.

49. Schwartz, *America's Germany,* 222; *EP,* XII, 179–82, 273–76.

behind the EDC plan, Eisenhower ensured that the critics of the plan could no longer dismiss it as militarily impractical. He and his advisers then took the plan and forged it into an instrument of their own liking. Addressing one final concern of U.S. Army Chief of Staff General J. Lawton Collins, it was arranged for Eisenhower to have "full power to organize and deploy European units as required by any military situation." He and Washington then pressed for quick results and received that in a fifty-page interim report.[50]

The way he gained this initial victory in the long-raging EDF battle was the way in which Eisenhower sought to gain the American troop withdrawals he desired. This was through the "*continuous [and] energetic [exertion] of American leadership*," which he saw as the tertiary mission of SHAPE.[51] The next question is how did Eisenhower hope to demonstrate this leadership and create the sense of unity that would allow the withdrawal of American troops?

The immediate answer was through the early infusion of American troops to solve the temporary problem of manpower shortages needed for deterrence, accompanied by a "major and special contribution . . . in the field of munitions and equipment."[52] This is the primary reason why Eisenhower agreed to the incredibly high force goal figures that emerged from NATO's crucial Lisbon Conference of February, 1952, not his involvement in inter- and intra-service rivalry as suggested by Ernest R. May.[53]

50. See *FRUS*, 1951, Vol. III, Pt. 1, pp. 820, 838–39, 843–46, 903–905, 937–38, 1269; and Schwartz, *America's Germany*, 225, 231.

51. *EP,* XII, 566. Emphasis added.

52. Cited in Francis A. Beer, *Integration and Disintegration in NATO: Processes of Alliance Cohesion and Prospects for Atlantic Community* (Columbus, Ohio, 1969), 94, 95.

53. May, "The American Commitment to Germany," 447. There is an inherent contradiction in May's argument. First, one needs to question why a man committed to the full integration of his headquarters would be party to inter-service rivalry. Eisenhower insisted not only on national integration but also on integration by service. The men picked to fill positions were picked on the basis of their being the best men for the job. Additionally, if Eisenhower were looking to increase the army's share of the defense budget by pushing for more soldiers in NATO, then why was he looking to bring the troops back home as quickly as possible? If the troops were to come home as Eisenhower planned, then they would become the targets of an economy-minded Congress, as May argues. The above is also the reason why Eisenhower encouraged the NAC to accept Turkey and Greece as members of NATO (see Kaplan, *The Enduring Alliance,* 50). Their divisions would go a long way in making up the shortfalls SHAPE was experiencing on its crucial southern flank. This was also the reason for German rearmament. The German divisions were needed to implement the "forward strategy" on the central front that the French had insisted on in the early phases of NATO's development. Indeed, that Eisenhower intended to use the EDF to send troops home is evidenced in a report filed with the British prime minister, Winston Churchill, by Anthony Eden, then deputy prime minister. It detailed a conversation Eden had with Eisenhower in which the general told Eden that he envisioned the EDF as a conduit to draw the American and British troops into reserve status. See Anthony Eden, *The Memoirs of Anthony Eden: Full Circle* (Boston, 1960), 36.

Another way to exhibit this leadership was to influence those bodies of the alliance that wielded the most authority. In 1951, as part of the Brussels Conference of the North Atlantic Council (NAC), NATO structures were reorganized to allow for the integration of the military element. At this time the SACEUR was made directly responsible to the Standing Group, who were responsible to the Military Committee, composed of the chiefs of staff from each signatory country. The Military Committee was responsible to the Council of Deputies, who reported to the highest organ of NATO, the NAC. The NAC was reorganized to accommodate the ministers of defense, economics, and state of each member country.[54]

Eisenhower saw the NAC as the body imbued with the authority that made it the proper vehicle for the expression of American leadership. He lobbied long and hard to encourage the NAC members to begin preparing public opinion for the acceptance of a rearmed Germany and a united Europe. Eisenhower believed that the best way to prepare public opinion was through the demonstration of unity of purpose. This could be accomplished with more frequent NAC meetings, at least on a quarterly basis.[55] He felt that these meetings were of such importance that they should occur with or without a set agenda.

The European ministers were not the only recipients of this lobbying effort. Eisenhower wrote numerous letters to Robert A. Lovett, the secretary of defense, and William Averell Harriman, the administrator of the Military Assistance Program. Both of these "wise men" were subjected to lengthy letters extolling the necessity for the exertion of American leadership in the NAC and NATO.[56] This was naturally linked to the frequency of the meetings. Eisenhower wrote, "NATO needs an eloquent and inspired Moses as much as it needs planes, tanks, guns, and ships. He must be civilian and he must be legion—he must speak to each of the countries, every day of the year—he must be the product

54. See Ismay, *NATO: The First Five Years, 1949–1954* (The Hague, 1954), 41–43; also Draft Memorandum prepared for John Ferguson of the Policy Planning Staff, July 16, 1951, and the ambassador in Turkey (Wadsworth) to the Secretary of State, September 24, 1951, in *FRUS, 1951*, III, 554, 578.

55. See Eisenhower to William Averell Harriman, June 12, 1951, in *EP,* XII, 345, 347; Eisenhower to Paul van Zeeland, September 11, 1951, p. 532; September 27, 1951, p. 584; Diary entry November 24, 1951, pp. 727-29. Also, the U.S. Delegation to the Seventh Session of the NAC to the acting secretary of state, September 15, 1951, in *FRUS, 1951,* III, 654.

56. That is, wise men in the sense given by Walter Isaacson and Evan Thomas, *The Wise Men: Six Friends and the World They Made, Acheson, Bohlen, Harriman, Kennan, Lovett, McCloy* (New York, 1986). This book looks at the lives of these six men and demonstrates how they shaped the postwar world through the positions they held, which were among the most crucial for deciding important questions of the direction of American national security policy.

of American leadership." [57] Eisenhower got his message through; at its yearly meeting in Ottawa, the NAC voted to begin meeting on a quarterly basis as opposed to its annual schedule. [58]

At this meeting, the NAC also established the Temporary Council Committee (TCC), composed of one representative from each allied country. These men were soon dubbed the "Wise Men." This group then named an executive bureau composed of the representatives of England, France, and the United States named the "Three Wise Men." [59] The TCC was charged with devising a means of reconciling the conflicting goals of military production and peacetime economic growth. [60] Its chairman, Harriman, had been serving as Eisenhower's unofficial liaison with Truman since the former's arrival in Paris. The two amassed a large body of correspondence. Among the topics discussed were two that would arise at the Lisbon Conference, where the TCC was to give its final report. One was the problem that Eisenhower was having with the chain of command and committee system of NATO. The other was the direction that the TCC's final report should take. [61]

Addressing the problem of support from the NATO structure, Eisenhower described the NATO channels of command, starting with the Standing Group and extending through the NAC, as being "well nigh useless." This worthlessness arose from the lengthy deliberations critical issues were subjected to. Decisions had to be cleared through all organs of NATO and the national staffs affected by a decision, and as Eisenhower said, "This we have to do daily." [62] He spelled out his problems with the NAC's subordinate body, the Council of Deputies. He stated that "as Shape [sic] I have no ministries to take over ministerial functions in finance, construction, policy, etc etc. The weak, unarticulated mechanism that tries to serve as the NATO overhead is futile." [63]

Eisenhower became increasingly critical of the support given him by the Council of Deputies. On July 20, 1951, Douglas MacArthur II, the counselor of

57. Letter from Eisenhower to Lovett, September 25, 1951, EP, XII, 568. For the need of more NAC meetings see ibid., 544, 546n8, 567, 569.

58. See Ismay, NATO, 43–44; FRUS, 1951, III, 654.

59. The members of the "Three Wise Men" were W. Averell Harriman, of the United States, who was named the group chairman, and the two co-chairs, Jean Monnet, a leading French economist and former deputy secretary of the League of Nations, and Hugh Todd Naylor Gaitskell, the British chancellor of the exchequer. Gaitskell was represented by Sir Edwin Plowden, the chairman of Britain's Economic Planning Board. See The U.S. Delegate on the TCC to the Secretary of State, October 12, 1951, in FRUS, 1951, III, 314–16.

60. Ismay, NATO, 44–45; Kaplan, The Enduring Alliance, 58–59.

61. Letter from Eisenhower to Harriman, March 14, 1951, EP, XII, 127–28.

62. Ibid.

63. Diary entry for July 11, 1951, in EP, XI, 341.

the American embassy in France and Eisenhower's political adviser, told the State Department that the Council of Deputies lacked "the organizational terms of reference, and level of representation which make for the most effective action."[64] Due to these problems, Eisenhower began discussing the need for a reorganization of NATO.

Eisenhower had a meeting with Harriman, Milton Katz, Charles Spofford, and General Alfred M. Gruenther, the SHAPE chief of staff. This influential group discussed a NATO reorganization with the aim of centralizing functions. The goal was to bring a lean efficiency to the organization. There were two objectives, first to "bring about a coordination and greater efficiency in American activity in the region, especially in directing all appropriate activities more effectively toward the purpose of building up collective security," and second, to "produce efficiency in the *Allied* machinery set up in NATO." The ideal solution, for the group, would be to have one man run the alliance on a regular basis.[65]

Prior to this meeting, Eisenhower had written Harriman about a discussion he had with the Belgian foreign minister, Paul van Zeeland. The major point Eisenhower made in this meeting was that he would like to see "*major*" policy handled at quarterly meetings, but "delegated *authority* must be exercised by the Deputies between quarterly meetings, and there must be a responsibility for submitting to the Council specific programs for approval."[66] The reforms enacted at Lisbon gave Eisenhower just what he was seeking. A secretary general was named and an integrated, international staff-secretariat was established to handle the daily business of the alliance.[67]

The other area of influence Eisenhower exerted at Lisbon was on the report of the TCC. He and Harriman discussed the report on several occasions during its inception. Shortly before he and Gruenther were to meet with the "Wise Men," Eisenhower detailed what he thought were the essential commodities in the collective security of Western Europe. Rather than focusing on economic and material factors, Eisenhower felt these men should look at areas where the West was "immeasurably stronger than the Iron Curtain countries." These areas were raw materials, the appeal of the Western cause, and the intelligence, productivity, and scientific skill of the western bloc's people. He went on to stress

64. The counselor of embassy in France (MacArthur) to the deputy assistant secretary of state for European affairs (Bonbright), June 20, 1951, in FRUS, 1951, III, 188–90; see also EP, XII, 117–23.

65. Eisenhower to Paul Gray Hoffman, ibid., 380. Emphasis in the original.

66. Letter, Eisenhower to Harriman, June 12, 1951, ibid., 345. Emphasis in the original.

67. See Ismay, NATO, 47–48, 55–65.

the need for building morale and stated, "I hope the wise men will see this. Certainly I'm going to try to *make* them see it." The importance of this was that Harriman would later cite these same elements, in slightly different language, as the assets that would enable the West to ensure peace.[68] Harriman presented Eisenhower with a final version of the report on December 14, 1951, prior to sending it to the member governments. Eisenhower replied the same day and declared that the report represented the first true statement of the dimensions of the necessary buildup in terms of an integrated military, economic, and political effort.[69] This was in spite of recommended force levels lower than both he and the Military Committee had approved.[70] As a concession to Eisenhower, and in keeping with his desire for a maximum effective force at the earliest possible date, the TCC established "firm" targets for 1952 and "provisional" targets for 1953. All others were "goals to be used for planning purposes to guide those early actions required to make possible the achievement of targets."[71]

Finally, Eisenhower indicated that the general approach of the plan supported the fulfillment of the mission NATO had entrusted him with, namely, the "building of balanced, combat effective forces at the maximum rate which the availability of resources will permit." He said the same of the program as envisioned for the next three years.[72] Eisenhower was pleased with the outcome of the Lisbon Conference. Not only had the TCC report set appropriate guidelines for the future but the NAC reorganized the civilian sector into a more efficient form and expanded the SACEUR's power in connection with the Standing Group.[73] It also ratified the EDC treaty, promising a German contribution to the defense effort.[74]

68. Diary entry for October 10, 1951, in *EP,* XII, 629. See *n*3 also.

69. Eisenhower to Harriman, December 14, 1951, in *EP,* XII, 788–90. A summary of the TCC's interim report can be found in *FRUS, 1951,* III, Pt. 1, pp. 389–92.

70. For a discussion of the force levels debate see Poole, *History of the JCS,* IV, 275–76.

71. Briefing Memorandum prepared for the secretary of state, December 17, 1951, in *FRUS, 1951,* III, 389. For a summary of TCC report see *ibid.,* 389–92, and Poole, *History of the JCS,* IV, 275–79.

72. Eisenhower to Harriman, December 14, 1951, in *EP,* XII, 788–89.

73. The SACEUR was now given expanded responsibilities for equipment and planning and logistic support. This was done over the objection that such an agreement would grant an international commander disproportionate authority over allocation of U.S. resources.

74. Diary entry, February 28, 1952, in Louis Galambos *et al.,* eds., *The Papers of Dwight D. Eisenhower* (Baltimore, Md., 1984) XIII, 1026–27. For more on the conference see the Final Communiqué of the Ninth Session of the NAC, February 26, 1952; the Supplementary Report of the TCC, February 8, 1952; and the Resolution by the NAC, February 23, 1952, in U.S. Department of State, *Foreign Relations of the United States, 1952–54,* Vol. V, Pt. 1, pp. 177–99, 217–18, 226–54; Acheson, *Present at the Creation,* 622–28; and Ismay, *NATO,* 50, 51, 55–56, 190–92.

When Eisenhower left NATO to run for president, the alliance's terms had been set. NATO was militarized, collective security was obtained, and the American presence assured with solid manpower and military assistance commitments. Eisenhower's impact was decisive, as he was both the agent of the Truman administration and a force in his own right because of his personal and Allied authority. He forged an effective integrated force and thus contributed to deterring the Soviets. Eisenhower also reassured the Europeans that they could depend on American support against Soviet aggression. By demonstrating this dependability, he and Truman rebuilt European morale.

Yet ironically, according to Eisenhower's own hopes for a *short-term,* or at worst *intermediate-term,* commitment of U.S. forces to Europe, he would have to be considered less than a success. Even though the Soviets were deterred and Europe was militarily integrated, NATO required the *long-term* commitment of American ground forces. This ran counter to Eisenhower's goal of withdrawing American forces in no more than ten years. From this perspective, Eisenhower failed, for American troops are still in Europe, forty years after Eisenhower's crucial shaping of NATO. Many factors contributed to this. The Europeans preferred social to military spending as long as U.S. forces provided the shield for the defense of Western Europe. Continuing financial crises kept the British and French from being able to afford costly ground troops. The Indochina War led to continuing French intransigence over German rearmament.[75] And gaps in force requirements could not be closed without a German contribution.

Eisenhower must share partial blame for not bringing American forces home within a ten-year time frame. His actions mirrored those of the Truman administration. These policies exhibited contradictions. Neither Eisenhower nor Truman realized that pushing for larger force levels led to an increasing spiral of American troop commitments to Europe. The Europeans either could not or would not reconcile increased defense spending with economic gains. Their unwillingness to pay for more troops left the Americans holding the bag. Either the United States made good the shortages, or the reason for their need would be questioned. Moreover, a decline in American credibility in terms of maintaining its commitments in Europe would certainly undermine Western security and NATO's *raison d'être.*

Eisenhower's role was central to all this. He spearheaded and then fed the growing force levels. His motive was to gain collective security by demonstrating American resolve with the infusion of American troops. This would reassure Europeans that America would play its part if they would play theirs. By saying that NATO needed ever more troops, Eisenhower reaffirmed the need for

75. Duchin, "Agonizing Reappraisal," 205.

American forces as long as the Europeans were stalling and German rearmament was postponed. The problem was that the Europeans, unwilling or unable to provide them, felt that America should.

Eisenhower sat in the middle. He ended up in an inescapable catch-22 situation. By calling for more troops, he forced the Americans to provide them, since Europe would not. But, he believed that these forces were required to encourage Europeans to honor their commitments. He possessed the means to remedy this situation. He was afforded full access to all Allied governments and military staffs. The Truman administration, under advice from George C. Marshall when secretary of defense, accepted Eisenhower's recommendations and requirements at face value.[76] With full access to all Allied governments and complete knowledge of Europe's very difficult economic and military situation, Eisenhower could have pushed the administration to realize that the United States would have to provide the majority of NATO ground forces for many years to come. By failing to admit that his policies tended to lead the United States into a long-term commitment to Western Europe, given the growing Soviet nuclear and conventional arsenals, Eisenhower prolonged the American presence indefinitely without ever acknowledging this trend to the American public. Thus he failed to adjust and realize his goal of an early American withdrawal from Europe. Yet given the ever-tightening American containment strategy and the growing militarization of American national security policy in the "ice age" of the cold war during Korea, Eisenhower may have had no other choice.

76. Paper prepared by the International Security Affairs Committee (undated) in *FRUS,* 1951, Vol. III, Pt. 1, pp. 193–97 and 193*n*1.

II Eisenhower as President: Domestic Policy

STANLEY I. KUTLER
Eisenhower, the Judiciary, and Desegregation:
Some Reflections

The constitutional struggles over race and civil rights dominate any discussion of President Dwight D. Eisenhower and the federal judiciary. Those conflicts, of course, transcended abstract constitutional doctrine and raised profound questions of power and social relationships in the United States. The Supreme Court touched off matters when it ruled in *Brown* v. *Board of Education,* in 1954, that racial segregation violated the equal protection of the laws clause of the Fourteenth Amendment. The Court thus repudiated its 1896 decision in *Plessy* v. *Ferguson,* legitimating segregation with that peculiarly contradictory phrase "separate but equal." For nearly six decades, this nation attempted to rationalize blatant racial discrimination in the traditional American language of equality.

The Eisenhower years marked a transition for American race relations. Coincidentally, the president of the United States had spent almost all of his adult life in the military, arguably the nation's most segregated national institution. Eisenhower's career, coupled with his longstanding experience and friendships in the South, made him highly dubious of the Supreme Court's decision. Yet, schooled as a traditional product of the military caste, Eisenhower also appreciated American constitutional norms. General Bruce Palmer, a former army vice-chief of staff and a historian of some note, contemptuously dismissed any notion that the military in 1974 might have aided Richard Nixon in his attempts to remain in power. Palmer recalled his irritation and resentment toward any such suggestion, insisting that his generation of military officers simply had been too well steeped in American constitutionalism.[1]

Eisenhower, of course, similarly respected that tradition. Throughout the

---

1. Robert Fredrick Burke, *The Eisenhower Administration and Black Civil Rights* (Knoxville, 1984), offers the most extensive treatment of Eisenhower's response to the growing civil rights movement in the 1950s. The Palmer episode is in Stanley I. Kutler, *The Wars of Watergate* (New York, 1990), 547. The general emphasized that he was speaking for his generation of officers and expressed some skepticism about contemporary junior officers. He specifically offered doubts about the commitments of such officers as Colonel Oliver North, one of the leading figures in the Iran–*contra* affair.

school segregation controversies of his presidency, Eisenhower consistently emphasized the need for maintaining the rule of law, social peace, and very crucially, the Supreme Court's role in interpreting the Constitution of the United States. His reluctance to specifically endorse the *Brown* decision undoubtedly weakened the immediate impact of the decision. But his personal views on race and segregation ultimately yielded to his commitment for maintaining constitutional order in the United States.

During the first arguments on public school segregation, in 1953, Chief Justice Fred Vinson, a Kentuckian, clearly opposed any frontal attack against southern school practices. Although he had found law and graduate school segregation unconstitutional, he was reluctant to extend those rulings to cover the entire educational system. But as the Court prepared to hear reargument on the issue, Vinson suddenly died, on September 8. Justice Felix Frankfurter, who had little respect for his colleague, later remarked to one of his former clerks, "This is the first indication I have ever had that there is a God." [2]

Eisenhower's subsequent appointment of California governor Earl Warren to replace Vinson in 1953 had more links to Practical Politics than to Providence. The choice apparently originated with a promise offered prior to the Republican National Convention in 1952. Eisenhower, locked in a bitter struggle with Senator Robert A. Taft for control of contested southern delegations, needed support, and his advisers turned to the California governor, promising Warren a Supreme Court seat when the first vacancy occurred. At the same time, the Eisenhower staff played a double game, dangling the vice-presidency in front of Richard Nixon in exchange for his undermining Warren's control of the California delegation—a matter that forever embittered Warren toward Nixon. When Vinson died, Eisenhower briefly flirted with the notion that the Chief Justiceship constituted an exception of his promise to Warren. The president considered other possible candidates—including, incredibly enough, former presidential candidate John W. Davis, then the lawyer of record for South Carolina in a pending school desegregation case. [3]

Warren's selection is one of the most significant and memorable acts of Eisenhower's presidency—whatever one's regard for Warren's opinions. In the particular area of race and civil rights, Warren skillfully massed his colleagues to maintain unanimity in such cases—sometimes at the cost of diluting doctrine. [4]

2. Richard Kluger, *Simple Justice* (New York, 1976), 591, 656.

3. Piers Brendon, *Ike: His Life and Times* (New York, 1986), 215; Stephen E. Ambrose, *Eisenhower: The President* (New York, 1984), 128–29.

4. Dennis Hutchinson, "Unanimity and Desegregation: Decision-Making in the Supreme Court, 1948–1958," *Georgetown Law Journal,* LXVIII (1979). The phrase "all deliberate speed," which supposedly established a guideline for the implementation of desegregation, offers a vivid

On occasion, Eisenhower expressed enormous satisfaction with his selection, but other negative, damning statements about Warren and the desegregation decision have haunted the president's historical record. He once remarked that Warren's appointment was "the biggest damn fool thing I ever did." Earlier, the president had told Attorney General Herbert Brownell that he hoped the Court would defer a desegregation decision until the next administration. "I don't know where I stand," he told Brownell a month after the Court held school segregation unconstitutional, "but I think that the best interests of the U.S. demand an answer in keep[ing] with past decisions."[5] Some might have a little trouble with that typical "Eisenhowerese," but in fact it amounted to nothing less than a clear preference for maintaining *Plessy* v. *Ferguson* as the law of the land.

Privately, Eisenhower told Warren that he opposed placing white girls in classrooms with black boys. Southerners, he told the new chief justice in 1954, "are not bad people. All they are concerned about is to see that their sweet little girls are not required to sit in school alongside some big overgrown Negroes." Nearly two years later, confiding in his diary, and perhaps with an eye to history, Eisenhower noted, "Of course I favor the elimination of segregation, because I believe that equality of opportunity for every individual in America is one of the foundation stones of our system of government."[6]

Eisenhower's biographers dutifully quote him on both sides of the fence—not an altogether unique phenomenon in the man's history, of course. But the president's record demonstrates—after some initial, almost fatal, hesitation—a clear commitment to enforcing federal court orders as if they were laws that he was constitutionally obligated to enforce. Disclaiming any interest in segregation or integration, he told an old friend in November, 1957, that he must uphold "specific orders of our Courts, taken in accordance with the terms of our Constitution as interpreted by the Supreme Court." Eisenhower's position starkly contrasts with Andrew Jackson's alleged retort to Chief Justice John Marshall's decision in the *Cherokee Nation* case: "John Marshall has made his decision, now let him enforce it." Eisenhower disagreed completely. "If the day comes when we can obey the orders of our Courts only when we personally approve of them, the end of the American system . . . will not be far off."[7]

---

example of the Court massing behind a convenient, but vague, slogan. Although Justice Frankfurter promoted the phrase, the chief justice embraced it rather readily.

5. Brendon, *Ike,* 279. Ambrose, *Eisenhower,* 129, concluded that Eisenhower "remained convinced" throughout his presidency that he had made the right choice in selecting Warren. The president's reactionary brother Edgar denounced Warren as a dangerous left-winger, while brother Milton considered Warren too much to the right.

6. Ambrose, *Eisenhower,* 190; Robert H. Ferrell, ed., *The Eisenhower Diaries* (New York, 1981), 313.

7. Robert Griffith, ed., *Ike's Letters to a Friend, 1941–1958* (Lawrence, Kans., 1984), 193.

Three days after the decision, the president observed that the Court had "spoken" and that he was sworn to obey the "constitutional processes in this country." But for the next two years, Eisenhower generally displayed caution on the merits of the issue itself. He counseled restraint to black leaders and urged the country to accommodate what he considered the moderate responses of such southern political leaders as Governor James Byrnes, of South Carolina, who called for calm, reason, and local solutions. In press conferences, Eisenhower talked about the "practical problem" of desegregation and the "very deep-seated emotions" involved. He also lent comfort to local control advocates when he praised the diffuse authority of tens of thousands of school boards as a "safeguard against centralized control and abuse of the educational system." The president pleaded for understanding of the southern white position. "The people who have this deep emotional reaction on the other side were not acting over these past three generations in defiance of law," he said. Instead, they had dutifully followed the Court's earlier approval of segregation and it would "take time for them to adjust their thinking and their progress to that."

By 1956, however, Eisenhower and his advisers realized that they had to publicly counter mounting southern calls for resistance. Nearly all southern legislators had signed the "Southern Manifesto," a not-so-subtle call for defiance of the Supreme Court's ruling. Local politicians took the cue and preached resistance, with far less subtlety. In March, the president—this time following Andrew Jackson's doctrine in another issue—specifically rejected a state's right to nullify federal law or court orders. And by that time, he began to allude more frequently to the notion that "the Constitution, as interpreted by the Supreme Court, is our basic law." Five months later, he added that "everybody knows I am sworn to uphold the Constitution. . . . That is my job," he told reporters. At that moment, however, Texas governor Alan Shivers, a Democrat who had supported Ike in 1952 and who did so during the then-current 1956 campaign, dispatched Texas Rangers to restore order in the Mansfield, Texas, school district, then under a federal court ruling to desegregate. The governor's idea of order was to instruct the Rangers to defy the court's decree and exclude the black children— all in the name of peace. The president meekly, even lamely, rationalized Shivers' action as a "locality's right to execute the police power." Furthermore, Eisenhower contended that in "the ordinary normal case" of keeping order, the federal government could not intervene unless the state proved unable to do so. During his press conference that day, the president specifically refused to endorse the *Brown* decision.[8]

8. Presidential Press Conferences, New York *Times,* May 20, June 30, November 24, 1954; February 9, 1955; March 1, March 15, March 22, August 9, September 6, 1956.

At that moment in political history, Governor Shivers satisfied the president that the state had maintained order. Perhaps it was good politics for Eisenhower and his advisers; but it created a precedent for other governors that eventually the president had to confront if he meant what he said about the Constitution, constitutional processes, and court orders. Some historians and biographers suggest that caution pervaded and dominated Eisenhower's behavior, whether in the military or political arenas.[9] The Texas affair can be understood as the politics of appeasement, or as reluctance, even naïveté, on Eisenhower's part—or perhaps both. But "jawboning" would not suffice. That simple response ran the risk of hardening a precedent into a principle of constitutional resistance—at odds with one that Eisenhower regularly proclaimed. And thus the stage was set for Governor Orval Faubus and the Little Rock crisis of 1957.

The politics of avoidance that Eisenhower attempted with Governor Shivers proved no match for Faubus' politics of opportunism. The president, whatever his intentions, unfortunately signaled vacillation and reluctance to confront the resistance Faubus stirred in Little Rock when the city's schools faced a federal court order for desegregation. Eventually, Eisenhower's advisers persuaded him that if he meant what he said about the Constitution and the role of courts, then he had no alternative but to resist Faubus and, if necessary, demonstrate his resolve with armed intervention. Eisenhower federalized the Arkansas National Guard, sent federal troops, and brought desegregation to Central High School in Little Rock. The president acted under authority first granted to George Washington in the 1790s, power that John F. Kennedy similarly used to implement federal court desegregation decrees. The courts, as Alexander Hamilton noted in *Federalist 78,* have "neither force nor will" of their own; their judgments are dependent upon voluntary compliance or upon the coercive power of executive authority.[10] Little Rock confirmed that observation.

Justice Felix Frankfurter, who had spent his legal career as a teacher and occasional advocate before joining the Supreme Court in 1939, once remarked (in obvious self-defense) that the correlation between prior judicial experience and one's record on the Supreme Court is exactly zero. The records of John Marshall, Louis Brandeis, and Hugo Black sustain Frankfurter's thesis. But some eminent jurists served on lower courts—Oliver Wendell Holmes, Stephen J. Field, and William J. Brennan come to mind. And, rest assured, we have had an am-

9. See, *e.g.,* Brendon, *Ike.*

10. Alexander M. Bickel's *The Least Dangerous Branch: The Supreme Court at the Bar of Politics* (New York, 1962) is perhaps the most useful contemporary account for understanding the nature and limits of judicial power.

ple number of mediocre justices who served with or without previous court experience.

For the past half century, Republican presidents (and President Clinton, a Democrat) generally have sought Supreme Court nominees with prior judicial experience. Seven of Franklin D. Roosevelt's appointments had no previous time on the bench (excluding Chief Justice Stone). Only one of Truman's four judges had judicial experience—the president preferring, as he once remarked, men with "political" experience.

With the exception of Warren, Eisenhower's Supreme Court appointments had judicial experience—and all proved unswerving in their commitment to the basic ruling in the *Brown* case. John Marshall Harlan, whose grandfather had been the lone dissenter in *Plessy,* Potter Stewart, and Charles Whittaker had served on the U.S. Circuit Court of Appeals. William J. Brennan, Eisenhower's lone Democratic appointee, had been a member of the New Jersey Supreme Court.

Eisenhower's selections, on the surface, appeared to be almost a conscious rejection of the New Deal–Fair Deal pattern for selecting judges. No senators with a somewhat radical reputation, no allegedly radical college professors, no bright young lawyer-professor types who rose to fame as tamers of Wall Street, no governors noted for tolerating such radical notions as sit-down strikes, and no old political cronies. But like FDR's appointees, Eisenhower's offered a varied mixture of doctrinal views.

Eisenhower's insistence on prior judicial experience took on new meaning for his Republican successors in the Reagan-Bush era. In Eisenhower's time, the idea seemed based on the desirability of having a jurist who knew the rigors and demands of judging—in contrast to so many of the Roosevelt appointees. Thirty years later, however, all the talk of experience merely veiled the need for insight into a judge's ideological positions and a means for applying a litmus test. Of course, all presidents have desired judges in their own image. The Reagan and Bush administrations have differed only in their overt, candid behavior in this regard, and perhaps their efficiency in finding such like-minded individuals.

The appointments of Warren, Brennan, Harlan, and Stewart—we will except Whittaker—certainly give Eisenhower an extraordinary record. We have had 107 Supreme Court justices. Most historians, I suspect, would include the Eisenhower quartet among the top third of the historically most significant justices. Two might even rank in the top 10 percent. But for the moment of the 1950s and the 1960s, when desegregation issues were in the forefront of federal court considerations, perhaps nothing proved more significant than Eisenhower's appointments to the vitally important Fifth Circuit Court of Appeals, whose jurisdiction consisted of old Confederate states. The Supreme Court, in its second *Brown* decision, had in effect given the lower courts responsibility for enforcing desegregation. Such was the task for those "lonely men," as they have been described, who ordered desegregation in their local districts, risking—and suffering—physical harm and social ostracization.

Let no one mistake or underestimate the heroic actions of the many southern federal district judges who brought about desegregation in their locales—such men as Frank Johnson and J. Skelly Wright must not be forgotten. The southern federal judges were a varied lot, but looming over them was the bank of fifth circuit judges, who staunchly supported or prodded the district courts to implement the new law of the land. And the circuit judges, in turn, buffered the Supreme Court from both enormous burdens and added political pressures. The fifth circuit, through the crucial years of the 1950s and 1960s, decidedly was an Eisenhower court.[11]

Elbert Tuttle grew up in Hawaii but moved to Atlanta when he was twenty-six. He quickly identified as a Republican, dismissing the Georgia Democratic party as paternalistic. For Tuttle, there was "nothing 'democratic' about it at all except the name." Tuttle created a successful general law practice in Atlanta, but beginning in the 1930s, he involved himself in civil rights and civil liberties cases. Most notably, he and his partner (former Brandeis clerk William Sutherland) successfully appealed Angelo Herndon's conviction under a Georgia criminal syndicalism law, a case that marked the Supreme Court's turn toward a more libertarian view of the First Amendment. John Minor Wisdom sprang from an aristocratic New Orleans background, went to Harvard, but returned to Tulane for law school. He developed a lively practice and became especially active in state Republican circles. As a young man, Wisdom had run afoul of the Huey Long machine, an event that led him to share Tuttle's disdain for the political monopoly of the Democrats.[12]

In 1951, Herbert Brownell, who later emerged as Eisenhower's campaign manager, brought Tuttle and Wisdom together to work in the "Draft Eisen-

11. J. W. Peltason, *Fifty-Eight Lonely Men: Southern Federal Judges and School Desegregation* (New York, 1961), offers a perceptive account of the difficult times for federal district court judges—in effect, "shock troops" for implementing the Supreme Court's decree in *Brown II* (1955).

12. *Herndon v. Lowry*, 301 U.S. 242 (1937). Jack Bass, *Unlikely Heroes* (New York, 1981), is a magnificent account of the fifth circuit's implementation and expansion of the *Brown* decision. It is a model for writing contemporary history, and I am greatly indebted to it. Also see Deborah J. Barrow and Thomas G. Walker, *A Court Divided: The Fifth Circuit Court of Appeals and the Politics of Judicial Reform* (New Haven, Conn., 1988), for an interesting account of how politics affected the fifth circuit bench.

hower" movement. With others, they formed the Southern Conference for Eisenhower, a group created to wrest power from local Republican elites who preferred to keep the party small and thereby dominate national political patronage. When Wisdom challenged the Taft Louisiana delegation in 1952, he assailed the ruling faction for having "studied and perfected the technique of stunting the growth of the party in Louisiana for purposes of control." Both Wisdom and Tuttle had active roles in the crucial convention battles over the validity of delegates' credentials. Those dramatic battles, featured on national television, enhanced the Eisenhower image of fresh, clean politics. The Eisenhower insurgents successfully challenged the Taft delegations, largely composed of old-line party regulars, and ensured the general's nomination.

For his efforts, Tuttle was approached to participate in the nomination of the vice-presidential candidate. In later life, he expressed relief that he was passed over. Like legions to follow, he developed a profound contempt for Richard Nixon.

Tuttle and Wisdom proved to be the new beneficiaries for national Republican patronage. A week after the *Brown* decision, the administration persuaded Tuttle to accept a seat on the Fifth Circuit Court of Appeals. In 1957, Eisenhower appointed Wisdom to the same bench. Tuttle eventually became chief judge, presiding over the circuit during the hectic civil rights battles of the 1960s. His leadership paved the way for that court's pioneering decisions in civil rights law. Wisdom, meanwhile, fashioned much of the doctrinal rationale that provided the basis for many Supreme Court decisions. A New Orleans aristocrat who resolutely maintained his ties to his exclusive, elite clubs, Wisdom nevertheless "transformed the face of school desegregation law." [13]

Two votes, of course, did not make a majority. In 1955, Eisenhower named John Robert Brown, a Houston lawyer and also a Republican activist. He regularly joined with Tuttle and Wisdom in resisting both state and private efforts to thwart desegregation. That same year, the president appointed Warren Jones, a Florida lawyer, to the court. Jones had been president of the Florida Bar Association and the Jacksonville Chamber of Commerce. While reluctant to chart new ground (as, for example, on the reapportionment issue), Jones generally accepted the new law on racial matters. Finally, Richard Rives, an Alabama friend of Justice Hugo Black's, who had sat on the fifth circuit since 1951, joined his new Republican colleagues in revolutionizing civil rights law. As a young lawyer and Democratic activist in Alabama—aligned with the national Democratic party and opposed to the future Dixiecrats—Rives had spoken out against injustice to blacks. "The chains we forge to shackle qualified Negroes . . . would

13. J. Harvie Wilkinson III, *From Brown to Bakke: The Supreme Court and School Integration, 1954–1978* (New York, 1979), 111.

not only breed resistance in the Negro, but, far worse, would rub a moral can-
cer on the character of the white man," he once wrote.[14] Years later, Jimmy
Carter extended Rives's metaphor when he argued that the 1964 Civil Rights
Act freed white southerners as well as black ones.

For their efforts, of course, these men, along with the federal district court
judges, burdened with the obligation of developing and enforcing new civil
rights realities, suffered social isolation and bitter recriminations in their native
land. How ironic and sad that the greatest denunciation should come from the
minions of Richard Nixon—the crown prince to Eisenhower's Modern Republicanism. When the Nixon administration actively sought a southerner to fill
a Supreme Court vacancy in 1969, Judge Wisdom received substantial support.
But Attorney General John Mitchell, one of the architects of Nixon's so-called
Southern Strategy—a strategy that consciously supported newly emergent
southern Republicans, who, in an earlier incarnation, had been the Dixiecrats
that led the struggles against court-enforced desegregation—dismissed any suggestion of Wisdom. "He's a damn left winger. He'd be as bad as Earl Warren."
From Warren and Wisdom to Nixon and Mitchell speaks volumes for the evolution of the Republican party.

Segregationist senator James Eastland later acknowledged that the "Fifth Cir-
cuit had done something that the Supreme Court couldn't do—that they
brought racial integration to the deep South a generation sooner than the
Supreme Court could have done it." Burke Marshall, who led the Civil Rights
Division in the Kennedy Justice Department, considered the dual roles of the
Republican-dominated circuit bench and the Democratic executive as crucial
for giving the controversial civil rights cases of the 1960s a less partisan flavor.
But times changed. When John F. Kennedy tried to promote Skelly Wright to
the fifth circuit, he could not circumvent Eastland's senatorial veto. Too late, in
any event, for Eastland to prevent the civil rights revolution shaped, in part, by
such southern judges as Wright. Fortunately, too, Eastland's writ could not
prevent Wright's appointment to the D.C. circuit—a place from which Wright
served the law and the nation with great distinction for years to come.[15]

We always measure desegregation battles in political and judicial terms, rigor-
ously case-bound, as it were. But we often do so while slighting other considerations, most notably that of both short- and long-term costs and implications.
In the short term, the South suffered severely from constant confrontation, court

14. Bass, *Unlikely Heroes,* 73.

15. *Ibid.,* 25, 332; David R. Goldfield, *Black, White, and Southern: Race Relations and Southern
Culture, 1940 to the Present* (Baton Rouge, 1990), 116.

battles, violence, and bad publicity over desegregation and civil rights. The resulting deficits shackled the South to its past, rendering it unable to free itself as the nation's neocolonial, economic backwater. The vibrancy of the new New South that we now know so well came with the massive influx of northern people, capital, and businesses—but they came only after the romantic notions of "massive resistance" and "Southern Manifestos" had been consigned to the ashcan of history. Jimmy Carter, the first southern president elected in more than sixty years, noted that the breakdown of segregation, and the subsequent civil rights legislation, "was the best thing that ever happened to the South in my lifetime." [16]

Gavin Wright, a shrewd observer of southern economic development and change, has noted the role of social peace in explaining the South's transformation in the past several decades. Climate, a disproportionate share of federal spending, the absence of labor unions, a favorable legislative impulse to lure new investment, and generous tax incentives all contributed to the massive upsurge in the attraction of capital and labor. Southern boosters also made a conscious effort to fashion a new image for the South. But without a scheme for public order—and that meant some measure of accommodation to racial equality and harmony—economic incentives alone would not work.

In 1940, the South constituted 29.4 percent of the population. Wartime migration, the continued postwar exodus north and south, and undoubtedly, the civil rights troubles of the 1950s and early 1960s resulted in stagnation and even decline as the Old Confederate states, plus several border ones, slipped to a little over 28 percent of the nation's total population. But by 1988, two decades of relative social peace had stimulated a 4 percent growth in the region's share. More dramatically, between 1965 and 1988, the South grew approximately 44 percent in population, compared to a national average of only 27 percent. The South even challenged the West as a magnet. Between 1940 and 1965, the western states increased 124 percent in population, but that rate dipped to only 57 percent for the years 1965–1988. The civil rights battles of the 1950s probably retarded growth, but they also affected political power. Arkansas, Alabama, and Mississippi lost congressional seats between 1950 and 1960, and each state had been distinguished by its militant resistance to desegregation. [17]

16. *Public Papers of the Presidents of the United States, Administration of Jimmy Carter, 1977* (Washington, D.C., 1978), II, 1328–29; Betty Glad, *Jimmy Carter: In Search of the Great White House* (New York, 1980), 324.

17. Michael Barone and Grant Ujifusa, *The Almanac of American Politics, 1990* (Washington, 1989), xxv. North Carolina also lost one seat during this period, but it is difficult to pinpoint social unrest as the cause in this case. By the 1960s, however, North Carolina's schools were in normal operation, and the state enjoyed unprecedented economic growth. Benjamin Muse, *Ten Years of*

Little Rock, Arkansas, had lured eight new plants to the area in 1957; in the next four years, following the school controversy, the city attracted no comparable enterprises. One industrial firm flatly dismissed Arkansas from consideration. "Our contacts with Arkansas have given us an unfavorable comparison" with other states. "We have no desire to be involved in the segregation problems of that state," the managers declared. The *Wall Street Journal* aptly summed up the situation in a May, 1961, headline: "Business in Dixie: Many Southerners Say Racial Tension Slows Area's Economic Gains." What was at stake for the advocates of a truly New South was, as Wright notes, not simply the protection of a feudal barony dominated by white men—as had typified the hollow successes of the New South of the late nineteenth century—but a need to attract new businesses and new capital. That required, Wright concluded, a demonstration that "their towns and cities . . . [were] safe, civilized communities," and their labor force well behaved. Such concerns were widespread. A southern commercial publication asked, "Will the new industries sought by the southern States be eager to build expensive plants in areas where the existence of public schools is in doubt, where tension and violence threaten, where public officials advocate political and economic reprisals against all who disagree . . . where the very maintenance of law and order is uncertain?" [18]

In the aftermath of the Little Rock imbroglio, business leaders in such cities as Atlanta, Dallas, and Charlotte banded together to anticipate desegregation and prepare their communities for peaceful compliance. Counterparts in Birmingham and New Orleans did nothing. The violence that later wracked the Alabama city severely damaged its image and potential for economic expansion. In New Orleans, the local chamber of commerce dismissed its press agent for his defense of the *Brown* decision. When New Orleans experienced a sharp decline in tourism in 1960, business leaders finally responded, calling on the community

Prelude (New York, 1964), 180. The census of 1990 projected eight states that would receive additional congressional seats, five of which were in the South: Florida, Texas, North Carolina, Georgia, and Virginia. Together, they gained ten seats out of a total shuffle of nineteen. Of the thirteen slated to lose seats, Louisiana was the only Deep South state, along with the border state of Kentucky. Each suffered one loss within the national shift of nineteen. Clearly, the South's political power and influence promised further enhancement. *Wall Street Journal,* November 29, 1990.

18. Gavin Wright, *Old South, New South: Revolutions in the Southern Economy Since the Civil War* (New York, 1986), 240, 255–56, 265–66; "A Call for Economic Leadership," *New South,* XI (1956), 1–2; James C. Cobb, *The Selling of the South: The Southern Crusade for Industrial Development, 1936–1980* (Baton Rouge, 1982), 122–25. Also see Elizabeth Jacoway and David R. Colburn, eds., *Southern Businessmen and School Desegregation* (Baton Rouge, 1982). I am indebted to Ellen Goldlust, my research assistant and graduate student, for leading me to a number of these sources. See her thesis, "The Civil Rights Wars: The Rise and Fall of Southern Resistance to Desegregation, 1954–1964" (M.A. thesis, University of Wisconsin, 1991).

to accept the school board's desegregation proposal. But it was too little, too late, as the city's agony over school desegregation in the early 1960s demonstrated —again, at great cost. Such painful experiences nevertheless were instructive. Promotional lures to attract new businesses and industries to the South implicitly promised a more moderate, a more accommodating, racial milieu.[19]

The South's economic and social transformation, and its new demographic profile, eventually led to an alteration of its political allegiances as well. Reconstruction following the Civil War has many meanings. One certainly involved an intensive Republican effort to gain political control, or at least competitive parity, in the South. The disfranchisement of blacks and the nation's disenchantment with Reconstruction aborted that goal by the 1880s and 1890s. From then until 1952, Republican presidential candidates carried southern states only in 1928, and those defections resulted from southern antipathy toward the Democratic candidate, Al Smith—a New Yorker, a Roman Catholic, and an anti-prohibitionist. Eisenhower in 1952, we now can clearly see, laid the basis for the political revolution of the latter half of the century, a revolution that has ironically reconstructed a new "Solid South," predominantly Republican in national elections.

Eisenhower had broken the Solid South, but his encroachment on the Democratic monopoly largely resulted from his own heroic, personable stature. His insistence on the preservation of domestic tranquillity and a recognition, however reluctant, that blacks were entitled to an equal measure of civil rights, doomed those who waved the standard for the maintenance of their White South Fortress. For a variety of reasons, mostly ideological and economic, the new southerners, and indigenous white southerners who benefited from the energies and largesse of the new, eventually flocked to the party of Eisenhower. And in some complicated turns of fortune and history, blacks in the South fell heir, not to the party of Lincoln and Eisenhower, but to that of their old oppressors and tormentors.

That change is filled with strange twists, ironies, and results. Eisenhower and his party supporters, particularly a younger generation, eagerly hoped to remold the South in a Republican image. The fuzzy contours of what Eisenhower and his speech writers called "Modern Republicanism" or "progressive conservatism" certainly enhanced the general's appeal.[20] Eisenhower nevertheless failed to provide sufficient coattails to aid the renascent party. But a base developed, one that Barry Goldwater, Richard Nixon, and Ronald Reagan nurtured to the

19. Cobb, *Selling of the South*, 130–45.

20. Dwight D. Eisenhower, *The White House Years: Waging Peace* (New York, 1965), 13–14; Arthur Larson, *A Republican Looks at His Party* (New York, 1956), 10–11 174–75, 198–203.

point of fulfilling the dream of the Republican radicals of the Reconstruction era—at least, the arithmetic part of the dream, if not the substance. In any event, the South is contested political turf today, a reality that has its roots in the civil rights issues of the 1950s.

Richard Nixon, that inveterate campaigner, left a legacy of unforgettable remarks and slogans. "Checkers," the "Pink Lady," "I can't stand pat"—all of these are memorable bits of Nixonia. Yet one of Nixon's embarrassing absurdities occurred in 1954 when he attempted to commandeer the Supreme Court's historic desegregation decision, *Brown* v. *Board of Education,* as the exclusive achievement of the Republican party. Now, riding the campaign trail, and conveniently forgetful of his long animosity toward Earl Warren, Nixon praised the decision that, he noted, had been fashioned by "a great Republican chief justice."

Nixon, as we well know, had contempt for Warren—and, in turn, Nixon was one of the public figures Warren regarded with rare overt disdain. Nevertheless, Vice-President Nixon unhesitatingly promoted the notion that *Brown* had been decided because the Court was led by a Republican chief justice. The irony here is that fourteen years later, Nixon spoke in unmistakable code language to signal to the White South that his support for blacks and civil rights had distinct limits. Nixon shamelessly campaigned for the presidency, attacking the Warren Court for its extreme views on civil rights and civil liberties. Irony, indeed, for Nixon won in part because of his oblique attitude toward *Brown* and its progeny. His mid-1950s enthusiasm for black civil rights belonged to an embarrassing history that Nixon preferred to obscure. Republican proprietary claims to the *Brown* decision notwithstanding, we must take historical notice that the ruling had some effect in transforming the old "Solid South" to the Solid Republican South.

Perhaps, given his ambivalence, Eisenhower hoped that a smile and good will would lubricate the gears for voluntary compliance with the Supreme Court's desegregation decree. That was not to be. Instead, Eisenhower's reluctantly imposed outside coercion, together with the more subtle forces for moderation from within, combined to take the Old South to a new place in the national polity and economy.

The civil rights war of post–World War II America has been bloody and costly. Pursuing the ideal of equality into reality brought a measure of pain and social disruption in its wake. In all this, of course, the federal judiciary proved indispensable, both for legitimating the struggle for equality and for providing a forum for the "peaceful resolution" of conflicts, as Chief Justice John Marshall promised more than a century earlier. However inadvertent or unintended, President Eisenhower shaped a judiciary that did just that and pushed the South toward including blacks as first-class citizens of the United States. He appointed an array of outstanding judges throughout the federal system, mostly Republicans from an older party tradition, who steadily advanced the cause of desegregation and civil rights in the late 1950s and in the next decade. We can only recoil in horror at what might have been without that vital critical mass of courageous jurists to legitimate a nearly century-old aspiration that the Constitution was color-blind and recognized no distinctions of caste.

What has happened since those changes in constitutional doctrine is another story.

WILLIAM L. O'NEILL
Eisenhower and American Society

In order to determine the influence of President Dwight David Eisenhower upon American society, we must first arrive at some sense of what that social order was like. A stereotype popular among writers and intellectuals at the time, and still cherished by many today, goes something like this: The 1950s was an age of mindless affluence and conformity, when people abandoned higher values and devoted themselves to consumer goods and drab suburban pleasures. Amid the Lonely Crowd, the Organization Man in his Gray Flannel Suit lived a life of quiet mediocrity. Women were more domestic than ever, and college students had become a silent generation, unlike during the heroic thirties.[1] According to this version, Eisenhower symbolized the age by being attractive and yet banal. As with most clichés, there are elements of truth here. The fifties were affluent by all previous standards, suburbs grew extravagantly, the birth rate soared, students were uninterested in politics, and Eisenhower, though highly regarded, was not a charismatic leader.

However, these clichés ignore most of what makes the period interesting— the fact that it was a golden age, the last and best years of that older America that vanished during the sixties. It was, to be sure, imperfect. Social welfare programs were extremely limited, medicare and medicaid lay in the future, while social security payments were so low that upon retirement those not otherwise provided for slipped into poverty. Most shocking of all by today's standards was the prevalence of racial segregation. In the South black Americans were segregated by law, in the North by established customs reinforced by public policy—such as the refusal of federal agencies to insure home mortgages in racially mixed neighbor-

1. Among the representative books that promoted this point of view are David Riesman et al., *The Lonely Crowd: A Study of the Changing National Character* (New Haven, Conn., 1950); William Whyte, *The Organization Man* (New York, 1956); and Sloan Wilson, *The Man in the Gray Flannel Suit* (New York, 1955). Contemporary texts frequently repeat the clichés popular in the fifties. Here is an example pulled literally at random from a shelf of textbooks. "This was the great age of conformity, when Americans seemed to want to emulate those around them rather than strike out on their own." Allan M. Winkler, *Modern America: The United States from World War II to the Present* (New York, 1985), 88.

hoods.[2] Most blacks, even when qualified for higher positions, were employed at the lowest levels. Racism had long been a scandalous betrayal of America's democratic principles, and remained so throughout the Eisenhower era. Other minorities were discriminated against too, including homosexuals and women, who, though not a minority, were unequal to men in law and, as employees, limited to a narrow range of poorly paid occupations.[3]

Despite these very important exceptions, the United States was, in other respects, healthier than today. In 1957 the rate of major crimes per 100,000 people was 5 murders, 39 robberies, and 65 aggravated assaults.[4] In 1988 the rate was 8.4 murders, 220.9 robberies, and 370.2 aggravated assaults.[5] More striking still is the remarkable fact that, as one historian points out, "Crimes against persons remained remarkably stable from 1940 to 1960, and the trend in homicide and non-negligent manslaughter was clearly downward."[6] In 1955 the divorce rate was 2.3 divorces for every 1,000 persons; in 1988 it was 4.8, down slightly from the all-time high of 5.2 achieved eight years earlier.[7]

What these later figures mean in practice is that about half of all marriages now end in divorce, as compared to fewer than 1 in 4 during the 1950s. They also mean that the percentage of children affected by divorce is vastly greater as well.

Divorces concluded in 1955 involved only 6.3 of every 1,000 children under the age of eighteen; in 1986 the figure was 16.8.[8] And, while there are many more children of divorce than before, there are many more illegitimate children, too. About 22 percent of all children born in 1988, out of a total of 3.91 million live births, were illegitimate, compared to something like 10 percent of children born in the 1950s—a time when it was very difficult to secure a legal abortion.[9] Were it not for the ease with which abortions may be gotten today, there would have been another 1 million illegitimate children born in 1988.[10]

2. On "red-lining" and similar practices see Kenneth T. Jackson, *Crabgrass Frontier: The Suburbanization of the United States* (New York, 1985), 197–218.

3. On women's legal inequalities as late as 1970, even after passage of the Civil Rights Act of 1964, which prohibited discrimination on the basis of sex as well as of race, see Jane J. Mansbridge, *Why We Lost the ERA* (Chicago, 1986), 45–59.

4. *Historical Statistics of the United States: Colonial Times to 1970* (Washington, D.C., 1975), 413.

5. *The World Almanac and Book of Facts, 1990* (New York, 1989), 848.

6. Eugene J. Watts, "Cops and Crooks: The War at Home," in Robert H. Bremner and Gary W. Reichard, eds., *Reshaping America: Society and Institutions, 1945–1960* (Columbus, Ohio, 1982), 296.

7. *World Almanac, 1990*, 839.

8. *Ibid.*, 840.

9. *Historical Statistics*, 52; *World Almanac, 1990*, 838.

10. "Social Science and the Citizen," *Society* (1990), 3. Births by unmarried white women

As a result of these high divorce and illegitimate birth rates, of 60.3 million children under the age of eighteen alive in 1988, almost 15 million were living in single-parent families—nearly all of them headed by women.[11] The great majority of such families were impoverished; in the 1980s, two-thirds of female-headed families received child welfare support, and two-thirds of the long-term poor were women.[12] Blacks have been damaged most by these changes. Today about 60 percent of black children are illegitimate, compared to 15 percent in 1940, and 47 percent of black families with children are headed by women, as against 8 percent in 1950.[13] As an institution, the black workingclass family has been destroyed, while the white family, though less severely impaired, is much sicker than in the fifties.

Generally, the United States is more tolerant than it used to be and more respectful of the rights of women and minorities. It also is more of a welfare state, the ill and the aged having gained most from the social programs of the sixties and seventies. On the other hand, this has meant shifting the burden of poverty from seniors to single mothers and their children. The United States is less sexually repressed than it used to be, but while the benefits of sexual freedom are real, they are hard to measure, unlike the drawbacks, which range from the huge increase in illegitimate births to the spread of venereal diseases. Drug addiction, relatively rare in the 1950s, has become a national scourge. Homelessness is new as well, a function to a considerable degree of housing being much more expensive in constant dollars than it was three decades ago. In 1950, housing costs, not including operating expenses, took 15 percent of the average family's income, whereas in the 1980s it ranged between one-quarter and one-third.[14]

Thus, while there have been important social gains since the 1950s, the losses

would have doubled had abortions been prohibited, and tripled for girls under fifteen. Black women had abortion rates more than twice that of whites.

11. *World Almanac, 1990*, 841.

12. For most mothers, divorce means instant poverty because alimony is seldom awarded and almost never paid, and because child support judgments, even though usually low, are seldom paid either. A 1982 census study found that in the first year after divorce only a third of all fathers pay the full amount of child support, while after ten years, 79 percent of fathers are paying nothing at all. The female single parent who works has an income that is on the average less than half that of her former spouse, but in a majority of cases bears most if not all of the child-rearing expenses. See Sylvia Ann Hewlett, *A Lesser Life: The Myth of Women's Liberation in America* (New York, 1986), 62-63. Not surprisingly, the fathers of illegitimate children rarely pay anything.

13. Nancy Woloch, *Women and the American Experience* (New York, 1984), 533–34.

14. In 1981, mortgage payments consumed 36.3 percent of median family income; in 1989, 25.2 percent. *World Almanac, 1990*, 829. In 1950 the cost of renting or paying a mortgage for a year averaged $455, while median family income was $2,990. *Historical Statistics,* 323, 297.

have been major as well. There is little point in trying to strike a balance between the two, since there is no going back to the fifties even if they were superior. For our purposes, the important thing is that the stereotype of the 1950s social order is not so much false as irrelevant. What seemed boring or monotonous or was taken for granted at the time—family togetherness, inexpensive housing, safe streets—are what we would give almost anything for if only they could be recovered. It is time to stop patronizing the fifties and admit that in the areas just discussed, they were preferable to our own time.

To what extent was President Eisenhower responsible for social conditions in the 1950s? The low crime and divorce rates, sexual responsibility, and family health in general were not the results of federal policy. The adequate stock of affordable housing was closely related to government programs and policies; however, these were already established when Eisenhower became president. Further, it must be admitted, Eisenhower did not understand the civil rights revolution and failed to meet its challenge. That he was unprejudiced personally and, by appointing Chief Justice Earl Warren to the Supreme Court, had an indirect responsibility for some of the positive changes make his record here all the more disappointing. The reasons for his failure are plain enough. Eisenhower was a child of the nineteenth century, and as such he did not believe that desegregation could, or should, be brought about by coercion. Further, he wished to gain support for Republican candidates in the previously solid but now fragmenting South. Thus, conviction and calculation alike prevented Eisenhower from doing more than the absolute minimum. As Stephen Ambrose puts it, "He missed a historic opportunity to provide moral leadership." In fact, until Little Rock in 1957 he provided almost no leadership at all "on the most fundamental social problem of his time." [15] That is a grave indictment, and also the worst thing to be said about Eisenhower's social policy.

In other areas Eisenhower did better, particularly as the custodian of existing programs. Thus, social security, aid to dependent children, and other social initiatives begun under Democratic presidents were continued by his administration—and in some cases even expanded. [16] His first two years in office were blighted by the Republican majority in Congress, which rejected his proposals for revising the anti-union Taft-Hartley Act, creating federally subsidized health insurance, and enlarging aid to education. When the Democrats regained control after 1954, his domestic program had easier sledding. As a result Social Se-

15. Stephen E. Ambrose, *Eisenhower: The President* (New York, 1984) 192.
16. On the particulars see Robert H. Bremner and Gary W. Reichard, eds., *Reshaping America,* especially Robert H. Bremner, "Families, Children, and the State," 3–32, and James T. Patterson, "Poverty and Welfare in America," 193–221.

curity coverage broadened, and spending for public health, medical research, and hospital construction more than trebled, from $290 million in 1954 to almost $1 billion in 1960. In 1958, Congress passed Eisenhower's National Defense Education Act, the most important federal contribution to schooling since the land grant colleges were established.

In these and other ways Eisenhower put together a respectable if not overwhelming package of social legislation. However, the most important thing about his approach to social issues was not his failure to launch a second New Deal—something that, as a moderate Republican, Eisenhower had absolutely no intention of doing—but that he preserved the gains of the first. Many Republicans still regarded the New Deal as temporary, and once in power it was their hope to destroy the social reforms of Franklin Delano Roosevelt. Instead, by maintaining Aid to Dependent Children, farm subsidies, Social Security, and the like, Eisenhower made them safely bipartisan, no longer in danger of being nullified as "socialistic" or "un-American."

All the same, Eisenhower was not a social reformer, which understandably annoyed liberals very much at the time, but ought to be viewed in a different light by historians, who are expected to have some perspective. It is unhistorical to fault Eisenhower for not being a social reformer when he never represented himself as one, and especially at a time when the majority of voters did not see reform as an urgent national objective. Far from being able to promote social change, Eisenhower had to struggle throughout his presidency against conservatives who were trying to take over the Republican party. After he was out of office, conservatives did so, yet Barry Goldwater's conservatism was not the same brand that Eisenhower had fought against, being notable for its commitment to internationalism and general lack of racism. In keeping conservatism at bay until it had improved, Eisenhower did something to benefit the quality of American public life that often goes unnoticed.

While Eisenhower's social policy was better than liberals have been willing to admit, his most important contribution to the health of American society was not any of the above but resulted from his management of the economy. By the time he became president, liberals had gotten used to prosperity and took economic success for granted. In fact, Eisenhower was criticized for failing to stimulate even more economic growth, since the rate of increase was lower in America than in many other industrial countries. Critics failed to allow for the fact that a highly developed economy will always have a lower rate of growth than a damaged one that is in the process of rebuilding—which was the state of America's foremost competitors, including Germany, Japan, and, in a different way, the Soviet Union.

John F. Kennedy made economic sluggishness a major theme of his campaign in 1960 and followed up as president by obtaining tax reductions on the theory that they would promote growth—against the advice of John Kenneth Galbraith, who called tax cuts "reactionary Keynesianism." It was his belief that tax reductions would lead to the production of more consumer goods, which were already abundant, at the expense of what the country most needed. "I am not sure," he remarked, "what the advantage is in having a few more dollars to spend if the air is too dirty to breathe, the water too polluted to drink, the commuters are losing out on the struggle to get in and out of the cities, the streets are filthy, and the schools so bad that the young, perhaps wisely, stay away, and hoodlums roll citizens for some of the dollars they save in taxes."[17] Galbraith's warning was ignored, and so began the irresponsible slide that culminated with President Reagan lowering the income tax ceiling from 70 to 28 percent and nearly tripling the national debt.

The economy today is nothing like as strong as it was under Eisenhower, and the social consequences of that decline have been dismal. In his day, America was a creditor, not a debtor, nation; inflation was extremely low—about 1.5 percent a year. And whereas today family income is just about what it was in 1973, and is that high only because a much higher percentage of mothers have entered the labor force, family income rose sharply during Eisenhower's eight years— a time when, unlike today, the typical family was supported by a single wage earner. Between 1953 and 1960, while the consumer price index rose by about 12 percent, median family income increased by more than twice as much.[18] In terms of such crucial performance areas as income growth, inflation, interest rates, and the like, the economy functioned better under Eisenhower than under any president who followed—save only Kennedy, whose tenure was too short for meaningful comparisons.

That this was not simply a function of momentum or good luck can be seen by looking at Truman's economics. Though the postwar period is usually thought of as one long surge of prosperity, it was during the Eisenhower years that this was most true. Between 1945 and 1950, income actually declined because, while wages and salaries rose by 23 percent, the cost of living went up by 36.2 percent. And in 1950, after the Korean War broke out, inflation, which had just eased, soared upward again.[19] The United States had advantages under both Truman and Eisenhower that were none of their doing. Because World War II had ravaged most

17. Quoted in Arthur M. Schlesinger, Jr., *A Thousand Days: John F. Kennedy in the White House* (Boston, 1965), 649.

18. *Historical Statistics,* 211, 303.

19. Susan M. Hartmann, *The Home Front and Beyond: American Women in the 1940s* (Boston, 1982), 8.

other economies, the United States was almost the only rich nation in an impoverished world. The United States was also remarkably self-sufficient—producing an oil surplus as late as 1960, for example; it did not depend heavily upon either exports or imports, and generated its own capital. Accordingly, unlike today, its economic well-being did not hinge upon decisions made in other countries.

Still, while Truman and Eisenhower functioned in substantially the same economic environment, their performances were radically different. Truman failed to control inflation after World War II and during the Korean conflict, while Eisenhower licked it at once by ending the war, reducing expenditures, and keeping taxes at a high level. There was nothing easy or automatic about this. The pressure to increase defense spending was especially acute, and perhaps only his general's stars enabled Eisenhower to prevent it. In 1957 a sharp recession led many to demand tax cuts, which Eisenhower avoided at the risk of being charged with lacking compassion for the jobless. Thanks to his resolve, budget deficits—as a percentage of gross national product—declined throughout Eisenhower's administration. In 1956 and 1957, there were surpluses, and the 1960 budget was balanced. No subsequent president has come anywhere near matching this record.

A prudent manager of the economy, Eisenhower was a wise investor, too. I have argued elsewhere that the postwar era as a whole may be seen as a time when domestic policy was chiefly concerned with physical reconstruction.[20] In 1945, there had been comparatively little private building for fifteen years and, except for war-related purposes, little public construction for five. In addition, a baby boom was under way that would place additional strain on the housing supply and require a great expansion of schools and related facilities. The housing crisis was solved by the time Eisenhower became president, so his special contribution was to build up the infrastructure—constructing roads and other facilities that do not earn profits themselves but without which no economy can flourish. In 1954 he pushed through the St. Lawrence Seaway, which in its first year of operation doubled the quantity of freight passing between Montreal and Lake Ontario. He sponsored numerous public works projects also, building dams and reservoirs and improving harbors.

Much the most important program was the Interstate highway system, which Eisenhower persuaded Congress to fund in 1956. The National System of Interstate and Defense Highways was the greatest public works project in history and would ultimately blanket the country with a 42,000-mile network. Critics complained that highways were killing passenger rail service, an alternate and environmentally superior form of transportation. This was true but irrelevant,

20. William L. O'Neill, *American High: The Years of Confidence, 1945–1960* (New York, 1986).

for most Americans prefer highways to railways, and if Eisenhower had gone against the grain of public opinion, he would have ended up with neither.

Eisenhower was a master builder, and the projects he supported would go on benefiting the economy for many years afterward. In fact, sad to say, the United States is still living off the infrastructure he built, since the country has not really expanded, or even maintained, what he started. Spending for infrastructure renewal has long been only a fraction of what it was in the 1950s, roads and bridges being allowed to crumble for the sake of holding down taxes, which is like a farmer eating his seed grain so as to reduce household expenses.

Eisenhower knew better, and if he had been president in the 1980s, the United States would now have a smaller defense establishment, higher income and lower social security taxes, a negligible budget deficit, a modest national debt, a lower rate of inflation, lower interest rates, and because of them, a favorable balance of trade, a stronger infrastructure, cheaper housing, and a more vibrant economy. This is not the same thing as enacting reforms, yet real economic strength offsets social problems to a considerable degree by reducing the amount of poverty. It also creates the means by which reforms can be funded later. Thus, it was the expanded infrastructure and booming economy Eisenhower bequeathed to Kennedy and Johnson that made the Great Society possible.

By the same token, economic mismanagement in the 1980s seems to have ruled out any chance of promoting social justice at home or abroad in the immediate future. Some critics have argued that this was the motive behind supply-side economics. The cost of servicing the national debt is now so high and income taxes so low that there is no money left to meet human needs, however urgent. This is probably to give President Reagan more credit for deviousness than he seems to warrant. Regardless of intent, the results stand. Weakening the economy, as Reagan did, makes anything constructive impossible. And by the same token, strengthening it, as Eisenhower did, creates many options.

What Eisenhower understood above all, and what needs to be understood today if we are to reverse our national descent, is that patriotism consists not in having the most weapons or the lowest taxes, but rather in building up economic strength, which is both the fundamental source of international power and the key to a decent society. Eisenhower was a great patriot, in every sense of the word, and though not a reformer as such, by wisely managing the economy he did more to ease or avert social problems than any postwar president except Lyndon Johnson —and, of course, without making Johnson's mistakes. We could use another president like Eisenhower.[21]

21. Curiously, in his revision of an earlier study by Elmo Richardson, Chester J. Pach gives Eisenhower only slight credit for his economic achievements, while asserting that President Truman, whose economics were notoriously poor, did about as well. Where Eisenhower is concerned the double standard refuses to die. See Chester J. Pach, Jr., and Elmo Richardson, *The Presidency of Dwight D. Eisenhower* (Lawrence, Kans., 1991).

Eisenhower and General Andrew Goodpaster, his staff secretary through both terms and the president's closest confidant and adviser.

Eisenhower and General George Marshall in 1943, the year President Roosevelt appointed Eisenhower Supreme Commander for the Allied landings in Normandy. Marshall stayed on as Roosevelt's principal military adviser in Washington because the president "could not sleep without having General Marshall in Washington."

Eisenhower and President Roosevelt in 1943 en route to a summit conference.

Eisenhower and Prime Minister Winston Churchill in 1944, inspecting troops of the 101st Airborne Division during Allied preparations for Operation Overlord.

The victors of World War II: Eisenhower and Marshall Zhukov in Leningrad in May, 1945.

Associated Press photograph

Eisenhower and the press in April, 1954.

Eisenhower, the first Supreme Allied Commander, Europe (SACEUR), inspecting the 2nd Armored Cavalry Regiments in April, 1951, with Generals Thomas Handy and Manton Eddy.

Eisenhower's fifth-grade class (1901) in Abilene, Kansas. Eisenhower is second from left on the first row.

Courtesy Dwight D. Eisenhower Library

Eisenhower talks to black GIs during World War II.

Eisenhower, Vice-President Richard Nixon, and Supreme Court Justice Earl Warren in February, 1954.

President Harry Truman and President-elect Eisenhower meet in the Oval Office in November, 1952.

United Press International photograph

Eisenhower and Soviet Premier Nikita Khrushchev at Camp David in September, 1959.

United Press International photograph

The architects of the new American nuclear strategy, Eisenhower and chairman of the Joint Chiefs of Staff Admiral Arthur Radford. Eisenhower is presenting Radford with the Distinguished Service Medal.

Eisenhower and Secretary of State John Foster Dulles during the Geneva Summit in 1955.

Courtesy Dwight D. Eisenhower Library

Eisenhower and President Charles de Gaulle in the Oval Office, April 22, 1960.

Courtesy Dwight D. Eisenhower Library

Eisenhower and Field Marshal Bernard Law Montgomery visit the battlefield at Gettysburg.

Courtesy Dwight D. Eisenhower Library

III EISENHOWER AS PRESIDENT: FOREIGN POLICY

ANNA K. NELSON

The Importance of Foreign Policy Process:
Eisenhower and the National Security Council

To understand both the foreign policy and the foreign policy process of the Eisenhower administration, it is necessary to return briefly to 1945 and the post-war years that followed.

After World War II, when the United States found itself in a cold war with the Soviet Union, it simultaneously decided that it was ill-equipped to fight this kind of war. This was not a war that was concerned only with military action. In the minds of American policymakers it was a war of ideology—a war marked by the fatal attraction of communism, the internal subversion of friendly governments, and the perilous effect of Soviet influence on the "periphery," those areas that continued to supply the resources necessary for the retention of U.S. military and industrial might.

This kind of war required a radical change in the formulation and implementation of foreign policy—a change symbolized by the phrase *national security policy.* Inspired by the examples set in World War II, the cold war solidified the importance of military strategy coordinated with psychological warfare, intelligence sources, and a strong industrial base. This was a war that required unprecedented coordination among government departments and agencies.

The National Security Act of 1947 recognized these changes and tried to implement the coordination. The National Military Establishment was created in an attempt to coordinate military policy through unification. The National Security Resources Board (NSRB) was created to assure that U.S. resources and industrial might would be equal both to the long haul of the cold war and the hot war that was sure to follow. A director of central intelligence and the Central Intelligence Agency (CIA) were established to coordinate intelligence and, in effect, beat the Soviets at their own game. Finally, the National Security Council (NSC) was created to coordinate all of the above, to act as chief advisory council to the president, and to assure that policy decisions would reflect the coordination process.[1]

1. Demetrios Caraley, *The Politics of Military Unification: A Study of Conflict and the Policy Process* (New York, 1966); Thomas F. Troy, *Donovan and the CIA: A History of the Establishment of the Central Intelligence Agency* (Frederick, Md., 1981); Harry B. Yoshpe and Stanley L. Falk, "The Economics

None of these coordinating agencies operated the way they were supposed to operate. The Truman administration was a period of trial and error, bureaucratic infighting, and State Department recalcitrance. Even though the cold war had heated up in Korea, when President Eisenhower was inaugurated it appeared that the United States was still not prepared for the kind of long-term efforts that lay ahead.

Eisenhower quickly strengthened the coordinating mechanisms in the NSC, supported a broad mandate for the CIA, and imposed a certain amount of discipline on the military establishment. An Office of Defense Mobilization (ODM), established after the outbreak of war in Korea, inherited the work of the NSRB, which was abolished early in the administration.

The most important coordinating mechanism—because Eisenhower chose to emphasize its significance—was the NSC. Throughout his administration, Eisenhower and members of his White House staff insisted that the president made his most critical national security policy decisions through the NSC. Due to the secrecy of the national security process, this claim was accepted and Eisenhower was subjected to much partisan criticism for conducting policy by committee.

Nor did the paper generated by the NSC and passed along to the Kennedy administration inspire confidence in the ability of Eisenhower to generate either fresh thinking or bold policy. One six-page memorandum prepared for McGeorge Bundy, Kennedy's incoming national security adviser, for example, reported that the NSC produced 187 numbered policy papers from 1953 to 1961. Nine versions of a basic national security policy paper were produced in those eight years, and 126 of the papers covered 37 geographic areas, countries, or regions (such as papers on Tunisia, Morocco-Algeria, and four on Antarctica). The seemingly endless burden of revising these papers served to prove the contention that the NSC had become a paper mill. Furthermore, many of the papers were replete with tedious platitudes. NSC-5602 concluded that "the basic objective of U.S. national security policy is to preserve the security of the United States, and its fundamental values and institutions." The so-called revisions were often very repetitive, thus supporting the disdain for policy by committee.[2]

of National Security," in *Organization for National Security* (Washington, D.C., 1965); Steven L. Rearden, *History of the Office of the Secretary of Defense: The Formative Years, 1947–1950* (Washington, D.C., 1984); U.S. Congress, Senate, Subcommittee on National Policy Machinery of the Committee on Government Operations, *Organizational History of the National Security Council* (Washington, 1960); Anna Kasten Nelson, "President Truman and the Evolution of the National Security Council," *Journal of American History,* LXXII (1985), 360–78.

2. Gordon Gray, Memorandum for the Record, January 17, 1961, Transition Series, Whitman File, in Dwight D. Eisenhower Library, Abilene, Kansas (hereinafter cited as EL); Memorandum

Convinced that such a static system could only inhibit a dynamic foreign policy, Kennedy and his advisers completely restructured the national security process, setting the stage for a system that emphasized an increasingly powerful national security adviser to the president, who was supported by a large White House policy staff. As a result, after Eisenhower the NSC would never again operate as it had been conceived.

We now know that Eisenhower's NSC process was just one part of a multi-faceted foreign policy process. In spite of Eisenhower's public insistence that his policy emanated from the NSC, all "operational" decisions were made in the Oval Office. The decision to withhold air power from the French at Dien Bien Phu, to require the British and French to withdraw from Suez, or to order the troops to Lebanon were decisions made in the president's office.

The role of the NSC apparatus was that of "planning" and "coordinating" policy. Thus the council had a planning board, an interagency group of high-level officials who met to prepare the papers and studies for council consideration, and an operation coordinating board (OCB), with the less specific function of policy coordination. Officials on the planning board were chosen by each of the agencies represented on the council, as well as those who attended council meetings in an advisory capacity. Unlike similar interagency groups formed in the Truman administration that were coordinated by the State Department, the work of the planning board was organized by the NSC staff and its meetings chaired by the executive secretary.

The function of the OCB was to assure the implementation of NSC policy and to coordinate psychological "warfare" among the agencies involved in the policy process. It had an independent staff, under the leadership of the national security assistant, and produced a number of papers and progress reports. The most significant part of the OCB process, however, was the weekly meetings of the OCB members, the undersecretary of state, deputy secretary of defense, director of the Foreign Operations Administration, director of the CIA, and the president's national security adviser. Information was exchanged and communication between the agencies improved.[3]

---

for Mr. Bundy and Mr. Rostow from George Weber, January 27, 1961, box 283, NSF, in John F. Kennedy Library, Boston (hereinafter cited as JFKL). Quote from Section A, NSC 5602, in Record Group 273, National Archives.

3. Anna Kasten Nelson, "The 'Top of Policy Hill': President Eisenhower and the National Security Council," *Diplomatic History,* VII (1983), 307–26; Fred I. Greenstein, *The Hidden-Hand Presidency* (New York, 1982); 124–30. Also see U.S. Congress, Senate, Subcommittee on National Policy Machinery of the Committee on Government Operations, *Organizational History of the National Security Council* (Washington, D.C., 1960); 455. As a result of its emphasis on psychological warfare, many documents describing the work of the OCB are either closed to researchers or heavily censored.

Meanwhile, the statutory members of the council (the president, vice-president, secretaries of state and defense, and directors for mutual security and the ODM) met virtually every week on a regular basis. Among the most illuminating documents included in the mammoth collection of national security records are the summaries of these NSC meetings. The council met 346 times in the 8 years of the Eisenhower administration, an average of about 43 meetings each year. In order to assure complete freedom of expression, verbatim minutes of meetings were not allowed. But from the very first meeting of the council, in the Truman administration, brief summaries of the discussions for the use of the president were prepared by the deputy executive secretary of the council, James Lay.[4]

A different notetaker took over in January, 1953, one who chose to capture nuances and subtleties, as well as the straightforward text. Did the new deputy executive secretary, S. Everett Gleason, take such copious notes because he was a historian, or because he assumed the president would want to use them to write his memoirs? Unfortunately, Gleason died before his notes became available, but in an interview some years ago, Gordon Gray, Eisenhower's last national security assistant, confirmed the fact that everyone in the council meetings, including the president, knew Gleason was there taking notes. They probably had no idea as to the extent of these notes. Not until Gleason resigned his position with the NSC did he bring to Eisenhower the pile of meeting summaries. If Gray's memory was accurate, Gleason was free to write as he wished because these notes did not, in fact, serve as the official report of meetings to the president. Unlike the summaries prepared for Truman, who rarely attended meetings until the onset of the Korean War, these summaries were prepared "for the record." Of course, writing for history may have generated other restrictions on a cautious civil servant such as Gleason.[5]

Several years ago, in an uncharacteristically intelligent response to declassification requests, the NSC decided to release these meeting summaries in an orderly fashion through systematic review. We now have meeting notes available through 1959, one year short of the end of the administration, although many of the summary notes for the second term have numerous pages still unavailable because of classification procedures. Nevertheless, a truly remarkable docu-

4. Yoshpe and Falk, *Organization for National Security,* 441; Memorandum for Mr. Bundy and Mr. Rostow from George Weber, January 27, 1961, box 283, NSF, in JFKL. Very brief summaries of the Truman NSC meetings can be found in the President's Secretary's Files, Harry S. Truman Library, Independence, Missouri (hereinafter cited as PSF, TL.)

5. Interview by the author with Gordon Gray, July 30, 1976. At the time of the interview some government historians with security clearances had read the summaries and could discuss their value if not their content.

mentary history of the Eisenhower NSC meetings is now available for research.

Although any number of researchers and writers have used the summaries of particular meetings to discuss, for example, U.S. relations with Indochina, NATO countries, China, or Latin America, no one has examined them to evaluate the role played by these NSC meetings within the totality of the policy process. Of course with countless pages of discussion still classified and no visible movement toward opening the files of those officials who actually wrote the papers under discussion, any assessment is bound to be temporary. Nevertheless, six years of summaries provide a window to almost three hundred of these meetings. They present an unprecedented opportunity to illuminate the effect of personalities, the interrelationship between president and advisers, and, in spite of the centrality of the Oval Office, the troubling national security issues of the era.

First, a few general observations. As one reads through these summaries, patterns soon emerge. Except for those meetings featuring reports on foreign travel by Dulles, Nixon, or others, and informational meetings on such topics as new weapons, every meeting agenda revolved around the numbered reports or previous NSC actions. Yet, often the most interesting discussions were those that ranged far afield from the papers that prompted them. Unfortunately, the national security assistants felt duty bound to interrupt the free-wheeling discussions of the participants in order to complete the task at hand, namely, the consideration of the papers under review.

Also, even though Eisenhower specified that Vice-President Nixon was to chair the NSC in his absence, Nixon was not a major player in these meetings, in spite of his statements to the contrary during the 1960 election campaign. He gained attention only when he reported on his trips abroad. Trips to Asia, the Middle East, and Latin America between 1953 and 1955, for example, allowed him to express opinions about Syngman Rhee and Korea or to support aid for Pakistan over India (interesting in light of President Nixon and Henry Kissinger's "tilt" to Pakistan). Otherwise, he rarely spoke up in meetings chaired by the president. When he did speak, his contribution was that of political expert, not foreign policy expert. Whenever there were questions about congressional intent, public opinion, or the Democratic party, the national security assistants or the president would specifically turn to Nixon.[6]

6. President Truman designated the secretary of state as chairman of the NSC meetings during his absence. Nixon's reports can be found in the 175th Meeting (December 15, 1953), 176th Meeting (December 16, 1953), 240th Meeting (March 10, 1955). For examples of Nixon the political expert see 135th meeting (March 4, 1953), 145th Meeting (May 20, 1953), 163rd Meeting (September 24, 1953). All meeting summaries cited in this paper are filed by meeting number and can be found in the Whitman File, EL.

Harold Stassen, an almost forgotten member of the administration, on the other hand, never failed to express an opinion and often spoke at length. Stassen, who is now known only as a perennial presidential candidate with a particularly ill-fitting toupee, held several positions in the administration. His long reports and comments in the council meetings projected a strong optimism, and unwavering support for the president. Early in the administration, he reported at length as director of the Mutual Security Administration. Later, he reported with the same enthusiasm as the president's special assistant on disarmament, but in neither case did anyone seem to pay much attention. Except when Dulles would strongly disagree, Stassen's comments on the various agenda items would usually be met by a change of subject. Rarely did other members of the council even address the issues he raised. The isolation of Stassen is truly striking. Even Eisenhower, who apparently never tried to squash the long comments, rarely took note of them. However, perhaps because the NSC meetings provided the one opportunity to express his views, Stassen never seemed to give up.[7]

Of course, like Dean Acheson before him, it was Dulles who dominated the NSC meetings. He presented lengthy accounts of his meetings abroad with foreign leaders. He was always given the opportunity to present the first comment on a new agenda item, and never hesitated to do so. Nor did he hesitate to express his opinion on matters involving strategic issues. The summaries suggest that Dulles never met a topic he thought beyond his ken.

Furthermore, again not unlike Acheson, Dulles did not always agree with his own representative on the planning board. Often this group of senior staff members from the various departments who were in charge of writing the papers could not agree on policy recommendations. When the planning board disagreements —or splits—were brought to the council, Dulles did not hesitate to abandon the State Department position. He usually was the person who came up with the compromise language, often negating the State Department position with new language.

When Dulles refused to compromise and when he chose to use all of his persuasive powers to influence the president and the council, the topic usually involved the United States and her European allies. Supported, of course, by Eisenhower's own inclinations, Dulles determined U.S. global policy in terms of its impact on U.S. relations with Western Europe. Indochina policy, for example, hinged upon U.S. attempts to influence France to join the European Defense Community. Even his objections to a civilian shelter program were based

7. 164th Meeting (October 1, 1953), 258th Meeting (September 8, 1955), 324th Meeting (May 23, 1957), 339th Meeting (October 10, 1957). On Stassen, also see H. W. Brands, Jr., *Cold Warriors: Eisenhower's Generation and American Foreign Policy* (New York, 1988), 138–62.

upon the psychological effect of such a program on U.S. allies in Western Europe.[8]

The summaries also indicate that Dulles regarded the NSC meetings as more public than private. The Dulles in the summaries is not the Dulles recently discovered in his letters or the private memos of telephone calls and conversations, but the public Dulles of *Life* magazine and congressional hearings. Thus, Dulles was not above treating the council to one of his more vehement anti-Communist "cold war" speeches when necessary, even though such speeches surely represented preaching to the converted.[9]

In general, the discussion summaries support the earlier characterization of the NSC as a device for building a consensus and generating a coordinated national security policy. However, in the first months of his administration, Eisenhower did use the NSC system to reexamine national security policies inherited from the previous administration.

Less than five months after taking office, Eisenhower asked his special assistant for national security affairs, Robert Cutler, to organize this reexamination. Soon dubbed Project Solarium after the location of the original meeting, the study was not conducted by the staff of the NSC but by consultants working under the aegis of the council. Three task forces were formed to evaluate three alternative courses of action for the new administration. Task Force A presented the case for the continuation of previous policies; Task Force B argued for "drawing a line," beyond which Soviet aggression would face an atomic attack; Task Force C argued for more determined efforts to "roll back" Communist achievements. The final paper that emerged from these three groups was presented to the council as NSC-162. After considerable disagreement between those who advocated economic restraint on the one hand and the advocates of a strong defense posture on the other, the final policy paper, NSC-162/2, advocated the protection of American national security through the preservation of a cautious and conservative economic policy coupled with a reliance upon nuclear weapons.[10]

8. 347th Meeting (December 5, 1957), 165th Meeting (October 7, 1953), 136th Meeting (March 11, 1953). Also see Richard Immerman, ed., *John Foster Dulles and the Diplomacy of the Cold War* (Princeton, N.J., 1990); Brands, *Cold Warriors*, 3–26. For Acheson's actions in NSC meetings see the brief summaries in the PSF, TL.

9. See, for example, the 336th Meeting (September 12, 1957), 343rd Meeting (November 7, 1957). Also see essays in Immerman, ed., *John Foster Dulles and the Diplomacy of the Cold War;* Brands, *Cold Warriors*, 3–26.

10. Summaries of the Task Force reports and accompanying documents can be found in U.S. Department of State, *Foreign Relations of the United States, 1952–1954*, II, 323–442. Also see H. W. Brands, "The Age of Vulnerability: Eisenhower and the National Insecurity State," *American Historical Review*, XCIV (1989), 963–89. See also the Brands and Wampler essays in this volume.

There were other instances when Eisenhower used the machinery of the council to gain the advice of outside consultants. Usually, the ensuing reports provided information but did not contribute directly to policy statements. Although often cited as an example of the NSC at work, Project Solarium was an exception that proved the rule.[11]

Although there was more continuity than change in the national security process from Truman to Eisenhower (in spite of the claims of Eisenhower stalwarts such as Robert Cutler and Gordon Gray, his national security advisers), the summaries tell us of one striking difference—one marking a clear distinction between the two administrations (and one that influenced all policy decisions). This difference is illustrated by the pervasive participation in council meetings of Eisenhower's secretary of the treasury. With the exception of Foster Dulles, George Humphrey, until his resignation in 1957, was the most important participant in the NSC meetings.

Truman put a cap on the military budget until the outbreak of the Korean War. The most famous of the NSC documents, NSC-68, was designed to discredit that cap, which was finally removed as a result of the war and the fear of Russian intentions that accompanied it. However, as the more cryptic NSC notes of the Truman period indicate, budgets were discussed within the context of congressional opposition or the political fallout from irate taxpayers. There was never any question in the minds of Truman and his advisers that the same American economy that managed to gear up for war in 1941 could also support the global responsibilities of the cold war. Encouraged by the economic projections provided by Leon Keyserling, neither the discussions of NSC-68 nor the extra military burdens imposed by the effects of the Korean War were hampered by concern over the capacity of the American economy.[12]

This carefree attitude toward the economy was not shared either by Eisenhower or his party. The president announced that under the new administration, both the secretary of the treasury and the director of the budget would participate in all NSC meetings and that all policy papers were to include budgetary

11. 133rd Meeting (February 24, 1953), 150th Meeting (June 18, 1953). Eisenhower raised the question of British-Egyptian negotiations at the former and the effect of the release of North Korean prisoners by Rhee at the latter.

12. Neither Keyserling nor Snyder particpated in the early meetings on NSC-68. See for example the 55th Meeting (April 21, 1950) and 57th Meeting (May 18, 1950). Keyserling did attend the 68th Meeting (October 2, 1950), but the cryptic notes only indicate that he urged the group to "speed up." Also see, for example, the discussion of NSC-114 on October 18, 1951, in PSF, TL. Nelson, "President Truman and the Evolution of the National Security Council," 360–78. John Prados, *Keepers of the Keys: A History of the National Security Council from Truman to Bush* (New York, 1991), like most of its predecessors, only briefly discusses the years 1947–1960.

appendices "to assure that the current and future financial implications of all policies under consideration were fully appreciated." [13]

For eight years the Eisenhower administration struggled with its firm commitment to budgetary restraint and its equally firm commitment to an American global presence to protect the free world and turn back the march of Soviet-dominated communism. The NSC was the battleground, the place where national security needs and federal budgetary limits had to compete. When participants wrote about the NSC function of integrating foreign policy decisions or coordinating policy, they were, perhaps unwittingly, referring to this constant struggle.

Hints of the ongoing debate can be gleaned from the policy papers and memoirs, but the summaries show how it dominated discussion after discussion in the council meetings. In almost every instance, debates on national security policy were debates on budget policy. For the most part, conflicting views were especially notable during discussions on basic national security policy, continental defense, the mutual security program, missile and space programs, and the uses of atomic energy.

Many of these discussions in the council were prompted by the lack of agreement within the planning board itself. While there were instances when these "splits" were between the Joint Chiefs of Staff and everyone else, most splits on basic national security policy papers were between Treasury and Budget on the one hand and other members of the planning board on the other. For example, NSC-5440/1, a paper to set basic national security policy, required the resolution of three splits. To a paragraph on the basic objective to preserve national security, Treasury and Budget proposed adding the phrase "without seriously weakening the U.S. economy." To a paragraph on economic assistance, they argued for adding a statement that the total level of economic assistance should be progressively reduced in the following years. Another paragraph on the preservation of a sound U.S. economy brought disagreement over whether the goal was to move toward a "substantial balance" between national security needs and budget receipts or a "complete balance" (that is, a balanced budget as an immediate goal). After considerable discussion, the council resolved such disputes, either by taking sides or writing new language. [14]

13. Supplementary Statement by Maurice H. Stans, U.S. Senate, GOC-NPM, box 72, Papers of Henry Jackson, University of Washington; Greenstein, *Hidden-Hand Presidency*, 14. In fact, Truman's secretary of the treasury, John Snyder, often came to NSC meetings, and after 1949 the NSC papers usually included budgetary appendices.

14. 230th Meeting (January 5, 1955). Also see 134th Meeting (February 25, 1953). Even the 155th Meeting (July 16, 1953) on "Solarium" was really a budget discussion. Also see the 166th Meeting (October 13, 1953), 269th Meeting (December 8, 1955), 322nd Meeting (May 10, 1957).

George Humphrey participated vigorously in these discussions. He used every possible opportunity to remind the council that the days of free spending were over. At one of the first meetings of the council, he "stated very emphatically his belief that from now on out this Government must pay its way." Increasing deficits, he warned, "would bankrupt the free world and force the United States itself to abandon its way of life." Basically, Humphrey argued, the Eisenhower administration must develop a completely different set of objectives than those of the previous administration. The following month Humphrey told the council that "if we must live in a permanent state of mobilization our whole democratic way of life would be destroyed in the process." [15]

Others could worry about the effect of budget deficits on Congress or the voters; Humphrey's dire warnings came from an abiding belief that the country would self-destruct if unbalanced budgets became the norm and the United States continued to spend money around the world. He did not hesitate to interject his views into almost every policy issue, because there were few that did not cost money. Thus he questioned the need for military bases in Spain, supported ICBMs and the capability for "massive retaliation," opposed giving money away to individual countries without adding it all up first, and opposed long-term economic aid projects such as the Aswan Dam.[16] Finally, in a longer speech than usual, he told the council that the United States could not defend every corner of the world but should learn to coexist with the Soviets on the basis of a balance of power. The United States, he continued, should concentrate on strengthening its position in areas such as South America, the Middle East, Japan, and Western Europe. Places like Quemoy and Indochina, he suggested, were not worth protecting. He also told the council that while the United States should make clear "we will not tolerate Communism anywhere in the Western Hemisphere," it should stop talking so much about democracy and support dictatorships of the right that were pro-American." [17]

It was Dulles who usually defended American global interests against the attacks of Humphrey, but Eisenhower, although basically agreeing with Humphrey's position, was quick to defend the necessity of a global policy. For example, he strongly disagreed with Humphrey's suggestion that the United States write off South Asia. Not only would it lead to the loss of the Middle East, Eisenhower argued, but when the Soviet Union "takes over an additional free country, the rate of the process accelerates." Although usually in control of his

15. 131st Meeting (February 11, 1953), 138th Meeting (March 26, 1953).

16. 144th Meeting (May 13, 1953), 258th Meeting (September 8, 1955), 311th Meeting (April 19, 1957), 268th Meeting (December 2, 1955), 237th Meeting (February 17, 1955).

17. 299th Meeting (December 21, 1954).

temper, at least once Eisenhower's exasperation with Humphrey seeps through the pages of the summary.[18]

Yet, we know from his private letters and public speeches that Eisenhower shared many of Humphrey's concerns. He often expressed the view that the defense of the United States depended as much upon its economic strength as its military strength. He could never accept the kind of budget requests submitted by the military services. They would so unbalance the economy that "controls" would have to be imposed, thus destroying the "values" we were fighting for. Responding to a suggestion that the nation needed both conventional forces and nuclear capability, Eisenhower immediately placed the issue in its economic context. If we accept massive increases in military budgets, he told the council in 1958, "We are going to maintain very much larger military forces than we have previously done. These methods would almost certainly involve what is euphemistically called a controlled economy, but which in effect would amount to a garrison state." Thus it would seem that Eisenhower, like his administration, was also of two minds.[19]

George Humphrey's role was to constantly remind, if not convince, other council participants, members of the planning board, the Joint Chiefs, and any others sitting in the back of the room, of the economic realities. As Humphrey prepared to leave the administration in the summer of 1957, Eisenhower noted at his last council meeting that they would miss his speech at every meeting.[20] Dulles, and possibly Stassen, on the other hand, educated all of them, including Humphrey, on the responsibilities of the United States in the face of Communist subversion and Soviet aggression.

These discussions, although budget oriented, reflect important policy decisions. (1) The administration strongly supported appropriations for mutual security, but it was a mutual security program that emphasized support for indigenous armies, hence future budget commitments would be cut and American soldiers could come home. German rearmament, NATO, and support for Diem's army in Indochina, for example, fit within this policy. (2) Appropriations were sought for foreign economic aid, but aid that emphasized short-term solutions instead of long-term commitments. Part of the decision to abandon the Aswan Dam on the Nile reflected the apparent requirement for a long-term commitment. (3) The so-called New Look stressed the value of nuclear

18. 233rd Meeting (January 21, 1955).

19. 164th Meeting (October 1, 1953), 364th Meeting (May 1, 1958). Humphrey had left the cabinet by 1958. In this instance Eisenhower may have been performing Humphrey's role.

20. 322nd Meeting (July 26, 1957). His replacement, Robert Anderson, is rarely heard in the meetings that followed.

weapons ("a bigger bang for the buck") over large armies and an expensive navy. (4) Even the decisions to encourage covert operations reflected their cost effective nature. (It should be noted that there is no indication that covert actions were ever discussed in council meetings, although deletions in the summaries of classified material could contain such discussions.)

Sometime around the middle of 1957 and the beginning of 1958, a subtle change occurs in the summaries of the council meetings. This partly reflects a change in participants. Robert Anderson, who replaced George Humphrey, is less free with his opinions. There are far fewer reminders of the imminent collapse of the U.S. economy. Gordon Gray, who replaced Robert Cutler as national security assistant, was more policy oriented and less paper bound. And after Sputnik put the Soviets in space, a new member of the administration, the special assistant for science and technology, James Killian, became an active participant in many of the NSC meetings.

But the topics for discussion also change. In among the discussions of U.S. relations with various countries and regions are lengthy informational sessions on the impact of new weapons systems, missiles, and satellites.[21]

The IRBM and ICBM had changed the nature of U.S. war plans. Because of the potential Russian capability to dispatch missiles across oceans, around the last half of the 1950s, the strategic community became obsessed with the fear of a Russian surprise attack. The United States, argued many of those at the Rand Corporation and other think tanks, had become vulnerable. While the United States had concentrated on its first-strike capability to deter the Soviets, it now had to concentrate on its vulnerability (especially to the Strategic Air Command) to a Soviet first strike and the possibility that as a result the United States would have no second-strike capacity. There were two aspects to U.S. vulnerability. If the Soviets did not fear a return strike, they were more likely to stage a preemptive attack when they had enough capability. Second, vulnerability to Soviet attack would probably prevent the United States from ever using its nuclear capability because there would be no way to protect its citizens. Thus it was argued that preparing for a second Soviet retaliatory strike meant protecting U.S. citizens through a shelter program.[22]

In the spring of 1957, under pressure from internal as well as external critics, Eisenhower appointed a blue-ribbon commission to study these strategic issues and report back to the NSC. This panel had an official name but is generally known by the name of its chairman, H. Rowan Gaither.

21. See for example, 382nd Meeting, October 13, 1958.
22. A nontechnical discussion of the changing views toward vulnerability can be found in Fred Kaplan, *The Wizards of Armageddon* (New York, 1983).

The Gaither Report, which reached the NSC as Sputnik sent ripples of shock throughout the country, proposed many controversial solutions to pre-pare the United States for the Soviet capability to retaliate. Not only did the re-port recommend building more than four times as many ICBMs by 1963 than were planned, it also seriously proposed a government-sponsored program to provide Americans with fallout shelters. The fallout shelter program was dis-cussed at length by the NSC before being abandoned. Aside from the cost, the ethical complications raised by the president seemed insoluble. Finally, Eisenhower agreed that "the over-all answer seemed . . . to be for this Gov-ernment to assure that no doubt whatsoever existed about the protection of our massive retaliatory capability." But given the goal of a balanced budget, that still meant 130 ICBMs rather than the 600 proposed by the Gaither Report, and the discussions continued.[23]

Although both Dulles and Eisenhower continued to dominate the proceed-ings, after 1957 the NSC was beholden for information to Killian and the var-ious military and technical personnel who could explain, inform, and judge the effects of these technological changes on American strategy. Even the budget discussions took on an entirely different cast when each time a Titan missile was fired, $15 million went with it. Council members continued to question the ef-ficacy of putting large sums into first-generation missiles when a new genera-tion would appear in a year or two. Meanwhile, Eisenhower probed, ques-tioned, and warned about centering all national production on military production. Yet, there was a subtle change, a weariness in the acceptance of the inevitable.[24]

The council summaries tell us little about the specific policy decisions made in response to the various crises of the administration. Although the NSC was informed and even discussed these crises, its function was to address the larger issues. For example, the critical studies on the situation in Indochina were ac-complished months before the battle at Dien Bien Phu. They formed the ba-sis for the administration's later support of the Diem government rather than the French in Dien Bien Phu. The decision not to fund the Aswan High Dam on the Nile was never brought to the NSC, but U.S. policy toward Egypt and Nasser had been delineated in papers that were skeptical of Nasser's ability to keep his country afloat. Similarly, when Khrushchev threatened Western access to Berlin in 1958, he turned attention back to the larger issue of Germany's role

23. 350th Meeting (January 6, 1958); 351st Meeting (January 16, 1958). Quote from 360th Meeting (March 27, 1958). The Gaither Report remained an internal NSC document, although its contents were "leaked" to Congress and the press.

24. 363rd Meeting (April 24, 1958).

in Europe. The NSC discussed the possibility of unification and neutralization (dismissing both) but not the contingencies surrounding the crisis.[25]

Whether long-range or immediate, however, policy decisions have to be implemented. This requires understanding of the issues, loyalty to the president, and coordinating the final decisions through personal networking within the various agencies. This is what Eisenhower wanted of the NSC organization, and that is what he got.

Throughout the Eisenhower years, attempts were made to answer the requests of the curious, the suspicious, and the critical by writing about the workings of the NSC without actually describing its highly secretive work. Cutler wrote of recommendations being "thrashed out" by the planning board. He told the Senate Subcommittee on National Policy Machinery (Jackson Subcommittee) that Eisenhower liked the council process, the methods of presentation, and the "vigorous arguments in front of him" at NSC meetings. Eisenhower assured Kennedy that while the council normally worked from an agenda, "any member could present his frank opinion on any subject."[26] But there is strong evidence that these descriptions were dismissed by congressional critics and supporters of the incoming Kennedy administration.

What these critics shared was the assumption that the process itself influenced the policy. The view that good process produces good policy has stimulated many a White House reorganization, and inspired many a scholarly article and monograph. But what the voluminous documentation of the Eisenhower administration seems to indicate is that policy can just as often influence process, a process that evolves to fit the parameters of policy set by the president.

Eisenhower was not interested in blazing new trails; they had been blazed. He wanted to keep them in good repair. That was one of the important NSC functions. Another was the coordination of all those agencies important to fighting the cold war. The ponderous efforts of the planning board usually served to re-

25. The NSC first discussed Indochina at the 138th Meeting (March 25, 1953). However, the most pertinent discussion can be found in meetings from January 8, 1954 (179th Meeting) through May 8, 1954 (196th Meeting). NSC-177 was the policy paper on Indochina.

At the 268th Meeting (December 2, 1955), the funding of the Aswan Dam was briefly discussed, but there is no reference to the reversal of that decision. See meetings from January 12, 1956 (272nd Meeting), to June 28, 1956 (289th Meeting).

Berlin was discussed in two "special meetings." The first was held after the 398th Meeting (March 5, 1959), the second before the 403rd Meeting (April 23, 1959).

26. Robert Cutler, "The Development of the National Security Council," U.S. Congress, Senate, Subcommittee on National Policy Machinery of the Committee on Government Operations; *Hearings on Organizing for National Security*, 584; "Account of My December 6th, 1960, Meeting with President-Elect Kennedy," box 11, Whitman Diary, Whitman File, in EL.

solve petty interdepartmental quarrels while coopting the participants into support of the final papers that defined general policy.

The council meetings were particularly useful because they provided several echelons of public officials with important information about world events. In addition, the participants absorbed the president's sense of priorities as well as those of his appointees. It was the ideal process for a cautious administration that preferred to respond to events rather than institute radical new policies. Thus, in spite of the policy meetings in the Oval Office, Eisenhower was probably sincere when he assured President-Elect Kennedy that the NSC "had become the most important weekly meeting of the Government." [27]

Historians and political scientists now laud the Eisenhower White House for its organizational and administrative system, and Eisenhower has been reassessed as a leader, politician, and statesman; yet his national security process was discredited by 1961 and subsequently discarded, never to be revived. [28]

If none of his successors chose to emulate Eisenhower's national security process, it may have less to do with his process than with his policies. Eisenhower was followed by activist presidents eager to make their mark on world affairs. Impatient with delay and determined to control the bureaucracies as well as the policy, they abandoned the NSC process and chose to coordinate policy through a national security adviser and an ever-growing White House staff. The public risk taking exemplified by the Cuban Missile Crisis, commitment of ground troops for an Asian war, overt interventionism illustrated by U.S. involvement in Nicaragua, and rapid full-scale military strikes such as those in Panama and the Middle East—all required this kind of White House hegemony. Unless the end of the cold war brings to office another kind of administration, the Eisenhower NSC process, like his policy, will never again be emulated—at least not in the foreseeable future.

27. "Account of My December 6th, 1960, Meeting with President-Elect Kennedy," box 11, Whitman Diary, Whitman File, in EL.

28. See, for example, Greenstein, *The Hidden-Hand Presidency.* President Richard Nixon promised a revival of the Eisenhower NSC system, but his appointment of Henry Kissinger as national security adviser effectively undermined such a revival. For information on the rise of the national security adviser and his staff, see Christopher C. Shoemaker, *The NSC Staff: Counseling the Council* (Boulder, Colo. 1991).

H. W. BRANDS
Eisenhower and the Problem of Loose Ends

Dwight Eisenhower brought to the office of the presidency an experience of international affairs unmatched in the twentieth century—perhaps unmatched since the days of John Quincy Adams. Eisenhower had seen how the world worked, and during the most tumultuous decade of the century he had played a signal role in that working. In no small part, because of his efforts the world had survived the multiple crises of the Second World War and the early cold war.

One consequence of this experience and these efforts was Eisenhower's elevation to the presidency. Another was a characteristic approach to crisis management. During one moment of great tension Eisenhower summarized his thinking on the subject in his diary. "I have so often been through these periods of strain that I have become accustomed to the fact that most of the calamities that we anticipate never really occur."[1] Repeatedly during his presidency, Eisenhower resisted calls to do something dramatic in response to fast-breaking developments. At certain times and places—Dien Bieu Phu in 1954, for instance, and Hungary in 1956—Eisenhower's propensity for letting events take their course served the United States and world peace well. In neither of these two instances could the outcome of the crisis be accounted a triumph for American diplomacy; yet Eisenhower understood the risks of erring on the side of activism, and he wisely accepted a minor setback rather than hazard a major disaster.

In other areas, though, Eisenhower's willingness to be guided by events created problems. Two examples illustrate the situation. The first involves Eisenhower's handling of the Taiwan Strait crisis of 1954–1955. In September, 1954, artillery of the People's Republic of China began shelling Nationalist Chinese positions on the island of Quemoy (now called Jinmen) in the Taiwan Strait. Certain Eisenhower administration officials, notably Joint Chiefs chairman Arthur Radford, urged an energetic response to this Communist provocation. Radford conceded that Quemoy and the other offshore islands lacked intrinsic

1. Diary entry for March 26, 1955, in Robert H. Ferrell, ed., *The Eisenhower Diaries* (New York, 1981). 296.

strategic value, but, speaking in the wake of the Western setback in Indochina, ratified just six weeks before at the Geneva Conference, the admiral argued that the free world could not step away from this latest Communist provocation. The loss of the offshore islands, Radford said, would discourage, perhaps fatally, the government of the Republic of China, and it would have spillover effects throughout the American alliance system. On the other hand, a robust defense of the islands would constitute what Radford called "a serious political and psychological reverse for the Communists and a corresponding lift for all anti-Communist forces in the Far East."[2]

The trouble with Radford's argument was that defending the offshore islands successfully would almost certainly require American counterattacks against mainland China. General John Hull, commander in chief for the Far East, described "a serious likelihood that the situation would progress rather swiftly to that of general hostilities with Communist China." In the event this likelihood materialized, Hull added, the United States must be prepared to use whatever force was necessary to achieve success, "including the use of atomic weapons."[3]

Eisenhower did not think much of the idea of going to nuclear war with China over the offshore islands. Beyond the chance of escalation to a major conflict with the Soviet Union, a nuclear assault on China would alienate the European allies, who had suffered near apoplexy when Truman had raised the possibility during the Korean War.

At the same time, though, Eisenhower appreciated the liabilities he would incur in allowing the People's Republic to take the islands. Not the least of these liabilities would be trouble with the China bloc in Congress. Majority leader William Knowland, the so-called senator from Formosa, hardly dictated Eisenhower's foreign policy: Eisenhower considered Knowland a complete ignoramus in matters of high policy, and after one particularly trying session with Knowland, Eisenhower remarked in his diary, "In his case there seems to be no final answer to the question, 'How stupid can you get?'" Yet, Knowland had a following—as his position as majority leader demonstrated—and Eisenhower preferred not to set him off.[4]

So the president sought to finesse the issue. He authorized efforts to pursue a ceasefire in the United Nations Security Council, while simultaneously agreeing to a mutual-defense pact with Chiang Kai-shek's Nationalist government.

2. Radford quoted in Washington to Manila, September 3, 1954, U.S. Department of State, *Foreign Relations of the United States, 1952–54* (Washington, D.C., 1985), XIV, 557 (hereinafter cited as *FRUS, 1952–54*).

3. Hull to JCS in Radford to Wilson, September 11, 1954, *ibid.*, 598.

4. Diary entry for January 10, 1955, in Ferrell, ed., *Eisenhower Diaries*, 291.

The former course would demonstrate America's desire for peace, the latter its determination to resist Communist expansion.

At this point two fresh problems arose. Chiang, still claiming authority over all of China, threatened to veto U.N. consideration of the strait affair. Equally troubling, he threatened to denounce the administration for appeasement. He expressed his dismay to the assistant secretary of state, Walter Robertson, whom Eisenhower dispatched to Taipei to gain Chiang's acquiescence. "Like all Asians," Chiang said, "the Chinese have watched the situation in Indochina closely. After the negotiations at Geneva, all of Indochina was surely doomed. The beginnings of negotiations with the Communists will eventually lead to the loss of Formosa." [5]

The second problem involved defining the area the United States should agree to defend. There was no doubt regarding Washington's commitment to the security of Taiwan proper. American strategists consistently judged Taiwan vital to holding the Pacific island chain that provided America's basic line of defense in the Far East. But should Eisenhower commit to defending the offshore islands, which lay just a few miles from the mainland and had almost nothing to do with holding Taiwan? This was the crux of the whole affair—and it was on this point that Eisenhower waffled. By a treaty initialed in November and ratified by the Senate early in 1955, the president pledged the United States specifically to defend only Taiwan and the nearby Pescadores; but a congressional resolution he submitted simultaneously with the treaty—and which Congress promptly accepted—granted him discretion to employ America military forces in the Taiwan Strait against preparations for an attack on Taiwan.

Would an invasion of Quemoy or its twin, Matsu, be interpreted as preparation for an attack on Taiwan? Eisenhower wasn't saying, because he had not decided. He would make that decision when the time came. A reasonable enough approach—except that it left the initiative with the Communists. Beijing reiterated its conviction that Taiwan was an "inalienable part" of China, and Premier Chou En-lai branded the Taiwan Resolution a "war message." [6]

In such an atmosphere, any assault on Quemoy would certainly give the appearance of an attack on Taiwan. Chiang, who had every reason to enhance this appearance, prepared to do precisely that by cramming Quemoy with 100,000 of his best troops. The soldiers would not suffice to defend the island against a

5. Memorandum of Conversation, October 13, 1954, file 793.5/10–1354, in Department of State records, National Archives.

6. Beijing in Noble Franklin, ed., Documents on International Affairs, 1955 (London, 1958), 445–46; Chou in British government to U.S. government, January 23, 1955, U.S. Department of State, Foreign Relations of the United States, 1955–57, II, 157 (hereinafter cited as FRUS, 1955–57).

determined Communist attack; moreover, their likely capture or death would ease the way to an invasion of Taiwan itself. This was Chiang's design: to tie the security of Quemoy as closely as possible to the security of Taiwan.

During the first three months of 1955, circumstances looked forbidding. Eisenhower admitted during a session of the National Security Council that American policy was in a condition of what he called "dangerous drift." The question of war or peace with China was largely out of American hands. If the Communists wanted war, he said, there was "nothing we can do to prevent it." Secretary of State John Foster Dulles, just back from Taipei, declared that the situation in the strait was "much more virulent" than the administration had realized. Dulles perceived what he described as "at least an even chance" of war, and he said the United States must gird itself for a "quite serious showdown." Dulles went even further, asserting that war was "a question of time rather than a question of fact." The secretary thought the administration should work on delaying the showdown, in order, as he put it, "to create a better climate for the use of atomic weapons." [7]

Arthur Radford, typically, considered the crisis an opportunity. The JCS chairman predicted that the United States would continue to have difficulties with China until the Communists got "a bloody nose." He thought now was as favorable a time as any to give them one. He advocated a stern warning to Beijing and Moscow that the United States would use "all means available" to defend the offshore islands. While the Communists pondered this message, the United States should get its nuclear weapons ready. [8]

Eisenhower refused to go that far, although he did talk up the possibility of using nuclear weapons in the area of the strait. The president declared, "In any combat situation where these things can be used on strictly military targets and for strictly military purposes, I see no reason why they shouldn't be used, just exactly as you would use a bullet or anything else." [9]

The crisis entered April, 1955, with the essential question—would the United States defend the offshore islands—unresolved. Fortunately for the Eisenhower administration, and for the peace of East Asia, Beijing chose to deescalate. At the Bandung Conference of Asian and African nations, Chou En-lai announced his government's desire to settle outstanding disputes with the

---

7. Memorandum of Discussion, January 20, 1955, *FRUS, 1955–57*, II, 69; Memorandum of Discussion, March 10, 1955, *ibid.,* 345: Memorandum for Record, March 11, 1955, John Foster Dulles Papers, in Eisenhower Library, Abilene, Kansas (hereinafter cited as EL).

8. Radford to Wilson, March 27, 1955, 091 China, Arthur Radford files, Joint Chiefs of Staff records, NA.

9. Quoted in Stephen E. Ambrose, *Eisenhower: The President* (New York, 1984), 239.

United States peacefully and proposed negotiations to end the crisis in the strait. Eisenhower seized the offer, and the threat of war receded.

Unfortunately, the fundamental issue remained unresolved. The administration claimed a victory in the affair—Dulles cited it as an example of his and the president's willingness to go to the brink of war to defend American interests—but such victory was strictly superficial and had far more to do with politics in the United States than with security in the Far East. Although Eisenhower had refused to commit the United States explicitly to the defense of the offshore islands, he had allowed the development of expectations to that effect. Having made such a big deal of the islands in 1955, he would almost be obliged to go back to the brink for them in the future should Beijing decide again that it needed an issue to rally the masses against the imperialists. This was exactly what happened in 1958, and the administration once more was forced nearly to war, in the same place over the same issue—and it achieved the same equivocal outcome.

The second illustration of the problem of loose ends relates to Eisenhower's attempts to implement the New Look policy of 1953. Better than any other president of the cold war era, Eisenhower recognized that American military strength rested on America's economic strength. The United States had won the Second World War—with help—not because of the great valor of its soldiers or because of the insight and cleverness of its generals—though Eisenhower was never one to downplay his own accomplishments—but because the United States had outproduced its enemies. Inheriting a defense budget ballooned by both the Korean War and, more fundamentally, by the imperatives of NSC-68 —the 1950 National Security Council paper that called for a tripling of American defense spending and served as a blueprint for the permanent mobilization of the country—Eisenhower sought to bring spending in line with America's capacity to produce over the long term.

A top-level review of American strategy during the summer of 1953—a time, not coincidentally, when Eisenhower succeeded in liquidating the Korean conflict—resulted in a new policy paper, NSC-162. As approved by the president, NSC-162 asserted bluntly that "excessive government spending leads to inflationary deficits or to repressive taxation," each of which undermined American security by damaging America's economy and hence America's "defense productivity." [10]

Capping defense spending, however, demanded choosing among different defense strategies. Under the regime of NSC-68 and the Korean War, the

10. NSC–162/2, October 30, 1953, *FRUS,* 1952–54, II, 577–97.

United States had attempted to meet aggression at the level at which the aggression took place. This required a capacity to wage conventional war to deal with peripheral aggression like that in Korea, and a capacity to wage nuclear war to deter direct aggression by the Soviet Union. Needless to say, this dual strategy entailed considerable redundancy and expense.

Eisenhower attempted to minimize the expense by putting all, or at least most, of America's eggs in a nuclear basket, so to speak. He authorized America's war gamers to assume the early use of nuclear weapons even in peripheral wars. As NSC-162 phrased the decision, "In the event of hostilities, the United States will consider nuclear weapons to be as available for use as other munitions."

The premise of the new policy was simple. By threatening nuclear retaliation, the United States would deter aggression in places like Korea just as the same threat had deterred aggression in central Europe. John Foster Dulles, in a widely noted speech at the beginning of 1954, described the policy as resting "primarily upon a great capacity to retaliate, instantly, by means and at places of our choosing." [11]

There were two problems with the policy of what quickly came to be called "massive retaliation." The first was that the policy, on its face, was incredible. Perhaps the United States conceived Berlin to be so crucial to American security that it would risk nuclear war to keep that city out of Russian hands. (Truman had responded to the blockade of 1948—when the United States still possessed a nuclear monopoly—with nothing more belligerent than transport planes.) But it boggled the mind to think that the American leadership would put New York in jeopardy to preserve Seoul or Saigon.

The second problem was that Eisenhower failed to make the New Look policy stick within the American defense establishment. The Pentagon had accepted the downgrading of conventional forces implicit in NSC-162 only with the utmost reluctance and only after the president intruded himself personally into the decision-making process. With its endless capacity for obstruction, the military bureaucracy, led by the army, which bore the brunt of the conventional cutbacks, dragged its feet. Even before NSC-162 arrived back from the printers, opponents of reliance on nuclear force succeeded in reopening the discussion Eisenhower's approval of NSC-162 supposedly closed.

Initially, the reconsideration involved nothing more than appropriate means for implementing the basic decisions enunciated by NSC-162. But means and ends soon became hopelessly confused as the foot draggers raised troublesome issues regarding calculations of the nature of the Soviet threat. No one—not

11. *Department of State Bulletin,* January 25, 1954, 107–10.

even Treasury Secretary George Humphrey or budget director Joseph Dodge, the leaders of those who advocated cutting conventional military forces—denied the need to protect America's nuclear retaliatory capacity. But they recognized that there were degrees of protection, and that the higher degrees came with higher price tags. They argued for simple sufficiency, contending that the United States could afford to lose a few nukes without mortally eroding its deterrent capacity.

But how many was a few, and how likely were the rest to survive a Soviet attack? For bureaucratic reasons as well as from simple prudence, the Pentagon preferred to err on the side of safety. To bolster its arguments, it drew some positively horrendous scenarios. In these pre–U-2, pre-satellite days, nearly anybody's guess at what the Soviets possessed and what they might soon possess was as good—or bad—as anyone else's. Until 1953, significant doubt had existed that hydrogen weapons could be sufficiently miniaturized to fit on the head of long-range missiles. By the beginning of 1954, the Eisenhower administration's experts reported to the president and the National Security Council that American scientists had solved the miniaturization problem. Recent experience indicated that the Russians could not be far behind. Some analysts thought they were ahead. All agreed that nuclear-tipped missiles would be nearly unstoppable, and that in a short time the United States would be at the mercy of the Soviet Union's trigger holders.

The debate over the vulnerability of the American nuclear deterrent, which eventually produced another policy paper, NSC-5422, was about more than merely how to defend the American nuclear arsenal. More fundamentally, it was about the whole concept of massive retaliation. If the concept had ever made sense, it now no longer did. Now the United States had to be prepared to commit national suicide to preserve peripheral interests in outlying areas. No one could take such a policy seriously.

The Pentagon pushed exactly this argument. Its draft of NSC-5422 declared that "in the face of possible nuclear balance in 1956–59, there is serious question whether the U.S., while maintaining maximum nuclear capabilities, can continue to place major reliance thereon." Consequently, the Pentagon draft continued, the United States must undertake to increase its conventional capabilities.[12]

Budget balancers Humphrey and Dodge disagreed violently. Humphrey was outraged—though not surprised—that the generals had the effrontery even to raise the issue again. As the treasury secretary complained to Eisenhower in a June, 1954, meeting of the National Security Council, the NSC had "long

12. Draft of NSC-5422, June 14, 1954, *FRUS*, 1952–54, II, 647–67.

since" decided to rely on nuclear weapons and to cut back conventionally. Looking to the president, Humphrey declared that it was "high time that this decision be enforced."

In principle, Eisenhower agreed. The president expressed annoyance that the issue was still being debated. It was "simply impossible" for the United States to "try to play safe in all the possible kinds of warfare." He said that if the administration accepted the views of partisans of limited war, as opposed to nuclear war, "We might just as well stop any further talk about preserving a sound U.S. economy and proceed to transform ourselves forthwith into a garrison state."

All the same, Eisenhower refused to get too worked up regarding debates over policy papers. Adopting his characteristic fabian approach, the president declared that he would defer decisions regarding the use of conventional or nuclear weapons until events required a decision. Then he would be guided by the merits of the individual case, rather than the guidelines of some abstract paper.[13]

These remarks indicated a softening of Eisenhower's commitment to the New Look. The commitment softened further as the president received new estimates of the consequences of nuclear war. In 1956 a special panel reported that the country could expect fifty million deaths and injuries in an initial exchange with the Soviets, while collateral damage would largely eliminate America's ability to keep fighting. Eisenhower found the report gravely sobering. It described, he said, "the most serious problem" that had ever faced the world. He added, "We should certainly revise our war plans."[14]

Doubt trickled down from the top. The Pentagon, spotting its opportunity, agitated for more of both conventional and nuclear weapons. Arthur Radford complained that the United States was giving friends and enemies alike the impression of "confusion and indecisiveness" among its leaders. Absent strong action—Radford suggested an immediate $3 billion increase in defense spending—this impression would damage American prestige and endanger American interests.[15]

George Humphrey again differed vigorously. The treasury secretary complained that nothing had "ever really been done to carry out this New Look policy." Humphrey added that the administration had allowed itself to be "led astray by scientists and by vested interests."[16]

Defense Secretary Charles Wilson confessed to sabotage within the ranks of

---

13. Memorandum of Discussion, June 24, 1954, *ibid.*, 686–98.
14. Memorandum of Discussion, February 7, 1957, Dwight Eisenhower Papers, in EL.
15. Radford to Wilson, March 12, 1956, Staff Secretary Records, in EL.
16. Memorandum of Discussion, March 28, 1957, Eisenhower Papers, in EL.

the Defense Department. The army, Wilson conceded, had been leaking anti–New Look information to the press.[17]

Eisenhower began to question whether his desire to strike a balance between military and economic strength would ever become a reality. At an NSC meeting in August, 1956, he wondered aloud whether the manpower ceiling of 2.5 million troops was too low—which was exactly what the Pentagon had been waiting to hear. A few months later, the president admitted to what he called a "sense of defeat" regarding his ability to implement his national security reforms.[18]

"Defeat" was too strong a word. For the most part Eisenhower held the line against big increases in defense spending. But his unwillingness to decide conclusively between conventional and nuclear weapons ultimately led—under his successors—to a position where the United States faced the worst of both worlds: the high cost of conventional forces and the high risks of relying on nuclear deterrence.

This last point raises an interesting question regarding how Eisenhower should be evaluated. Eisenhower's procrastinating leadership style produced no disasters during his presidency and, aside from the Taiwan crises, not even very many close calls. If the loose ends he left lying around entangled anyone, they did not entangle him.

Should Eisenhower be blamed for what came after him? The nonresolution of the offshore islands question caused few problems after Eisenhower left office, but the arms race continued to accelerate, costing trillions of dollars and spreading a dark cloud of uncertainty over the future of the human race—a cloud that still exists, despite the easing of superpower tensions in the past few years. How much of this buildup should be charged against Eisenhower's account?

Or to take another example: How much responsibility should Eisenhower bear for the Vietnam War? He prudently said no to American military intervention in 1954. But he left the door open to subsequent military intervention, and by throwing America's support to the Diem regime he created the conditions that led directly to American escalation during the 1960s.

At one level it is unfair to blame Eisenhower for decisions made by his successors, whether about the arms race or about Vietnam. The most one can ask of presidents is that they do well during their terms in office. They cannot be expected to determine the future also.

17. *Ibid.*
18. Memorandums of Discussion, August 16 and 17, 1956, and March 28, 1957, Eisenhower Papers, in EL. See also the Wampler essay in this volume.

On the other hand, presidents should remember that they live within the stream of history, and that the rocks they place in the stream shape the currents their successors have to contend with. Ironically, Eisenhower's failures in this regard may have resulted from his very strengths. Eisenhower, had he served that long, could have said no to the pace the arms race acquired during the 1960s and 1970s. With his stature as a military leader he could have shrugged off charges of weakness on defense. He could have said no to escalation in Vietnam during the 1960s just as he said no in 1954.

Unfortunately, Eisenhower's successors were not Eisenhower, and what he might have done they could not. Or, rather, they thought they could not, which was even worse, since it prevented their trying.

The problem is hardly peculiar to Eisenhower—which is why it is worth studying. To cite an example of recent and continuing concern: Ronald Reagan accomplished much during his eight years as president. Among his accomplishments, however, was driving the spike of antagonism to taxes—even at the expense of previously inconceivable budget deficits—so deeply into the bedrock of the American political landscape that it will take years to dig it out. Bridges may crumble and school systems disintegrate, but we will still be reading George Bush's lips.

Reagan's gifts, such as they were, differed greatly from Eisenhower's. Yet each would have done better by the country if he had given more thought for those who would come after.

GÜNTER BISCHOF

Eisenhower, the Summit, and the Austrian Treaty, 1953–1955

On March 5, 1953, Soviet dictator Josef Stalin unexpectedly died. This opened an unanticipated window of opportunity for the West to initiate an easing of East-West tensions. On March 15, only ten days later, Stalin's apparent successor, Georgi Malenkov, the chairman of the Council of Ministers, announced Soviet readiness to settle peacefully and by mutual agreement all unresolved or disputed matters with the United States.[1] How would the West respond to this seemingly dramatic turn in Soviet foreign policy?

While Winston Churchill quickly and persistently pleaded for a quick and informal summit to test the sincerity for "peaceful coexistence" of the new Kremlin leadership, the new Republican administration of Dwight D. Eisenhower refused to be stampeded into negotiations with the Soviet Union and continued to pursue hard-line cold war policies of no talks and no concessions. Six weeks after Stalin's death, Eisenhower made a gesture. Instead of agreeing to meet the new Kremlin leadership face to face, he delivered a speech, calling for concrete Soviet "deeds" to prove that Malenkov was serious about "peaceful coexistence." Signing of the Austrian peace treaty was made a crucial item on Eisenhower's list of "deeds" expected from the Soviets.

The Austrian treaty had been on the unresolved East-West agenda ever since the outbreak of the cold war in 1946–1947. By 1953, the Austrians were prepared to enter any form of negotiations with the Soviet Union as long as it would bring them their nation's independence. Unlike their suspicious Western guardians, the new administration of conservative chancellor Julius Raab was prepared to seize any straw and take advantage of Stalin's death. While Eisenhower refused to negotiate with Malenkov, the Austrians tested the new leader-

The author would like to thank his University of New Orleans colleagues Stephen E. Ambrose and Joseph Logsdon, Anna Kasten Nelson of The American University, and Saki Dockrill of King's College, London, for their useful comments on earlier drafts of this paper. A Krupp Foundation grant from the Center for European Studies and the Charles Warren Center's Kohn Fund, both of Harvard University, as well as an award from UNO's Research Council, have made research for this paper possible.

1. U.S. Department of State, *Foreign Relations of the United States, 1952–1954*, VIII, 1130*n*2 (hereinafter cited as *FRUS, 1952–54*).

ship in the Kremlin directly—whether they would be willing to negotiate bi-
laterally about the withdrawal of occupation forces and the signing of the Austrian treaty. Washington disdained this Austro-Soviet bilateral diplomacy but
could do little about it. In April, 1955, Austro-Soviet diplomacy culminated in
a bilateral summit meeting of sorts in Moscow. This breakthrough in direct personal contacts with the Kremlin quickly led to the final five-power negotiations,
the signing of the Austrian State Treaty, the subsequent four-power evacuation
of the country, and the Austrian declaration of neutrality. It was the emancipation of Austrian diplomacy in the wake of Stalin's death—the "new looks" in
the Kremlin and on the Ballhausplatz—that led to this dramatic breakthrough
in the spring of 1955. After ten years of four-power occupation, the Austrians
did not miss any opportunities. In the process they also proved to the world
that one could do business with the Soviet Union.

Coming after the "ice age" of the cold war, 1953 had the potential of being
a year of great opportunities in easing East-West tensions. During the first half
of 1953, new leaders appeared on the stage of international politics. In January,
the Republican Eisenhower administration replaced the Democratic Truman-
Acheson team. On March 5, Stalin died.[2] A month later in Austria, Raab, from
the People's party, replaced Leopold Figl as chancellor of the durable Conserv-
ative-Socialist coalition government. Bruno Kreisky, the young state secretary in
the Foreign Office, brought a fresh infusion of realistic thinking into Austrian
foreign policy. In September the West Germans reelected Konrad Adenauer as
chancellor, who was expected to complete the integration of the Federal Republic into the Western defense system.[3]

Between 1950 and 1953, Austria had become a "secret ally" of the West.[4]

2. Stephen E. Ambrose, *Eisenhower: The President* (New York, 1984), 44–103; Martin Gilbert,
Never Despair (Boston, 1988), 805–28, Vol. VIII of Randolph S. Churchill and Martin Gilbert,
Winston S. Churchill.

3. Manfried Rauchensteiner, *Die Zwei: Die Grosse Koalition in Österreich, 1945–1966* (Vienna,
1987), 183–200; Gerald Stourzh, *Geschichte des Staatsvertrages, 1945-1955: Österreichs Weg zur
Neutralität,* 3rd ed. (Graz, 1985), 81–90. See also the various essays in Alois Brusatti and Gottfried
Heindl, eds., *Julius Raab: Eine Biographie in Einzeldarstellungen* (Linz, 1986); Bruno Kreisky, *Zwischen
den Zeiten: Erinnerungen aus Fünf Jahrzehnten* (Berlin, 1986), 430 ff.

4. This is Gerald Stourzh's judgment. See his "The Origins of Austrian Neutrality," in
Neutrality: Changing Concepts and Practices, ed. Alan T. Leonhard (Lanham, Md., 1988), 39–40. For
the origins of Austria's political and economic Western orientation in the early phases of the cold
war, see Günter Bischof, "Between Responsibility and Rehabilitation: Austria in International
Politics, 1940–1950" (Ph.D. dissertation, Harvard University, 1989), 292–525, and Josef Leidenfrost,
"Karl Gruber und die Westorietierung Österreichs nach 1945," in *Für Österreichs Freiheit: Karl
Gruber—Landeshauptmann und Aussenminister, 1945–1953,* ed. Othmar Huber and Lothar Höbelt
(Innsbruck, 1991), 101–20. For Austria's ideological and cultural Western integration in the early

While Austria profited from the pro-Western foreign policy of the staunch anti-Communist Austrian foreign secretary, Karl Gruber, with massive American economic aid, it did not regain its independence. East-West tensions made progress on an Austria treaty almost impossible during the cold war, when the Korean War was fought and the nuclear arms race exploded. In the absence of any great power agreement, Gruber practiced what might be called a "diplomacy of pestering," by reminding the great powers that Austria was part of the unresolved cold war agenda.[5]

In the spring of 1952, the Western powers had failed to accomplish the long overdue four-power evacuation of Austria with their proposal for a drastically "abbreviated treaty" (Kurzvertrag). The British, the French, and the Austrians considered this short treaty, drafted by the State Department, as an American propaganda instrument. So did the Soviets; they refused to discuss the American proposal, since it obviated their extensive economic claims against Austria. In the fall of 1952, Gruber brought the unresolved Austrian issue up for discussion in the U.N. General Assembly.[6] But nothing was accomplished, and by the end of 1952 the deadlock between the great powers over the Austrian treaty persisted.[7]

In 1953, a dramatic change in Austrian foreign policy came about. This was a result of the alleviations in the Soviet occupation regime in Austria, which were part and parcel of the new look in the Kremlin's foreign policy. The Soviet high commissioner in Vienna was replaced by an ambassador; they stopped making the Austrian government pay for Soviet occupation costs; they discontinued trade restrictions between the zones of occupation; and they ended censorship

cold war, see Oliver Rathkolb, "Die Entwicklung der U.S.-Besatzungskulturpolitik zum Instrument des Kalten Krieges," in *Kontinuität und Bruch 1938–1945–1955: Beiträge zur österreichischen Kultur- und Wissenschaftsgeschichte,* ed. Friedrich Stadler (Vienna, 1988), 35–50.

5. For "diplomacy of pestering" see Günter Bischof, "'Austria and Moscow's Wiles': The Western Powers, Neutrality and the Austrian Peace Treaty, 1952–1955," paper presented at the conference, "The United States and West European Security, 1950–1955," Harvard University, 1987, and Günter Bischof, "Karl Gruber und die Anfänge des 'Neuen Kurses' in der österreichischen Aussenpolitik 1952–53," in *Gruber,* ed. Huber and Höbelt, 151–54.

6. On the abbreviated treaty and the U.N. initiative see Audrey Kurth Cronin, *Great Power Politics and the Struggle over Austria, 1945–1955* (Ithaca, N. Y., 1986), 115–19; Stourzh, Staatsvertrag, 71–81; Manfried Rauchensteiner, *Der Sonderfall: Die Besatzungszeit in Österreich 1945 bis 1955* (Graz, 1979), 299–314; Oliver Rathkolb, "Von der Besatzung zur Neutralität," in *Die bevormundete Nation: Österreich und die Alliierten, 1945–1949,* ed. Günter Bischof and Josef Leidenfrost (Innsbruck, 1988), 377–90; Bischof, "Karl Gruber und die Anfänge des 'Neuen Kurses,'" in *Gruber,* ed. Huber and Höbelt, 144–54.

7. About the last rounds of serious 1949 treaty negotiations in Paris and London, see Bischof, "Austria in International Politics," 727–821.

and gave back Austrian properties such as the huge Danube power plants that they had seized in 1945–1946 as "German assets." The new chancellor, Raab, explicitly praised the Soviets for these concessions. He remarked, "One should not pinch the tail of the Russian bear when it stands in the midst of the Austrian garden."[8] In the process of welcoming the new look in the Kremlin, Raab began the emancipation of Austrian foreign policy from Western tutelage. Richard H. Davis, the counselor of the American embassy in Vienna, recognized the essence of the new departure in Austrian foreign policy: "A certain show of independence from the United States on the part of the Austrian Government is a natural accompaniment to its policy of encouraging Soviet concessions."[9]

When the Western powers failed to revive regular four-power Austrian treaty talks in 1953, the Austrians seized the initiative, testing the idea of neutrality as an option for regaining Austrian independence.[10] Beginning in 1952, in a number of informal behind-the-scenes contacts, Soviet diplomats had hinted that Austrian neutrality would constitute a "guarantee" for the Soviets against Austrian participation in Western defense planning. In June, 1953, Gruber went a step further in these bilateral diplomatic contacts. He asked Jawaharlal Nehru, the neutralist Indian prime minister, to act as go-between with the Kremlin. Upon Gruber's urging, India's ambassador in Moscow, K. P. S. Menon, asked Molotov, the Soviet foreign minister, whether it would be "useful if Austria were to give an undertaking [sic] of neutrality." Molotov answered that "it would be useful but not enough." He added, "Declarations can be given today but withdrawn tomorrow."[11] Much to the dislike of the Western powers, Gruber nevertheless went public and announced that Austria's future policy would stay "free of military alliances."[12]

Raab's foreign policy was characterized both by growing independence from

8. Rauchensteiner, *Die Zwei,* 201–203; Stourzh, *Staatsvertrag,* 81–83; Ludwig Steiner, "Die Aussenpolitik Raabs als Bundeskanzler," in *Raab,* ed. Brusatti and Heindl, 212–14. Philips E. Mosley was quite in tune with most American observers, whose attention was riveted on events in Germany, when he failed to mention the Soviet concessions in Austria while discussing the new flexibility in Kremlin diplomacy after Stalin's death in *Foreign Affairs,* repr. in *The Kremlin and World Politics: Studies in Soviet Policy and Action* (New York, 1960), 363–81.

9. Davis dispatch sent by Ambassador Thompson to Department of State, August 25, 1953, *FRUS* 1952–54, Vol. VII, Pt. 2, p. 1987.

10. Stourzh, *Staatsvertrag,* 74–76; Cronin, *Great Power Politics,* 112–15, 125-26.

11. On the origins of Austro-Soviet bilateral diplomacy, see the collection of documents from the Austrian Foreign Office, *Österreich und die Grossmächte: Dokumente zur Österreichischen Aussenpolitik, 1945–1955,* ed. Alfons Schilcher (Vienna, 1980), 154–63, 176–77. See also Stourzh, *Staatsvertrag,* 86–88; Cronin, *Great Power Politics,* 126; Bischof, "Gruber und die Anfänge des 'Neuen Kurses,'" in *Gruber,* ed. Huber and Höbelt, 161–68.

12. Cited in Stourzh, *Staatsvertrag,* 89–90.

Western tutelage and increased friendliness toward the new Kremlin leadership and the Soviet representatives in Vienna. Unlike his predecessor, Figl, Raab assumed the initiative in foreign affairs despite his personal inexperience in the diplomatic arena. Raab relied heavily on the advice of Norbert Bischoff, Austria's experienced, long-time ambassador to Moscow, who had good channels of communication into the Kremlin. By 1953, Gruber's anti-Soviet, pro-Western policies had become a liability for Raab's new path toward careful equidistance between East and West; the abrasive, pro-American Gruber no longer fit into Raab's new look.[13] In November, 1953, Raab seized the opportunity to fire Gruber after the unpredictable Tyrolean published, while still in office, a volume of "memoirs" attacking the occupation powers. Gruber's departure from the Ballhausplatz probably was also designed to send a message to Moscow.[14]

The Western powers were highly suspicious of Austria's bilateral diplomatic maneuvers with the Kremlin. They worried about the repercussions a "neutralization" of Austria might have on Adenauer's Germany. Between 1953 and 1955, German rearmament and the integration of the Federal Republic into the Western defense system was at the top of the Western diplomatic agenda. The Anglo-American capitals viewed anything that might interfere with this priority with alarm.[15] It is hardly surprising that the French in particular feared "damaging repercussions" on Germany by a neutralization of Austria.[16] The Soviets, for their part, had been making a number of diplomatic offers since 1952 to unify and neutralize Germany.[17] Ever since the West had adopted plans to rearm and integrate the Germans in a European Defense Community, the Kremlin had been working to block a German rearmament and Western integration.

After Stalin's death, behind the scenes the Western powers filtered plans on whether a new round of high-level four-power negotiations over the unresolved

13. Alfred Maleta, personal interview, Vienna, May 27, 1986.
14. Gruber's consolation prize was the ambassadorship in Washington. See Steiner, "Aussenpolitik Raabs," in *Raab,* ed. Brusatti and Heindl, 215–16; Rauchensteiner, *Die Zwei,* 222–23; Bischof, "Gruber und die Anfänge des 'Neuron Kurses,'" in *Gruber,* ed. Huber and Höbelt, 169–70.
15. On the intensive EDC debates in the Western camp, see Rolf Steininger, "John Foster Dulles, the European Defense Community, and the German Question," in *John Foster Dulles and the Diplomacy of the Cold War,* ed. Richard H. Immerman (Princeton, 1990), 79–108; Saki Dockrill, "The Evolution of Britain's Policy Towards a European Army, 1950–1954," *Journal of Strategic Studies,* XII (1989), 38–62.
16. Harrison Memorandum of Conversation with the French minister Crouy-Chanel, May 12, 1953, Foreign Office 371/103762/CA 1071/123, Public Record Office, Kew, Richmond, England (hereinafter cited PRO).
17. Rolf Steininger, *Eine vertane Chance: Die Stalin-Note vom 10. März 1952 und die Wiedervereinigung* (Berlin, 1985).

cold war agenda (Germany, Korea, Austria, Vietnam, nuclear weapons, etc.) ought to be initiated.[18] The leaders of state had not gathered for a summit since Potsdam in 1945; the foreign ministers had not met since 1949. In any of these meetings, the Austrian treaty, which the powers had been negotiating through interminably dreary meetings since 1946, would be an item high up on the agenda.[19]

The Eisenhower administration was shocked to find the American government inadequately prepared for the contingency of Stalin's death.[20] Eisenhower reported to his cabinet a day after Stalin's death that the U.S. government had no contingency plans for Stalin's death: "What we found was that the result of 7 years of yapping [plans were supposed to be prepared as early as 1946] is exactly ZERO [*sic*]. We have no plan. We don't even have any agreement on what difference his death makes. It's—well, it's *criminal,* that's all I can say" (emphasis in the original). Emmet J. Hughes, Eisenhower's speech writer, who recorded the president's outburst in his diary, added, "And no one felt like contradicting."[21] To make matters worse for Washington crisis management, the United States had no ambassador in Moscow at the time. By March, 1953, George Kennan, who had been declared persona non grata in 1952, had not been replaced. In spite of this emergency, the McCarthyites held up the Senate confirmation of "Chip" Bohlen, one of the premier U.S. experts on the Soviet Union, for the entire month of March.[22]

18. Walt W. Rostow describes how people like himself and C. D. Jackson were starting to think about a more comprehensive U.S. psychological warfare program, including the contingency of Stalin's death, even before Eisenhower was elected. After Stalin's death they advocated that the Eisenhower administration set a positive initiative toward the new Kremlin leadership and engage in direct negotiations to end the cold war confrontation in Central Europe; see *Europe After Stalin: Eisenhower's Three Decisions of March 11, 1953* (Austin, Tex., 1982), 35–45.

19. See, for example, CC 48 (53), August 10, 1953, CAB [Cabinet Records] 128/26, Part II, in PRO. The Austrian issue had a firm place in the Rostow initiative; see Rostow, *Europe After Stalin,* 39, 41, 56–57, 60, 63.

20. Steven Fish, "After Stalin's Death: The Anglo-American Debate Over a New Cold War," *Diplomatic History,* X (1986), 334–36. See also Francis MacDonnell, "The American Response to Stalin's Death: A Study in the Eisenhower Style of Leadership," Seminar Paper, Harvard University, 1985.

21. March 6, 1953, folder "Diary Notes of Meetings, Oct. 1951–1953," box 1, in Emmet John Hughes Papers, Mudd Library, Princeton University. The official minutes of this cabinet meeting confirm Hughes's diary entry, albeit in more restrained language: "The President told the Cabinet that no specific plan for Government action or policy had been developed in advance, despite continuous talk since 1946 about the possibility of Stalin's death." See *FRUS, 1952–1954,* VIII, 1098. On further American analyses of Soviet policy after Stalin's death, see *ibid.,* 1099–1139.

22. On the Senate fight over Bohlen's confirmation, see Günter Bischof, "Before the Break: The Relationship Between Eisenhower and McCarthy, 1952-1953" (M.A. thesis, University of

The Kremlin surprised the scrambling Eisenhower administration with a peace offensive. On March 15, Malenkov announced that there was no dispute between the Soviet Union and the United States that "cannot be decided by peaceful means, on the basis of mutual understanding."[23] This unexpected offer was inspired by the fact that "Stalin's successors needed to find some accommodation with the West, since a confrontation in the nuclear age was far too dangerous," as the Soviet expert Alec Nove has noted.[24]

Behind the scenes, a divided Eisenhower administration discussed whether to initiate direct negotiations and encourage changes in Kremlin foreign policy. By mid-March the president decided to send positive signals. He noted, "There are new governments in two great countries. The slate is clean—now let's begin—AND LET'S SAY WHAT WE'VE GOT TO SAY SO EVERY PERSON ON EARTH CAN UNDERSTAND IT" [sic].[25] But Secretary of State John Foster Dulles did not deem the Kremlin's post-Stalin peace offensive a sincere effort. Dulles thought the Soviets were acting from a position of weakness; so no concessions should be made, no four-power meeting held, no major presidential speech given. Dulles feared that any positive response to the new look at the Kremlin "would indefinitely delay progress" on the European Defense Community and German rearmament.[26]

In spite of Dulles' intransigence, Eisenhower was determined to test Soviet sincerity. He told his speech writers to prepare a major address and make concrete offers to which the Soviets could respond. In his famous speech before the American Society of Newspaper Editors, on April 16, President Eisenhower called upon the Soviets to back up their sincerity for peace with actual deeds. Ending hostilities in Korea, reducing armaments, ending the division of Germany and Europe, and signing the Austrian treaty were on the list.[27]

New Orleans, 1980), 107-24; Michael Ruddy, *The Cautious Diplomat: Charles E. Bohlen and the Soviet Union, 1929–1969* (Kent, Ohio, 1986), 109–24.

23. As chairman of the Council of Ministers, Malenkov was the apparent heir to Stalin; in reality he was only *primus inter pares,* and after the trial of Beria and the rise of Khrushchev, Malenkov lost his leadership position, in February, 1955. See the chapter on Malenkov by Roy Medvedev, *All Stalin's Men* (London, 1983), 140–63; *Soviet Diplomacy and Negotiating Behavior: Emerging New Context For U.S. Diplomacy,* 96th Cong., 1st Sess., Committee on Foreign Affairs, Special Studies on Foreign Affairs Issues (Washington, D.C., 1979), I, 259–80.

24. Alec Nove, *Stalinism and After: The Road to Gorbachev,* 3rd ed. (Boston, 1989), 121.

25. March 16, 1953, Diary, box 1, in Emmet J. Hughes Papers, Princeton University.

26. Rostow, *Europe After Stalin,* 6–8, 113–14.

27. Coming early in Eisenhower's first term and constituting a first response to the changes in the Kremlin, there are probably few presidential addresses with such a long and complicated gestation period as the April 16 "Chance for Peace" speech. For the final draft of the speech, see *FRUS,* 1952–1954, VIII, 1147–55. For a discussion of the psychological warfare approaches that

While Eisenhower reacted very cautiously to Malenkov's offer of "peaceful coexistence," the British prime minister, Winston Churchill, approached the changes in the Kremlin with much greater enthusiasm, sensing the potential for an historic breakthrough in easing cold war tensions.[28] He hoped to end the division of Europe by dealing directly with the new and internationally inexperienced Kremlin leadership. The old and ailing Churchill saw great promise in an informal summit meeting. He wanted to renew his wartime contacts with people like Molotov in the Kremlin.[29] This was the same Churchill who had warned Roosevelt and Eisenhower in 1944–1945 about the threats of Soviet expansionism in Central Europe and who helped start the cold war with his famous "iron curtain" speech.[30] Now Churchill had grown weary of cold war confrontations and scared of the awesome threat of thermonuclear warfare and wanted to be remembered in the history books as the great peacemaker.

Only six days after Stalin's death, Churchill suggested a summit meeting with the new Kremlin leadership. On April 5, he suggested to Eisenhower that "we ought to lose no chance of finding out how far the Malenkov regime are prepared to go in easing things up all around." On April 12, Churchill noted that "a new hope has . . . been created in the unhappy, bewildered world." He warned the president, "It would be a pity too if a sudden frost nipped spring in the bud." [31] Churchill even contemplated going alone to Moscow on a "solitary

---

went into the speech, see the W. W. Rostow memorandum of May 11, 1953, *ibid.*, 1173–83. For early speech drafts, see the folder in box 2, in Hughes Papers, Princeton University. For disagreements within the Eisenhower administration over how to respond to the conciliatory Soviet gestures after Stalin's death, see March and early April entries, Hughes Diary, box 1, in Hughes Papers, Princeton University. For a discussion of the speech, see Ambrose, *Eisenhower: The President*, 77–96; Deborah Welch Larson, "Crisis Prevention and the Austrian State Treaty," *International Organization*, XLI (1987), 35–39. The best analysis of the speech, including a reprint of the principal documents, is Rostow, *Europe After Stalin*.

28. The most complete treatment now available of Churchill's heroic and futile struggle to persuade Eisenhower to meet the Soviets in a summit is *The Churchill-Eisenhower Correspondence, 1953–1955*, ed. Peter Boyle (Chapel Hill, 1990) (hereinafter cited as *Correspondence*).

29. This point is stressed by John Lukacs in a review of Boyle's *Correspondence* that is highly critical of Eisenhower. See *New York Times Book Review*, February 10, 1991, pp. 3, 26–27. "Anthony and I have done a lot of business with Molotov," Churchill told Eisenhower on March 11, 1953, in *Correspondence*, 31.

30. Fraser J. Harbutt, *The Iron Curtain: Churchill, America and the Origins of the Cold War* (New York, 1986).

31. In his March 11 letter, Churchill had added: "I have the feeling that we might both of us together or separately be called to account if no attempt were made to turn over a leaf so that a new page would be started with something more coherent on it than a series of casual and dangerous incidents at the many points of contact between the two divisions of the world." See letters of March 11 and April 11 and 12, 1953, in *Correspondence*, 31, 40–45. See also Sir Michael

pilgrimage"; he prepared a draft telegram to Molotov asking the Soviet foreign minister whether he "would like me to come to Moscow so that we could renew our own war-time relation." [32] Eisenhower, who feared for the solid Western front regarding Moscow, quickly talked Churchill out of dispatching the telegram, cautioning him that "anything the Kremlin could misinterpret as weakness or overeagerness on our part would militate against success in negotiation." Eisenhower warned his old friend that a solitary pilgrimage for good will alone could only be misinterpreted by both the allies and the American Congress. [33]

Churchill's efforts culminated in his famous speech of May 11. He addressed the House of Commons, proposing an alternative approach to the new leadership in the Kremlin, much more positive and encouraging than Eisenhower's hesitant Chance for Peace speech. Churchill stressed that individual issues like a Korean armistice or the conclusion of an Austrian treaty could be settled immediately, even without a general settlement of differences. But Churchill went a step further and pleaded for direct negotiations without delay in an informal summit conference. Such a conference should be confined to "the smallest number of powers and persons possible" and should not be hampered by rigid agendas or hordes of zealous experts. [34]

Not only Eisenhower and the State Department but also British foreign minister Anthony Eden as well as the British Foreign Office were appalled by Churchill's free-wheeling initiative. [35] Eisenhower privately surmised that Churchill wanted to relive the days of World War II, when he and Roosevelt and Stalin could direct the affairs of the world from their "Olympian platform." The American president argued that "in the present international complexities, any hope of establishing such a relationship is completely fatuous." [36]

Anthony Eden and the Foreign Office opposed a summit for similar reasons.

Howard, "Churchill: Prophet of Détente," Eighth Crosby Kemper Lecture, March 25, 1990, pp. 3–4.

32. Churchill added: "I should of course make it clear I was not expecting any major decisions at this informal meeting but to restore an easy and friendly basis between us such as I have with so many other countries," Churchill to Eisenhower, May 4, 1953, in FRUS, 1952–1954, VIII, 1169, repr. in Correspondence, 48.

33. Eisenhower to Churchill, May 5, 1953, in FRUS, 1952–54, VIII, 1170–71, repr. in Correspondence, 49–50.

34. Gilbert, Never Despair, 829–31.

35. Churchill's close associates increasingly worried about the prime minister's "senility," especially after his June stroke. See Howard, "Churchill: Prophet of Détente," 7.

36. For Eisenhower's long diary entry of January 6, 1953, on Churchill's World War II nostalgia, see Robert H. Ferrell, ed., The Eisenhower Diaries (New York, 1981), 222–24.

They argued that the Soviets would abuse a summit without a fixed agenda as a pretext for interminable negotiations to block the ratification of the European Defense Community and German rearmament. Any summit before the ratification of the EDC threatened prospects for quick German rearmament. Churchill's solitary pilgrimage to Moscow, without a clear agenda, would threaten Western bargaining positions, bring disharmony into the united Western front, threaten the reelection prospects of Adenauer in the Federal Republic, and give the Kremlin new opportunities to block ratification of the EDC treaty.[37]

Why did Eisenhower so vehemently oppose a summit in 1953? At a time when the Republican right wing was attacking the Yalta summit and its legacy, a Soviet summit meeting by a Republican president would have met violent opposition from the anti-Communist McCarthyites.[38] And, as Walt Rostow has argued, Eisenhower also lacked Churchill's "confident eagerness" when it came to professional diplomatic negotiations with the Soviets. And, Dulles, his principal foreign policy adviser, acted as a formidable roadblock whenever the president contemplated bold new departures in dealing with the Communist foe.[39]

Beyond the uncompromising Dulles and some hysterical senators, Eisenhower also encountered firm resistance on the summit idea from other advisers. C. D. Jackson, his psychological warfare adviser, reminded the president that during the Bermuda summit—offered to the prime minister as a consolation prize—he would have to demonstrate American leadership by containing Churchill's unilateral diplomatic activity and stalemating the Soviet peace offensive, which threatened to split the Western alliance. The American leadership role, argued Jackson, should not be "sacrificed because of a very human feeling of decency and generosity toward an opinionated old gentleman who is still sufficiently sharp and selfish to grab every advantage with bland assurances of unwavering support."[40]

---

37. Gilbert, *Never Despair,* 827–45; Robert Rhodes James, *Anthony Eden: A Biography* (London, 1986), 365; Anthony Seldon, *Churchill's Indian Summer: The Conservative Government, 1951–55* (London, 1981), 396–401; David Carlton, *Anthony Eden* (London, 1981), 333–36.

38. For Eisenhower's craven 1953 approach to McCarthy, see Bischof, "Before the Break." Lukacs argues that by 1953, Eisenhower had to adapt his ideology to the McCarthyites and therefore resisted a direct approach to the new leadership in the Kremlin; see *New York Times Book Review,* February 10, 1991. See also Howard, "Churchill: Prophet of Détente," 7.

39. Rostow, *Europe After Stalin,* 4–75.

40. Jackson added: "It is evident that we must seek to emerge from the Bermuda conference with the free world in the highest state of unity possible, so that we may go forward together either (a) to force the issue militarily in Korea, and/or (b) to negotiate with the Russians (the Four Power

Eisenhower also encountered resistance to a summit from his allies. In a letter to the American president, Adenauer pleaded for a firm Western front and reminded Eisenhower that "unity among the Western Allies and concerted action on their part was an essential prerequisite for a successful solution of the tension between East and West." Adenauer insisted that a summit meeting be preceded by a meeting of the Western foreign ministers' deputies, where an agenda could be set in consultation with German diplomats.[41] But the unexpected East German workers' uprising on June 17 stopped all talks for a summit for a while, and after the Soviets crushed it, cold war tensions again were heating up.

In spite of Churchill's entreaties, Eisenhower refused to meet the Soviets for a summit in 1953. Instead, he suggested a Western summit on Bermuda in June. But a stroke on June 24 incapacitated Churchill. As a consequence the Bermuda summit had to be postponed until December, 1953.[42] When Eisenhower, Churchill, and Laniel, the French premier, met at Bermuda, they at last agreed to resume negotiations with the Soviets. Yet it would not be a meeting of the heads of state as Churchill had hoped. Instead, the Americans insisted on a foreign ministers conference, where Molotov could be tested about Soviet sincerity on the German and Austrian questions.

In the course of this meeting, Eisenhower shocked the British with his revealing remarks on the Soviets. Churchill's private secretary, John Colville, recorded in his diary: "[Eisenhower] said that as regards the P.M.'s belief that there was a New Look in Soviet Policy, Russia was a woman of the streets and whether her dress was new, or just the old one patched, it was certainly the same whore underneath. America intended to drive her off her present 'beat' into the back streets." [43]

Given such uncouth imagery, it is hardly surprising that Eisenhower refused to sit at the negotiating table with the Kremlin leaders. Half a year later Eisen-

---

Conference is something that is going to happen with or without Churchill's pushing, and we should reverse our own frame of mind and our own planning so that it ceases to be a Sword of Damocles and becomes something that we can turn to our advantage). " See C. D. Jackson memorandum to the President, June 3, 1953, folder "Jackson C. D. 1953 (2)," box 21, Administration Series, Ann Whitman File, in Dwight D. Eisenhower Library, Abilene, Kansas (hereafter cited as EL). On C. D. Jackson's important role as a gadfly in formulating Eisenhower's foreign policy, see H. W. Brands, Jr., *Cold Warriors: Eisenhower's Generation and American Foreign Policy,* (New York, 1988), 117–37.

41. Letter, Adenauer to Eisenhower, May 29, 1953, in folder "Germany 1953 (3)," box 13, Diary Series, Ann Withman File, EL.

42. Gilbert, *Never Despair,* 846–57.

43. John Colville, *The Fringes of Power: 10 Downing Street Diaries, 1939–1955* (New York, 1985), 683. Howard downplays this remark and instead stresses Churchill's "senility" ("Churchill: Prophet of Détente," 6-7).

hower confirmed his view of the Soviet leaders when he confided his "utter lack of confidence in the reliability and integrity of the men in the Kremlin." [44]

Churchill suspected that Dulles was the cause of such American priggishness when he told his physician, Lord Moran, that Eisenhower was Dulles' "ventriloquist's doll," adding, in tears, "This fellow [Dulles] preaches like a Methodist Minister and his bloody text is always the same: That nothing but evil can come out of a meeting with Malenkov." Then the old Churchill came close to admitting defeat. "Dulles is a terrible handicap," Churchill complained bitterly and noted, "Ten years ago I could have dealt with him. Even as it is I have not been defeated by this bastard. I have been humiliated by my own decay." [45] These deep personal divisions among the Western leaders may go a long way to explain why the Soviets were never met at the bargaining table in 1953.

American intransigence to meet the Soviets at the negotiating table made diplomatic progress on the Austrian question impossible in 1953, in spite of hopeful signs from the Kremlin. Eisenhower's refusal to meet Malenkov and Molotov for a summit did not allow any dramatic unfreezing of East-West tensions, even though the Korean armistice agreement was signed in July. Dulles' personal determination to rearm Germany and complete ratification of the EDC effectively blocked any movement on the foreign ministers' level. The Austrians had no opportunity to get on the international agenda, since negotiations on the foreign ministers deputies' level were made impossible by the American insistence on the abbreviated treaty. [46]

When the Austrian government took matters in its own hands, in 1953, suggesting a declaration of neutrality in return for Soviet withdrawal of troops, the Western powers felt hard pressed. The British argued that it was time to separate the Austrian from the German question. While a neutralization of Germany would be a major "reversal of Western policy," this would not be the case with Austrian neutrality. [47] Dennis Allen, the head of the Foreign Office's Cen-

44. Eisenhower to Churchill, July 22, 1954, in *Correspondence*, 163.

45. Gilbert, *Never Despair*, 936; Howard, "Churchill: Prophet of Détente," 7.

46. The Western Allies and the Austrian government had been urging the State Department to drop their short draft treaty. Eisenhower characterized the short draft as one of the "straitjackets which we have inherited from the past Administration." In order to prevent an American isolation in the Austrian treaty matter, Dulles reluctantly suggested to the National Security Council that he be authorized to resume negotiations on the basis of the long draft. The United States formally withdrew the ill-fated short draft treaty in August. See discussion in 142nd NSC meeting, April 30, 1953, *FRUS*, 1952–54, Vol., VII Pt. 2, pp. 1956–60; Bischof, "Gruber und die Anfänge des 'Neuen Kurses,'" in *Gruber*, ed. Huber and Höbelt, 160f.

47. Hancock minute, May 24, 1953, FO 371/103762/CA 1071/137, in PRO.

tral Department, doubted that "in practise the effects in Germany of a neutralization of Austria need be so serious as the French fear." [48] He warned that one
had to be careful not to fall into the trap of "What goes for Austria goes for Germany." Frank Roberts, the Foreign Office undersecretary for Germany, argued
that the Soviet Union wanted to hold the Austrians hostage, "until they can bargain them against western concessions over Germany." [49] But the British realized
that they could not publicly oppose Austrian neutrality if the Soviets were finally
prepared to sign an Austrian treaty. Only a demilitarized Austria and power vacuum in Central Europe would be unacceptable. [50]

The American position toward Austrian neutrality developed in a similar direction. In the minds of American policymakers, the Austrian issue was totally
overshadowed by German rearmament. The Policy Planning Staff in the State
Department opposed the inclusion of Austrian neutrality in the State Treaty
"because it might serve as a precedent for the German peace treaty and prevent
a united Germany from joining EDC, as we presume might be Germany's desire and intent." [51]

The basic American disagreements over a neutralization of Austria can best
be discerned from a crucial debate in the National Security Council in October,
1953, in which the Pentagon was pitted against the State Department. [52] The
chairman of the Joint Chiefs of Staff, Admiral Arthur Radford, vigorously resisted "the neutralization of Austria as contrary to U.S. interests." He summarized the views of the American military establishment: "A neutralized Austria
would greatly weaken us in Europe." Radford particularly feared the effects of
a neutralization of Austria on Germany, and "a neutralized Germany
would be much more serious." [53]

Dulles disagreed and in this instance displayed remarkable sensitivity toward
the Austrian situation. His view resembled the British position. If the Austri-

48. Allen minute, May 13, 1953, FO 371/103762/CA 1071/123, in PRO.

49. Roberts minute, May 22, 1953, FO 371/103762/CA 1071/137, in PRO.

50. Strang to Roberts, October 31, 1953, FO 371/103768/CA 1071/303, in PRO.

51. Memorandum by Beam of the Policy Planning Staff to the acting director of the Office
of Western European Affairs (Knight), September 28, 1953, *FRUS, 1952–54*, Vol. VII, Pt. 2, pp.
1901–1902. For a more detailed discussion of State Department views on a neutralization of
Austria, see also Rauchensteiner, *Die Zwei,* 210–16.

52. In 1949, the Pentagon and Foggy Bottom had gone through a similar controversy over the
signing of an Austrian State Treaty. In the end President Truman had to resolve the issue himself.
See Audrey Kurth Cronin, "Eine verpasste Chance? Die Grossmächte und die Verhandlungen im
Jahre 1949," in *Die bevormundete Nation,* ed. Bischof and Leidenfrost, 347–70.

53. Memorandum of Discussion of the 166th Meeting of the National Security Council,
October 13, 1953, and NSC-164/1 of October 14, 1953, *FRUS, 1952–53,* Vol. VII, Pt. 2, pp. 1911,
1918. On the U.S. military see also Rauchensteiner, *Die Zwei,* 217–19.

ans wanted to become neutral in return for a treaty, the Americans could not stop them. He, too, was against neutralization, but "the decision in the long run would depend on the Austrians themselves. Dulles concluded that if the Americans refused to sign the treaty, "an embittered Austria would never prove a reliable ally for the United States." The United States could not impose its point of view, either on the Austrians or on the French and British, if they went along with the Austrians.[54] A pragmatic Dulles tried to avert being pushed into an isolated corner on the Austrian issue.[55]

Eisenhower was equally pragmatic when it came to Austrian neutrality. His only stipulation was that if Austria became neutral, it would have to be an armed neutrality.[56] In January, 1954, shortly before Dulles went to the Berlin Council of Foreign Ministers, Eisenhower cautioned the secretary of state: "He could see no objection to the neutralization of Austria if this did not carry with it the demilitarization. If Austria could achieve a status somewhat comparable to Switzerland, this would be quite satisfactory from a military standpoint."[57] Eisenhower shared the views of the Pentagon that what was unacceptable after the final withdrawal of occupation forces was a military vacuum in Austria.[58]

54. *FRUS*, 1952–54, Vol. VII, Pt. 2, pp. 1910–11. The basic American position toward a neutralization of Austria was outlined in NSC-164/1 of October 14, 1953, *ibid.*, 1914–22. Rathkolb has also pointed out the importance of this meeting; see "Von der Besatzung zur Neutralität," in *Die bevormundet Nation*, ed. Bischof and Leidenfrost, 391–93. Rauchensteiner only briefly mentions the earlier version, NSC-164; see *Die Zwei*, 214.

55. On Dulles' pragmatism on the issue of neutrality, see Günter Bischof, "Dulles and Austrian Neutrality," Proceedings of the Dulles Centennial Conference, 1988, Princeton University; Brands's essay on Dulles in *Cold Warriors*, 18–24; *Dulles and the Diplomacy of the Cold War*, ed. Immerman; Gerald Stourzh, "Towards the Settlement of 1955: The Austrian State Treaty Negotiations and the Origins of Austrian Neutrality," *Austrian History Yearbook*, XVII–XVIII (1981–82), 179–80. Similarly, for the Third World, Dennis Merrill has shown in the case of India how Dulles' "moral absolutes gave way to increased tolerance for the nonaligned perspective." See his "Eisenhower, Dulles, and India: Accommodating Immoral Neutralism, 1953–1958," a paper presented at the American Historical Association annual convention, 1987.

56. Governor Stassen, Eisenhower's administrator for Mutual Security Aid, had already foreshadowed this solution in the October NSC meeting when he argued that "the status of neutrality did not necessarily imply disarmament," adding: "What we want to avoid above all else, especially in Germany, is the combination of neutralization with disarmament." See *FRUS*, 1952–54, Vol. VII, Pt. 2, p. 1961.

57. Memorandum of Breakfast Conference with the President, January 20, 1954, folder "Meetings with the President 1954 (4)," box 1, White House Memoranda Series, John Foster Dulles Papers, Princeton University. See also Gerald Stourzh, *Die Furche*, April 19, 1985, pp. 6–7, and Gerald Stourzh, "The Origins of Austrian Neutrality," in *Neutrality: Changing Concepts and Practices*, ed. Leonhard, 45; Cronin, *Great Power Politics*, 134; Rathkolb, "Von der Besatzung zur Neutralität," in *Die bevormundete Nation*, ed. Bischof and Leidenfrost, 393–94.

58. The American military establishment had discussed the rearmament of Austria earlier. See Rauchensteiner, *Die Zwei*, 218–20. Rauchensteiner is correct in stressing that the Americans were

In late January, 1954, for the first time since Paris in 1949, the foreign ministers convened in Berlin. Dulles still was less than eager to sit at the negotiating table with the Soviets. But Berlin offered him the opportunity to size up the Soviet diplomats and "to demonstrate to the world that the United States did seek peace," as Richard Immerman has argued.[59] If nothing else, Berlin would offer propaganda opportunities by once again demonstrating Soviet intransigence to the world.

Next to the German question, where the Soviets rejected the "Eden Plan" by making no concessions on the main issue of free elections, Austria was the principal item on the agenda. At the Council of Foreign Ministers in Berlin, Dulles presented the basic American position that the Eisenhower administration had internally agreed to: "A neutral status is an honorable status if it is voluntarily chosen by a nation. Switzerland has chosen to be neutral, and as a neutral she has achieved an honorable place in the family of nations. Under the Austrian state treaty as heretofore drafted, Austria would be free to choose for itself to be a neutral state like Switzerland. Certainly the United States would fully respect its choice in this respect, as it fully respects its choice in the respect of the Swiss nation." Dulles added that in "special circumstances" self-chosen neutrality was acceptable, but a neutralization imposed from the outside was not.[60]

In Berlin, Molotov was still not prepared to sign a treaty with Austria and evacuate the country as the price of Austrian neutrality.[61] The Austrian formula for neutrality tabled in Berlin was a proposal of not allowing any military bases on Austrian soil, and not joining any future alliances. But Molotov linked a final pullout of occupation troops from Austria with the conclusion of a

---

only willing to grant Austria a neutral status if she was armed—"for the Americans neutrality was strictly conditioned on Austria's rearmament" (*ibid.*, 218).

59. Richard Immerman, "The United States and the Geneva Conference of 1954: A New Look," *Diplomatic History,* XIV (1990), 47–48.

60. Nineteenth Plenary Session, February 19, 1954, *FRUS,* 1952–1954, Vol. VII, Pt. l, pp. 1088–89. For a draft of this statement, with Dulles' handwritten changes, see Draft of Statement by John Foster Dulles, February 13, 1954, folder "Berlin Four Power Conference of Foreign Ministers, 1954," box 78, Dulles Papers, Princeton University. It is almost certain that Dulles drafted this statement by himself. Personal interview with Robert Bowie (director of the Policy Planning Staff), February 25, 1988, and Phyllis Macomber (Dulles' personal secretary), February 26, 1988, at Princeton University.

61. The Soviets had been developing a positive view on neutrality in general and nonalignment in particular since the early 1950s. On the changing Soviet views on neutrality and nonalignment, see Margot Light, *The Soviet Theory of International Relations* (New York, 1988), 229–37. On a sketch of Molotov, see Medvedev, *All Stalin's Men,* 82–112.

German peace treaty.[62] Waiting for a German peace treaty, however, meant waiting for Godot. Molotov's intrasigence apparently was rooted in his unwillingness to give up any territory that the Red Army had conquered in World War II.[63]

After his return from Berlin, Dulles reported to the National Security Council that the Austrians were prepared to "neutralize their country." He added that Molotov had brushed the hint aside in the most brutal fashion and that the Austrian foreign minister, Figl, and his delegation had walked out of the council chambers "almost in tears." Dulles concluded, "Neutralization is no substitute for the European Defense Community, as many Western Europeans believed or would like to believe."[64]

The Berlin CFM reaffirmed Eisenhower in his views that the new Kremlin leadership was not prepared to make major diplomatic concessions in the international arena in general and on the Austrian treaty in particular. This confirmed the American president in his view that negotiations with the Soviets would lead nowhere and were only exercises for the superpowers to jockey for propaganda advantages. Yet, Churchill, recovered from his stroke of the previous year, continued his pressure to meet Malenkov in a friendly summit. At a time when the British decided to build their own H-bomb and when American H-bomb tests in the Pacific demonstrated the utter destructiveness of the new nuclear bombs, Churchill's anxiety about thermonuclear war greatly increased. The prime minister kept pestering Eisenhower over "a personal meeting between Three." He pleaded with the president: "Men have to settle with men, no matter how vast, and in part beyond their comprehension, the business in hand may be. He added, "I can even imagine that a few simple words, spoken in the awe which may at once oppress and inspire the speakers, might lift this nuclear monster from our world."[65]

At the end of June, 1954, Churchill traveled to Washington to plead one

62. On Molotov's objections (after Figl's presentation) in the 18th meeting of February 12, 1954, see *FRUS, 1952–54*, Vol. VII, Pt. I, pp. 1061–65. On summaries of the Berlin CFM, see Stourzh, *Staatsvertrag*, 116–25, and Cronin, *Great Power Politics*, 129–36. Dulles cabled home to Eisenhower that Molotov's presentation had destroyed all lingering hopes for an agreement on Austria. See Dulles to Eisenhower, February 13, 1954, in folder "February 1954 (1)," box 2, Dulles Herter Series, Ann Whitman File, EL.

63. In a 1958 conversation with Raab, Khrushchev blamed Molotov personally for this intransigence and his failure to follow the Kremlin's "new course." See Kreisky, *Zwischen den Zeiten*, 472. See also Vojtech Mastny, "Kremlin Politics and the Austrian Settlement," *Problems of Communism*, XXXI (1982), 37–51.

64. Memorandum of Discussion at the 186th NSC meeting, February 26, 1954, *FRUS*, 1952–54, Vol. VII, Pt. I, p. 1222.

65. See Churchill to Eisenhower, quoted in Gilbert, *Never Despair*, 959–60; *Correspondence*, 109–11.

more time for a summit meeting. There was one issue where the Russians could make a quick concession—agreeing to an Austrian treaty. He argued that signing an Austrian treaty was "a dream," and added, "If I were a Russian I should think it would be good politics." [66] Eisenhower disagreed. He argued that "we had gone very far with Molotov in trying to get an Austrian treaty," and he remained "skeptical about the possibility of getting it by this method." [67]

Churchill was certain, however, that "all the world" desired a summit that might ease tensions between East and West and bring peace.[68] A meeting with the Soviets and the conclusion of an Austrian treaty became the *idée fixe* for the single-minded prime minister. He saw it as the final great mission before his retirement. On his trip back to England on the *Queen Mary*, Churchill told his associates that "he was decided on an expedition to Russia, where he would ask freedom for Austria as an earnest of better relations." For this he was prepared to meet the Soviets at Vienna.[69] Without further consulting either Eisenhower or the British cabinet, Churchill proceeded to prepare a telegram proposing talks to the Soviet leaders; this time he sent it. Molotov responded right away with a friendly cable informing Churchill that his proposal "met with sympathetic acknowledgment in Moscow." He added, "We feel that such a personal contact may serve to carrying out a broader meeting on the highest level, if it is accepted by all parties which are interested in easing the international tension and in strengthening peace." [70]

But domestic pressure from Anthony Eden and the British cabinet—some members even threatened resignation—convinced a reluctant Churchill in the end to abandon his dream for a summit with the Soviets. Churchill's critics in the cabinet continued to worry that in such a high-level meeting the Soviets would try to prevent German rearmament and the establishment of the European Defense Community. Eden argued that in a bilateral meeting with the Soviets, there was no prospect for agreements, since the Soviets continued to hold an uncompromising attitude.[71]

66. See the Eisenhower-Churchill conversation during their Washington meeting, June 26, 1954, in Gilbert, *Never Despair*, 1002. On the ups and downs of Washington talks see also Colville, *The Fringes of Power*, 692–95.

67. Eisenhower-Churchill meeting, June 26, 1954, folder "June 1954 (1)," box 2, Ann Whitman Diary Series, in EL; Gilbert, *Never Despair*, 1006–1007; *Correspondence*, 151.

68. He added: "Fancy that you and Malenkov should never have met, or that he should never have been outside Russia, when all the time in both countries appalling preparations are being made for measureless mutual destruction" (Churchill to Eisenhower, August 8, 1954, *Correspondence*, 167).

69. See diary entry of July 2, 1954, in Colville, *The Fringes of Power*, 697; Gilbert, *Never Despair*, 1012.

70. Churchill to Eisenhower, July 7, 1954, in *Correspondence*, 152–53.

71. After Churchill's telegram to Molotov, spirited discussions over the constitutionality of

Eisenhower continued to be convinced that a summit would "serve no useful purpose." The president detected no Soviet "deeds" that might demonstrate the Kremlin's will to coexist peacefully.[72] The searing battle with McCarthy during the recently concluded Army-McCarthy hearings and the pressure from the China lobby after the Indochina settlement in the Geneva Conference did not encourage the president to make diplomatic gestures to any Communists. Eisenhower ventured to explain his "conscious or subconscious mind" to Churchill: "I am certain that you must have a very deep and understandable desire to do something special and additional in your remaining period of active service that will be forever recognized as a milestone in the world's tortuous progress towards a just and lasting peace." He concluded, "Nothing else could provide such a fitting climax to your long and brilliant service."[73]

In the face of such formidable opposition from friends and allies, the prime minister at last was compelled to give in. There would be neither a preparatory bilateral meeting with the Soviets (Vienna was bandied about as a likely site) nor a summit. This also meant that there would be no further chance to conclude the Austrian treaty during a high-level meeting, as Churchill had envisioned all along.

Meanwhile, the international landscape was changing dramatically to the disadvantage of the Soviet Union. German rearmament remained the central issue in European politics. On August 30, 1954, the French National Assembly at last ended the long charade and voted down the EDC treaty; Soviet obstructionism seemed to have triumphed. But the British had developed contingency plans. Anthony Eden quickly engineered the alternative solution of a direct integration of the Federal Republic into the Western defense system. In the Paris Accords of October, 1954, the Western powers pressed ahead with directly integrating German military contingents into NATO.[74]

Churchill's approach ensued in the cabinet. Could the prime minister initiate a major foreign policy proposal without consulting the cabinet? Churchill's initiative also threatened good relations with the United States and the other Allies; see the "confidential Annexes" ("Top Secret") to the cabinet conclusions of the July 8, July 9, July 13, July 23, and July 26, 1954, cabinet meetings, CC 50 to 54 (54), CAB 45128/27, Pt. II, PRO; see also Gilbert, *Never Despair*, 1012–32. In his correspondence with Eisenhower, Churchill continued to stress that "an undertaking to ratify the Austrian Treaty in which their conditions have been agreed, and to liberate Austria and Vienna from Russian military domination" would be high on the agenda (*ibid.*, 1028).

72. Eisenhower noted that no Soviet "deed" could be expected on the Austrian issue ("nothing but an evil purpose can prevent their liberation of Austria"). See Eisenhower to Churchill, July 7 and 12, 1954, in *Correspondence*, 153–54, 160–62.

73. Eisenhower to Churchill, July 22, 1954, in *Correspondence*, 161.

74. Churchill commented after the French Assembly rejected the EDC, "The throwing out

Not surprisingly, the ensuing Soviet propaganda campaign against the Paris accords and German membership in NATO was intense. But German rearmament was a forgone conclusion.[75] Early in 1955 it became clear that the Paris agreements would be ratified in Bonn and Paris. After this major diplomatic defeat, the Kremlin was forced to reasses its foreign policy.[76] The backdrop of German rearmament and Western integration is crucial to understanding the developments in the Austrian question.

During 1954, the Austrian question had continued to remain hostage to great power disagreements and to Western priorities with German rearmament. In the absence of a summit, or any other forum for East-West negotiations, the Raab government could only wait and see whether the Kremlin might be prepared to enter bilateral negotiations with Austria. Raab insisted that contacts with the Soviets must not cease, "even if the prospects were bleak."[77] Raab continued his policy of mollifying the Soviets in his speeches, despite a renewed Soviet propaganda campaign claiming that the western powers were remilitarizing their Austrian occupation zones with the intent of annexing Western Austria to NATO. Moscow issued warnings about the dangers of a "new *Anschluss*"—"a short hand term at the time for the suspected Western objective of integrating Austria into the emerging Western security system," as Kurt Steiner has argued.[78]

Raab managed to keep the diplomatic channels open with Soviet ambassador Ilyichev.[79] At the end of 1954, he repeated that his government was "ready to negotiate what, when and where it might be possible." He reconfirmed with the Soviets that "some kind of declaration of neutrality" would not be excluded from Austrian thinking, nor would a slowed-down staged withdrawal of occu-

---

of EDC is a great score for the Russians" (see Gilbert, *Never Despair,* 1055). On the 1954 Western diplomacy on West German rearmament, see Steininger, "Dulles," in *Dulles and the Diplomacy of the Cold War,* ed. Immerman, 86–108. See also the essays by Stephen E. Ambrose and Hermann-Josef Rupieper in Bruno Thoss and Hans-Erich Volkmann, eds., *Zwischen Kalten Krieg und Entspannung: Sicherheits- und Deutschlandpolitik der Bundesrepublik im Mächtesystem der Jahre, 1953–1956* (Boppard am Rhein, 1988), 25–33, 179–209. For a detailed examination of the British role, see Saki Dockrill, "Britain and a West German Contribution to NATO," 233–378, and Saki Dockrill, "Britain and the Settlement of the West German Rearmament Question in 1954," in *British Foreign Policy, 1945–56,* ed. Michael Dockrill and John W. Young (London, 1989), 149–72.

75. Kurth Cronin, *Great Power Politics,* 136–42.

76. Bruno Thoss, "Modellfall Österreich? Der österreichische Staatsvertrag und die deutsche Frage 1954–55," in *Zwischen Kalten Krieg und Entspannung,* ed. Thoss and Volkmann, 93–107.

77. *Ibid.,* 98.

78. Kurt Steiner, "Negotiations for an Austrian Treaty," in *U.S.-Soviet Security Cooperation: Achievements, Failures, Lessons,* ed. Alexander L. George *et al.* (New York, 1988), 72; Stourzh, *Staatsvertrag,* 126–29.

79. For Austria in 1954, see Rauchensteiner, *Die Zwei,* 228–58.

pation troops (a variant of the proposal suggested by Pierre Mendès-France, the French premier, before the United Nations in December, 1954).[80] Yet Raab left no doubt about the basic Austrian position, demanding "the removal of all foreign troops within a set period [of time]." The Austrian chancellor thus rejected Molotov's Berlin condition of linking the final troop withdrawals from Austria to the conclusion of a German peace treaty.[81] Not expecting any substantive East-West talks before the solution of the German rearmament question, however, the Raab government firmly supported the ratification of the Paris Agreements. Raab realized that future Austrian neutrality would only benefit from a strong Western security system including the Federal Republic.[82]

In a conversation with Geoffrey Wallinger, the British ambassador in Vienna, Raab reported a talk he had with the Soviet ambassador. The Russians probably would be upset over the Paris agreements for some time, noted Raab, because they were so "fear-ridden over the prospect of West-German rearmament." But after a time they would get used to the new situation created by the Paris agreements, "and then they might become more negotiable." [83] Raab, in short, counseled patience, the best of diplomatic virtues.

In 1955, Raab's persistence finally paid off. On February 8, Malenkov was demoted from his position of leadership, and Molotov gave a lengthy keynote address before the Supreme Soviet. He announced that he saw no reason "for any further delay in concluding a state treaty with Austria," if she undertook "not to join any coalitions or military alliances." [84] Molotov lured the Austrians into

80. Mendès-France wanted to gain more political support at home by designing a French role as mediators in East-West tensions. He recognized a major problem in the fact that the West left all initiatives in East-West diplomacy to the Soviets. To bring movement into the Austrian Treaty question, in a speech before the United Nations in November, 1954, he proposed the compromise solution of a staged withdrawal of the occupation troops from Austria over a period of eighteen to twenty-four months after the signing of the Austrian Treaty (as opposed to three months envisioned in the Austrian treaty draft). See Thoss, "Modellfall Österreich?" in Zwischen Kalten Krieg und Entspannung, ed. Thoss and Volkmann, 100–107; Stourzh, Staatsvertrag, 128–29; René Girault, "La France dans les Rapports Est-Ouest au Temps de la Présidence de Pierre Mendès-France," in Pierre Mendès-France et le Mendénisme: L'Expérience Gouvernementale (1954–1955) et sa Postérité, ed. François Bedarida and Jean-Pierre Rioux (Paris, 1985), 255–59.

81. Wallinger to Harrison, December 31, 1954, FO 371/117779/R 1017/1, in PRO. The Foreign Office observed that the Austrians appeared to be intensifying their pressure in the Allied Council and with the Russians to end the occupation. Stow minute, January 6, 1955, ibid.

82. Thoss, "Modellfall Österreich?" in Zwischen Kalten Krieg und Entspannung, ed. Thoss and Volkmann, 99–100.

83. Wallinger to Harrison, December 31, 1954, FO 371/117779/R 1017/1, in PRO.

84. Stourzh, Staatsvertrag, 131–32; Cronin, Great Power Politics, 145–47; Mastny, "Kremlin Politics," 41–42.

bilateral negotiations, telling them that "it would depend mainly on Austria" if they wanted to reach conclusion of the treaty. If Austria and the Soviet Union could reach an agreement, argued Molotov, "the others would find it difficult to say no" (exactly what the British Foreign Office and Dulles had predicted in the fall of 1953). Over the next six weeks Raab's personal confidant, Austrian ambassador Bischoff in Moscow, was busy probing the exact meaning of Molotov's words in bilateral diplomatic contacts in Vienna and Moscow.[85]

These decisive rounds of bilateral diplomacy culminated in the highly successful Austro-Soviet summit in Moscow. The Kremlin invited a high-level Austrian delegation to talks in Moscow. From April 11 to 15, Chancellor Raab, Vice-Chancellor Adolf Schärf, Foreign Secretary Figl, and State Secretary Kreisky accomplished the decisive breakthrough in intense negotiations with the entire Kremlin leadership. The Soviets demanded Austrian neutrality as the decisive guarantee against incorporation either within Germany or in the Western defense system. Austrian neutrality should be armed similar to that of Switzerland. The Soviets did not stipulate that neutrality had to be written into the treaty. The Soviets also made decisive concessions in the unagreed economic clauses of the treaty. The results of the Moscow talks were written down in a memorandum.[86] Only one month after the breakthrough in the Austro-Soviet Moscow summit, the foreign ministers signed the Austrian treaty, on May 15.[87]

How did the Western powers view these bilateral Austro-Soviet negotiations that led to the signing of the treaty? The Western powers were highly frustrated over their loss of initiative on the Austrian question, observing the hectic Austro-Soviet bilateral diplomacy from the sidelines. The British Foreign Office felt that the Austrian diplomats were "no match" for the Soviet bullies and not up to "Moscow's wiles." Left to their own devices, the Austrians were "in an appallingly vulnerable situation *vis-à-vis* the Russians," argued the Foreign Office. British experts felt that the Soviet initiative on Austria represented just another "facet of the campaign to prevent the entry into force of the Paris Agreements." They wanted to cause "delay and confusion in the Western camp" and tempt the West into four-power talks in order to then raise the German question and stop German rearmament.[88]

85. On this frantic bilateral diplomacy see the selection of Austrian Foreign Office papers, *Österreich und die Grossmächte*, ed. Schilcher, 236; Stourzh, *Staatsvertrag*, 132–38.

86. Stourzh, *Staatsvertrag*, 142–63.

87. Based on the long draft treaty of 1949, the ambassadors of the four powers and the Austrian representatives had cleared up the open issues in early May. The Austrian Parliament passed a constitutional law on Austria's "permanent neutrality" after the Allied forces had withdrawn. For these final rounds of negotiations, see Stourzh, *Staatsvertrag*, 163–72.

88. Record of Conversation, Harrison and the Austrian ambassador, Schwarzenberg, March

American concerns differed little from the British ones. Dulles conceded that the Moscow invitation had to be accepted by the Austrian government. But he was deeply concerned that the Soviets wanted to use the Austrian question as a "back door" to reopen the German question. Dulles maintained his clear sense of priorities when he reminded the Austrians that a four-power meeting was inconceivable before the ratification of the Paris agreements. Dulles also warned the Austrians that Moscow was a "dangerous place to go to alone" and cautioned Raab that he should not think he could go to Moscow and speak for the Western powers.[89] Llewellyn Thompson, the American ambassador in Vienna, agreed with Dulles that the Soviet moves on Austria had to be seen in conjunction with their final attempt to block the ratification of the Paris agreements.[90] President Eisenhower argued even after the Austrian breakthrough at Moscow that "the Soviet gambit on Austria was definitely made with Germany in mind as the real target."[91]

In the spring of 1955, the Austrian issue still lingered in the shadow of Germany. The new leadership in the Kremlin had its own strategic, political, and economic reasons for signing an Austrian treaty in spite of the unilateral German rearmament by the West. Nikita Khrushchev, the emerging new Soviet leader, apparently was prepared to cut losses and demonstrate his sincerity over "peaceful coexistence" with the dramatic Soviet concessions on Austria.[92] Charles Bohlen, the U.S. ambassador in Moscow, argued that the Soviets realized German rearmament could no longer be stopped.[93] The cold war mindset in the West, however, simply could not imagine the Soviet Union making any positive offer that was also in the Soviet interest, given that the Western powers also had to withdraw their own troops from Austria. Before the Austrian delegation went to Moscow in April, 1955, the Western powers were understandably much more concerned about West German integration into NATO than the quick conclusion of the Austrian treaty. Austria's priorities, however, were

8, 1955, FO 371/117786/RR 1071/33; Harrison to Nutting, March 18, 1955, RR 1071/43; Wright minute, 15 March 1955, RR 1071/34, in PRO.

89. Memorandum of conversation, Dulles, Gruber, *et al.,* March 25, 1955, U.S. Department of State, *Foreign Relations of the United States, 1955–57,* V, 16–19 (hereinafter cited as *FRUS, 1955–57*). See also Raab's consultations with his ambassadors in Vienna, March 28, 1955, in *Österreich und die Grossmächtel,* ed. Schilcher, 250–64.

90. Thompson to Dulles, April 4, 1955, in 663.001/4-455, box 2662, RG 59, National Archives.

91. 245th NSC meeting, April 21, 1955, *FRUS, 1955–57,* V, 52–54.

92. See Khrushchev's explanation to Raab, cited in Kreisky, *Zwischen den Zeiten,* 472.

93. Bohlen to Dulles, April 8, 1955, in 863.001/4-855, RG 59, NA. See also Bohlen to Dulles, March 31, 1955, in *FRUS, 1955–57,* V, 26.

the opposite; the Austrians grasped at every straw to get their treaty and independence. This time, the Austrian government did not allow its own interest to be sacrificed to the Western agenda on Germany.

After the signing of the Austrian treaty, Dulles returned to the United States and tried to claim the laurels for the conclusion of the treaty. On May 17, in a joint television appearance with the president, he reported to the American public the dramatic breakthrough in Central Europe: The German integration into NATO had been completed and the Austrian State Treaty signed. He proudly called it "just one of those breaks that come, if you keep on steadily, steadily, keeping the pressure on." He speculated that Austrian freedom would be contagious to Austria's neighbors behind the iron curtain.[94] The same day, Dulles told the Senate Foreign Relations Committee that "the Austrian Treaty is definitely recognized everywhere as being the first fruit of the consummation of the Western European policy and bringing Germany into NATO."[95] Two days later, Dulles told the National Security Council that the diplomatic success in Germany and Austria was a result of the Western policy of toughness in the wake of Stalin's death and ventured the following speculation: "It had been quite apparent to him, as a result of the achievements of the United States and its alliances—including the bringing of Germany into NATO and other manifestations of strength—the Soviets had effected a complete alteration of their policy. Their policy had been hard and was becoming soft. The Iron Curtain is going to disappear. In the future there will be no more sharp line between the free world and the Soviet bloc. The sharp line will be replaced by a fuzzy area."[96]

The Hungarians supposedly listened to Dulles. But the Eisenhower administration, facing dual crises in Budapest and in Suez in the fall of 1956, was not prepared to intervene and support the Hungarian insurgents, nor were they bailing out the British and French. Contrary to Dulles' predictions, the iron curtain did not disappear, at least not for another thirty-five years.

Contrary to traditional historiography, it was not Western toughness that led to the Austrian breakthrough, but the changes in the Kremlin after Stalin's death and the cheeky but subtle Austrian responses to them. In 1953, Eisenhower and Dulles were facing a very conservative and ugly mood in the American pub-

94. For text of the Dulles television address, see "An Historic Week," *Department of State Bulletin,* May 30, 1955, pp. 871–76.

95. Report by the Secretary of State, May 17, 1955, 84th Congr., 1st Sess., 1955, *Executive Sessions of the Senate Foreign Relations Committee (Historical Series)* (Washington, D.C., 1978), VII, 500.

96. Discussion of the 245th NSC meeting, May 19, 1955, box 7, NSC-Series, Ann Whitman File, in EL.

lic. Eisenhower's April 16 speech signaled a cautious approach to the new look in the Kremlin. His refusal to meet Malenkov for a summit meeting, as well as Dulles' reluctance to negotiate with Communists, never gave the new Kremlin leaders a good opportunity to demonstrate their sincerity for peaceful coexistence, as Churchill was demanding. We will never know whether it was one of the great missed opportunities for ending the cold war early.[97] Or, is Michael Howard correct when he argues that Churchill's call for a summit was "premature"? After all, Howard adds, "Stalin might be dead, but the grip of Marxist Leninist ideology remained unshaken in Moscow."[98] A general détente following a quick summit after Stalin's death represents one of the great "might have beens" of the Eisenhower presidency.

Eisenhower contained the Communists with great determination. In 1953, Eisenhower's tough stance pushed the Koreans to sign an armistice. In 1954, he acceded to the division of Vietnam negotiated at Geneva. In the spring of 1955, he countered the Chinese Communist attacks on Chiang Kai-shek's Nationalists in the offshore islands crisis with the threat of nuclear retaliation. He sped up the nuclear arms race with the Soviets. His greatest triumph came with the completion of West German rearmament in the spring of 1955.

After showing his toughness in dealing with the Communists, Eisenhower finally settled for a summit with the Soviets. More than two years after Stalin's death, the president finally overcame "his own reluctance and Dulles' resistance" when agreeing to meet the new Kremlin leadership for negotiations in Geneva in July, 1955.[99] With the Korean armistice and Russian withdrawal from Austria, Eisenhower no longer could ignore the Soviet "deeds" that he had demanded in April, 1953. Moreover, during his trip to Europe in early May, Dulles had encountered a "tremendous demand" for a summit meeting among U.S. allies. In the American planning for the Geneva summit, the basic ambivalence of the Eisenhower-Dulles team in dealing with the Soviets comes through again. On the one hand, Ronald Pruessen argues that they opened up to the idea of serious negotiations and were not as diametrically opposed to "testing" the Soviets in Geneva as traditional clichés have it. Inside the White House, they were discussing rolling back the iron curtain in Eastern Europe and debating nuclear free zones in Central Europe.[100] On the other hand, the fact remains that "the pres-

97. Rostow tends to think it was. See *Europe After Stalin,* 69–83. See also Lukacs in *New York Times Book Review,* February 10, 1991.

98. Howard, "Churchill: Prophet of Detente," 9.

99. Piers Brendon, *Ike: His Life and Times* (New York, 1986), 306.

100. Ronald W. Pruessen, "Beyond the Cold War—Again: 1955 and the 1990s," *Political Science Quarterly,* CVIII (1993). For the new scholarship on Dulles, stressing his non-ideological pragmatism as well as the complexity of his thoughts and actions, see the introduction and con-

ident was as vigorous a cold warrior as the secretary," as Piers Brendon has put it.[101] Dulles remained more averse to negotiations with the Soviets, making sure that no major concessions would be made. "I, of course, see serious disadvantages in any meeting of the President with the heads of the Soviet Union," Dulles wrote from Europe, "but in the form proposed which is merely to consider whether or not ways and means can be found to settle differences and *not to reach any substantive decisions, probably the harm is held to a minimum*" [emphasis added.][102] Geneva, indeed, is remembered as a summit for its atmospherics ("the spirit of Geneva") rather than for any major substantive breakthrough on the East-West agenda.

When Eisenhower went to Geneva, Eden had replaced Churchill as British prime minister. Churchill had retired in April, 1955, for health reasons. Eisenhower wrote his old friend—whom he admired like no other living man, yet whose dogged persistence in engineering a summit had exasperated him in the course of 1953–1954[103]—"I cannot escape a feeling of sadness that [the summit's] delay brought about by the persistent hostile attitude toward NATO has operated to prevent your personal attendance at the meeting."[104] But Churchill knew that American intransigence as much as "Soviet hostility" prevented the staging of an earlier summit.

In the spring of 1953, Eisenhower linked a summit with the new Kremlin leaders to Soviet concessions on issues like the Austrian treaty. Yet when it came to negotiations, the Eisenhower administration pursued the conclusion of the

clusion by Richard H. Immerman and the essays in *John Foster Dulles and the Diplomacy of the Cold War,* ed. Immerman.

101. Brendon, *Ike,* 306.

102. Dulles to Department of State, May 8, 1955, in *FRUS, 1955–57,* V, 170–71. See also Dulles to London Embassy, May 23, 1955, *ibid.,* 193–95. In his preparatory meeting Dulles concentrated on how Soviet propaganda could be countered most convincingly. Memorandum of Conversation, May 20, 1955, *ibid.,* 189–93. Eisenhower, however, ignored Dulles' advice to keep an "austere countenance" in the presence of the Russians at Geneva. See Michael Beschloss, *Eisenhower: A Centennial Life* (New York, 1990), 130.

103. Eisenhower's mixed views about Churchill come through in letters to his old confidant "Swede" Hazlett, to whom he wrote letters after the Bermuda Summit: "At times Winston seemed to be his old and hearty self, full of vim and determination. At others he seemed almost to wander in his mind." See Eisenhower to Hazlett, December 24, 1953, in *Ike's Letters to a Friend, 1941–1958,* ed. Robert Griffith (Lawrence Kans., 1984), 114. In a discourse on great men in history, Eisenhower judged Churchill as coming "as near to fulfilling the requirements of greatness in any individual that I have met in my lifetime." See Eisenhower to Hazlett, December 8, 1954, *ibid.,* 140.

104. Quoted in *Correspondence,* 213.

Austrian treaty only half-heartedly. In view of such American intransigence to negotiate with the new Soviet leadership, Austrian willingness to test the "new look" in the Kremlin after Stalin's death became crucial. While the Eisenhower administration watched from the sidelines, Austrian behind-the-scenes contacts led to direct bilateral negotiations with Moscow and the conclusion of the Austrian treaty. It was the boldness of the diplomacy of Vienna's Ballhausplatz, then, that led to the April, 1955, Austro-Soviet summit and the conclusion of the Austrian State Treaty; this Soviet "deed" clinched the Geneva summit.

After 1953, the powerless Austrian government emancipated itself from the tight control of Western tutelage and started to pursue a more independent course between East and West. With the new look in its foreign policy, the Raab government demonstrated that the impotent had leverage in the cold war. There were opportunities for diplomatic breakthroughs in the changing international environment of 1953–1955. The Eisenhower administration, with its strong priorities in German rearmament, a strong nuclear posture, and general European security, did not deem it wise to rush toward negotiations with the new Kremlin leadership by testing peaceful coexistence in Austria right away. Thus, we will never know whether a summit meeting in 1953–1954 might have eased superpower tensions and initiated a period of détente between East and West long before the 1970s. In Robert Divine's judgment, Eisenhower's foreign policy achievements were negative in nature. "He ended the Korean War, he refused to intervene militarily in Indochina, he refrained from involving the United States in the Suez crisis, he avoided war with China over Quemoy and Matsu, he resisted the temptation to force a showdown over Berlin, he stopped exploding nuclear weapons in the atmosphere." [105] To this one might add: He did not intervene in bilateral Austro-Soviet negotiations leading to the conclusion of the Austrian treaty.

105. Robert A. Divine, *Eisenhower and the Cold War* (New York, 1981), 154.

Robert A. Wampler

Eisenhower, NATO, and Nuclear Weapons: The Strategy and Political Economy of Alliance Security

One of the enduring images of Dwight D. Eisenhower is that of the Supreme Commander who oversaw the Normandy landing in 1944 and the subsequent liberation of Europe from Nazi occupation. Less well known, but arguably just as important, was the central role he played in laying the foundations for planning a quite different war in defense of Europe, which, if it had come to pass, would have had repercussions far wider and more deadly than World War II. In October, 1951, Eisenhower, in his new role as the first Supreme Allied Commander Europe (SACEUR) for NATO, along with his main U.S. planners at Supreme Headquarters Allied Powers Europe (SHAPE), began to obtain critical information from the U.S. Joint Chiefs of Staff about the atomic weapons his command could plan on using to defend Europe. Three years later, NATO would take the fateful step of authorizing Eisenhower's successor, Alfred Gruenther, to prepare his plans on the assumption that atomic weapons would be used to meet a Soviet attack.

Four decades later, we are witnessing the terminus of a critical arc in postwar history, the far end of which was rooted in these plans begun under Eisenhower in 1951. With the fall of the Berlin Wall, German reunification, and the transformation of the former Soviet Union, the nuclear basis upon which NATO has safeguarded European security during the cold war is undergoing rapid reevaluation. President Bush has initiated the withdrawal from Europe of significant numbers of U.S. theater nuclear weapons previously earmarked for NATO defense, and the alliance itself has rewritten its basic strategy, relegating to history the prior planning premised upon Flexible Response and the threat of escalating use of nuclear weapons to deter a Soviet attack.[1]

This remarkable juncture in world events brings both the opportunity as well as the need to reexamine the manner in which nuclear weapons became committed to the defense of Europe and integrated into the strategy, planning, and

---

1. On these developments, see "NATO Transforming Collective Defense Arrangements (excerpts) [May 28–29, 1991] and U.S. Disarmament Initiatives (excerpts from President George Bush's nationally televised address), 27 September 1991," *Survival*, XXXIII (1991), 372, 567–69; and Baltimore *Sun*, November 8, 1991, Sec. A, p.2.

policies of NATO during the critical decade of the 1950s. The significance of this process is clear when one considers that in 1952, Ike was told he could plan on having 80 atomic weapons with a nominal yield of 20 kilotons available for tactical use in Europe; six years later, the numbers had grown to 2,500-kiloton-range and 50-megaton-range weapons, not to mention the 800-kiloton-range and 100-megaton-range weapons earmarked for the Supreme Allied Commander Atlantic.[2] These weapons were in turn linked to a strategy laid down in NATO document MC-14/2, adopted in 1957, which usually has been viewed as NATO's adoption of the U.S. strategy of massive retaliation.

These developments were in large part rooted in the process begun by Eisenhower while SACEUR, and then continued during his presidency. The progressive nuclearization of NATO strategy, embodied in two statements of basic alliance strategy—MC-48 of 1954 and MC-14/2 of 1957—were presided over and in many ways encouraged by both the president and his secretary of state, John Foster Dulles. This fact resulted in the judgment, pressed both at the time and subsequently by historians, that the Eisenhower administration by its actions (or inactions) led NATO to a dangerous over-reliance upon nuclear weapons by the time it left office.

The past decade, however, has seen a proliferation of studies revising our understanding of the Eisenhower administration, and in particular its foreign and defense policies. We are now much more aware of the nuances and ambivalences underlying these policies, belying the seemingly more bellicose and simplistic public pronouncements that informed earlier studies. As John Lewis Gaddis has said, the result is an "unexpected" John Foster Dulles, a sobriquet that can be applied to the entire administration, especially when one looks at the new evidence brought to light regarding its policies with respect to nuclear weapons.[3]

Indicative of this new evidence are two statements, both made by Dulles, the

2. For the 1952 figures, see Memorandum, Rear Admiral W. G. Lalor to Eisenhower, January 28, 1952, CCS 471.6 (4-18-49)(section 7), in Record Group 218, National Archives. For the 1958–59 figures, see Memorandum for U.S. Representative to the Standing Group from Colonel H. L. Hillyard (secretary to the JCS), September 22, 1958, CCS 092 Western Europe (3-12-48)(2)(section 118), in RG 218, NA.

3. The Gaddis discussion of Dulles is found in John Lewis Gaddis, "The Unexpected John Foster Dulles: Nuclear Weapons, Communism, and the Russians," in Richard H. Immerman, ed., *John Foster Dulles and the Diplomacy of the Cold War* (Princeton, N.J., 1990), 47–78. This collection is a good introduction to recent scholarship on the diplomacy of the Eisenhower administration and provides useful summaries of prior critical scholarship of this diplomacy. The basic work on the development of nuclear strategy under Eisenhower is in David Alan Rosenberg, "The Origins of Overkill: Nuclear Weapons and American Strategy, 1945–1960," *International Security*, VII (1983), 3–71.

supposed high priest of nuclear brinkmanship, which reflect a less dogmatic attitude about nuclear weapons. At a press briefing in December, 1956, Dulles held that present NATO planning did *not* mean the use of atomic weapons would be automatic, but was forced to admit that the likelihood of this would only increase as planning was based on their use. Against this seemingly inexorable momentum in NATO planning, Dulles argued that there must be alternatives to nuclear retaliation — the alliance could not put all of its eggs in the nuclear basket. Repeating a warning he had given to his fellow ministers during the recent NATO meeting in Paris, Dulles stressed that the only certainty was that one could not be sure what the nature of a future war would be. He feared that if NATO assumed that a future war would be nuclear, and then based all its planning upon fighting just that type of war, the Soviets would take advantage of this fact and adapt their strategy to circumvent NATO planning and capabilities.[4]

Moreover, Dulles' concerns over this nuclear momentum in NATO planning were augmented by its potential consequences for Eisenhower's desire to effect a better division of burdens within the alliance. At the recent NATO meeting, U.S. allies had betrayed an unmistakable desire to arm NATO forces with nuclear weapons, as well as a belief that in most if not all cases of Soviet aggressive actions, NATO's response would include nuclear weapons. These clear signs of how the allies were reading (or misreading in the U.S. view) NATO strategy prompted Dulles to warn Eisenhower, "I fear we are getting into trouble by insisting on the one hand that almost any kind of aggression must be met by nuclear weapons and on the other hand that we alone will have the nuclear weapons. I fear this is going to leave us carrying the bag alone so far as the defense of Europe is concerned."[5]

Revealed by these statements are tensions that plagued U.S. policy on nuclear weapons and alliance strategy as it sought to promote what it viewed as the proper use of these weapons to address the intertwined political, military, and economic problems at the heart of NATO defense. Throughout the 1950s, both Eisenhower and Dulles underwent a process of education in these matters, as the limitations of nuclear weapons to address these problems became ever clearer. Yet, at the same time, a seemingly relentless process continued by which nuclear

4. POLTO 1427, McCardle to Department of State, December 15, 1956, lot file 62D181, box 11, file 819, in RG 59, released to the author by the Department of State under Freedom of Information Act request (hereinafter cited as FOIA).

5. DULTE 19, Dulles to Eisenhower, December 14, 1956, lot file 62D181, box 11, file CF 820, in RG 59, FOIA. This cable also appears in the published Foreign Relations series, but with the quoted passage deleted. See also U.S. Department of State, *Foreign Relations of the United States,* 1955–57, IV, 162–63 (hereinafter cited as *FRUS, 1955–57*).

weapons came to have a prominent and even predominant role in NATO strategy by the end of the Eisenhower administration.

Eisenhower, Dulles, and their policy advisers, as noted earlier, played a leading role in framing the strategy and planning underlying this process; the other side of this story—the growing doubts about the implications of this deepening reliance upon nuclear weapons in terms of strategy and the political economy of alliance strategy, that is, the burdens the United States and its allies should bear in the common defense—must be seen in light of the role played by allied pressures for the progressive nuclearization of NATO strategy, and the manner in which the imperatives of allied diplomacy served to shape this process and set limits upon U.S. ability to guide NATO strategy, planning, and burden sharing in the direction it felt was strategically, politically, and economically correct.

Ike's imprint upon U.S. planning for the defense of Europe, and the important place given atomic and nuclear weapons in these plans, can be traced back to the very beginnings of NATO. In 1949, the Joint Chiefs of Staff (JCS), responding in large part to guidance issued by Eisenhower, who was then the acting JCS chairman, drew up a new emergency war plan that gave greater attention to the problem of defending Europe. In line with the new U.S. commitments to West European defense assumed under the North Atlantic Treaty signed that year, Eisenhower stressed that U.S. security now required working to ensure, at the earliest time possible, the ability to hold a line along the Rhine against Soviet attack upon Western Europe. Following Eisenhower's directive, the JCS, starting in mid-1949, prepared OFFTACKLE, a Joint Outline Emergency War Plan covering the first two years of a war.[6] Approved by the JCS in late 1949, OFFTACKLE laid out a concept for operations that, echoing earlier plans, gave priority to a strategic offensive in Europe. In the early stages of a war, this offensive would consist solely of strategic air operations against the Soviets, using both atomic and conventional bombs. Following Eisenhower's views, these operations now included the new goal of retarding Soviet advances in Western Europe.[7]

Two years later, in 1951, Eisenhower again took up the task of planning for Europe's defense when he accepted the newly created NATO post of SACEUR

6. Kenneth Condit, *The Joint Chiefs of Staff and National Policy, 1947–1949* (Wilmington, Del., 1979), 294–96, Vol. II of *The History of the Joint Chiefs of Staff;* Steven L. Rearden, *The Formative Years, 1947–1950* (Washington, D.C., 1984), 365, Vol. I of *History of the Office of the Secretary of Defense;* JSPC 877/56, April 21, 1949, P&O 381 TS (Section III) (Cases 21–40), P&O TS 1949–50 Files, in RG 319, NA.

7. Condit, *The Joint Chiefs of Staff and National Policy, 1947–1949,* 297–302; Walter S. Poole, *The Joint Chiefs of Staff and National Policy, 1950–1952* (Wilmington, Del., 1980), 161–62, Vol. IV of *The History of the Joint Chiefs of Staff.*

and tackled the complex job of integrating atomic weapons into alliance strategy. SACEUR and the American officers in the new NATO commands at SHAPE became closely involved with the problem of harnessing America's atomic deterrent, embodied in the Strategic Air Command (SAC), to Europe's defense. The importance of this to Eisenhower was clear; as he stressed to the JCS, "The employment of atomic weapons constitutes one of the most significant means which SACEUR can utilize in fulfilling his mission, [so] it is important that he have all necessary authority in the planning and control of atomic operations in his area."[8]

Under his direction in the years 1951–1952, much progress was made in laying the basis for atomic planning within SHAPE; the JCS provided briefings and informational pamphlets on atomic weapons and operational procedures to SACEUR and his staff. Working with General Lauris Norstad (USAF) and General Alfred Gruenther, who were SACEUR's commander in chief, Allied forces, Central Europe, and chief of staff, respectively, Eisenhower hammered out with U.S. Air Force chief of staff Hoyt Vandenberg and SAC commanding general Curtis LeMay principles to govern coordination of SHAPE's operations with those of SAC. Perhaps most important, Eisenhower pressed to establish clearly his command prerogatives in the planning and carrying out of atomic operations in the NATO theater. As a result, after lengthy debate with the JCS, one of Eisenhower's last acts as SACEUR before returning to the United States to run for president was to tell his major U.S. commanders in NATO to begin work on the first atomic weapons annex to SACEUR's emergency war plan.[9]

The next major step in the nuclearization of NATO strategy came during Eisenhower's first term as president. Much has been written about the New Look defense policies instituted under Eisenhower, and the emphasis given to nuclear weapons under these policies.[10] NCS-162/2, the basic statement of this

8. Message, SHAPE to CINCEUR, CINCNELM, CINCUSAFE, May 15, 1992, 092 Western Europe (3-12-48)(section 145), in RG 218, NA.

9. I discuss these developments in greater detail in *NATO Strategic Planning and Nuclear Weapons, 1950–1957* (College Park, Md., 1990), 4–8, and "Conventional Goals and Nuclear Promises: The Truman Administration and the Roots of the NATO New Look," in *NATO: The Founding of the Alliance and the Integration of Europe,* ed. Francis H. Heller and John R. Gillingham (New York, 1992), 363–65.

10. There are a number of good studies of the Eisenhower administration's New Look and its origins. The best general account of its development can be found in John Lewis Gaddis, *Strategies of Containment: A Critical Appraisal of Postwar American National Security Policy* (New York, 1982), 127–64. Also very useful for its treatment of the nuclear strategy and weapons planning consequences of the New Look, which is of particular relevance to this essay, is Rosenberg, "The Origins of Overkill," 27–35. Documentation on the development of the New Look can be found in *FRUS,* 1952–54, II, 236 *passim.* The role of the JCS in these developments is disucssed in Robert

new policy, made clear the prominent role nuclear weapons would play in U.S. strategic planning: "Within the free world, only the United States can provide and maintain . . . the atomic capability to counterbalance Soviet atomic power. Thus, sufficient atomic weapons and effective means of delivery are indispensable for U.S. security. . . . In the event of hostilities, the United States will consider nuclear weapons to be as available for use as other munitions." [11]

The U.S. atomic capability was also seen as a major contribution to the security of U.S. allies: "The major deterrent to aggression against Western Europe is the manifest determination of the United States to use its atomic capability and massive retaliatory striking power if the area is attacked." [12] As the JCS pointed out to the secretary of defense, Charles Wilson, this policy would call for the U.S. not only to back up West European defense with its strategic atomic capabilities but also to provide tactical atomic support for U.S. or allied forces whenever the use of these weapons would be militarily advantageous. The Joint Chiefs clearly believed these weapons would be advantageous, as JCS chairman Arthur Radford told Wilson that "the tactical atomic support which can be provided our allies will become increasingly important in offsetting present deficiencies in conventional requirements." [13]

This policy could only be carried out if America's allies recognized and accepted the central role atomic weapons played in deterring Soviet aggression, and supported this strategy by agreeing to the use of their territory where needed as bases for the launching of the U.S. strategic counteroffensive. As Dulles stressed during NSC discussion on NSC-162/2, the United States had to find a way to remove the taboo from the use of nuclear weapons. Eisenhower agreed, saying they needed to convince allies of the desirability of using these weapons. [14] This desire to bring the NATO allies to a closer understanding of

J. Watson, *The Joint Chiefs of Staff and National Policy, 1953–1954* (Wilmington, Del., 1986), 1–37, Vol. V of *History of the Joint Chiefs of Staff*.

11. NSC 162/2, *FRUS,* 1952–54, II, 583, 593.

12. Ibid., 585.

13. Memorandum, Radford to Wilson, December 9, 1953, CJCS Radford 381 Military Strategy and Posture; and Memorandum, Radford to Joint Chiefs re Security within the Baghdad Pact, February 7, 1956, CJCS Radford CM-1956 (245-56 through 419-56), both in RG 218, NA. The flip side of the JCS view was that U.S. allies would be required to provide the major share of the ground forces needed for their defense; see Memorandum, Radford to Joint Chiefs, February 7, 1956.

14. NSC-162/2, NSC-583, NSC593; discussion at the 165th meeting of the NSC, October 7, 1953, *FRUS,* 1952–54, II, 533–34. Eisenhower received some reassurance about his concerns when, during this same NSC meeting, Army Chief of Staff Matthew Ridgway reported that both West German Chancellor Konrad Adenauer and British Prime Minister Winston Churchill had told him in great confidence that they would approve the use of bases in their countries for launching atomic attacks in the event of war (*ibid.*).

U.S. nuclear strategy was in turn linked with administration plans to expand the sharing of nuclear weapons information with allies. The president forcefully drew attention to this link in the NSC, arguing, "Since you are asking your allies to take some pretty terrible risks in standing with you, it was certainly incumbent upon you to give them some good idea of the magnitudes which would be available for their defense. In short, we should be in a position to reveal to them the nature and character of the military impact that our atomic weapons would have against an enemy attack." [15]

Eisenhower and Dulles clearly recognized the magnitude of the problems facing the United States in shifting NATO planning onto an atomic basis. In December, 1953, Eisenhower told the NSC, "We, more than any other people . . . have accepted the atomic age in which we now all live. Many European people are lagging far behind us and think of themselves only as the defenseless targets of atomic warfare." Dulles agreed, pointing out that "while we regarded atomic weapons as one of the great sources of defensive strength, many of our allies regarded the atomic capability as the gateway to annihilation." [16]

The process of educating America's allies about the necessary role for nuclear weapons in NATO defense took a critical step forward with the New Approach studies initiated by Alfred Gruenther, Eisenhower's former chief of staff at SHAPE, who became SACEUR himself in the summer of 1953. These studies, begun in late 1953, were rooted in a complex tangle of military, political, and economic factors, involving the persistent "gap" problem plaguing NATO in its efforts to raise the forces required by the Lisbon force goals adopted in 1952; growing interest within the United States and its allies, particularly the United Kingdom, in turning to nuclear weapons, especially anticipated tactical weapons, as the solution to the economic burdens of deterrence and defense; long-standing army critiques of air force and SAC strategic nuclear planning as it related to the defense of Europe; and, most immediately, a study carried out by the previous SACEUR, Matthew Ridgway, which planners within SHAPE found

15. Memorandum of Discussion at 173rd meeting of the NSC, December 3, 1953, Dwight D. Eisenhower Papers as President, Ann Whitman Files (hereinafter cited as EP-AWF), NSC Series, box 5, folder: NSC Summaries of Discussion, 173rd Meeting of the NSC, Dwight D. Eisenhower Library, Abilene, Kansas (hereinafter cited as EL). For a more detailed discussion of early Eisenhower administration policy developments with respect to nuclear weapons information sharing as part of the New Look, see chapter 8 of Robert A. Wampler, "Ambiguous Legacy: The United States, Great Britain, and the Foundations of NATO Strategy, 1948–1957" (Ph.D. dissertation, Harvard University, 1991).

16. Memorandum of discussion at 174th meeting of the NSC, December, 11, 1953, *FRUS, 1952–54,* II, 451–52.

flawed in its analysis of the impact of nuclear weapons upon NATO strategy and force needs.[17]

Carried out in 1954, Gruenther's New Approach studies involved a probing analysis of the impact of strategic nuclear weapons upon the course of a general war, the consequences of this for defensive operations in NATO Europe, and the manner in which the introduction of tactical nuclear weapons into NATO forces would compel a fundamental reassessment of battlefield strategy and doctrine, force composition, and requirements.[18] The primary analysis and conclusions of the first phase of Gruenther's studies were embodied in MC-48, which was approved by NATO in December, 1954. This step, which was strongly supported by the Eisenhower administration, firmly placed NATO strategy on a nuclear basis. In summary, MC-48 declared:

1. Superiority in atomic weapons and the capability to deliver them would be the most important factor in a future war.

2. Surprise would be of even greater importance in a nuclear war.

3. War was likely to open with an initial phase of intensive exchange of nuclear weapons, which would be of short duration. (A subsequent, less intense phase might follow, but the results of the first phase were likely to be decisive of the outcome of the war.)

4. The best defense against atomic attack was the allied ability to retaliate immediately at the source of the attack.

5. Priority had to be given to forces that could effectively contribute to the initial, and likely decisive, phase.

6. Provided that certain minimum measures were implemented (the provision to SACEUR of an integrated atomic capability and an adequate alert system) and a West German contribution was available, SACEUR could provide a successful defense forward of the Rhine-Ijssel line.

7. And most important, it was essential that NATO forces be able to use nuclear weapons from the outset and that SHAPE be authorized to plan on this assumption.[19]

Though the United States decided in late 1954 not to press at that time for NATO agreement on prior authorization for SACEUR's use of nuclear weapons, Eisenhower and his advisers were clear in their own minds that in the

17. The background to the New Approach studies is discussed in detail in Wampler, *Ambiguous Legacy,* chapters 5 and 8. The army's criticisms of air force and SAC strategic nuclear planning are also well documented in Marc Trachtenberg, *History and Strategy* (Princeton, N.J., 1991). 153–60.
18. A detailed discussion of the New Approach studies in 1954 can be found in Wampler, *Ambiguous Legacy,* chapter 9.
19. JP (54)99(Final), 2 December 1954, DEFE 6/26, Public Records Office, Kew, Richmond, England (hereinafter cited as PRO).

event of war, political considerations must not be allowed to block the implementation of SACEUR's plans. Eisenhower felt that the NATO allies would have to accept that the power to order the use of nuclear weapons could not be held solely by the North Atlantic Council and that SACEUR would have to be given some latitude for decision in an emergency. Moreover, the Eisenhower administration was determined that its NATO allies should clearly realize that agreement to MC-48 did not in any way diminish the United States' right to take unilateral action and use nuclear weapons if circumstances prevented taking the time to obtain NATO concurrence. Regardless of language in MC-48 to the effect that the final decision to use nuclear weapons was not prejudged by NATO's approval of the paper, the United States was determined there should be no doubt as to the dangerous consequences if a NATO ally should try to impose a veto on actions that the U.S. considered essential to its own security or that of NATO.[20]

Dulles laid out the reasoning behind the U.S. position in a press conference after the NATO meeting that approved MC-48.

> [It] is not possible to make in advance the decision as to just when atomic weapons will be used and whether they will be used for tactical purposes or strategic purposes. All of these decisions have to be left for decision in the light of events. . . . If your deterrent measures are so restricted that the potential enemy could feel reasonably confident that you would be subject to political delays and inhibitions, you lose your deterrent power and make more and more likely a deterrent to be ineffective. It must be something that the potential aggressor thinks will work and work quickly. If you so enmesh it with political machinery and requirements to action which many times cannot work or work only after great delay, then you lose the main purpose of it which is not to fight a war but to prevent a war.[21]

In subsequent years, the Eisenhower administration continued its efforts to educate the NATO allies on the proper role of nuclear weapons in NATO strategy. Regardless of the compelling logic of their views in American eyes, Eisenhower realized that implementing them presented the United States with many complex and perplexing problems. As he warned Radford, a fervent advocate of the greater efficiencies and economies to be gained by faster integra-

20. Memorandum for Admiral Radford, (n.a.), December 8, 1954, CJCS Radford, 092.2 NAT, in RG 218, NA; Watson, *The Joint Chiefs of Staff and National Policy, 1953–1954*, p. 317. The need for the United States to retain the freedom to use its nuclear weapons was stressed to Eisenhower in his meeting with Radford, Wilson, and Dulles on December 8 (*ibid*).

21. Record of Background Press Conference by the Secretary of State, December 16, 1954, *FRUS, 1952–54*, V, 542–47.

tion of nuclear weapons into U.S. and allied forces, these things had to be done gradually and without undue haste. As matters stood two years after the adoption of MC-48, Eisenhower felt the United States had made real progress in convincing its allies of the validity of its views on nuclear weapons: The NATO allies were now "clamoring" for the United States to share these weapons with them, when only a few years earlier they had "recoiled in horror" at the idea of using nuclear weapons.[22]

Dulles, however, realized that matters were not so clear-cut, and he had harbored worries about the implications of the strategy NATO had adopted, despite its seeming necessity. The confident mien he assumed when discussing the political problems inherent in any alliance decision to use nuclear weapons (such as telling the Canadian foreign minister, Lester Pearson, in late 1954 that the "whole problem has a certain artificial aspect in that it involves constitutional and political problems which are virtually impossible of solution in the abstract but which are as a rule determined without difficulty by events themselves") was belied by private troubled musings about the implications of the course NATO had set upon.[23] Even as the United States worked to secure NATO's adoption of MC-48, Dulles grasped two essential consequences of this step: The United States would now be *"morally committed to maintain in Europe forces for using these weapons or to supply such weapons to the other NATO countries,"* and the United States and its NATO allies needed to "explore urgently the possibility of maintaining sufficient flexibility in NATO forces to avoid exclusive dependence on atomic weapons, without losing their deterrent effect, so as to give the Europeans some sense of choice as to the actual character of warfare. *Otherwise the strategy will strain the will to fight and spur neutralism."* [24]

Dulles' concerns about the fundamental tension between the need for and fear of nuclear weapons were well grounded and deepened in the years ahead. Dulles remained convinced that only nuclear weapons provided the United States with the needed global power at a bearable cost. However, the apparently unstoppable growth in Soviet nuclear capabilities was, as net evaluation analyses detailing the likely consequences of future nuclear wars with the USSR made painfully clear, leading to a future in which the United States would be in-

22. Discussion at the 284th meeting of the NSC, Thursday, May 10, 1956 (dated May 22, 1956), EP-AWF, NSC Series, box 7, folder 284th Summary of Discussion, May 10, 1956, in EL.

23. Memorandum of conversation by Livingston Merchant, December 19, 1954, *FRUS, 1952–54,* V, 560.

24. "Basic National Security Policy" (Suggestions of the Secretary of State), November 15, 1953, *FRUS, 1952–54,* II, 775 (emphasis added). As can be seen, there is a strong similarity between Dulles' first point and the point Radford made to Wilson later the same year, as discussed earlier in this essay.

creasingly more vulnerable to Soviet nuclear strikes. The U.S. strategy of relying upon NATO allies to hold the forward line in Europe until SAC could carry
out its mission would be brought into greater question by this trend if the allies
came to doubt the United States either would be able to retaliate to a Soviet first
strike or be willing to court national suicide in defense of Europe. The dilemma
facing the United States was compounded by the fact that allied fears that the
United States would not act coexisted with horror at the consequences if it did
act. Dulles feared that repugnance to the use of nuclear weapons could grow to
the point that America's value as an ally would be undermined, putting at risk
the reliability of U.S. allies and the availability of foreign bases for SAC operations. This repugnance could also work to deny the United States allied support
in meeting limited threats, given the ongoing integration of tactical nuclear
weapons into U.S. forces.[25]

The Eisenhower administration sought to adopt its policies to address these
concerns. This can be seen in NSC-5602, the basic statement of national security policy adopted in 1956. NSC-5602 reaffirmed the need to maintain an effective U.S. nuclear retaliatory force, secure from any threat of neutralization by
the USSR, and firmly supported militarily and politically by U.S. allies. Now,
however, and in tension with the foregoing, there was recognition that even as
nuclear weapons were integrated into U.S. and allied forces, these forces must
not become so dependent upon nuclear capabilities as to create dangerous inflexibilities in the available responses to threats. As NSC-5602 asserted, the coming of nuclear parity would put a premium on the ability to respond flexibly to
aggression, particularly local or limited in nature, lest the West's choices be reduced to impotence or the use of force in such as way as to create fears of global
war and nuclear devastation in the minds of the American people or their allies.[26]

The translation of these general precepts into specific policies to guide the
ongoing education of the allies and adaptation of NATO planning to the
needs of the nuclear concepts outlined in MC-48 was made ever more difficult
by the deepening worries and proliferating uncertainties, both within the U.S.
government and among other NATO members, about the implications of im-
pending nuclear plenty and potential parity between the West (that is, the United
States) and the USSR. As the mounting numbers of nuclear weapons and their

25. Memorandum by Dulles, January 22, 1956, EP-AWF, Dulles-Herter Series, box 5, folder
Dulles, J.F., January, 1956, in EL. On the net evaluation studies of hypothetical future nuclear exchanges with the USSR, which were presented to Eisenhower in January, 1956, see Eisenhower Diary Entry, January 23, 1956, Nuclear History Collection, National Security Archives (hereinafter
cited as NHC-NSA) Washington, D.C.

26. NSC-5602/1, March 15, 1956, in NHC-NSA.

growing prominence in military planning led some to doubt the continued need for substantial ground forces in NATO, the parallel fear was growing that the price of nuclear economy would be a choice between surrender in the short run and Armageddon in the long run. Both strains of thought could wreck the consensus upon strategy and the alliance cohesion necessary if NATO was to carry out its primary missions of deterrence and defense.

As the administration grappled with these dilemmas, there was no one strategy or policy that would perfectly mesh the contending military, political, and economic imperatives of a viable defense and deterrence strategy. Further complicating the debate was the manner in which efforts to address the problem of allied fears about nuclear weapons overlapped with efforts to answer the second, related issue—whether NATO still needed substantial ground forces as the alliance moved into an era of nuclear plenty. Efforts to address these issues came to center on two general positions. Some in the administration came to hold that NATO should move to a strategy of full reliance upon nuclear deterrence, keeping only those ground forces needed to deal with quite limited threats. For others, the military and political dictates of deterrence and defense still mandated sizable alliance "shield" forces if NATO was to meet the threat of major war as well as the lesser challenges that might proliferate with the coming of nuclear parity.[27]

The tensions, uncertainties, and ambiguities inherent in this situation provided ample room for disagreement, as the administration sought to determine

27. This debate within the Eisenhower administration on the relative merits of deterrence and defense is discussed at length in Wampler, *Ambiguous Legacy,* chapter 11. While there were nuances and overlaps in arguments that make it difficult to pigeon-hole individuals in the different camps, in general Robert Bowie (Assistant Secretary of State for Policy Planning), Edwin Martin (the Deputy U.S. Permanent Representative to NATO), and Robert Kranich (a long-time officer in State's Office of European Regional Affairs with extensive NATO experience) exemplified those who argued that the alliance should begin to move toward a more explicit reliance upon nuclear deterrence. On the other side can be placed Joseph Wolf (state adviser on NATO Affairs) and Ridgway Knight (a State Department adviser at SHAPE), who made the case for providing the necessary forces, nuclear and conventional, to wage an effective defense and holding action against major attack as well as to deal with lesser threats. All of these men fully recognized the unresolved tensions lurking in their own positions as well as those on the other side. For representative expressions of the contending views, see Memorandum by Bowie, Analysis of "Community Control of Atomic Weapons," January 3, 1956, and Memorandum by Bowie for the Secretary of State, "Sharing of Control of Atomic Weapons," January 4, 1956, both in NHC-NSA; Memorandum, Martin to Timmons re Need for NATO Ground Forces in Western Europe, June 8, 1956, enclosed with Memorandum, Martin to Timmons, same subject, June 13, 1956, 740.5/6-1356; Memorandum by Kranich, "A Deterrence Strategy for NATO," June 29, 1956, 740.5/6-2956; Memorandum by Wolf, March 15, 1956, 740.5/3-1556; and Letter, Knight to Timmons, June 21, 1956, 740.5/6-2156; all in RG 59, NA.

the requirements for both deterring and waging a nuclear war with the Soviets, as well as for securing the necessary flexibility to meet lesser threats. These disagreements came to a head in early 1956 when the JCS struggled to hammer out a consensus on the strategic concepts to guide U.S. military preparations for future conflicts, both global and limited. The battleground was the Joint Strategic Objectives Plan for 1960. On one side stood JCS chairman Arthur Radford, who, with the air force and navy chiefs, held that by basing all planning on the use of nuclear weapons and providing for the worst case—all-out war with the Soviets—the United States would also be ready to meet lesser threats. On the other side stood Maxwell Taylor, army chief of staff, who argued that the growth in U.S. and Soviet nuclear stockpiles would result in a situation of mutual deterrence making all-out war very unlikely, but limited wars much more likely. This new strategic situation, Taylor insisted, required U.S. forces to have greater flexibility to deal with such threats.[28]

In the end, it took Eisenhower's intervention to resolve this debate within the JCS, and the final resolution was clearly marked by the president's own firm views about the issues involved. In large part, these views were framed by Eisenhower's concerns about the U.S. economy. The strategic debate being waged in the spring of 1956 was intimately linked with a running battle between Eisenhower and the JCS over what the latter argued were the requirements for meeting U.S. national security needs and alliance commitments. Pressed by the escalating costs of modernizing America's nuclear retaliatory force and the claims of allies for aid, Eisenhower was determined to hold U.S. military spending to a level stabilizing at around $37 billion, and within this limit he had firm convictions about what America could and should do.[29]

These convictions guided the resolution of the debate within the JCS as well

28. This debate, its antecedents and outcome, is discussed in Rosenberg, "The Origins of Overkill," 40–43. For documents on this debate, see Memorandum, Radford to Twining, Taylor, Burke, and Pate, March 28, 1956, re Strategic Concept and Use of U.S. Military Forces, CJCS Radford 381 (Military Strategy and Posture), in RG 218, NARS; Memoranda of Conversation with the President by Goodpaster, May 14 and 24, 1956, EP-AWF, Dwight D. Eisenhower Diary Series (hereinafter cited as DDE Diary), box 15, folder May, 1956, Goodpaster, EL.

29. Eisenhower's ongoing struggle with the JCS to keep military spending in line and the upward pressures being exerted by the demands of strategic force modernization and allied calls for aid can be seen in the following: Memorandum of Conference with the President on March 13, 1956, by Goodpaster (dated March 14, 1956), EP-AWF, DDE Diary, box 13, folder March, 1956, Goodpaster; Memorandum for the President from Wilson, March 29, 1956, White House Office to Office of the Staff Secretary, Subject Series, DoD Subseries, box 2, folder Budget, Military (2); Discussion at the 285th Meeting of the NSC, Thursday, May 17, 1956 (dated May 18, 1956), EP-AWF, NSC Series, box 8, folder 285, Meeting of the NSC, May 17, 1956; and Memorandum of Conversation with the President, May 18, 1956, by Goodpaster, EP-AWF, DDE Diary, box 15, folder May, 1956, Goodpaster; all in EL.

as the subsequent translation of the precepts laid down in NSC-5602 into U.S.-NATO policy, and clearly revealed Eisenhower's personal understanding of the nature of future threats, both limited and total, and America's proper role in preparing for them. In essence, Eisenhower was determined to avoid the economic and political quagmires of limited wars, and to place reliance upon massive retaliation to deal with global war. So far as the issue of flexibility to deal with lesser threats was concerned, he had firmly decided that the United States would not tie its forces down in limited wars around the Soviet periphery. The United States should not get involved in a "small war" beyond a few Marine battalions or army units, he told Radford; if the conflict grew to anything resembling Korean War proportions, then to his mind it was a clear case for using nuclear weapons. He believed planning should proceed on the assumption that tactical nuclear weapons would be used in any small war, and he had no fear that the use of these weapons would inevitably escalate into a full-scale war.[30]

Regarding global war, Eisenhower took little comfort in arguments that nuclear parity would bring mutual deterrence. Though he agreed that awareness of the mutual devastation that would ensue from any nuclear war would reduce materially the possibility of war, he would not rule out war resulting from miscalculation, and he felt it unsafe to predict that, should the West and East ever become locked in a life-and-death struggle, both sides would have the sense not to use nuclear weapons. As Eisenhower foresaw it after digesting the results of the aforementioned net evaluation studies on the results of various nuclear war scenarios presented to him in early 1956, a future war would likely fall into two phases: In the first, the United States must seek to avoid disaster, while in the second, it would carry the fight to the enemy in a final conclusion, which he felt could be anything from a stalemate to another Thirty or Hundred Years' War. Eisenhower firmly believed that any war between the United States and the USSR would be nuclear, repeatedly declaring his determination, if the need should arise, to use these weapons. As he told the JCS, "Massive retaliation, although the term has been scoffed at, is likely to be the key to survival."[31]

Eisenhower made clear that his view of future wars and threats carried cer-

30. Memorandum of Conferences with the President by Goodpaster, May 14, 24, 1956, EP-AWF, DDE Diary, box 15, folder May, 1956, Goodpaster, EL.

31. Memorandum for the Record by Goodpaster, February 10, 1956, re Conference of Joint Chiefs of Staff with the President, February 10, 1956, NHC-NSA; Letter, Eisenhower to Churchill, April 27, 1956, EP-AWF, DDE Diary, box 14, folder April, 1956, Miscellaneous (1); and Letter, Eisenhower to Montgomery, May 2, 1956, EP-AWF, DDE Diary, box 15, folder May, 1956, Miscellaneous (5), both in EL; and Memorandum of Conference with the President, May 24, 1956, by Goodpaster, NHC-NSA.

176 / Robert A. Wampler

tain firm conclusions about the proper role of the United States, particularly within NATO, in preparing for both. As he saw it, the United States should focus on building up the indigenous defenses of regions in the world. For NATO, this meant that the United States should be the "central keep" behind the alliance's forward forces, concentrating on providing the already immensely expensive nuclear retaliatory forces and assisting the allies in carrying out the necessary integration of nuclear weapons into their forces. While he was now ready to admit that political necessity constrained the United States to keep forces in Europe for some time, he argued that to the degree that NATO strategy dictated greater stress on ready D-Day forces, the allies should be pressed to do more to carry their weight in the alliance.[32]

Beyond this, though, Eisenhower wanted to gain more flexibility in the current arrangements in line with his understanding of the proper allocation of burdens within NATO, allowing the United States to balance better its diplomatic and economic responsibilities and keep faith with the "fair share" principle that Dulles had pledged in 1954 would govern America's contribution to NATO.[33] One avenue that seemed to offer substantial promise for providing such flexibility, in Eisenhower and Radford's view, was the prospect of "streamlining" U.S. ground divisions through the introduction of tactical nuclear weapons, thus in theory reducing both size and costs but not overall effective combat power.[34]

Implementing these precepts and goals of Eisenhower presented a difficult diplomatic problem for the United States, which fell upon the shoulders of Dulles. The task facing the secretary was to frame a U.S. policy that would address his president's deeply held convictions, yet somehow avoid the perils and pitfalls created by those, both within the U.S. government and among its allies,

32. Memorandum for the Record by Goodpaster, February 10, 1956; Memorandum of Conference with the President on March 13, 1956, by Goodpaster; Discussion at the 285th Meeting of the NSC, May 17, 1956; Memorandum of Conversation with the President by Goodpaster, May 18, 1956; and Memorandum of Conference with the President, May 24, 1956, by Goodpaster, all in NHC-NSA.

33. For Dulles' statement of the U.S. commitment to keep forces in Europe as part of the "fair share" of its responsibilities to NATO, see Final Act of the Nine-Power Conference Held in London Between the Twenty-Eighth of September and the Third of October, Nineteen Hundred and Fifty Four, Annex IIA: Extemporaneous Statement by the United States Secretary of State (The Hon. John Foster Dulles) at the Fourth Plenary Meeting, FRUS, 1952–54, V, 1357–61.

34. On the Eisenhower administration's interest in streamlining through the introduction of tactical nuclear weapons, see Secretary Dulles' News Conference of July 18, 1956, Dulles Papers, box 100, folder Atomic Energy and Disarmament, and Letter, Dulles to Adenauer, August 11, 1956, Dulles Papers, General Correspondence and Memoranda Series, box 2, folder Strictly Confidential A-B(1), both in EL; and Memorandum of a Conversation, Department of State, Washington, August 13, 1956, Subject: NATO Force Levels, FRUS, 1955–57, IV, 93–95.

who either held different views or misconstrued U.S. policy regarding the proper role for nuclear weapons in NATO strategy. The summer and fall of 1956 provided a textbook example of the complex maneuverings demanded to navigate such a course. On the one hand, the United Kingdom renewed a long-standing campaign to shift NATO strategy to a more explicit reliance upon nuclear deterrence, with a corresponding substantial cut in the alliance's SHIELD forces, motivated in large part by the need to reduce the economic burdens of the British commitment to European defense.[35] On the other hand, the perpetually suspicious German chancellor, Konrad Adenauer, was in an uproar over the rumored Radford Plan to drastically reduce U.S. forces in Europe and feared that the United States and United Kingdom were engaged in a conspiracy to base NATO defense solely on nuclear weapons. As he made clear to all who would listen, such a step would be both perilous and pernicious, undermine his domestic political standing based upon his commitment to German rearmament, create dangerous inflexibilities in NATO's ability to respond to less than all-out threats, and place Europe's security solely in the hands of a U.S. nuclear guarantee that Adenauer seemed constantly to doubt.[36]

In the last half of 1956, Dulles strove to hammer out a consensus within the administration upon what he saw as the proper principles to guide U.S. policy on NATO strategy. As suggested earlier, his efforts were complicated by the need to address Eisenhower's desire to begin reducing the size of the U.S. military establishment in Europe, without leading Bonn, Paris, and other allied capitals to fear that America was abandoning the Continent and taking up a "peripheral strategy." Further difficulties arose from the efforts of Defense Secretary Wilson and JCS chairman Radford to get a policy decision in favor of making immediate substantial U.S. force withdrawals. Radford's role represented another element in this policy mix—his belief, shared by Eisenhower and the United Kingdom, that nuclear weapons would permit extensive streamlining of U.S. ground forces without any serious diminution of military effectiveness. One of Dulles' imperatives was to ensure that NATO strategy did not promote a destabilizing overdependence upon nuclear weapons, and continued to state the need for sizable SHIELD forces, able to respond to lesser threats in Europe with or without nuclear weapons as the situation demanded.[37]

35. These British efforts are discussed in detail in Wampler, *Ambiguous Legacy*, chapters 11–13.

36. For a discussion of the Eisenhower administration's problems with Adenauer in 1956 over U.S. and NATO nuclear strategy, see Wampler's "Educating Adenauer: The Eisenhower Administration, Germany and the Diplomacy of Alliance Strategy," in *Die doppelte Eindämmung: Europäische Sicherheit und die Deutsche Frage in den Fünfzigern*, ed. Rolf Steininger *et al.* (Munich, 1993).

37. These developments are discussed in depth in Wampler, *Ambiguous Legacy*, chapter 12, Basic documents outlining the course of the administration debate include Memorandum of a Con-

Finally, Dulles secured agreement to practically all of the essential points that he wanted incorporated in a statement of U.S. policy on NATO strategy. As approved by Eisenhower in October, 1956, and later presented to NATO, U.S. policy acknowledged the central role of the strategic nuclear retaliatory force (largely provided by the United States) in deterring and if need be meeting a major Soviet attack. Also reaffirmed was the alliance's need for substantial SHIELD forces, to protect its nuclear retaliatory forces in Europe and to hold against a Soviet attack until the strategic nuclear retaliation took effect, as well as to deal with the possibility of limited conventional aggression, a primary concern of Adenauer's, without unnecessarily unleashing a major nuclear war.[38]

To secure this victory, Dulles had to hold fast against the efforts of Wilson and Radford to sell nuclear weapons as the answer to Eisenhower's desire to cut the U.S. defense burden in Europe. Dulles came down hard against such a simple solution, arguing, "It was one thing for us to rely on the new look, not being subject to insurrectionary or conventional attack as the Europeans are, and it is something else to propose it for the Europeans." In the end, Eisenhower was forced to admit the wisdom in Dulles' call for a cautious approach. Concerning U.S. forces in Europe, Eisenhower remained firm that the United States had to use "every art of statecraft" to educate the Europeans on American thinking about its forces, but insisted that no move could be made now to remove troops, given the damaging impact this would have upon the NATO allies, and especially on Adenauer's position. With respect to the chancellor's fears that the United States might be increasingly deterred by the prospect of Soviet nuclear attacks from using its nuclear capability in defense of Europe, the president also reaffirmed that the U.S. planning would proceed on the basis that "if the Soviets invade, atomic weapons would be used."[39]

These decisions thus guided the United States as it sought to hold off competing rationales for NATO strategy and to ease allied worries over the U.S. commitment to Europe. In this effort it received great assistance from SACEUR, Alfred Gruenther, who in his final New Approach studies sought to reaffirm the strategic need for substantial NATO SHIELD forces in the coming era of nu-

versation, Department of State, Washington, August 13, 1956, Subject: NATO Force Levels, 93–95; Draft Memorandum (re U.S. response to British proposals), September 26, 1956, 740.5/9-2656, and Memorandum, C. Burke Elbrick and Douglas MacArthur II to John Foster Dulles re Review of NATO Strategy and Withdrawal of Forces, September 27, 1956, 740.5/9-2756, both in RG 59, NA; Memorandum from the Secretary of State to the President, October 1, 1956, and Memorandum of Conference with the President, October 2, 1956, both in *FRUS,* 1955–57, IV, 96–102.

38. Memorandum from the Secretary of State to the President, October 1, 1956, and Memorandum of Meeting with the President, October 2, 1956, both in *FRUS,* 1955–57, IV, 96–102.

39. Memorandum of Meeting with the President, October 2, 1956, *ibid.,* 101–102.

clear plenty both to support the deterrent against all-out attack as well as to deal with lesser threats.[40] U.S. policy and SACEUR's studies served to shape the new Political Directive adopted by NATO in December, 1956, to guide NATO's military planning, and the ensuing restatement of alliance strategy, MC-14/2, which was adopted in the spring of 1957.[41]

MC-14/2, in seeking to adapt the nuclear strategy devised by the New Approach studies to the issue of nuclear parity with the USSR and the uncertain dangers this portended, laid out a demanding task for SACEUR and the alliance. Only recently have substantial sections of this long-classified and key statement of NATO strategy been opened to scholars, so it is useful as well as important here to provide excerpts from its critical passages. As its statement on NATO's overall strategic concept reaffirmed:

> Our chief objective is to prevent war by creating an effective deterrent to aggression. The principal elements of the deterrent are adequate nuclear and other ready forces and the manifest determination to retaliate against any aggressor with all the forces at our disposal, including nuclear weapons, which the defense of NATO would require.
>
> In preparation for a general war, should one be forced upon us . . . we must first ensure the ability to carry out an instant and devastating nuclear counteroffensive by all available means and develop the capability to absorb and survive the enemy's onslaught.[42]

Beyond this worst-case scenario, MC-14/2 also called upon NATO to pursue what can be seen as flexible response-style capabilities, while at the same time explicitly ruling out limited war with the USSR in Europe:

> The Soviets might . . . conclude that the only way in which they could profitably further their aim would be to initiate operations with limited objectives, such as infiltration, incursions or hostile local actions in the NATO area, covertly or overtly supported by themselves, trusting that the Allies in their collective desire to prevent a general conflict would either limit their reactions accordingly or

40. Gruenther's final study, which assessed SACEUR's long-range force needs looking to the early 1960s, is discussed in Wampler, *NATO Strategic Planning and Nuclear Weapons*, 26–34, and Wampler, *Ambiguous Legacy*, chapter 13.

41. For a detailed discussion of the drafting of and debate over MC-14/2, see Wampler, *Ambiguous Legacy*, chapter 13 and Conclusions. A recent article, drawing upon a number of the same documents, has also pointed out the flexible response aspects of MC-14/2. See John S. Duffield, "The Evolution of NATO's Strategy of Flexible Response: A Reinterpretation," *Security Studies* (1991), I, 132–56.

42. JCS 2305/257, *ca.* October 24, 1960; attached to CM-17-60, Memorandum for the Secretary of Defense from L. L. Lemnitzer, October 28, 1960, re NATO Long Range Planning, CCS 9050/3000 NATO (August 29, 1960)(section 104), in RG 218, NA.

not react at all. Under these circumstances NATO must be prepared to deal immediately with such situations without necessarily having recourse to nuclear
weapons. NATO must also be prepared to respond quickly with nuclear weapons
should the situation require it. In this latter respect . . . if the Soviets were involved
in a local hostile action and sought to broaden the scope of such an incident or to
prolong it, the situation would call for the utilization of all weapons and forces at
NATO's disposal, since in no case is there a NATO concept of limited war with
the Soviets.[43]

The dilemma facing Dulles and the United States, however, was that even
as the majority of the alliance members voiced agreement that NATO required strong SHIELD forces to provide the flexibility Dulles emphasized, the
discussion on the new Political Directive revealed that these same allies viewed
the SHIELD forces and NATO's response to most if not all threats in predominantly nuclear terms. The Dutch defense minister, Cornelius Staf, set the tone
when he argued that the only way to strengthen the SHIELD forces was to
provide them with atomic weapons. Holding it was necessary that all national
forces have atomic weapons at their disposal in Europe, "so they can be used op-
erationally at the will of NATO commanders," Staf argued that tactical nuclear
weapons should be integrated at the corps or army levels, with the warheads
remaining in the hands of the nations now possessing them.[44]

German defense minister Franz-Josef Strauss seconded Staf, both on giving
NATO commanders pre-authorization to use nuclear weapons and on the need
to make tactical nuclear weapons available, down to the divisional level. The
French defense minister, Maurice Bourges-Manoury, presented a somewhat
more nuanced position, citing the need for both nuclear weapons to implement
the forward strategy to prevent Europe from being overrun and strong SHIELD
forces to deter and meet a Soviet surprise attack waged with conventional
weapons, which NATO assessments of the Soviet threat accepted as a possibility. But on the other hand, noting the danger of how a swift Soviet occupation
of Western Europe might lead to hesitancy to use nuclear weapons within
NATO, he also stressed that this assessment of the Soviet threat underlined as
well the need for firmness of intention to use these weapons.[45]

43. Memorandum for Secretary McElroy from Twining, April 9, 1958; CCS 092 Western Europe (3-12-48)(2)(section 104), in RG 218, NA.

44. Telegram from the U.S. Delegation at the North Atlantic Council Ministerial Meeting to
the Secretary of State (POLTO 1422), December 14, 1956, FRUS, 1955–57, IV, 150–51; and the
same document, found in lot file 62D181, box 11, file CF819, in RG 59, FOIA. This latter copy
of the telegram is vital, as it includes crucial passages indicating the general desire to equip NATO
forces with nuclear weapons and to give NATO commanders predelegated authority to use these,
which were deleted from the copy in the FRUS volume.

45. POLTO 1422, December 14, 1956 (FOIA copy).

Dulles sought in the ensuing discussion on the text of the new Political Directive to correct this overemphasis, in his view, upon the nuclear side of NATO's defense equation. Undoubtedly, the clear intent of Strauss and other NATO defense ministers to give NATO commanders the capability and the authority to use nuclear weapons instantly in response to a Soviet attack reflected the allies' concern to ensure that this response *would* occur, regardless of possible U.S. hesitations in the face of its own heightened vulnerability to Soviet nuclear strikes. Steps in this direction, however, could limit the alliance's capability to respond flexibly to a wider range of threats without using nuclear weapons. As Dulles firmly believed, NATO must not place its sole reliance upon nuclear weapons, even if it must place its main reliance upon them. Conventional forces were necessary, and the secretary of state made it amply clear that the burden of supplying these forces should increasingly be taken on by the European NATO members, among whom he singled out Germany.[46]

Yet, despite his forceful restatements in Paris of the need to secure adequate SHIELD forces to give NATO this flexibility, and his warnings that NATO must not put all its eggs in the nuclear basket, Dulles, as indicated at the beginning of this paper, had to admit it was becoming increasingly likely that the use of nuclear weapons would be automatic, as NATO planning was based upon the use of these weapons.[47] Beyond the perilous military consequences of such inflexibility, Dulles also harbored the concerns, revealed in his message to Eisenhower, that this trend could leave America "holding the bag alone so far as the defense of Europe is concerned."[48] Such a result, needless to say, would ill suit Eisenhower's sense of America's "fair share" of Europe's defense responsibilities.

The problem facing Dulles and the United States was how to reconcile the tensions produced by the conflicting demands of alliance members that nuclear weapons would be used when they (that is, the allies) agreed it was necessary, but also to ensure that they would *not* be used if they felt the situation did not call for it. NATO strategy was pitting the understandable U.S. insistence that its hands not be tied in the event of a crisis against the equally understandable allied insistence upon a voice in their fates. In Dulles' mind (and it should be noted also in the view of Alfred Gruenther and his successor as SACEUR, Lauris Norstad), this issue was intimately interwoven with the aforementioned need for greater flexibility in NATO's military capabilities. As noted, as far back as 1954 Dulles had seen the pressing need to explore the possibility of maintaining suf-

46. POLTO 1422 (*FRUS* version), 153–54.
47. POLTO 1427, McCardle to Department of State, December 15, 1956, lot file 62D181, box 11, file CF 819, in RG 59, FOIA.
48. DULTE 19, December 14, 1956 (FOIA version).

ficient flexibility in NATO forces to avoid an exclusive dependence on atomic weapons and to give the Europeans some sense of choice as to the means of their defense, lest NATO's nuclear strategy foment neutralism.[49]

The question was how to square the circles of contending U.S. and allied interests in controlling nuclear weapons. As Dulles saw it, the United States retained flexibility and discretion in two ways. First, he repeatedly impressed upon the NATO allies that the United States could make no commitment not to act without consulting them. There could be times when the United States would have to act very quickly, and thus would be unable to consult with its allies before taking what it viewed as essential actions, up to and including the use of its massive nuclear retaliatory power.[50] The capacity to act quickly was also protected by existing predelegated authority to use nuclear weapons. As Dulles told the West German foreign minister, Heinrich von Brentano, late in 1957, there was one exception to the general principle that the use of nuclear weapons was a political decision—a situation in which a ground force was attacked. If the commander of this force had tactical nuclear weapons, Dulles said he already had authority to use them to prevent the destruction of his command.[51]

Beyond this, Dulles also began to consider the possible delegation of nuclear authority in NATO to SACEUR, as a means both of addressing the serious political problems surrounding allied concerns that the United States would not act and getting the United States out of "holding the bag" for European defense, as he had put it. Beyond meeting the evident interest of the allies in such a move, it would also be in accord with the long-standing efforts of successive SACEURs, going back to Matthew Ridgway, for preauthorization to use nuclear weapons in an emergency, an effort that had already attained a substantial degree of success as the result of decisions taken by the NAC in 1954 and 1956.[52]

49. "Basic National Security Policy" (Suggestions of the Secretary of State), November 15, 1956, 775. The growing interest of Gruenther and Norstad in securing a greater capacity for flexible responses to a wider range of possible threats to NATO security is discussed in Wampler, *Ambiguous Legacy,* and Wampler, *NATO Strategic Planning and Nuclear Weapons, 1950–1957,* 26–34, 42–43.

50. Dulles had made this point clear from the time when NATO first adopted its nuclear strategy in 1954. See his comments, noted earlier, in Record of Background Press Conference by the Secretary of State, December 16, 1954. For a restatement of this position in 1957, see Memorandum of Conversation (Dulles and West German Foreign Minister Von Brentano), November 23, 1957, *FRUS, 1955–57,* IV, 191.

51. Memorandum, Reinstein to Jones *et al.,* December 19, 1957, 762.00/12–1957, in RG 59, NA. There is evidence that a degree of predelegated authority was also given to certain senior U.S. military commanders, including the commander-in-chief of SAC, in the event time or circumstances did not permit a decision by the president; see Scott D. Sagan, *Moving Targets; Nuclear Strategy and National Security* (Princeton, N.J., 1989), 142.

52. The exact degree of predelegated discretionary authority granted to SACEUR at this time is unclear from the available records. In 1954, the NAC had ruled that while SACEUR should seek

By 1957, Dulles was arguing that it might be desirable to give Norstad in his capacity as the U.S. military leader in NATO the authority to use nuclear weapons in his theater of responsibility. He felt that it would be more reassuring to America's allies in Europe to keep this authority at a high level and specifically with Norstad, in whom the Europeans had confidence. Of equal interest was Dulles' remark that though there was a lot of "stuff" that the United States had implied about the authority to use nuclear weapons remaining a political decision, he believed the United States was not stuck with this.[53]

Dulles' zealous protection of U.S. prerogatives and his wish to increase SACEUR's authority in the nuclear sphere had the full support of Eisenhower, whose strong opposition to allowing political considerations to block the implementation of SACEUR's plans or military action that the United States deemed necessary for its own security has already been noted.[54] Similarly, his interest in increased nuclear sharing with its NATO allies, both as a means of addressing the political problems attendant to the control issue as well as to develop greater flexibility and combat overreliance upon massive retaliation, were the logical continuation of policies adopted during the first New Look in 1953–1954.

Behind the renewed interest in pursuing these possibilities was the unceasing growth in Soviet nuclear capabilities. By 1957, the growing Soviet nuclear stockpile and technical developments in the U.S. stockpile were leading Dulles to reassess the applicability of massive retaliation to NATO, even as MC-14/2 was reaffirming NATO's reliance upon this strategy to meet the worst case threat. He expressed his views succinctly to Adenauer and other visiting German officials in the spring of 1957, telling them:

its political guidance before employing his forces in NATO territory, he need only do so when he deemed it "appropriate." In 1956, this ruling was reaffirmed and expanded, stating that SACEUR need not request guidance for "moves of a routine or administrative nature or *in cases of emergency where the degree of urgency precludes following the full procedure*" (emphasis added); see COS(56)377: Briefs for the 14th Session of the NATO Military Committee, October 11, 1956, DEFE 5/71, in PRO. Against this seemingly clear-cut delegation of authority must be placed, however, the concerns voiced by German Defense Minister Strauss in 1957 that NATO needed a single military headquarters with the authority, in the event of a Soviet attack, to use the weapons at its disposal without "processing requests to fifteen members through NATO Ambassadors"; see Memorandum for the Record by Clark L. Ruffner, November 12, 1957, re Conversation held in Bonn between Prescott Bush and German Minister of Defense Strauss, White House Central Files (Confidential Files), box 46, folder NATO (2), in EL.

53. Memorandum, Dulles telephone call to General Cutler, April, 27, 1957, John Foster Dulles Papers, Telephone Conversations and Memoranda, box 12, folder March-August 30, 1957(4), in Princeton University Library.

54. See the discussion above at pp. 169–73.

He believed that the defense of Germany and Western Europe cannot be left entirely to the deterrent of massive atomic counter-attack. Depending on the situation, there would be powerful moral considerations against a massive retaliation on Moscow which would annihilate millions of people. There was a definite development, however, toward nuclear tactical weapons with far greater power than conventional tactical weapons. The time would arrive fairly soon, though it had not arrived yet, when forces equipped with such weapons, if stationed in a national border, might make virtually impossible invasion by hostile forces. Though this development was by no means yet complete, the Secretary believed that the trend was therefore away from defense by massive retaliation and toward defense by tactical atomic weapons.[55]

Dulles expanded upon these ideas in an article published in the influential journal *Foreign Affairs* in October, 1957, in which he pointed to recent nuclear tests that raised the possibility of developing nuclear weapons whose destructiveness and radiation effects could be confined to predetermined targets. As a result, he argued, it might be feasible to place less reliance upon massive retaliation and more on defense by mobile forces possessing tactical nuclear weapons. Such a shift would entail certain necessary changes in military and political policies, Dulles held. So long as NATO security relied almost solely upon massive retaliation, this meant almost sole dependence upon the United States. But as nuclear weapons became more tactical in nature and so more adaptable to area defense, this would naturally lead to a desire by qualified allies to participate more directly in this defense, as well as a greater assurance this nuclear power would be used when needed.[56]

Clearly, it was this conjoining of military, political, and economic concerns that motivated the Eisenhower administration's positive response to French proposals in the spring of 1957 for the creation of a NATO atomic stockpile, and the parallel U.S. proposal to provide IRBMs to certain NATO nations (to be chosen by SACEUR) that would make use of this stockpile. Nuclear sharing, however, was only part of a possible answer, so long as allied doubts persisted

55. USEL/MC/6: Memorandum of Conversation, May 4, 1957, re Middle East, Defense Strategy, EP-AWF, Dulles-Herter Series, box 6, folder Dulles, J. F. May, 1957, in EL.

56. John Foster Dulles, "Challenge and Response in United States Policy," *Foreign Affairs,* XXXVI (October, 1957), 25–43. Dulles had earlier outlined his developing ideas on the need for flexibility in a talk that he gave to the Service Secretaries Conference in Quantico, Virginia, in June, 1956. See Draft Outline: Secretary's Talk at Quantico, June 14, 1956, in NHC-NSA. The importance with which these ideas were viewed in the State Department is seen in the prominence they were given in a lengthy briefing paper on NATO strategy prepared for the 1957 NATO Heads of Government conference. See PRS B-2/51: Background Paper—NATO Defense Policy and Strategy, December 4, 1957, White House Central Files (Confidential Files), box 46, folder NATO

about the strategy these weapons would serve. These doubts would only deepen as SACEUR continued to emphasize that NATO had to be prepared to initiate nuclear operations immediately upon attack, if not preemptively, for there to be any hope for survival and success, however these might be defined. From Ridgway's study on, SACEUR's atomic strike plans were aimed at targets that could retard the ability of Soviet bloc forces to advance into Europe and to deliver atomic strikes on NATO forces. Logic dictated, as it did in the development of U.S. strategic strike plans, that as the means of delivering nuclear weapons accelerated and the pace of war increased thereby, the most effective way of striking these counterforce targets, and thus the best and perhaps sole way of assuring any possibility of victory, was in preemption upon warning of attack. The coming of the missile age only served to sharpen further the horns of this dilemma, thus militating against the political desire for flexibility even as it increased it.[57]

However compelling the military and technological imperatives behind this logic, the resulting strains upon alliance cohesion, the growing doubts about the continuing credibility of the U.S. nuclear guarantee, and the added impetus for other allies to take up the British example and develop their own national nuclear capabilities (the French under de Gaulle being the classic case, and the prospect of a nuclear Germany being the classic fear) were just as compelling in driving Dulles and Norstad to find some way to divorce NATO security from these seemingly intractable dilemmas plaguing massive retaliation. Given these circumstances, Dulles in 1958 returned to the possibility that tactical nuclear weapons might offer some means of supplementing massive retaliation and allow both the United States and NATO to avoid becoming prisoners of a "frozen" strategic concept. The United States had to develop a doctrine to guide the use of the tactical nuclear weapons it was developing, he asserted, for the decision to "press the button" was an awesome thing, and the possibility such a de-

---

57. By way of illustration, SACEUR's Emergency Defense Plan for 1958 expanded upon the responsibilities of commanders authorized to release and expend nuclear weapons on preplanned targets. SACEUR's Atomic Strike Plan under this EDP consisted of a Scheduled Plan directed against Soviet atomic delivery capabilities within SACEUR's area of responsibility; a Counter Radar Program of automatic attacks against certain radar and control centers; and an Interdiction Program against targets whose destruction was likely to have a major impact on the movements of enemy forces. See JP(57)127 (Final): SACEUR's Emergency Defense Plan-1958, November 8, 1957, DEFE 4/101, in PRO. To carry out these strikes, SACEUR for planning purposes could assume that during 1958–1959 he would have available 2,500 weapons with yields in the kiloton range, and 50 with yields running into megatons. This was in addition to the 800 kiloton-range and 100 megaton-range weapons SACLANT could assume having available. See Memorandum, Hillyard to U.S. Representative–Standing Group, September 22, 1958.

cision would not be taken had to be recognized. Unless the alliance could devise some alternative strategic concept encompassing the potential of these new weapons, Dulles warned, NATO could not be held together more than a few more years.[58]

These ineluctable constraints and recondite dilemmas surrounding U.S. policies and objectives for NATO bore heavily upon the Eisenhower administration as it closed out its days. Not surprisingly, Eisenhower's greatest frustration was with his failure to get the Europeans to take on more of the burdens of local defense in NATO, and he let no opportunity pass to recount his long history of disappointment in this regard. As he told Dulles and the undersecretary of state, Christian Herter, in late 1958, after one such peroration, the United States would stick to its commitments, but should ask the European governments to what extent they intended to keep leaning on the United States. The idea that the United States was an inexhaustible reservoir of support, despite its undeniable utility in the cold war, could no longer be realistically considered applicable, he warned.[59]

For his part, Dulles in his final months brooded darkly over NATO's overall future prospects, prompted by his reading of West European public opinion in the wake of Khrushchev's renewed assault upon the status of Berlin. Ever since the adoption of MC-48, this contingency had been seen as the most likely to reveal the faultlines at the heart of an alliance strategy that relied upon nuclear weapons. Now, the likelihood that public fear of nuclear war would bar NATO governments from risking a land operation to keep open Western access to Berlin led Dulles to wonder if Western Europe was really defensible at all. No amount of power could provide a deterrent if there was no will to use it when necessary, he felt. The United States possessed this will, Dulles believed, but it seemed to be lacking in Europe, where some feared the United States was eager to provoke a "showdown" with the Soviets, in which the allies would bear the brunt of the risks. Given this situation, he feared that the administration's entire NATO concept and U.S. participation in it would require "drastic review."[60]

58. Memorandum for the Record by A. J. Goodpaster re Meeting in the Office of the Secretary of Defense on April 7, 1958 (dated April 9, 1958), and Memorandum of conference, June 17, 1958, by R.C. (Robert Cutler), both in White House Office to Office of the Staff Secretary, Subject Series, Alpha Subseries, box 21, folder Nuclear Exchange (September 1957–June 1958)(3), in EL.

59. Memorandum of Conversation with the President on December 12, 1958, by John S. D. Eisenhower (dated December 15, 1958), in NSA-NHC.

60. "Thinking Out Loud," by John Foster Dulles, January 26, 1959, John Foster Dulles Papers, White House Memoranda Series, box 7, folder White House Correspondence—General, 1959, in EL. The Berlin crisis of 1958–59 and the Eisenhower administration's response are discussed in detail in Marc Trachtenberg, *History and Strategy,* 169–234. Though he did not refer to it in the above

Dulles did not live to carry out such a review, as he finally succumbed to the cancer afflicting him in May, 1959. His successor, Christian Herter, did initiate an overall review of NATO policies, resulting in the last proposal drawn up by the Eisenhower administration to address the interlocking dilemmas surrounding NATO strategy and the proper roles of the United States, its allies, and nuclear weapons in this strategy. To provide a focus and recommendations for this review, Herter in 1960 brought in Robert Bowie, Dulles' former head of the policy planning staff and adviser on nuclear weapons issues, who had returned to teaching at Harvard University. Drawing upon political and military specialists within and outside government, Bowie prepared a report on "The North Atlantic Nations: Tasks for the 1960's," which he submitted in August, 1960. At the heart of this report was Bowie's proposal to link and reconcile the U.S. goals of reducing its defense burdens within NATO and securing a greater alliance capability for flexible response with the NATO allies' desire for a greater say in the alliance's nuclear capability.[61]

Rejecting tactical nuclear defense and limited nuclear war as politically unacceptable options for the alliance, Bowie outlined the essential elements of a new arrangement between the United States and its allies. The essence of this new bargain would be U.S. agreement to provide NATO with a Polaris submarine fleet to serve as a NATO nuclear force, which would operate free of U.S. veto to defend against a Soviet attack upon Western Europe, but only if the Europeans agreed to provide the additional SHIELD forces necessary to raise the nuclear threshold, and thus assure that this new NATO nuclear force would only be used as a last resort to a major Soviet assault upon Europe. This arrangement,

---

memorandum, Dulles likely was also reacting to the widespread public interest in various schemes for disengagement and nuclear-free zones in Europe that were being advanced by a wide variety of individuals and nations, ranging from George Kennan to Britain's Labour Party to the Polish government to the USSR, with the expected comparable range in specifics and motivations. Kennan's ideas, presented in the 1957 Reith Lectures in England, were later published in his *Russia, the Atom and the West* (New York, 1957). A detailed discussion and assessment (from the British point of view) of the various major plans for disengagement and/or nuclear-free zones in Europe can be found in MD/P(58)17: Report of the Military Disengagement Working Party, January 31, 1958, FO 371/135628, in PRO.

61. "The North Atlantic Nations: Tasks for the 1960's—A Report to the Secretary of State," August, 1960 (the Bowie Report), copy provided to the Nuclear History Program by Dr. Robert R. Bowie. The NHP has published the Bowie report in its entirety, along with an introduction by Dr. Bowie on the background and preparation of the report as Nuclear History Occasional Paper 7 (College Park, Md., 1991). The background and genesis of the Bowie Report, which gave rise to the abortive Multilateral Force proposal under the Kennedy and Johnson administrations, is discussed in John Choon Yoo, "Three Faces of Hegemony: Eisenhower, Kennedy, Johnson, and the Multilateral Force" (Senior honors thesis, Harvard University, 1989).

Bowie believed, would not only address NATO's political and military problems but also the U.S. desire to head off French, and potential German, nuclear aspirations.[62]

The Eisenhower administration had little time to act upon Bowie's proposals. Herter unveiled the idea of selling U.S. Polaris submarines to the NATO allies at the December, 1960, NATO ministerial meeting, linking the proposal for a new NATO nuclear force to America's growing balance of payments problems with Europe and warnings of possible withdrawals of U.S. forces from Europe if these difficulties could not be resolved.[63] The fate of Bowie's proposals, most notably in the form of the rechristened Multilateral Force, however, would lie in the hands of the new Kennedy administration, which entered office just after this NATO meeting, bringing with it a decidedly different approach to alliance strategy and nuclear sharing.[64]

Our understanding of the Eisenhower administration has been colored by the critiques that scholars outside of government, such as Henry Kissinger as well as by officials of the Kennedy and Johnson administrations and subsequent scholars, have made of its policies. A general theme running through these critiques has been the judgment that the heavy reliance upon nuclear weapons and massive retaliation in U.S. and NATO strategy at the end of the 1950s was the desired end of the Eisenhower administration, or at least a path that it had within its power to avoid. The essence of this viewpoint was captured by Arthur Schlesinger, Jr. Charging Dulles' policies were marked by his exclusive reliance upon nuclear power, Schlesinger held that by 1961, "Washington had been persuading Western Europe for a decade of the infallibility of nuclear protection." It was up to Kennedy and his forceful secretary of defense, Robert McNamara, to devise a new strategy of flexible response, "brilliantly designed to reduce the threat of nuclear war and to cope with the worldwide nuances of communist aggression."[65]

62. *Ibid.*

63. Letter, Dirk Stikker to Dean Acheson, January 9, 1961, Dean Acheson Papers, State Department and White House Advisor, March 1961 Series, box 85, Post Administration Files, Harry S. Truman Library, Independence, Missouri.

64. In addition to the Yoo thesis cited earlier, see also Jane Stromseth, *The Origins of Flexible Response: NATO's Debate over Strategy in the 1960s* (London, 1988), and the earlier study by John D. Steinbrunner, *The Cybernetic Theory of Decision: New Dimension of Political Analysis* (Princeton, N.J., 1974), for discussion of the subsequent fate of the MLF proposal.

65. Arthur M. Schlesinger, Jr., *A Thousand Days: John F. Kennedy in the White House* (Boston, 1965), 299, 852–53. The classic exposition of the Kennedy-McNamara defense policies is Alain C. Enthoven and K. Wayne Smith, *How Much Is Enough: Shaping the Defense Program, 1961–1969* (New

As I have sought to show, however, behind the public images of a president and his secretary of state, enamored of nuclear weapons as the means to get "more bang for the buck," lay a much more sophisticated as well as ambivalent personal grasp of the ambiguities surrounding the role of nuclear weapons in alliance diplomacy and strategy that infused the policy objectives of the administration. The emphasis upon nuclear weapons in the Eisenhower New Look must be seen in the alliance context of this policy. As viewed by Eisenhower and Dulles, the political economy of NATO security put differing demands upon its members, and as discussed, the primary role of the United States was to provide the strategic nuclear force for deterring and if need be defending against a major Soviet attack. Insofar as alliance solidarity, economics, and military planning dictated, the administration stood ready to aid its allies in the integration of nuclear weapons into their forces and to seek some instrument for sharing control of the alliance's (if not America's) nuclear might. To the degree that NATO needed sizable SHIELD forces to secure the capability to respond more flexibly to lesser threats, Eisenhower and Dulles both plainly saw this as a responsibility resting upon the European allies.

As I have sought to demonstrate, there were formidable obstacles astride the road to implementing this dispensation of the "fair shares" of alliance duties. For example, Dulles and Adenauer might find themselves in hearty agreement on the need to avoid a dangerous overreliance upon nuclear weapons, but Adenauer's persistent need for reassurance about the U.S. nuclear guarantee only served to underscore the nuclear aspect of NATO defense. In similar fashion, the strong support Strauss and other NATO defense ministers gave to equipping NATO forces with nuclear weapons and giving their commanders predelegated

---

York, 1971), which presented a similar view of the policies of the Eisenhower administration; see especially pp. 117–21 on NATO. Two works that played important roles in setting forth the accumulating criticism of the Eisenhower administration's nuclear policies, in particular with respect to NATO, were Henry A. Kissinger, *Nuclear Weapons and Foreign Policy* (New York, 1957), 269–315 especially; and Robert Endicott Osgood, *NATO: The Entangling Alliance* (Chicago, 1962). Osgood in particular served to guide subsequent scholarship on NATO, with his identification of NATO strategy under Eisenhower with an undifferentiated massive retaliation. Later studies that followed Osgood in this identification include J. Michael Legge, *Theater Nuclear Weapons and the NATO Strategy of Flexible Response* [R–29264-FF] (Santa Monica, Calif., 1983), 5; and Stromseth, *The Origins of Flexible Response,* 15, 18. Stromseth and David Schwartz do discuss Dulles' growing ambivalence about the viability of massive retaliation for NATO, and Schwartz in particular identifies some of the early roots of NATO's later strategy of Flexible Response in the late 1950s. Still, their studies portray Dulles as continuing to stress nuclear weapons, in particular tactical nuclear weapons, as the means to flexibility, and the Eisenhower administration overall as unsympathetic to NATO's need for greater conventional flexibility, a view with which I obviously disagree. See Stromseth, 18–22; David N. Schwartz, *NATO's Nuclear Dilemmas* (Washington, D.C., 1983), 137–42.

authority to use these only served to help push NATO down the road toward a situation in which, as Dulles admitted, immediate use of nuclear weapons could come to be the defining aspect of the alliance's response to threats, regardless of SACEUR's efforts to secure a broader range of options.

So, in the end, Eisenhower and Dulles' hopes both to achieve a better ordering of the relative burdens of defense within NATO and to secure for the alliance the means to pursue options between acquiescence and nuclear holocaust in response to the prospective wider range of Soviet threats ran aground upon the deep-rooted concerns not just of Adenauer but of the rest of the alliance to tie the United States firmly to the defense of Europe. To the degree that both men hoped to affect some economies in the costs of America's defense commitments through the integration of tactical nuclear weapons, it was only natural that the allies would want to take similar steps. To the extent that the presence of U.S. forces in Europe became a central symbol of the U.S. commitment to NATO, Eisenhower's treasured hopes of shifting more of this burden to the allies would have to be deferred.

Finally, to the extent (which was great) that the U.S looked to its allies to provide the forces necessary for more flexible responses to less than all-out threats, success or failure rode on the ability, or willingness, of the allies to shoulder this burden. The persistent failure, not only of the allies, but of the United States itself, to provide the forces Norstad argued he needed to secure such flexible response capabilities, when combined with the intent of the allies to emulate the United States in nuclearizing their own forces (the most prominent examples of which being the United Kingdom and France), resulted in the "nuclear addiction" that critics charged marked NATO strategy in 1961, when the Kennedy administration took over. As this paper argues, however, this de facto reliance upon nuclear weapons did not reflect the aspirations of the Eisenhower administration or of SACEUR. Only now can we begin to see the degree to which not only the Kennedy administration but subsequent chroniclers of the Eisenhower era misjudged this inheritance as the preferred goal of its predecessors, when it should more accurately be seen as the imperfect best that they could achieve, given the need to temper their goals with the differing interests and views of America's allies.

GORDON H. CHANG
Eisenhower and Mao's China

At his last meeting with the press as president of the United States, Dwight Eisenhower was asked what his greatest disappointment had been in office. Eisenhower confessed that it was the failure to achieve a "permanent peace with justice." He went on to explain. He did not rue initiatives he had failed to take nor lament decisions perhaps unwisely made during his eight years in office. Rather, Eisenhower attributed the continuing high level of tension in the world to the bellicosity of Mao Tse-tung and his fellow Chinese Communists. He said: "During the entire first four years, I think, the Red Chinese were constantly threatening war, saying they were and they were not only threatening, but often making moves in that direction and at the same time the Russians were saying, 'We are going to support our Red China allies.'"[1]

Indeed, the Chinese Communists had frustrated the Eisenhower administration from beginning to end. From Korea—Eisenhower's top problem upon entering office in 1953—to the defeat of the French at Dien Bien Phu, Vietnam and the rising Communist insurgency in Southeast Asia, through two crises in the Taiwan Strait, and finally to rising turbulence in the international Communist movement as a result of the militancy of the Chinese in the emerging Sino-Soviet split, China had been an especially vexing and dangerous adversary for the administration of President Dwight David Eisenhower. During the 1950s, the Eisenhower administration repeatedly discussed the possibility of general war with China and the use of nuclear weapons. If he had been asked at his last press conference what was America's number-one enemy, the answer would likely have been, "Communist China."

Thus, it is fitting to devote some attention to assessing Eisenhower's experience with China. I will focus mainly on his presidency and refer just in passing to his pre-presidential experiences with China. First, I will examine some of the traditional historical views about Eisenhower and China and then review what the new documentary evidence has revealed that has allowed us to have a more sophisticated understanding. And last, I would like to launch into a somewhat

1. Press Conference of January 18, 1961, *Public Papers of the Presidents of the United States: Dwight D. Eisenhower, 1960–1961* (Washington, D.C., 1960–61), 1043.

speculative but hopefully intriguing endeavor: I will compare Dwight Eisenhower with his chief adversary, Mao Tse-tung, especially as political-military strategists.

There is one thing that the Eisenhower public record, the traditional, somewhat partisan critical view of his presidency that emerged during and immediately after his administration, and the more recent revisionist reinterpretation of Eisenhower all share in common—that is, the conviction that the former president had a particular dislike of the Chinese Communists.

Even before he became president, Eisenhower seemed to accept the conservative Republican position on China that was voiced in the late 1940s during the defeat of Nationalist leader Chiang Kai-shek in the Chinese civil war. Before a group of legislators in June, 1951, Eisenhower stated that he considered the fall of China to the Communists in 1949 to be "the greatest diplomatic defeat in this nation's history." [2] During the 1952 presidential campaign, he frequently condemned the Truman administration for "losing" China.[3] Eisenhower's view was not simply partisan, however, for he did personally harbor a special dread of Chinese communism. His image of China under communism, he privately told his cabinet during discussion of his inaugural address, was "one of claws reaching out to grab anyone who looked as though he had five cents." [4] His imagery was typical of those days in America, when Asian villains appeared as fiendish demons. From his first state of the union address, where he announced what appeared to be a major change in foreign policy, that is, the "unleashing of Chiang Kai-shek" to harass the mainland, to his visit to Taiwan where he engaged in a public love-fest with Chiang in the last months of his administration, Eisenhower gave the impression that he was a steadfast supporter of the Chinese Nationalists and implacable foe of Chinese communism.[5]

The administration's actions and statements gave no substantive hint of a contrary opinion. In his first months in office, Eisenhower ordered that word be passed to Beijing that he was considering use of atomic weapons if an armistice was not soon reached in Korea. Then in 1954, after the ceasefire, his principal national security advisers repeatedly recommended—five times in one year—that he militarily intervene again in Asia, even with the use of nuclear weapons against the Chinese mainland or along its periphery.[6] Eisenhower did not adopt

2. Blanche Wiesen Cook, *The Declassified Eisenhower: A Divided Legacy* (Garden City, N.Y., 1981), 108.

3. Stephen E. Ambrose, *Eisenhower: Soldier, General of the Army, President-Elect, 1890–1952* (New York, 1983), 530–34.

4. Robert J. Donovan, *Eisenhower: The Inside Story* (New York, 1956), 9.

5. Herbert S. Parmet, *Eisenhower and the American Crusades* (New York, 1972), 194–95.

6. Stephen E. Ambrose, *Eisenhower: The President* (New York: 1983), 213, 229.

these bellicose recommendations, for he was sensitive to the dangers of becoming involved in a land war in Asia once again, and instead he pursued other anti-Communist courses of action to maintain American interests. Still, his administration quickly gained the reputation that it was prepared to use all the weapons at its disposal to deter the threat of Chinese aggression in Asia.[7]

The two offshore island crises involving Quemoy and Matsu, in the Taiwan Strait off the China mainland, brought the United States closer to general war than perhaps any other incidents during the Eisenhower administration and became symbolic of the intransigence of the administration's general China policy. The two crises, the first lasting eight months from the fall of 1954 through the spring of 1955, and the second occurring over several weeks in 1958, had eerie similarities.[8] From the U.S. perspective, both crises were initiated by Beijing, with the probable intention of seizing clusters of islands off the mainland shore that were held by Chinese Nationalist forces. The islands were not more than a few miles away from important harbors and sea routes. In both cases, Washington feared that Communist shelling of the small bits of land presaged a possible all-out attack on Taiwan, the last redoubt of Chiang Kai-shek and his defeated remnants from the Chinese revolution. And in both cases, the United States publicly and fully committed its forces to the support of Chiang's defense of Taiwan and territories related to the defense of the island. The Eisenhower administration, in both cases, came under severe domestic and world criticism for apparently injecting the United States back into the Chinese civil war and bringing the country to the brink of war over territory of extremely dubious value. And in both cases, Eisenhower concluded that because of American resolve and display of military might, war did not occur. During the 1955 crisis, Eisenhower announced in public his opinion that he did not see why atomic weapons couldn't be used like a bullet or any other munition. It was also during this crisis that the administration gained from Congress what became known as the Formosa Resolution, which gave the president a virtual blank check for the use of American military forces in the defense of Taiwan and the related Pescadores Islands. This was a precedent-setting move that substantially eroded Congress' responsibility for committing the United States to war and opened the way for the disastrous Gulf of Tonkin Resolution in 1964.

These incidents, combined with such highly publicized events as the refusal of John Foster Dulles, Eisenhower's secretary of state, to shake Chinese pre-

7. See James Shepley, "How Dulles Averted War," *Life*, January 16, 1956.

8. The following discussion of the offshore island crises is largely based on my book *Friends and Enemies: The United States, China, and the Soviet Union, 1948-1972* (Stanford, Calif., 1990), 116–42, 182–94.

mier Chou En-lai's hand at the 1954 Geneva Conference, the administration's prohibition of American reporters from visiting China in 1956 and 1957, and Dulles' public judgment that Chinese communism was a "passing and not perpetual phase," created the impression that Eisenhower was obdurately hostile toward the People's Republic of China.[9] In contrast to the Soviet Union, with which Eisenhower had pursued serious arms control measures and with whose top leaders he had met at several summits, China seemed to be an illegitimate international pariah. It expressed no indication of a willingness to lessen its hostility, let alone consider any change from the policy of recognizing the Chiang Kai-shek government as the sole, legitimate government of the Chinese people.

Critics of the Eisenhower administration charged that its China policy was unrealistic toward the most populous country on earth and dangerously attached to an unpredictable ally in the person of Chiang Kai-shek, whose only hope to regain his former glory was through war between China and the United States. Moreover, critics, Democrats as well as some Republicans, believed that the Eisenhower hard line toward China only helped cement the Sino-Soviet alliance, a strained partnership in the eyes of some. American flexibility toward China, it was suggested, might erode the Sino-Soviet alliance by showing the Chinese there was a Western alternative to dependence upon the Soviet Union.

Historians in the 1960s and 1970s arrived at similar conclusions about the Eisenhower record on China. They interpreted the hostility as based upon an emotional and myopic anti-communism. If it had not been for Eisenhower's hard line toward China, it was charged, the United States might have been able to reduce tensions in Asia, which could have led to an earlier exploitation of Sino-Soviet tensions, an interest in which helped lead Richard Nixon to Beijing in 1972, and possibly even an avoidance of the Vietnam tragedy—America's entrance into the quagmire was to stop alleged Chinese Communist expansionism in Southeast Asia. Arthur Schlesinger, Jr., respected historian and confidant of John F. Kennedy, suggests that Eisenhower's inflexibility on China even prevented the Kennedy administration from seeking a new China policy. According to Schlesinger, Eisenhower told President-elect Kennedy, in their last meeting before the inauguration, that he hoped to support the new administration on all foreign policy issues. Eisenhower warned the new president, however, that he would return to public life if Communist China threatened to enter the United Nations.[10]

9. U.S. Department of State, *Foreign Relations of the United States, 1955–57*, III, 558–66.

10. Foster Rhea Dulles, *American Policy Toward Communist China, 1949-1969* (New York, 1972), 130–87; Adam Ulam, *Expansion and Coexistence: The History of Soviet Foreign Policy, 1917–67* (New York, 1968), 613–27; Arthur M. Schlesinger, Jr., *A Thousand Days: John F. Kennedy in the White House* (Boston, 1965), 443.

But as more of the documentation about the internal life of the Eisenhower administration becomes known, we are developing a deeper and more complex sense of Dwight Eisenhower's views of China.

Take, for example, his policy toward Nationalist China. Despite all outward appearances, the Eisenhower administration did not have an untroubled relationship with Chiang Kai-shek. In fact, Eisenhower had little regard for the Nationalist leader and found him a troubling gadfly rather than a loyal ally.[11] Eisenhower did not trust Chiang, disdained his abilities, and doubted that he would ever return to the mainland. Eisenhower's support for the Nationalists on Taiwan was unwavering, but Eisenhower never labored under the illusion, dear to the Republican conservatives and Chiang himself, that the Nationalists would soon, if ever, reverse the verdict of the Chinese revolution.

Moreover, Eisenhower carefully controlled Chiang's machinations in the offshore island area. He tried to get Chiang to reduce his garrisons on the offshore islands or withdraw from them entirely when conditions permitted. Despite his early rhetoric about "unleashing Chiang," Eisenhower kept the reins tightly on Chiang to ensure that the United States would not be drawn into a wider conflict in the region. Eisenhower's support for Chiang was part of the general policy of containment of communism but reflected no special love for the Nationalists. In turn, the evidence now shows that Chiang and the Nationalists were never at ease with Eisenhower.

As regards the Communists on the mainland, Eisenhower actually toyed with thoughts about possibly less rigid policies toward them as early as the end of the Korean War. In late 1953, he reviewed U.S. policies and mused about the seating of the Chinese Communists in the United Nations, and U.S. recognition.[12] Throughout the 1950s, he favorably discussed among his advisers the advisability of opening limited Japanese and other non-Communist trade with the mainland. Western trade might help undermine the ruling Communist group, in Ike's view, by exposing the Chinese masses to the riches of the capitalist world. Moreover, trade might also encourage fissures in the Sino-Soviet alliance.[13] The Republican line on China trade at this time was complete embargo.

What is even more interesting is that the documentary evidence now confirms what had only been quietly rumored during the Eisenhower presidency: that Eisenhower himself believed it might have been possible for the United States to encourage Communist China to break away from the Soviets. He was convinced that the Communist alliance was an unnatural one and that under the

11. The following is based largely on my *Friends and Enemies,* 81–174.
12. Ambrose, *Eisenhower,* 99.
13. Chang, *Friends and Enemies,* 106–107.

right conditions China might end its ties with the Soviets. He wondered what might bring about such a split.[14] Other immediate considerations, such as the need to continue to sustain the Chiang Kai-shek regime and the perceived threat of the growing Communist movement in Southeast Asia, blocked progress toward an improvement in U.S.-China relations. Nevertheless, Eisenhower's confirmed anti-communism did not blind him to the possibilities of exploiting intra-Communist tensions in the long run. Despite his administration's constant public railings about "international communism," Eisenhower did not assume that China and the Soviet Union composed a monolithic bloc.[15]

Regardless of its relationship with Moscow, however, Eisenhower was still deeply worried about Communist China's independent threat to American interests. Discussions in the National Security Council in March, 1959, reflected the difficulty the Eisenhower administration had with China as an independent adversary. The record of these dramatic top-level meetings has only recently been declassified.

The National Security Council was the most important body in the Eisenhower administration, and its discussions helped the president determine fundamental policies regarding war and peace. In March, 1959, the NSC discussed the wording of a major draft policy paper entitled NSC-5904, "U.S. Policy in the Event of War." The discussion centered around the question of what the United States should do in the event of general war with the Soviet Union. The State Department objected to proposed language that seemed to commit the United States to waging war automatically against the eastern bloc countries and China in the event of hostilities between the United States and the Soviet Union. Christian Herter, who had taken over the State Department after Dulles' death, argued that some of the eastern bloc countries might actually take the opportunity of general war to rebel against Soviet domination.[16]

Eisenhower, according to the record of the meeting, "immediately expressed disagreement with Secretary Herter." Eisenhower conceded that Herter might be right about the eastern bloc countries, but not about Communist China at all. According to the record, Eisenhower said, "If the U.S. got into a disastrous nuclear war with the Soviet Union and in the course of the war simply ignored Communist China, we would end up in a 'hell of a fix.'" He continued later in

14. Donovan, *Eisenhower: The Inside Story,* 132; Chang, *Friends and Enemies,* 115.

15. See David Mayers, "Eisenhower and Communism: Later Findings," in Richard A. Melanson and David Mayers, eds., *Reevaluating Eisenhower: American Foreign Policy in the Fifties* (Urbana, Ill., 1987), 88–119.

16. Summary of Discussion of the 398th meeting of the NSC, March 5, 1959, box 11, Ann Whitman NSC Series, Eisenhower Papers, in Eisenhower Library, Abilene, Kansas (hereinafter cited as EL).

the meeting, saying that he could not foresee the United States becoming involved in an all-out nuclear war with Moscow and permitting Beijing to stay on the sidelines to "develop, after perhaps forty years, into another Soviet Union." Eisenhower drew a sharp distinction between the eastern bloc countries and China, which was a "willing partner" in international communism, in his view. Even if China sat out a war between the United States and the Soviet Union, the president said, the United States would have to "disarm and remove the threat of Communist China. We simply could not just ignore a Communist China which remained untouched and intact. . . . To do so would be unrealistic in the extreme." The essential thing, Eisenhower pointed out, was that in the event of general war, the United States had to ensure that both the USSR and China were "incapable of further harming the U.S. after the end of hostilities." Eisenhower's argument did not assume that China would automatically enter hostilities with the Soviets against the United States; rather, he assumed its independence from Moscow.

Even though Eisenhower had thought he had made himself clear, the discussion continued at the next NSC meeting on the same topic. Again, Eisenhower made the same points as he had in the earlier meeting. The result of these harrowing discussions was that U.S. policy drew a clear distinction between the Soviet Union and China on the one hand and the eastern bloc countries on the other. The final position paper included a notation that was sanguinary in its implications: "It is assumed that the peoples of the Bloc countries other than the USSR and Communist China are not responsible for the acts of their governments and accordingly so far as consistent with military objectives military action against these countries should avoid non-military destruction and casualties." Unstated but obvious, however, is that the U.S. military would not be hampered by concerns for civilian death and destruction in war against the Soviet Union and China.[17]

This discussion helps explain, if Eisenhower was privately willing to consider more flexible policies toward the mainland, why there was no change in the implacable policy toward China. For one, Eisenhower's comments about a change in China policy among his associates within the administration never amounted to more than musings, and much more on Eisenhower's mind was the independent threat China represented to American interests. There were also other

17. Summary of Discussion of the 399th meeting of the NSC, March 12, 1959, box 11, Ann Whitman NSC Series, Eisenhower Papers, EL. There was no discussion in the NSC on this occasion about whether the United States would have to take on the Soviet Union if there was war with China. During the offshore island crises of 1955 and 1958, administration officials contemplated war with China, but did not assume that the Soviets would become directly involved.

important interests and concerns. The United States could not simply jettison Chiang on Taiwan, and mainland China itself seemed wedded to a policy of hostility toward the United States. Eisenhower knew it took two to tango, and Beijing was still in no mood to dance.

Nevertheless, Eisenhower kept open the possibility for an eventual two-China solution, a solution whereby the United States would be able to deal with the Communist government on the mainland of China and the Nationalist government on Taiwan as separate entities. Eisenhower did not believe that Chiang Kai-shek represented the Chinese people and even anticipated eventual recognition of the mainland government. A so-called two-China solution was anathema to both the Communists and Nationalists (each claimed it was the sole, legitimate government of the Chinese people), but it was what the Eisenhower administration quietly prepared the way for.[18]

All in all, Eisenhower remained wary of both Chinese and Nationalist Chinese. One suspects that this caution profoundly colored his assessment of U.S-China relations and made him reluctant to take initiatives relating to the China area. Eisenhower's suspicion was itself rooted in an American attitude of superiority that looked down upon nonwhite peoples of the world. Eisenhower was at best insensitive to the condition of blacks in America, and was known to engage in racial jokes as president. He believed in a racial hierarchy of humankind.[19] On a number of occasions he expressed his belief that Orientals were devious and thought in ways profoundly different than Westerners.[20] Eisenhower's attitudes were linked, in fact, to his close association with Asia during the first part of his military career, and here it might be useful to review some of Eisenhower's early experiences with Asia.

Although Eisenhower is better known for his career in Europe, he had become familiar with much of Asia before World War II. Near the end of his life, Eisenhower recalled that it was an event in Asia that first awakened him to the reality beyond his home and Kansas. He remembered his uncle Abraham Lincoln Eisenhower's "glee" in hearing the news of Commodore Perry's victory over the Spanish fleet in Manila Bay during the Spanish-American War. As Eisenhower wrote, "I do not know just what day we got the news in Abilene but the smell of gunpowder and victory was in Uncle Abe's nostrils."[21] Perhaps it was

18. Nancy B. Tucker, "John Foster Dulles and the Taiwan Roots of the 'Two Chinas' Policy," in *John Foster Dulles and the Diplomacy of the Cold War,* ed. Richard Immerman (Princeton, N.J., 1990), 235–62; Chang, *Friends and Enemies,* 144–49.

19. Harold R. Isaacs, *The New World of Negro Americans* (New York, 1964), 45–46; Michael H. Hunt, *Ideology and U.S. Foreign Policy* (New Haven, Conn., 1987), 162–64; Chang, *Friends and Enemies,* 170–74.

20. Ambrose, *Eisenhower,* 102, 125–26; Chang, *Friends and Enemies,* 171–72.

21. Dwight D. Eisenhower, *At Ease: Stories I Tell to Friends* (Garden City, N.Y., 1967), 65.

that memory that inspired the West Point cadet Eisenhower to seek a post in the Philippines, perhaps the lowest priority in terms of preference among cadets. In 1935, at the age of forty-five, he finally got his wish and was stationed for four years in the Philippines with the staff of Douglas MacArthur.[22] These years were the heyday of American colonialism in the Philippines, and Eisenhower was likely affected by the attendant racism. His personal diaries at the time contain expressions of impatient frustration with Filipinos. He observed with exasperation that while in the Philippines he had "learned to expect from the Filipinos . . . a minimum of performance from a maximum of promise."[23]

While in Asia, he also had the opportunity to visit China itself in 1938 and again in 1946. From January to March, 1942, he was deputy chief for the Pacific and Far East, a position which was concerned with strategic planning and operations of the war in Asia. After the war, as chief of staff of the Army, he was well aware of the difficulties of the Marshall mission to China and visited Nanking in May, 1946.[24] During these trips it seems that Eisenhower developed impressions he kept for life. For one, he was struck by China's huge population. He, like many of his generation, saw China's masses as an ominous and threatening horde, a yellow peril. "China is a great mass of human beings, hundreds of millions," he observed as president. "Those of you who have traveled through China I know have been as astonished as I have that so many people could live in such a space." As he later stated in his memoirs, China's leaders were "absolutely indifferent to the prospect of losing millions of people" and that the Chinese held "peculiar attitudes" toward human life.[25] With such beliefs about the Chinese, it is no wonder that Eisenhower expected the worst from Asia throughout his life.

In closing, I want to explore a topic that might sound offbeat, but which I think may be intriguing. I want to compare Dwight Eisenhower and Mao Tse-tung, protagonists in the 1950s. Historians often compare leaders like Churchill and Roosevelt, Stalin and Hitler, but as far as I know there has been no effort to compare Ike and Chairman Mao; perhaps the immense contrast between the two men appears so great that one might assume that an effort at comparison

22. Eisenhower, *At Ease,* 111, 229–30.

23. Robert H. Ferrell, ed., *The Eisenhower Diaries* (New York, 1981), 11–12, 23–26; Ambrose, *Eisenhower,* 125.

24. Alfred D. Chandler, Jr., ed., *The Papers of Dwight D. Eisenhower: The War Years* (Baltimore, Md., 1981), I, 180ff.

25. *Public Papers of the Presidents of the United States: Dwight D. Eisenhower, 1954* (Washington, D.C., 1955), 182; Dwight D. Eisenhower, *The White House Years: Waging Peace* (Garden City, N.Y., 1965), 369.

would be futile if not facile.[26] The popular image of Ike is that he was rather bland, colorless, a company man, unlike Mao, who is thought of as a charismatic revolutionary and messianic tyrant. But a comparison of the two helps highlight the qualities of the two leaders and may even help explain why the two countries under their respective leadership became such bitter enemies.

To begin with, one finds some remarkable parallels in their early personal lives. They were of almost the same age: Ike was born in 1890 and died in 1969; Mao was born in 1893 and died in 1976. They were both products of small communities in their countries' heartlands: Kansas and its wheat, Mao's Hunan Province and its rice. Their families were linked to the land, frugal, and somewhat better off than many others in their communities. They were not poor but neither were they prosperous. Their fathers were authoritarian, distant, prone to beating their children, and apparently unliked. Their mothers were kindly and, in the recollections of the two men, the greater parental influence on them.[27] As young men, both were preoccupied with their physical strength, exercised assiduously, and associated early with the military. Mao was a private in a revolutionary army at the age of eighteen, two years younger than Ike when he entered West Point.[28] Both men then devoted the rest of their lives to what one might loosely call public life: For Ike, it was the U.S. Army, supreme command of European Allied forces in World War II, and then the presidency of the United States in 1952; for Mao it was the Communist party, the Chinese revolution, which was mainly a military struggle, and then the chairman of the People's Republic of China in 1949. Both men coincidentally also had brief but important experiences with university life, Ike with Columbia and Mao with Peking University.

One could go on to compare further their upbringings, marriages, personal lives, military careers, associations with friends and colleagues, work methods, and so on. There are some fascinating comparisons, in fact. I was intrigued, for example, by Stephen Ambrose's description of Ike in the introduction of the second volume of his two-volume biography of Eisenhower. Ambrose writes (one might mentally substitute "Mao" for Ike's name in the following passage):

> Eisenhower is at the center of events. Just as in Overlord, when he was the funnel through which everything had to pass, the one man who was responsible for the whole operation, so too as President, he was the one man who could weigh all the

26. Mao Tse-tung's name does not even appear in the indexes of two of the major biographies of Eisenhower. See Parmet, *Eisenhower and the American Crusades,* and Ambrose, *Eisenhower.*

27. On Ike's childhood, see Ambrose, *Eisenhower,* 13–36; on Mao, see Edgar Snow, *Red Star over China* (New York, 1968), 126–38.

28. See Stuart Shram, *Mao Tse-tung* (New York, 1967), 34–37.

factors in any one decision—the political repercussions, the effect on foreign policy, the economic consequences, and the myriad of other considerations involved—before acting. . . .

[Eisenhower] wanted to be in the position in which he could have a maximum influence on events. He liked making decisions. The primary reason was that he had such complete self-confidence that he was certain he was the best man in the country to make the decisions.[29]

But what I would like to focus on here is some comparison of Ike and Mao as strategists. By strategist I mean one who is concerned with the relationship of military means and national political ends. The extraordinary military careers of the two men gave them unique qualities as political leaders and later as adversaries when they were the leaders of their countries.[30] Roosevelt, Truman, Kennedy, and all other modern-day presidents of the United States had no comparable military experience to Eisenhower's; nor did Churchill, Stalin, or Khrushchev have either Ike's or Mao's field, organizational, and command experience leading millions of soldiers.

What we know about Mao and his work as the leader of China is rather limited, certainly considerably less than what we know about Ike. Nevertheless, some general comparisons of the men as strategists can be advanced. First, perhaps one obvious but not trivial observation can be made: Neither man was mystified by the military and what military force could and could not do. Both clearly understood that military considerations were always subordinate to political ends. One of Mao's best-known aphorisms was that the party always commands the gun.[31] Throughout his career, he frequently had to oppose what was called the purely military point of view in the revolution. Ike too was never intimidated by his military advisers during his administration. He felt no hesitation in rejecting their advice—a man with less military experience might not have been as confident in his own opinion and decisons to buck the military professionals.[32] Both men refused to accept the recommendations of their military commanders during confrontations in the Taiwan Strait, for example, and kept decisions about the operations in their own hands.[33]

29. Ambrose, *Eisenhower*, 9–10.

30. See Kenneth W. Thompson, "The Strengths and Weaknesses of Eisenhower's Leadership," in *Reevaluating Eisenhower*, ed. Melanson and Mayers, 17–25.

31. See John Shy and Thomas W. Collier, "Revolutionary War," in *Makers of Modern Strategy* ed. Peter Paret (Princeton, N.J., 1986), 839. Also see Arthur Huck, *The Security of China: Chinese Approaches to Problems of War and Strategy* (New York, 1970), 53–65; Chong-pin Lin, *China's Nuclear Weapons Strategy: Tradition Within Evolution* (Lexington, Ky., 1988), 18–21.

32. For a comparison of Eisenhower and Kennedy, see Ambrose, *Eisenhower*, 638.

33. Eisenhower occasionally became involved in decision making concerning specific military

All the same, both men understood the efficacy of the use of military means to achieve specific national security purposes and were not hesitant to use military force or the threat of military force to achieve specific ends. One thinks of Ike's threatened use of the atomic bomb to end the Korean War, his deployment of the Marines in Lebanon, and the CIA in Iran, Guatemala, and elsewhere. Of the evidence we now have, we also know that Mao employed military force in the Taiwan Strait less to achieve traditional military ends, such as gaining territory, than as a political instrument to probe the state of Nationalist China–U.S. relations.

Ike and Mao, as strategists, were also both keenly sensitive to popular opinion and actively sought in their own ways to cultivate domestic support and influence world public opinion. In the 1950s, both generally remained widely popular at home, which permitted them to pursue foreign policy aims with fewer constraints than other leaders would later face in China and in the United States. But Ike and Mao understood they were international leaders, who by their spoken word and gesture could influence millions around the world. Mao had messianic claims, and Eisenhower too was acutely sensitive about his public image, his legacy to history, and his responsibility as leader of the "free world."

Closely linked to this sensitivity to public opinion was their attention to what one might call the psychological aspect of international politics. Mao was a master in conducting psychological-political warfare during the revolution—his writings are full of essays concerning propaganda, ideological, and cultural work. Mao's concern for these areas came from his conviction that the human element was central in the conduct of war, both in leading one's own forces and in defeating the enemy. On his part, Ike was the first American president to make psychological warfare a regular and high-level instrument of foreign policy.

And perhaps because of this sensitivity to the psychology of politics, both Mao and Ike favored cultivating deliberate ambiguity in their military and political campaigns, especially in the several crises between the United States and China in the 1950s. It has never been completely clear why and for what purposes Beijing initiated the two offshore island crises in 1955 and 1958. On the other hand, Eisenhower also tried to maintain a degree of ambiguity in America's commitment to Chiang Kai-shek. Ike maintained this flexibility in opposition to the almost universal opinion of his military and political advisers, who wanted the president to define explicitly what the United States would or would not do given certain conditions.

matters, such as gun emplacements, weaponry, and tactics to oppose landing forces. See Goodpaster notes of March, 1955, NSC Meeting, 16 March 1955, Ann Whitman International Series, box 9, Formosa, Visit to CINCPAC [1955] (1), in EL.

There is another fascinating comparison of the two leaders concerning the basic relationship of war and peace. The Eisenhower administration is known for practicing what was called "brinkmanship," taking the country to the verge of war to achieve political ends and, paradoxically, it seemed, to maintain peace. Dulles explained this philosophy: "The ability to get to the verge without getting into war is the necessary art. If you cannot master it, you inevitably get into war. If you try to run away from it, if you are scared to go to the brink, you are lost." [34]

Mao's statement about imperialism and the atom bomb being "paper tigers" is similarly inspired. By paper tigers, Mao meant that war and the atom bomb were real threats and could kill people; one had to take them seriously *tactically*. But Mao encouraged his followers to despise war and the enemy *strategically*, firmly believing such an attitude was necessary to deflate the arrogance of the enemy and deter his threat. If, on the other hand, one is intimidated by the enemy and the threat of war, one is already defeated. [35] The conduct of the two offshore island crises, which brought the two countries to the edge of war but were both firmly controlled by their leaders, is evidence of this philosophy. In a sense, their strategic sensibilities were mirror images of one another. [36]

One, of course, can overstate the parallels of Ike and Mao as strategists. Ike's strategic approach was largely characteristic of Western traditions in strategy. He emphasized the massing of immense firepower and the efficacy of weaponry, nuclear or conventional, in war. As he stated on several occasions, one should avoid war, but if one must go to war, one should go into it with no holds barred, believing that firepower was decisive. [37] As president, he tended to make firm distinctions between war and peace, offense and defense, and enemy and friendly

34. Shepley, "How Dulles Averted War." Eisenhower himself once said about fearing war, "I have one great belief; nobody in war or anywhere else ever made a good decision if he was frightened to death. You have to look facts in the face, but you have to have the stamina to do it without just going hysterical." He made this statement during the 1955 offshore island crisis. Ambrose, *Eisenhower*, 239.

35. Mao Tse-tung, "Talk with the American Correspondent Anna Louise Strong," in *Selected Readings* (Peking, 1971), 345–51. Also see Mao Tse-tung, "Problems of Strategy in China's Revolutionary War," in *Selected Works* (Peking, 1963), I, 233–39.

36. Eisenhower and Mao never had any direct contact with one another. Eisenhower's public comments about Mao were always predictably disparaging. What Mao's opinions were of Eisenhower, one can only speculate. However, Mao once said to Richard Nixon, during his first trip to China, that he, Mao, liked "rightists. . . . I am comparatively happy when these people on the right come into power" (Richard Nixon, *Memoirs* [New York, 1978], 562). Mao was being his usual cryptic self, although on other occasions he suggested a reason for his preference: Rightists were less deceptive than liberals and seemed to represent the monopoly capitalists more openly.

37. *Ibid.*, 376–77.

positions. He tended to see the holding and winning of territory as decisive and a zero-sum game.

Mao, in the Asian tradition of strategy, emphasized man over weapons, deception, and fluidity. Chinese strategists historically blurred the distinctions between war and peace, offense and defense, and interior and exterior lines. Territory was less important than time and psychological advantage.

The differences between Ike and Mao reflect in many ways the different philosophies of Clausewitz, the most famous Western thinker of war and strategy who lived in the nineteenth century, and Sun-tzu, China's most important strategist, who lived around 500 B.C., the time of Confucius. Mao was familiar with both. To give you just a taste of the philosophy of Sun-tzu, let me quote a brief passage from his treatise, *The Art of War:* "Now an army may be likened to water, for just as flowing water avoids the heights and hastens to the lowlands, so an army avoids strength and strikes weakness. And as water shapes its flow in accordance with the ground, so an army manages its victory in accordance with the situation of the enemy. And as water has no constant form, there are in war no constant conditions."[38] Water is the metaphor for the army in Asian military thought, while steel is usually the metaphor in Western conceptions.

Lastly, I also wonder if the differences between the two men derive from the fundamentally different strategic positions of the United States and China. Eisenhower's responsibility in World War II was to restore the predominance of the United States and then as president to maintain its global hegemony. Mao was a revolutionary his entire life; he devoted the first half of his life to seizing power and then to constructing a radical socialist society and elevating China in the family of nations. Eisenhower was preeminently a leader of the status quo; Mao was never content with the status quo, even after the revolution.

Despite these immense differences in military tradition, strategic position, and personal temperament, there are some intriguing comparisons, as I have tried to point out. One wonders to what extent these parallels contributed to the animosity in U.S.-China relations in the 1950s. The legacy of Korea, the foment in Indochina, and the continuing Chinese civil war in the Taiwan Strait were fundamental sources of conflict, certainly. But Mao and Ike were also strangely contrasting and certainly capable adversaries. Their strategic approaches, similar as they may have been in odd ways, may have unwittingly heightened tensions and frustrations on both sides. And yet, with good fortune, after Korea, neither Dwight Eisenhower or Mao Tse-tung again committed his armed forces to wage war against those of his formidable opponent.

There is one last thing the two men shared and which linked them in an

38. Sun Tzu, *The Art of War,* trans. Samuel B. Griffith (New York, 1963), 101.

ironic way: They both played a major role in the life of another man who helped change the geopolitical complexion of the world. Eisenhower and Mao both contributed to building the career of a man named Richard M. Nixon.

Thomas A. Schwartz

Eisenhower and the Germans

I n light of two recent events, the subject of Dwight David Eisenhower and his relationship to his wartime enemy and subsequent peacetime ally, the German people, is particularly appropriate. Indeed, these two events have had a considerable impact on the content of this article, both in interpretation and emphasis. The first event is the peaceful reunification of Germany in October, 1990. Before November 9, 1989, the day the Berlin Wall came down, no one would have predicted German reunification taking place in 1990, the year of the Eisenhower centenary. To students of America's diplomatic history, the Eisenhower administration is recognized as having made the German question one of the central elements of its foreign policy, and the close relationship between the Presbyterian secretary of state, John Foster Dulles, and the German Catholic chancellor, Konrad Adenauer, came to symbolize the religious and crusading character of the cold war of the 1950s. Most important, President Eisenhower and Secretary Dulles were strong supporters of Germany's reunification within the NATO alliance, a policy attacked at the time and since as either duplicitous or, at best, "fatally inconsistent."[1] Many German historians, such as Rolf Steininger and Josef Foschepoth, have argued that the Eisenhower administration's refusal to consider a neutral, demilitarized Germany prevented the reunification of their country and perpetuated the division of Europe.[2] Whether the events of 1989 and 1990 will affect this interpretation is unclear—after all, a reunified Germany is now a member of NATO, the position that critics of Eisenhower thought was unrealistic—but the argument that the Eisenhower administration's policies intensified the cold war and the division of Germany is likely to remain.

The second event deals more directly and personally with Eisenhower and has generated considerable controversy. In the recently published book *Other Losses,* James Bacque charges that Eisenhower, as head of the American mili-

1. Anne Marie Burley, "Restoration and Reunification: Eisenhower's German Policy," in *Reevaluating Eisenhower,* ed. Richard A. Melanson and David Mayers (Urbana, Ill., 1987), 220–38.

2. For a recent statement of Steininger's views, now translated into English, see Rolf Steininger, *The German Question* (New York, 1990).

tary occupation in 1945, deliberately allowed the starvation of up to one million captured German soldiers in the immediate aftermath of the war.[3] This is a crime that Bacque compares to those of the Nazi regime itself. The dramatic nature of the book's charges earned for it enormous publicity, including television documentaries in Britain, Canada, and Germany. However, Eisenhower's biographer Stephen Ambrose, reporting on the results of a recent conference of experts convened to examine Bacque's book, reports that the "work is worse than worthless," a book that is "spectacularly flawed in its most fundamental aspects."[4]

Nevertheless, the juxtaposition of the two events highlights the extraordinary change that took place in American foreign policy toward Germany in the years after 1945, a change in which General and then President Eisenhower was deeply involved. The United States reversed its policy toward Germany almost 180 degrees within three years' time, and went from bombing Germany and killing Germans—something that Eisenhower did quite well and with the approval of his countrymen—to protecting the city of Berlin from the Russian blockade, incorporating West Germany in the Atlantic alliance, and making the reunification of Germany a major demand of American foreign policy, something Eisenhower also did quite well and with the approval of his countrymen, both as NATO supreme commander and president.

This essay will attempt to explore two aspects of Eisenhower's relationship to the Germans. The first aspect will be the central issues involved in the diplomatic relationship between the United States and the Federal Republic of Germany during Eisenhower's presidency. Many of these issues, such as German rearmament, membership in NATO, the role of nuclear weapons, the crises over Berlin, reunification, and neutrality, have provoked heated debate among diplomatic historians. The second aspect that the essay will reflect on is the personal and biographical element in Eisenhower's relations with the Germans, in which one can discern a profound ambivalence toward Germany and the Germans. Eisenhower had immense admiration for the achievements of Germany and yet a deeply felt disgust with Nazi barbarity. Dealing with the dynamism and power of Germany—for good and for evil—would mark much of Eisenhower's public career.

Although it may be dangerous to make too much of this, Eisenhower was himself of German descent. The Eisenhower family could trace its ancestry to the

---

3. James Bacque, *Other Losses* (London, 1990).

4. Stephen E. Ambrose, "Ike and the Disappearing Atrocities," *New York Times Book Review,* February 24, 1991, p. 35. See also the recent volume, Günter Bischof and Stephen E. Ambrose, eds., *Eisenhower and the German POWs: Facts Against Falsehood* (Baton Rouge, 1992).

region of western Germany known as the Palatinate, with the name stemming from *Eisenhauer,* meaning iron hewer or ironsmith. Eisenhower's German ancestry was on both sides of the family; his mother's maiden name was Stover and her family also came from the Palatinate. Eisenhower's ancestors came to America in the 1740s both to escape the religious persecution of their Mennonite, pacifist sect and to seek economic opportunity.[5] They settled in the ethnically and religiously heterogeneous colony of Pennsylvania, becoming part of the Pennsylvania Dutch (or more accurately, Deutsch), which constituted almost a third of the young colony's population. By 1790, the family name had been Anglicized and appeared in the first American census.

Dwight Eisenhower was not far removed from the German background of his family. His grandfather, Jacob, the familial patriarch, preached his sermons in German to the River Brethren, their sect of Mennonites, and it was Jacob who moved the three hundred members to Abilene, Kansas. Eisenhower's father, David, could read and speak German, but refused to do so around the house. (He himself broke from the family tradition by attending college to study engineering.) He gave no encouragement to his sons to study German. As one of Eisenhower's earliest biographers, Kenneth Davis, put it, David seems "to have deliberately cut the ties of language and, to some extent of custom, which bound him to the Old World. He wanted his children to be, in quite an exclusive sense, American."[6]

Whether one can draw any conclusions about Eisenhower's later perspectives on the Germans from his family background and ancestry is difficult to say. It is clear that Ike always thought of himself as an American and rarely noted or commented upon his German background. But it is worth noting this connection, because for a man of Eisenhower's generation, for whom conflict with Germany would mark his life, his ethnic origins must have seemed a bitter irony.

Eisenhower's early military career brought him little contact with modern Germany.[7] In the First World War he was bitterly disappointed that his orders to go overseas arrived at the same time as the November, 1918, armistice. He spent

5. Kenneth S. Davis, *Soldier of Democracy* (Garden City, N.Y., 1945), 10–11. This early biography of Eisenhower has the most detailed treatment of Ike's German roots.

6. *Ibid.,* 49.

7. Eisenhower's choice of careers also broke decisively with the pacifism of the River Brethren, and contains a certain degree of ambivalence toward Germany. On the one hand, his chief concern as a member of the military would be to defeat Germany in two world wars. On the other hand, the American military he joined venerated the models provided by Germany, especially the coordination and teamwork displayed by the German General Staff. Eisenhower's subsequent insistence on the elimination of the German General Staff in 1945 may have been influenced by this knowledge.

the interwar years in various postings in Panama, Washington, and the Philippines, with only a year's stay in Paris in the late 1920s. Far removed from the European scene, Eisenhower rarely commented on the events of this troubled time. But when Germany invaded Poland in 1939, Eisenhower's observation turned out to be particularly prophetic. In a letter to his brother Milton from the distant outpost of Manila, Eisenhower blamed the war on Hitler, the "power-drunk egocentric . . . one of the criminally insane" and predicted that "unless [Hitler] is successful in overcoming the whole world by brute force, the final result will be that Germany will have to be dismembered." [8]

During the war, Eisenhower developed an intense hatred of Nazi Germany and the Germans. He expected the Germans to fight to the bitter end, an expectation that Ambrose credits, at least in part, to Ike's knowledge of his stubborn and never-quit "German heritage." [9] But as admirable as German tenacity might be in the abstract, in war it brought only more destruction and death. In the summer of 1944, in a letter to his wife, Eisenhower wrote, "Don't be misled by the papers. Every victory is sweet—but the end of the war will only come with the complete destruction of the HUN forces. . . . There is still a lot of suffering to go through. God I hate the Germans." [10] Eisenhower expected German resistance to last well beyond any rational point, and even expected that his army would be faced with guerilla resistance in Germany after the occupation.

His hatred only increased as American forces entered Germany and he saw firsthand the results of German rule. On April 15, 1945, he wrote Mamie that "the other day I visited a German internment camp. . . . I never dreamed that such cruelty, bestiality, and savagery could really exist in this world! It was horrible." [11] He told General Marshall that he insisted on seeing the camps personally to be in a position to refute any future charges of "propaganda," and he saw to it that reporters and visiting dignitaries saw the same evidence. [12] At the surrender of the German Army, Eisenhower refused to shake hands with the defeated German generals. In his book *Crusade in Europe,* the general denounced the custom of treating all professional soldiers as "comrades in arms," adding that "for me World War II was far too personal a thing to entertain such feelings. . . . Never before [were] the forces that stood for human good and men's rights . . .

8. Kevin McCann, *Man from Abilene* (Garden City, N.Y., 1952), 52–53.
9. Stephen E. Ambrose, *Eisenhower: The President* (New York, 1983), 332.
10. John S. D. Eisenhower, ed., *Letters to Mamie* (Garden City, N.Y., 1978), 204, 210.
11. *Ibid.,* 248.
12. Ambrose, *Eisenhower,* 400.

confronted by a completely evil conspiracy with which no compromise could be tolerated. . . . Only by utter destruction of the Axis was a decent world possible." [13]

Proceeding from these attitudes, Eisenhower favored a hard peace with the defeated Reich. Although he was not the author of the Morgenthau Plan—a plan that among other things called for the destruction of Germany's industry and its reduction to a pastoral or agricultural state—Henry Morgenthau, the secretary of the treasury, claimed that he had gotten some of his ideas from a conversation with Eisenhower in August, 1944. Morgenthau put his plan in a book, *Germany Is Our Problem,* and sent it to Eisenhower in October, 1945, with the signed inscription that he hoped the book "may be of some assistance to you in solving the German problem." [14] Eisenhower promised to read it immediately and had a thousand copies sent to various members of military government. The general later explained that while he had not favored "pastoralization of Germany," he believed that "the German people must not be allowed to escape a personal sense of guilt" and that Germany's war-making capability and the German General Staff needed to be "utterly eliminated. [15]

Not only did Eisenhower favor a hard peace but he also had no sympathy for those who argued that the Allies should use the surrendering German soldiers as part of an anti-Communist drive against the Soviet Union. The general was convinced that four-power cooperation would be the basis for future peace, and that good relations with the Russians were essential. This conviction led to his decision to refuse to rush toward Berlin and to reject Churchill's suggestion that he delay the withdrawal of American soldiers from East Germany to the lines of their occupation zone. Eisenhower, as Ambrose has put it, was eager to show "good will" toward the Russians. [16] Only a few years later, Ike would try to claim that he recognized the beginnings of the cold war in Russian behavior and had warned against the impracticality of the occupation arrangements. In fact, Eisenhower believed in the possibility of such cooperation and sought to make it work. The same held true for the man who served Eisenhower in Germany, Lucius D. Clay. In a recently published biography, Jean Edward Smith argues

13. Dwight D. Eisenhower, *Crusade in Europe* (Garden City, N.Y., 1948), 156–57.

14. A reproduction of this signed inscription can be found in Manfred Pohl, *Wiederaufbau* (Frankfurt, 1973), 226. There is some irony in the fate of the book that Morgenthau gave to Eisenhower. Through a quirk of fate that is still somewhat mysterious, the book ended up in the possession of Hermann J. Abs, one of the leading German bankers and an architect of Germany's recovery after the war. It became a possession that Abs prized and was quite pleased to show young graduate students. Personal interview with Hermann J. Abs, Frankfurt, June 16, 1983.

15. Ambrose, *Eisenhower,* 422.

16. *Ibid.,* 401.

strenuously that Clay followed the same path as Eisenhower, hoping that American military cooperation with the Soviet Union would have "a happy and definite effect upon the whole question of whether communism and democracy could find a way to get along in the same world." [17]

General Clay did influence Ike in softening some of his views on the occupation, particularly the nonfraternization decrees and the question of rebuilding certain German industries. Clay told Eisenhower that some industrial recovery in Germany would be essential to European recovery. However, Eisenhower remained absolutely convinced of the necessity of wide-scale de-Nazification—a position that would lead him to remove General Patton as commander of the Third Army when Patton said, "The Nazi thing is just like a Democratic and Republican election fight." Eisenhower remained adamant, telling Patton that "the United States entered this war as a foe of Nazism; victory is not complete until we have eliminated from positions of responsibility and in appropriate cases properly punished, every active adherent to the Nazi Party." [18]

During the war, Eisenhower had been willing to collaborate with unsavory characters such as Admiral Darlan and the Vichy regime in North Africa. With the Germans he seemed to hold to a rigid and unbending determination to root out Nazism. But even here Eisenhower's incurable optimism and perhaps his ambivalence about his ethnic ancestors came to expression. In a speech given in Frankfurt on October 1, 1945, shortly before leaving Germany, Eisenhower said, "The success or failure of this occupation will be judged by the character of the Germans 50 years from now. Proof will come when they begin to run a democracy of their own and we are going to give the Germans a chance to do that, in time." [19] Even Eisenhower would be surprised by how quickly "in time" would turn out to be.

After he left Europe in 1945, and over the next five years, as the army's chief of staff and then president of Columbia University, Eisenhower kept abreast with the rapid change in American thinking toward the Soviet Union. As Soviet behavior in Eastern Europe and elsewhere soured Americans on cooperation with the Kremlin, and as the Germans seemed to support American policy in their actions during the Berlin blockade, Eisenhower's views changed as well. He told a Council on Foreign Relations study group that the United States could not treat West Germany as a neutral state, as this would drive that country into the arms of the Soviet Union and increase the number of enemies facing America. [20]

17. Jean Edward Smith, *Lucius D. Clay: An American Life* (New York, 1990), 253.

18. Ambrose, *Eisenhower*, 423.

19. Eisenhower, as quoted in Burley, "Restoration and Reunification," 237.

20. Michael Wala, *Winning the Peace: Amerikanische Aussenpolitik und der Council on Foreign Relations, 1945–1950* (Stuttgart, 1990), 167.

He attempted to revise his earlier positions on such issues as the Morgenthau Plan and four-power control in Germany, making it appear that he had known all along that cooperation with the Russians was hopeless.

In late 1950, after the outbreak of the Korean War, Truman turned to Eisenhower to become NATO's first supreme commander. In that position one of the first problems Eisenhower faced was the harsh controversy over the American demand for—and the French opposition to—the rearmament of West Germany. The Americans argued that Europe could not be defended without the Germans, and that one could not expect American soldiers to be committed to such an indefensible position. In reply, the French contended that it was too early—only five years—to talk about rearming the Germans, and that such a new German Army risked provoking war with the Soviet Union. The sharp crisis within the alliance affected German public opinion as well, where considerable numbers either rejected rearmament completely or sought to use the American demand to extort more concessions from the West.[21]

Although he wanted to bring Germany into the Western fold, Eisenhower thought the Truman administration had bungled the approach to German rearmament. The American demand had allowed the Germans to "blackmail" the West. Eisenhower worried that Americans had "been talking too much about [the Germans] and have made them cocky about their importance in the picture." A less zealous courtship would find the Germans "anxious to get in on the side of Western Europe."[22] Eisenhower was determined not to be an overly anxious suitor. When in January, 1951, the general went to Europe on a morale-raising tour, he initially refused to go to Germany. Only reluctantly, and at the urgent request of High Commissioner John McCloy, did Eisenhower change his itinerary and agree to visit. Once in Bonn, however, his personal demeanor and warmth conveyed his acceptance of the Germans as a potential ally. Eisenhower even made it a point to shake hands with former generals Hans Speidel and Adolf Heusinger, Chancellor Konrad Adenauer's new military advisers.[23] The American affirmed publicly that he had "come to know that there is a real difference between the regular German soldier and officer and Hitler and his criminal group. . . . For my part, I do not believe that the German soldier as such

21. Thomas Alan Schwartz, *America's Germany: John J. McCloy and the Federal Republic of Germany* (Cambridge, Mass., 1991), 145–49.

22. Eisenhower's comments were made in his report to the cabinet. Meeting of the Cabinet, January 31, 1951, Matthew J. Connelly Papers, box 1, in Harry S. Truman Library, Independence, Missouri.

23. Hans Speidel, *Aus unserer Zeit: Erinnerungen* (Berlin, 1977), 285–86. Eisenhower approached the two Germans and said, "Ah, the generals," and shook their hands. Speidel recounted that this small gesture had brought a "certain reconciliation" almost immediately.

had lost his honor." While certain individuals had committed "despicable acts," this did not reflect on the "great majority of German soldiers and officers." Eisenhower also told the Germans that despite his hatred of Germany in the last war, he was now prepared to say, "Let bygones be bygones." [24]

Although Eisenhower's statements about the German Army scored some political points, they were not historically accurate. Historians have effectively demolished the older argument that the Wehrmacht fought the honorable fight while the SS alone committed atrocities. The Wehrmacht was both involved in, and acquiesced toward, Nazi atrocities. [25] The July 20 plot against Hitler, in which men like Speidel were associated, provided the basis for the rehabilitation of German soldiery, a rehabilitation that involved suppressing many unpleasant realities about the Wehrmacht's behavior. In Eisenhower's defense, one must remember that much of the proof of such behavior was not brought out until the 1960s. However, his cavalier absolution of the Germans may have been more harmful. Coupled with McCloy's pardoning of several war criminals only a week later, the American behavior helped legitimate a German desire to bury the Nazi past. For much of the 1950s, the United States demonstrated relatively little interest in the continued pursuit and prosecution of Nazi war criminals, and did not encourage the Germans in the difficult task of "coming to terms with the past" ("Vergangenheitsbewältigung").

Eisenhower also assured German leaders that he "would not tolerate second class membership" in any army that he led, and that the German contribution would have to be made "on a free will basis without any pressure from outside." [26] Eisenhower said he wanted no "hired mercenaries" or, as he put it, "no Hessians." (This was a peculiar way to express the concern, but reflective of how thoroughgoing Ike's Americanization was that he failed to appreciate the irony of such words to a German audience.) [27] Eisenhower also reaffirmed his interest in German soldiers, but emphasized that "a political base must be established for the German nation, which would enable the German people to wholeheartedly support a German contribution." [28] The general worked closely with McCloy to

24. U.S. Department of State, *Foreign Relations of the United States, 1951*, III, 446 (hereinafter cited as *FRUS, 1951*) and Eisenhower Press Conference, January 20, 1951, Pre-Presidential Correspondence, 16–52, folder McCloy, box 75, Eisenhower Library, Abilene, Kansas (hereinafter cited as PPC and EL).

25. Jürgen Förster, "The Wehrmacht and the War of Extermination Against the Soviet Union," *Yad Vashem Studies*, XIV (1981), 7–34, and Volker R. Berghahn, "Wehrmacht und Nationalsozialismus," *Neue Politische Literatur*, I (1970), 44–52.

26. *FRUS, 1951*, III, 401–402.

27. When Eisenhower made this statement, he was in Frankfurt, the capital of the German state of Hesse.

28. Memorandum of Conversation at SHAPE Headquarters, March 22, 1951, TSGR box 4, in RG 466, McCloy Papers, National Archives, and *FRUS, 1951*, III, 1030–32.

devise a politically workable approach to German rearmament, one that would create the basis for some form of compromise between the French and the Germans. Despite his statements about bygones being bygones, Eisenhower could still remember his own wartime feelings. He expressed an understanding for the French concern for security, pointing out that "if his son had been tortured by the Germans [as the French minister of defense Jules Moch's had been], he would not be very sympathetic towards the Germans." [29]

Such concerns led Eisenhower to begin to support the concept of a "European Army," an idea formulated by the great French internationalist Jean Monnet and proposed by the French government as the Pleven Plan. This proposal, to combine the armies of France, Germany, and other continental European states under a single command, was designed by the French to prevent the reemergence of an independent German national army and the German General Staff. Monnet designed it to further the unification of Europe as well, a goal he had sought with the Schuman Plan, the proposal to join the coal and steel industries of France and Germany. The French government also saw the Pleven Plan as a politically acceptable way to delay German rearmament. But the plan drew the scorn of most military professionals, who viewed it as completely unworkable and ridiculous. Eisenhower later acknowledged that he had shared these feelings, calling the French proposal as "cockeyed an idea as a dope fiend could have figured out." [30]

However, during his first six months in Europe, Eisenhower's perspective changed. He observed the continuing disunity, bickering, and weakness of the Western European states. In early June, 1951, he confided to his diary that "I am coming to believe that Europe's security problem is never going to be solved satisfactorily until there exists a U.S. of Europe. . . . I think that the real and bitter problems of today would instantly come within the limits of capabilities in solving them if we had this single government." The general also believed that such a United Europe would allow America to reduce its aid "both in amount and duration," a concern that Eisenhower expressed repeatedly over the next years. In Eisenhower's view, it would be a "tragedy to the whole human race" if such a European union did not come about. "With this one problem solved—all lesser ones would soon disappear." [31]

29. McCloy to Eisenhower, January 31, 1951, PPC, 16–52, folder McCloy, box 75, in EL. For Eisenhower's views in mid-March, Memorandum of Conversation at SHAPE Headquarters, March 22, 1951, TSGR box 4, in RG 466, McCloy Papers, NA, and *FRUS,* 1951, III, 1030–1032.

30. Meeting of President Truman and General Eisenhower, November 5, 1951, Eben Ayers Papers, Folder EDC and the Contractuals, box 6, Truman Library, Independence, Missouri.

31. Eisenhower added, "I believe *inspired* leaders could put it across. But everyone is too cautious, too fearful, too lazy and too ambitious (personally)." Eisenhower Diary, June 11, 1951, DDE Diary Series, EL.

Eisenhower soon became a tireless advocate of the European Defense Community (EDC), the renamed version of the European Army, as the way to both strengthen Europe and bring Germany into the Western alliance. He was convinced that "a solution of the problem of European defense is impossible unless we have solved the German problem," and that the creation of a united Europe afforded the safest way, as he put it, to show "Germany how definitely her national interests will be served by sticking and working with us."[32] The general's intervention in this issue proved decisive in overcoming the remaining objections of both the Pentagon and the State Department, both of whom feared the potential for delay inherent to the proposal. At the end of July, 1951, the United States adopted the EDC as its official policy on German rearmament.[33]

In striving to create such a united Europe, Eisenhower resolved whatever final doubts he might have had about bringing the Germans into the West. In one sense, the goal of a united Europe appealed to Americans as a kind of skeleton key, unlocking the solution to a number of problems at once, and most important, providing a type of "dual containment." The Soviet Union could be kept out, and Germany kept in Europe, but with neither able to dominate the Continent. For Eisenhower and other Americans of German descent, there may have been a personal element to the support for Europe. They may also have seen in the plan to make Germans into good Europeans the chance to change or temper some of those German national characteristics that had caused the world so much trouble, in the same way as assimilation into the larger American community had allowed German-Americans to become the staunch defenders of democracy.

When he became president, in 1953, Eisenhower remained adamantly in favor of the European Defense Community as the method of securing a German contribution to Western defense. It was also, along with the Atlantic alliance, the principal method for organizing the West. Eisenhower continued to see the EDC as a way to contain both Soviet expansionism and German nationalism. He reassured reluctant French leaders that this strategy would "integrate [the Germans] in a federation from which they could not break loose." The creation of a strong and united Europe would also allow the United States to shed some of its most expensive burdens, including the large number of its soldiers stationed

32. Eisenhower Diary, July 2, 1951, DDE Diary Series, EL, and *FRUS*, 1951, III, 8838–39. The diary also contains some of the previously mentioned Eisenhower revisionism, as he regretted the "mistakes" of 1945 and noted how he warned against such treatment of Germany. One would never guess from the diary entry that Ike had shared in these sentiments.

33. *FRUS*, 1951, III, 849–52.

in West Germany.[34] Eisenhower's commitment to the EDC, and to the German government of Chancellor Konrad Adenauer, which supported the proposal, were important reasons why his administration did not show more interest in Winston Churchill's suggestion that the allies open up talks with the Soviet Union after the death of Stalin in March, 1953. Eisenhower argued that such talks could be misinterpreted "as weakness or overeagerness on our part [that] would militate against success in negotiation."[35] Eisenhower wanted the Germans locked into the West before attempting a four-power settlement, an approach that critics felt precluded any agreement with the Soviet Union.

Both Eisenhower and his secretary of state, John Foster Dulles, also rejected the notion that membership in the EDC prevented German reunification. Eisenhower told Adenauer that it was his "conviction that the strengthening of the Federal Republic, through adoption of the EDC, the contractual agreements and further progress in the integration of Western Europe, can only enhance the prospects for the peaceful unification of Germany."[36] After the Soviet suppression of the rebellion in East Germany in June, 1953, Eisenhower noted that events in East Germany might develop to a point that it might even "become impossible for the Communists to hold the place by force." What the Soviets might then do, however, Eisenhower did not speculate. German historian Hermann Rupieper, on the basis of recently opened archives, makes it clear that the president was prepared to negotiate some form of demilitarized zone arrangement and other security controls on Germany if that would lead to a Soviet pullback from East Germany.[37] (These arrangements were not that different from those accepted by Gorbachev in 1990.)

34. U.S. Department of State, *Foreign Relations of the United States,* 1952–1954, V, 1783 (hereinafter cited as *FRUS,* 1952–1954). See Ambrose, *Eisenhower,* 70–71, 119–121, for Eisenhower's conviction about the need to reduce the American commitment.

35. Martin Gilbert, *Never Despair* (Boston, 1988), 828, Vol. VIII of Gilbert, *Winston S. Churchill.* See also the Bischof essay in this volume.

36. Eisenhower's letter to Adenauer, dated July 23, 1953, is in *FRUS,* 1952–1954, VII, 491–94.

37. Eisenhower's musings about the Soviets being unable to hold Germany militarily are found in a letter to the British field marshal Bernard Montgomery dated July, 2 1953, and quoted in Frank Ninkovich, *Germany and the United States: The Transformation of the German Question Since 1945* (Boston, 1988), 102. These musings about revolution in East Germany brought a quick visit from the French ambassador, who was concerned lest the president seem to be relying on violence rather than negotiations to bring about a German settlement. Memorandum of a Conversation with the secretary of state, July 29, 1953, in *FRUS,* 1952–1954, VII, 498. For the Eisenhower administration's interest in a demilitarized zone arrangement, see Hermann-Josef Rupieper, "Deutsche Frage und europäische Sicherheit: Politisch-strategische Überlegungen 1953/1955," in *Zwischen Kalten Krieg und Entspannung,* ed. Bruno Thoss and Hans Erich Volkmann (Boppard am Rhein, 1988), 181–90.

Paradoxically, although they doubted the Russians would agree, Eisenhower and Dulles remained confident that reunification was a realistic possibility in the first half of the 1950s. Both insisted that reunification could only safely take place within a more politically united Europe.[38] In the American view, European integration was the key to stability in Europe and "the best means of solving Europe's economic, political, and defense problems." At the same time that a united Europe would constitute "a counterpoise, not a menace, to the Soviet Union," it would exercise "a strong and increasing attraction on Eastern Europe, thus weakening the Soviet position there and accelerating Soviet withdrawal from that area." German reunification would also have this dual impact on the cold war. The only acceptable solution was "a unified democratic Germany allied to the free world," which would "represent a major step in rolling back the iron curtain."[39]

These perspectives on German reunification led the Eisenhower administration to look unfavorably upon a neutralized Germany as a solution. A neutral Germany would be cast loose from its secure mooring within the West, and likely to try to play off both sides in the cold war for its own advantage. The West would lose German strength, both economically and militarily, as well as face the serious strategic and military problems that would be posed by a withdrawal of American forces from Germany. Despite the dangers of a neutral Germany, Washington did acknowledge that if the Soviets were to concede free elections *and* the right of a reunited Germany to affiliate itself with the West, the United States would have to accept the "minor risk" that the Germans might choose neutrality over Western alignment.[40]

(Eisenhower himself, though he demonstrated more understanding and sympathy for neutralism than his secretary of state, told the Indian prime minister Nehru that he had grave doubts "that a people as dynamic as the Germans could ever successfully be treated as neutrals." One wonders if Eisenhower believed that neutralism was only best for lethargic or "undynamic" peoples. What conclusion must Nehru have drawn?)[41]

38. For a discussion of these views, see Rolf Steininger, "John Foster Dulles, the European Defense Community, and the German Question," in *John Foster Dulles and the Diplomacy of the Cold War* ed. Richard H. Immerman (Princeton, N.J., 1990), 79–80.

39. These conclusions can be found in NSC-160/1, dated August 17, 1953, in *FRUS, 1952–1954*, VII, 510–20.

40. *Ibid.*, 510–20. Among the difficulties created by a unified neutral Germany would be one cited by General Collins. "We could scarcely expect the French to accept six American divisions. . . . Where would these forces go, and how would we defend Germany against a Russian advance?" *Ibid.*, 505.

41. Dwight D. Eisenhower, *The White House Years: Waging Peace* (New York, 1965), 112.

Neutralism seemed a minor risk because of the stunning success of Adenauer in the German elections of September, 1953. Eisenhower's changed view of the Germans stemmed in part from his respect for the "iron-willed Chancellor," who placed his faith and political future in the hands of the American-led alliance.[42] In April, 1953, Adenauer made his first of many trips to the United States, meeting with President Eisenhower and laying a wreath at Arlington National Cemetery. His warm reception from American dignitaries became part of his campaign film, and Adenauer welcomed the strong public endorsement he received from Dulles, who proclaimed that the chancellor's defeat would be disastrous.[43] To American observers, Adenauer's victory and Germany's resurgence made the pursuit of European integration all the more pressing, as it was necessary to tie Germany to the West while the indispensable but elderly Adenauer was still guiding German policy. As the assistant secretary of state, Livingston Merchant, put it, "Adenauer's success in leading Germany back along [the] road of sanity and to integration in Western Europe is an historic opportunity to resolve the German question."[44]

Because of Adenauer's importance in American eyes, the elderly chancellor acquired a quasi-veto power over American policy toward Germany. When the European Defense Community finally went down to defeat in the French Assembly, Eisenhower and Dulles were determined to restore Germany's sovereignty and rearm Germany quickly within NATO, an arrangement that was seen as essential to Adenauer's political survival. At the subsequent Geneva discussions with the Soviet Union, in 1955, Eisenhower remained distrustful of the Soviet proposal for a disarmed and neutral Germany, at least in part because, as Eisenhower put it, "we had obligations to Adenauer and the Federal Republic of Germany. No matter how harmless a Soviet proposal might appear, we were determined to do nothing that might injure the Chancellor or weaken Western resolution to sustain freedom in the German Republic."[45] In the same way, when word leaked in 1956 of a plan devised by the chairman of the Joint Chiefs, Admiral Radford, to replace American troops in the Federal Republic with increased reliance on nuclear weapons, a proposal that Eisenhower had long favored, the chancellor's strenuous protests helped stymie the initiative.[46] As one

42. Dwight D. Eisenhower, *Mandate for Cahnge, 1953–1956* (Garden City, N.Y., 1963), 397.
43. See Hans Jürgen Grabbe, "Konrad Adenauer, John Foster Dulles, and West German–American Relations, in *Dulles and the Cold War,* ed. Immerman, 109–132.
44. For Adenauer's growing popularity, see Elisabeth Noelle and Erich Peter Neumann, *The Germans: Public Opinion Polls, 1947–1966* (Allensbach, 1967), 256–57. For Merchant's assessment of Adenauer, see Rupieper, "Deutsche Frage," 190.
45. Eisenhower, *Mandate for Change,* 523.
46. Burley, "Restoration and Reunification," 232.

of the last actions in his administration, Eisenhower even enthusiastically backed a plan to create some type of European nuclear force (along the same lines as the once-defeated European Defense Community), both to encourage European unity and also to provide the Germans with an equal voice in the most important decision on their defense, the question of whether to use nuclear weapons.[47]

Eisenhower was proud of his administration's success in Germany, bringing at least the Western half of the country into NATO and establishing a successful democracy. He was impressed with Germany's transformation from a conquered and ravaged land to "a rehabilitated and equal member of the Western alliance," referring to it as a "near miracle—a shining chapter in history." On a trip to the Federal Republic in 1959, Eisenhower confessed astonishment "at the extent to which American styles had influenced the country in dress, manners, and even billboards."[48] Eisenhower's reaction to the new West Germany of his time was shared by many American leaders of his generation. They saw in the Federal Republic of Germany America's most compliant and loyal ally in Europe, a "little America," and they took what the historian Fritz Stern has termed "a strong, almost proprietary interest in the Alliance and most especially German-American friendship."[49]

Eisenhower's solicitude for Adenauer and his pleasure in seeing Germany's transformation did not lead him to abandon his hope for an end to the cold war, which still seemed at its coldest in Berlin. When in November, 1958, the Soviet premier, Nikita Khrushchev, announced that the time had come to "renounce the remnants of the occupation regime in Berlin," and triggered the first in the series of crises over the divided city, Eisenhower sought a settlement that preserved allied rights but sought to defuse the tension. The problem the Soviets faced in that divided city was essentially the same that would ultimately cause the demise of their German client, the late and unmourned German Democratic Republic. The GDR lacked political legitimacy and was losing its most productive citizens to the West through the escape valve of Berlin. Khrushchev's proposal to turn the control of the city over to the East Germans was a desperate attempt to shore up that regime and embarrass the West.

47. Eisenhower, Memo of Conversation, August 3, 1960, White House Office Files, Office of the Staff Secretary, Subject File, box 4, Department of State, box 4, in EL. The most complete published account of the "Multilateral Force," as the proposed nuclear-sharing idea was called, is in John Steinbrunner, *The Cybernetic Theory of Decision* (Princeton, N.J., 1974). See also the Wampler essay in this volume.

48. Eisenhower, *Waging Peace*, 416.

49. Fritz Stern, "German-American Relations and the Return of the Repressed," in James Cooney *et. al., The Federal Republic of Germany and the United States* (Boulder, Colo., 1984), 238.

The Eisenhower reaction was captured by Stephen Ambrose when he noted that the president "let Khrushchev know that although he was standing firm, he was willing to negotiate Berlin's status."[50] There were some initial indications of "softening"—Dulles entertained both the idea of considering the East Germans as agents of the Soviet Union, and of a reunification plan that did not involve free elections. However, by early 1959, there was a stiffening in the administration's position. Eisenhower insisted that any change in Berlin's status include the entire city, and not just its Western half. The administration also made plans to resist any East German takeover of Soviet responsibilities. Ike even hinted at the possibility of threatening the use of nuclear weapons, as when he told the National Security Council in January, 1959, that "Khrushchev should know that when we decide to act, our whole stack will be in the pot."[51]

Khrushchev abandoned his initial ultimatum, agreeing to a summit meeting with Eisenhower in September, 1959. The meeting led to the "Spirit of Camp David" and an easing of the crisis, as Khrushchev agreed to remove his time limit in return for a Western willingness to negotiate. By this time Dulles had died, and Eisenhower may have been changing his own view about German reunification. In a discussion with Llewellyen Thompson, the ambassador to the Soviet Union, in October, 1959, Eisenhower acknowledged that he was increasingly "coming to the view that complete reunification of the two parts of Germany is not going to be achieved early."[52] Eisenhower, who had long wanted the West Germans to adopt a more conciliatory policy toward East Germany, involving things like educational exchanges and increased travel, had no doubt that West Germany's freedom and economic prosperity would prove enormously enticing to the East. He hoped to move Adenauer away from his rigid policy of nonrecognition toward East Berlin, though he did not want to do this at the expense of West Berlin's freedom. It is doubtful that Eisenhower would have sacrificed some type of East-West accord solely over a German issue, despite the importance he placed on Adenauer's West Germany. How far Eisenhower may have gone with that sentiment was never made clear, as the plans for a Paris summit crashed along with the U-2 spy plane in the Soviet Union.

The Eisenhower administration sought a transformation of Germany and Europe. Eisenhower wanted to see Germany reunified in the context of a united Europe and the Western alliance. The events of 1989 and 1990 achieved at least part of that vision. The question over the next years for historians may well be

50. Ambrose, *Eisenhower*, 502.
51. *Ibid.*, 503.
52. *Ibid.*, 544.

whether the United States should have taken more risks during Eisenhower's presidency to defuse the cold war, whether a different strategy might not have brought an earlier end to the division of Europe. But if the Eisenhower administration's rigidity on the position of reunification contributed to delaying that process, should we judge this so critically? Would a neutral Germany in the 1950s have made a contribution to peace? Perhaps so. However, neutrality in the midst of cold war tensions would not have been an easy status to preserve, and the Germans of the 1950s were not those of 1990. The legacy of Nazi ideas was still powerful, and surveys in the 1950s showed that most Germans still believed that Germany's best time in recent history had been during the first years of the Nazis, and that a sizable minority still believed the proposition that Nazism was a good idea badly carried out, and that Hitler was a great German leader. Eisenhower may have been right in 1945, that it would take fifty years to judge Germany's development of democracy. Indeed, I would argue that the passage of time allowed political and economic liberalization to proceed within Germany, making reunification much less dangerous for Europe. The passage of time also allowed for the Gorbachev revolution in the Soviet Union, effectively ending the cold war and making neutrality an irrelevance.

Finally, perhaps the Eisenhower administration's rigid stance on reunification reflected the continuing ambivalence about Germany. Despite the widespread support for reunification in American opinion polls, the United States had other foreign policy priorities, such as preserving stability in Europe and maintaining its defense against the Soviet Union, that militated against action or risks on reunification. It seems to me that the Eisenhower administration will be much more vulnerable to attack on its policies in other regions of the world. In Europe the administration was probably as successful as Soviet foreign policy and internal conditions allowed it to be. In this sense, despite the ambivalence of his feelings toward his ancestral land, Dwight D. Eisenhower will be seen as having played a central role in transforming Germany's position in Europe and providing an answer to the German question.

STEVEN F. GROVER

U.S.-Cuban Relations, 1953–1958:
A Test of Eisenhower Revisionism

F ew scholars have utilized Dwight D. Eisenhower's relations with Cuba in the
historiographical debate over his presidential leadership. Those who have examined Eisenhower's response to events in Cuba typically use January, 1959—
the month that Castro marched triumphantly into Havana—as their jumping-
off point.[1] Although U.S.-Cuban relations from that time until shortly before the
close of Eisenhower's second term were marked by much diplomacy and
therefore are highly instructive, one also must look before 1959 because Castro

The author thanks Professor Thomas Schwartz of Vanderbilt University and, especially,
Professor Günter Bischof of the University of New Orleans for their guidance, as well as former
assistant secretary of state for inter-American affairs Richard Rubottom for granting me permis-
sion to quote from his oral history, done by the Columbia University Eisenhower Oral History
Project.

1. Richard E. Welch, Jr., *Response to Revolution: The United States and the Cuban Revolution,
1959–1961* (Chapel Hill, N.C., 1985), Morris H. Morley, *Imperial State and Revolution: The United
States and Cuba, 1952–1986* (New York, 1987), and Stephen G. Rabe, *Eisenhower and Latin America:
The Foreign Policy of Anticommunism* (Chapel Hill, N.C., 1988), only glance at the Eisenhower
administration's pre-1959 relations with Cuba. Focusing mostly on Eisenhower and Christian
Herter's response to Castro once the bearded revolutionary came to power, Welch puts insufficient
weight on the earlier pivotal roles of the U.S. assistant secretaries of state for inter-American affairs
and ambassadors to Cuba. Although Morley devotes more attention to these important actors in
his comprehensive diplomatic history, he does not address the sugar controversy described in this
essay and does not factor his results into the Eisenhower debate. See Morley, *Imperial State and
Revolution*, 40–71. Rabe's landmark study of Ike's relations with Latin America, on the other hand,
was broad in scope and focused on U.S.-Cuban relations from 1959 to 1961. See Rabe, *Eisenhower
and Latin America*, 117–73.

Alan H. Luxenberg was the first to analyze Castro's ascent to power under the rubric of
Eisenhower historiography. See "Did Eisenhower Push Castro into the Arms of the Soviets?"
Journal of Interamerican Studies and World Affairs, XXX (1988), 37–72. However, Eisenhower fares better in Luxenberg's study than he would otherwise for two reasons. First, Luxenberg bases his study
almost entirely on secondary literature. Consequently, he overlooks diplomatic bungles that marked
every level of the United States' Cuban policy-making apparatus. Second, Luxenberg places little
merit in the popular criticism that Eisenhower propped up unpopular, undemocratic, anti-
Communist regimes in the Third World because, in his opinion, "There are limits as to the extent
to which [the United States] can expect to bring its form of democracy to other countries, for the

did not spontaneously rise to power in Cuba; his power grew throughout the Eisenhower presidency.

The lack of scholarly attention to U.S.-Cuban relations during the Eisenhower administration, both before 1959 and in general, is surprising. The rise of Fidel Castro created a crisis in Washington. It was "the most important single development in U.S.–Latin American relations in the late 1950s," in the words of postrevisionist H. W. Brands, Jr.[2] The State Department believed that amicable relations with Cuba were essential to U.S. security and regarded Castro as a menace to Cuban stability as early as 1956.[3] Richard Rubottom, Eisenhower's assistant secretary of state for inter-American affairs from June, 1957, until September, 1960, attached "extraordinary interest" to Cuba.[4] Although Opera-

---

desire for democracy must come from within and cannot be imposed from without" (*ibid.*, 64).

2. H. W. Brands, Jr., *Cold Warriors: Eisenhower's Generation and American Foreign Policy* (New York, 1988), 45.

3. As the Latin American experts at the State Department saw it, "The geographic location of [Cuba] with its large, easily defensible harbors . . . off our coast at the crossroads to the Caribbean and Gulf trade, not to mention its proximity to the Panama Canal, makes control of the island strategically significant to us." "Selected Aspects of US-Cuban Relations," Department of State Intelligence Report, No. 6393, August 19, 1953, p. 1. These experts also sought to keep Cuba economically and strategically safe because of U.S. investments on the island, which had soared to $750 million under Cuban president Fulgencio Batista. Americans controlled 25 percent of Cuban bank deposits, 40 percent of the sugar industry, 50 percent of the public railways, 80 percent of the utilities, 90 percent of the mines and the cattle ranches, and nearly 100 percent of the oil refineries. William Appleman Williams, *The United States, Cuba, and Castro: An Essay on the Dynamics of Revolution and the Dissolution of Empire* (New York, 1962), 21–22. Next to Canada, Cuba was America's most important source of nickel, a mineral of immense wartime value. "Requirements for Chief of Mission," Embassy and Consulate Administration file, box 1 (Office of Middle-American Affairs [Cuba], 1955—1955 Agriculture to Passport), in Record Group 59, National Archives. Approximately $100 million was invested in Cuba's American-owned Nicaro Nickel Plant. "Telephone Conversations of Mr. Rubottom with Various Persons in the White House and the Department Regarding the Cuban Situation," October 24, 1958, 1958-Cuba file, box 5, Records of Richard Rubottom, 1958—American and Foreign Power to D, in RG 59, NA.

In July, 1956, the lower echelons of the State Department expressed suspicion that Castro was a Communist. See "Cuban Governmental Allegations that Fidel CASTRO Ruz, Recently Arrested in Mexico, was in Contact with Communists and had Revolutionary Plans," July 19, 1956, 737.00/1-656 file, box 3075, 1956–59 Central Decimal file, in RG 59, NA. By October, 1957, the State Department had reason to fear that Castro posed a serious threat to the Batista regime. In that month, the American consulate in Santiago, Cuba, transmitted to the State Department reports from eastern Cuba of the Batista regime's "utter inability to eliminate the Fidel Castro menace." "Political and other events in the Southern part of Oriente Province," October 22, 1957, 737.00/10-157 file, box 3077, 1955–59 Central Decimal file, in RG 59, NA.

4. "RRR files used in Cuba hearings 12/31 and 1/3—Senate Subcommittee," 1958 Cuba file,

tion SUCCESS, the CIA-sponsored coup that removed Jacobo Arbenz from power in Guatemala, has provided a sophisticated case study of the sort called for by Eisenhower scholars, the scrutiny of U.S.-Cuban relations from 1953 through 1958—not dominated by a single covert operation (an event by its very nature more a test of the CIA than of the White House), but comprised of intertwining diplomatic, economic, and political forces—provides a more sound basis for evaluating Eisenhower.[5]

This essay aspires to begin filling the historiographical void covering the Eisenhower administration's response to Cuba before Castro's revolutionary triumph. Part I focuses on Eisenhower's handling of the sugar controversy of 1954–1956, which was prompted by the American sugar states' attempt to modify the 1948 Sugar Act in a manner more favorable to themselves and less favorable to Cuba. Part II examines all policy-making levels of the U.S. response to Castro.[6] As will be shown, the examination of primary sources relating to Cuba arrives at an end that Robert Divine did not anticipate when, out of "sympathy for a badly underrated President," he made his clarion call for archival research that would establish "Eisenhower's place in history."[7] Although most of the blame for the United States' myopic response to Castro during the 1950s lies with the U.S. ambassadors to Cuba, the "impotence" of U.S. policy—to quote Wayne Smith—truly "ran all the way to the top."[8]

---

box 5, Records of Richard Rubottom, 1958—American and Foreign Power to D (Misc.), in RG 59, NA.

5. For accounts of the American intervention in Guatemala, see Richard H. Immerman, *The CIA in Guatemala: The Foreign Policy of Intervention* (Austin, Tex., 1982); Stephen Schlesinger and Stephen Kinzer, *Bitter Fruit: The Untold Story of the American Coup in Guatemala* (Garden City, N.Y., 1983); and Blanche Wiesen Cook, *The Declassified Eisenhower: A Divided Legacy* (Garden City, N.Y., 1981), 217–92.

Revisionists and postrevisionists alike have called for more focused studies of the Eisenhower administration's policies, especially toward the Third World. See, *e.g.,* Fred Greenstein, *Leadership in the Modern Presidency* (Cambridge, Mass., 1988), 107, and Rabe, *Eisenhower and Latin America,* 2.

6. One must examine all levels of the U.S. decision-making apparatus because, as Brands opines, "in the diplomacy of the 1950s, implementing and formulating foreign policy required a supporting cast that collectively often exerted as much influence as [Eisenhower and Dulles] did on that policy's final form." *Cold Warriors,* ix.

7. Robert A. Divine, *Eisenhower and the Cold War* (New York, 1981), viii–ix.

8. Wayne Smith, *The Closest of Enemies: A Personal and Diplomatic Account of U.S.-Cuban Relations Since 1957* (New York, 1987), 37. Wayne Smith, a professor of Latin American studies at the Johns Hopkins School of Advanced International Studies, was a junior officer in the U.S. embassy in Havana from July, 1958, until the United States severed diplomatic relations with Cuba in January, 1961.

I. The Sugar Controversy

The first test of Eisenhower's understanding of Cuba came two full years before Fidel Castro entered the Sierra Maestra. When domestic cane and beet producers from the so-called sugar states of the South and West (Louisiana, North Carolina, Florida, Colorado, and Utah) found their inventories overflowing in mid-1954, they pleaded for immediate modifications of the 1948 Sugar Act (as amended in 1951) that would permit them to supply a larger percentage of the U.S. market for sugar.[9] The Department of Agriculture, and sugar-state legislators who considered their own political futures intertwined with the fate of the producers, lobbied assiduously for Eisenhower's support of the sugar producers' plan.[10] Pitted against this powerful lobby were the Cuban government and the U.S. Department of State, which was more concerned with preserving order in an island only 90 miles south of Florida than with safeguarding one domestic industry's unabated prosperity.[11] Cuban officials justifiably feared that the modification of the Sugar Act to the benefit of American producers would mean a reduction in Cuba's supply of sugar to the United States.[12] If Cuba's share of the U.S. market dropped, the Cuban government would have to lower sugar prices to remain competitive. Because the wages of Cuban sugar workers were pegged by law to the price of sugar, their wages would drop, they would become disgruntled, and opposition groups would grow. Caught between the competing interests and principles of the Cuban government and the State Department (on the one hand) and the sugar states and the Department of Agriculture (on the other), Eisenhower thus faced a first-rate dilemma.

9. Sugar Act of 1948, Public Law 140, 82nd Cong., 1st Sess., United States Code Congressional and Administrative Service (hereinafter cited as USCCAN) (St. Paul, Minn., 1951), I, 303–305. Sugar-state interests felt that the 1948 act unfairly prohibited them from increasing their sugar sales, while domestic sugar consumption grew, but permitted Cuba to make out like a thief. For example, Frank Kemp, the president of the Great Western Sugar Company, the largest beet sugar manufacturer in the United States, publicly asserted that the Sugar Act put the American sugar industry "in a straitjacket." "Beet Producers Seek to Amend Sugar Act," New York *Times,* February 5, 1955, p. 24.

10. See "Sugar States Seek Rise in U.S. Quotas," New York *Times,* January 8, 1955, p. 24.

11. A few isolated members of Congress, led by Representative Albert Morane, a Connecticut Republican, also advocated the preservation of Cuba's sugar quota. A member of the House Foreign Affairs Committee, Morane concluded that a reduction in Cuba's quota not only would destabilize the island but also would deflate the large Cuban market for American foodstuffs and manufactured goods. C. P. Trussell, "Report on Sugar Backs Cuba Trade: Economic Mission Counsels Congress to Ignore Drive for Curbing of Imports," New York *Times,* January 24, 1955, p. 10.

12. See "Cuba to Cut Sugar Wages: Level of Pay Will Be Pegged to Lower Price of Product," New York *Times,* January 19, 1953, p. 14.

The sugar conflict surfaced in mid-1954 when Aurelio Concheso, the Cuban ambassador to the United States, learned of the sugar states' campaign to change the Sugar Act. He reminded the State Department that when the U.S. Congress had amended the Sugar Act in 1952, forcing the Cuban government to radically curtail its sugar production from 7 million to 4.75 million tons, unemployment on the island "had reached dangerous heights." [13] Concheso warned that "any further reduction of Cuba's quota in the American market will reduce [Cuba's] production to a level that will seriously endanger its economic and social stability." [14] Echoing Concheso's concerns, Arthur Gardner, the U.S. ambassador to Cuba, advised Henry Holland, the assistant secretary of state for inter-American affairs, that Cuba's economy was "in a precarious state" and that "the shock of an amendment in the Sugar Act would furnish . . . ammunition" to Batista's political opponents. [15] Secretary of State John Foster Dulles inferred from these warnings that the revision of the Sugar Act to Cuba's detriment would expose the island to Communist infiltration. He wrote a memo to Eisenhower predicting that the sugar-state legislators' proposal "might easily tip the scales to cause revolution in Cuba and would certainly increase instability and promote anti-American feeling and communist activity in the Caribbean area. It would be a blow to the Cuban economy already suffering from the curtailment of sugar production and lower prices." [16]

Dulles' premonition convinced Eisenhower to leave the Sugar Act intact until its expiration, on January 1, 1957. Indeed, so certain was Eisenhower that Cuba's stability would be threatened by a reduction in its sugar quota that he was

13. Memorandum of Conversation, "Possible Amendment of Sugar Act," May 30, 1954, Cuba 1954-55 file, box 2 (Country file—Brazil to Chile), Records of Henry F. Holland (hereinafter cited as RHFH), in RG 59, NA.

14. "Proposals to amend the 1948 Sugar Act to the Detriment of Cuba," *Embajada de Cuba,* June 8, 1954, Gabriel Hauge 1952–55 (5) file, box 18, Administrative Series, Ann Whitman File, Eisenhower Library (hereinafter cited as AWF and EL). This document also appears in Dulles, June, 1954 (3) file, box 2, Dulles-Herter Series, in AWF, EL.

15. Memorandum of Telephone Conversation, "Proposed Changes in Sugar Act—Effects in Cuba," May 28, 1954, Cuba 1954–55 file, box 2 (Brazil-Chile Country file), RHFH 1953–56, in RG 59, NA. For additional efforts by Gardner to impress upon Holland during the sugar controversy the gravity of Cuba's economic situation, see Arthur Gardner to Henry Holland, January 18, 1955, Sugar January–May file, box 2 (Point 4 to Wheat), Records of the Office of Middle American Affairs (hereinafter cited as ROMAA), in RG 59, NA; and Memorandum of Conversation, "Revision of Sugar Act," June 8, 1955, Cuba 1954–55 file, box 2 (Brazil-Chile Country file), RHFH, in RG 59, NA.

16. Memorandum from Dulles to Eisenhower, "Proposed Modification of the Sugar Act Unwise and Unfair," June 7, 1954, Dulles, June, 1954 (3) file, box 2, Dulles-Herter Series, in AWF, EL.

prepared to jeopardize his own popularity in the sugar states within one year of the 1956 presidential election. When Agriculture Secretary Ezra Taft Benson, the leader of the sugar state lobby, warned Eisenhower in late January, 1955, that a delay in accommodating the sugar states would have political ramifications, Ike responded: "I tend to agree with your idea that it would be better to deal with these matters in an off year rather than in an election year. However, it is equally important that we do nothing that looks like we are 'running out on our agreements' [with Cuba.]" [17] On Henry Cabot Lodge's advice, Eisenhower also tried to persuade Benson that it was in the long-term best interests of American agriculture that Cuba remain politically and economically stable. [18] In an "eyes-only" memorandum, the president urged Benson "not [to] forget [that American] agriculture . . . will suffer badly if any of our close neighbors would experience economic collapse and possible Communistic domination." [19]

The sugar conflict reached its boiling point in April of 1955. On the heels of Vice-President Nixon's promise to Batista that Cuba's quota would not be changed prematurely, senators Wallace Bennett, a Utah Republican, and Allen Ellender, a Louisiana Democrat, on April 1 introduced a bill, cosponsored by forty-six other senators, giving domestic producers the right to supply more than two-thirds of estimated increases in sugar consumption between 1955 and 1962. [20] Cuba's quota would be drastically cut from 8.35 to 2.7 million tons. [21] The Cuban Congress registered its displeasure that same day by unanimously approving a resolution that decried the state of U.S.-Cuban commercial relations. [22] Predictably, the bill also irked the White House and the State Department. When all parties met in order to negotiate a compromise, the Agriculture Department and the domestic sugar industry rejected the State Department's proposal that Cuba's

17. The President to the Secretary of Agriculture (Benson), January 26, 1955, U.S. Department of State, *Foreign Relations of the United States, 1955–57,* VI, 781 (hereinafter cited as *FRUS, 1955–57*).

18. See "Notes on certain points raised by Cabot Lodge," Feb. 5, 1955, DDE Diary, February, 1955 (2) file, box 9, DDE Diary Series, in AWF, EL.

19. Eyes Only—Personal Memorandum for the Secretary of Agriculture, February 5, 1955, DDE Diary, February, 1955 (2) file, box 9, DDE Diary Series, AWF, EL.

20. See Memorandum for the Files, "Meeting on Sugar Between Mr. Waugh; Mr. McConnell of Agriculture; Mr. Callanan and Mr. Hoyt," February 17, 1955, Sugar January–May file, box 2 (Point 4 to Wheat), ROMAA, Richard Rubottom Correspondence, in RG 59, NA; "Nixon Reassures Cubans; Says U.S. Sugar Quota Will Not Be Cut for 2 Years," New York *Times,* February 9, 1955, p. 36. "48 Senators Sign Sugar Quota Bill," New York *Times,* April 2, 1955, p. 27. Twenty-eight nearly identical bills already had been introduced in the House.

21. Assistant Secretary of State for Inter-American Affairs (Holland) to the Administrative Assistant to the President (Hauge), May 13, 1955, *FRUS, 1955–57,* VI, 805.

22. *Ibid.*

quota be raised to 8.4 million tons, which would have preserved Cuba's growing percentage of the market. Eisenhower in turn "rebelled" both at the sugar-
state legislators' compromise figure of 8.3 million tons and suggestion that the
revised Sugar Act go into effect in 1955. He accused the Agriculture Department
of being "sympathetic to the Hill" despite its obligations to him.[23]

The White House and State Department's resolve began to pay off in July,
1955, when the sugar-state legislators agreed to permit Cuba to continue supplying 96 percent of the United States' foreign quota. On July 30, the House
passed H.R. 7030 by a vote of 194 to 44. The bill amended the Sugar Act such
that, beginning in 1956, market quotas above 8.35 million tons would be divided
equally by domestic and foreign producers. In 1957, the foreign suppliers would
receive a statutory quota of 175,000 tons and, depending on consumption increases, an additional 45,000 tons each subsequent year.[24]

Two days later, however, the Senate Finance Committee amended H.R. 7030
so that any increase in U.S. consumption above 8.3 million tons would be supplied 55 percent by domestic producers and 45 percent by foreign countries (25.6
percent by Cuba and 19.4 percent by the full-duty countries). This revised bill,
S.R. 1635, was unacceptable to Eisenhower and the State Department. In testimony before the Senate Finance Committee on January 16,1956, Assistant
Secretary Holland emphasized the negative effects that S.R. 1635 would have on
Cuba's easily destabilized economy. The senators responded favorably. On February 9, the committee approved an amended bill that allotted to Cuba a 33.8
percent share of increases in consumption above 8.35 million tons, effective
retroactively to January 1, 1956.

Both this figure and this date conformed to Eisenhower's position. Any increase in consumption beyond 8.35 million tons would be divided 55 percent to
domestic and 45 percent to foreign suppliers. Most important, Cuba's share of
the allotment in 1956 would remain at 96 percent. After 1956, Cuba's share of
the American market would drop to 29.6 percent but because U.S. consumption
of sugar was growing, there would be no decline in Cuba's absolute sales.[25] On
May 17, Congress passed the bill as the Sugar Act of 1956.[26] The compromise

23. Record of Conversation between Eisenhower, Sherman Adams, and Gabriel Hauge, June
1, 1955, Gabriel Hauge 1952–55 (2) file, box 18, Administrative Series, in AWF, EL.
24. Memorandum of a Conversation, "Sugar Legislation," July 22, 1955, *FRUS, 1955–57*, VI,
825.
25. Sugar Act of 1948, Amendment and Extension, 84th Cong., 2nd Sess., USCCAN (St.
Paul, Minn., 1956), II, 2594, 2599.
26. *Ibid.*, I, 263–68.

legislation "breezed" through both congressional houses in less than ninety minutes.[27] Eisenhower signed it on May 29, 1956.[28]

Eisenhower played his cards right throughout the sugar controversy. Though no party spoke of the compromise in such clear terms, the sugar-state legislators waited until 1956 to enact the revised Sugar Act in return for a greater share of the U.S. market. They saved face, their state economies were relieved, and the United States lived up to its international obligations. The Cuban government, too, had little, if any, reason to complain: The actual tonnage of sugar that Cuba would market in the United States would increase substantially because American consumption of sugar was growing rapidly.[29]

Contrary to Agriculture Undersecretary Morse's fear, Eisenhower did not reach his views of the proposed modifications of the 1948 Sugar Act "without . . . sufficient information before him." [30] After carefully weighing State Department and Agricultural Department arguments, he decided that the domestic sugar industry's problems should not be relieved at Cuba's expense. In siding with the State Department against congressional entreaties, Ike not only displayed an intuitive understanding of Cuba's precarious sugar monoculture, he also showed a willingness to sacrifice his own popularity for the benefit of sound foreign policy. This was no small sacrifice, either. Eisenhower's reelection bid was only months away; he knew from Gabriel Hauge and Sherman Adams that sugar was "*the* important subject" in the West.[31]

One might argue that Eisenhower's limited efforts to sway non-sugar-state legislators from siding with the domestic sugar producers—the sugar-state legislators themselves were obviously beyond such persuasion—buttresses Burton Kaufman's theory that Ike exercised limited presidential power by resigning himself to congressional protectionism.[32] More likely, however, Ike's conciliations

27. "Congress Passes Bill to Raise Sugar Quotas, Keep Subsidies," New York *Times,* May 18, 1956, p. 33.

28. "President Signs Sugar Quota Bill; Law Extended Through '60 Raises Level for Domestic Beet and Cane Growers," New York *Times,* May 30, 1956, p. 25.

29. Sugar Act of 1948—Amendment and Extension, 84th Cong., 2nd Sess., USCCAN (St. Paul, Minn., 1956), II, 2599.

30. Memorandum of Conversation, "Revision of Sugar Act," February 2, 1955, *FRUS, 1955–57,* VI, 825.

31. Record of Conversation between Eisenhower, Sherman Adams, and Gabriel Hauge, June 1, 1955, Gabriel Hauge 1952–55 (2) file, box 18, Administrative Series, in AWF, EL (emphasis in original).

32. Kaufman argues that Eisenhower's reverence for the separation of powers "required that the White House not trespass too far onto Congressional domain." Burton I. Kaufman, *Trade and Aid: Eisenhower's Foreign Economic Policy, 1953–1961* (Baltimore, Md., 1982), 8. Kaufman does not address the Sugar Act controversy.

(which included a rejection of his veto option) resulted from political pragmatism. Why, he asked himself, alienate Congress over this issue and thereby narrow his chances of making inroads on future, more significant issues? With Democrats controlling both congressional chambers, Eisenhower had to save his aces. In Stephen Ambrose's words, "The combination of a Democratic Congress and a Republican administration meant that precious little in the way of domestic legislation could be passed." [33]

II. Diplomatic Shenanigans

[It was] tragic . . . during those critical years, having two ill-prepared people [in Cuba], no matter how honorable their intentions were, and how fine their loyalty to their country undoubtedly was. They were simply not the skilled type of diplomat that we needed in a situation of that kind. [34]

—Richard Rubottom, assistant secretary of state for inter-American affairs, June, 1957–September, 1960

On July 26, 1953, about six months after Eisenhower's inauguration, Fidel Castro led a contingent of 165 students in a failed attempt to capture the Moncada Barracks in Santiago de Cuba. His 15-year jail sentence came as good news to the U.S. embassy in Havana, which had pegged him as an "extremely ambitious and ruthless opportunist, obviously not adverse to violence when it serves his purpose." [35] Weeks later, Eisenhower appointed Arthur Gardner as U.S. ambassador to Cuba. Gardner had been Truman's assistant treasury secretary from 1947 to 1948 and a substantial contributor to Eisenhower's 1952 campaign. A businessman all his life, Gardner was "woefully inadequate in the knowledge of diplomacy," to quote Ruby Hart Phillips, the New York *Times*'s Havana correspondent. [36]

During Gardner's four-year ambassadorship, he became so "chummy" with Batista—he even played weekly canasta games and posed unabashedly for photographs with the loathed dictator—and distanced from the everyday Cuban that he underestimated the strength of Batista's political opposition. Cubans not holding powerful positions in government or business quickly grew to hate

33. Stephen E. Ambrose, *Eisenhower: The President* (New York, 1984), 219, 252.

34. Richard R. Rubottom, oral history, 49.

35. Telegram from Embassy, Habana, to State Department, "Transmitting Report from Consulate at Santiago de Cuba on Political and Economic Conditions in Oriente Province," October 13, 1953, microfilm frame 00179, reel 4, Central Decimal file 737.00, in RG 59, NA.

36. Ruby Hart Phillips, *Cuba: Island of Paradox* (New York, 1960), 311.

Gardner.[37] Batista, realizing that his closeness to the U.S. ambassador legitimated his rule, but nevertheless concerned that their friendship could be counterproductive, once admitted, "I'm glad Ambassador Gardner approves of my government but I wish he wouldn't talk about it so much."[38] The State Department urged Gardner to establish friendly relations with Batista's leading political opponents. But he never did.[39] Consequently, Batista assumed that the United States would support him through thick and thin; he felt no heat to accommodate any of his political opponents' demands that he improve economic conditions and human rights in Cuba.

That made Cubans all the more receptive to Fidel Castro, who by mid-1954, as Tad Szulc notes, "had become Cuba's most famous political prisoner and, increasingly, a factor in national politics."[40] When a reporter from the Cuban magazine *Bohemia* interviewed him in June, 1954, Fidel was highly critical of Batista and spoke of his plans to continue the revolution after his release from jail. Though the interview gave Castro immense exposure on the island, Gardner did not report it to the State Department.[41]

In November, 1954, Batista won Cuba's presidential election, but hardly by popular mandate. Protesting Batista's control of the election boards, the opposition parties—including the Auténtico party with its reputable candidate, Dr. Ramón Grau San Martín—had refused to participate in the election. Only 40 percent of the Cuban electorate had voted. Still incarcerated, Castro could not run against Batista; nevertheless, as Hugh Thomas notes, "he was already an unseen candidate, the spirit of liberty incarcerated and of Martí reincarnated."[42] In February, 1955, Vice-President Nixon visited Batista in Havana. He embraced Batista and, in a toast, likened him to Abraham Lincoln.[43] Upon his return to Washington, Nixon told Eisenhower's cabinet that Batista was renouncing his

37. Rubottom, oral history, 49; George Black, *The Good Neighbor: How the United States Wrote the History of Central America and the Caribbean* (New York, 1988),104.

38. Quoted in Phillips, *Cuba: Island of Paradox,* 325.

39. John Cabot to Arthur Gardner, November 6, 1953, Cuba country file, box 1, RJMC, in RG 59, NA. To Gardner's credit, however, he strongly endorsed the plan of John Hoover, the Cuban consul general, to reopen a consular office in Camagüey, Cuba. This office would later prove vital to informing the State Department on day-to-day revolutionary activities in Cuba's interior. See Arthur Gardner to Henry F. Holland, March 15, 1955, Cuba 1954–55 file, box 2 (Brazil-Chile country file), RHFH, in RG 59, NA.

40. Tad Szulc, *Fidel: A Critical Portrait* (New York, 1987), 856.

41. *Ibid.,* 341–42.

42. Hugh Thomas, *Cuba: The Pursuit of Freedom* (New York, 1971), 856.

43. Nixon's toast to Batista (February, 1955), Nixon Papers, series 362, cited in Stephen G. Rabe, "Dulles, Latin America, and Cold War Anticommunism," in *John Foster Dulles and the Diplomacy of the Cold War,* ed. Richard H. Immerman (Princeton, N.J., 1990), 172.

old despotic ways. Batista, he reported, was "a very remarkable man" and was now "desirous of working for Cuba rather than himself, and is greatly concerned with the social development of the country." [44]

Feeling in firm control of Cuba's military and wishing to resurrect his international reputation, Batista in May, 1954, released Castro and his rebel band from prison. Their release spurred a burst of anti-Batista riots throughout Cuba. Fidel and his brother, Raúl, fled to Mexico when rumors spread that Batista was planning to murder them. [45] In October, Castro left Mexico for a six-week speaking tour in the United States, raising funds for his new insurrection against Batista. When he returned to Mexico, a *Bohemia* article pinpointed him as Batista's prime opponent. Other Cuban politicians, the article theorized, suffered from a "*Fidelista* complex. . . . [They] feel dwarfed by the shadow of Fidel Castro that is becoming gigantic." [46] As Christmas, 1955, neared, Castro supporters distributed tens of thousands of pamphlets with the 26th of July movement's slogan ("In 1956, We Will Return Or We Will Be Martyrs") and spray-painted "MR-26-7" (Movimiento Revolucionario July 26) throughout Cuba. [47] Oblivious to Batista's mounting opposition, however, Ambassador Gardner cabled to Secretary Dulles that the Cuban people were "politically apathetic" and that there was "no evidence [that the] insurrectionary groups have [a] large following." [48]

Accompanied by eighty-two other revolutionaries, Castro reinvaded the island in December, 1956, only to be ambushed by Batista's forces as they set ashore. Sixty-three of the Fidelistas were killed, but Fidel, Raúl, the Argentine revolutionary Ernesto "Che" Guevara, and fifteen others miraculously survived. Without food and weapons, they fled into the wilderness of the Sierra Maestra in southeastern Cuba. [49] While the rebels endeared themselves with the Sierra Maestra peasants (decades-long victims of Rural Guard brutality), Ambassador Gardner perceived no threat to Batista, whose forces included a 40,000-man army, the Cuban National Police, and the Rural Guard. [50] Nevertheless, Batista proved unable to extirpate the rebels, who were joined by the countryside peasants in their first victories against Rural Guard outposts at La Plata and El Uvero.

44. Minutes of Cabinet Meeting, March 11, 1955, Cabinet Meeting of 11 March 1955 file, box 4, Cabinet Series, in AWF, EL.

45. Szulc, *Fidel,* 323, 347, 410.

46. Quoted *ibid.,* 373.

47. *Ibid.,* 375.

48. Telegram from the ambassador in Cuba (Gardner) to the secretary of state, October 16, 1956, *FRUS, 1955–57,* VI, 836.

49. Louis A. Pérez, Jr., *Cuba Between Reform and Revolution* (New York, 1988), 291.

50. Szulc, *Fidel,* 410.

Gardner, however, remained convinced that the Cuban people would not suc-
cumb to Fidelismo. Contradicting his prior argument that Cuba's sugar quota
should not be cut because the island's economy was weak and capricious,
Gardner claimed that Cubans were too well-off to want governmental change.
He told Henry Holland that the island was "enjoying high-level prosperity."[51]
Holland agreed.[52]

Meanwhile, Castro's insurgency gained momentum. Because Castro was
helped by *campesinos,* the strength of his rebel army extended far beyond the
eighteen regulars who filled its ranks when New York *Times* reporter Herbert
Matthews interviewed him in February, 1957. Thus, when Castro duped the
American correspondent into thinking that he led a phalanx of troops, the effect was not a far cry from the truth.[53] In his report to the State Department
about Matthews' visit with Castro, Ambassador Gardner focused mostly on exposing inaccuracies in Matthews' articles.[54] Although it is debatable whether
Gardner's estimate of Castro's strength was more accurate than Matthews', it is
indisputable that Matthews' scoop had caused Cubans to *perceive* that Castro's
power was snowballing, a fact that Gardner overlooked in this report and in future reports to the State Department.[55] Nonetheless, Gardner did concede that
the Castro rebels "seem socialistic and nationalistic, and have talked vaguely of
agrarian reform, socialization of profits, industrialization of Cuba by Cubans.
... they are hell-bent on change, and led by an unusual man—dedicated, fanatical, impractical, possibly megalomaniac."[56] This is not to say that Gardner
regarded Castro as a substantial threat to Batista. On the contrary, the ambassador argued that "the controversy over whether or not Fidel Castro is alive is
of no real importance."[57]

As Castro's 26th of July movement continued to liberate eastern Cuba in
early 1957, State Department and CIA analysts concluded that Batista was stand-

51. Telegram from the ambassador in Cuba (Gardner) to the secretary of state, October 16,
1956, *FRUS, 1955–57,* VI, 835.

52. See Memorandum from the assistant secretary of state for inter-American affairs (Holland)
to the secretary of state, "Cuban Political Situation," May 8, 1956, *FRUS, 1955–57,* VI, 832.

53. See Szulc, *Fidel,* 448.

54. "Situation in Cuba: Articles in New York *Times* by Herbert L. Matthews," February 28,
1957, 737.00/1-157 file, box 3076, in RG 59, NA.

55. According to Tad Szulc, Matthews' articles elevated Castro to "hero status." *Fidel,* 452.
Cubans were able to read Matthews' articles, reprinted in Cuban newspapers, because Batista had
just lifted press censorship from Cuba. *Ibid.*

56. "Situation in Cuba: Articles in New York *Times* by Herbert L. Matthews."

57. From Arthur Gardner to Richard Rubottom, February 28, 1957, 1957-Cuba file, box 2
(Costa Rica to L), Records of Richard R. Rubottom (hereinafter cited as RRRR), in RG 59,
NA.

ing on weak legs.[58] The State Department requested Ambassador Gardner's resignation in June, 1957, soon after Gardner foolishly joined International Telephone and Telegraph officials in ceremonially presenting Batista with a golden telephone as a token of their appreciation for his allowing the Cuban Telegraph Company, an ITT subsidiary, to raise its rates by 20 percent.[59] Perhaps, however, Gardner's sanguine reports already had influenced Assistant Secretary Rubottom into thinking that Castro's revolutionary program would not be well received by Cubans. In an October, 1957, news conference, Rubottom hypothesized: "Let's assume . . . that [Castro intends to expropriate American property and nationalize Cuban industry]. I honestly don't think that the Cuban people as a whole, who are a relatively well-off people, including the working class, are anti–private investment or anti–United States. I just think that . . . runs counter to rather deeply ingrained Cuban character and attitude."[60] Evidently, Rubottom placed greater trust in Ambassador Gardner's analysis than in Herbert Matthews' opinion that the assistant secretary would be "amazed at [Castro's] supporters among all walks of Cuban life."[61]

Eisenhower would have been wise to replace Gardner with an ambassador who would be less prone to diplomatic impropriety and more attuned to popular Cuban sentiment. Instead, he chose Earl E. T. Smith. As Assistant Secretary Rubottom has recalled:

> Earl E. T. Smith . . . was the only ambassador to a country in Latin America about whom I was not consulted in advance. I never will forget going up to Secretary Dulles's office one day and being told that Gardner was out and that Earl E. T. Smith was going to take his place, and I was rather dumbfounded because of course the country was extremely important. Castro was already fighting in the hills and to have had this kind of appointment without any consultation with those of us who were professionally involved, at my level, let alone below me—I thought it was rather unusual, to put it mildly.[62]

Eisenhower appointed Smith—a descendant of one of Massachusetts' oldest families, a staunch Republican, and an affluent Wall Street financier without experience in international relations—because of his substantial donations to

58. "National Intelligence Estimate: Political Stability in Central America and the Caribbean through 1958," April 23, 1957, *FRUS, 1955–57*, VI, 629.

59. ITT was an American company; Rabe, *Eisenhower and Latin America,* 120.

60. "Background Press and Radio News Conference," 12, October 13, 1957, Membership in Various Organizations to Speeches file, box 3, RRRR, in RG 59, NA.

61. Memorandum of Telephone Conversation between Rubottom and Matthews, "Cuban Matters," February 28, 1957, 737.00/1-57 file, box 3076, in RG 59, NA.

62. Rubottom, oral history, 47–48.

Ike's presidential campaigns.[63] Leonard Hall, the chairman of the Republican National Committee, had considered Smith an "active" Republican and had recommended him to Eisenhower.[64] Dulles thought Smith a better man for the job than Charles Bohlen, then U.S. ambassador to Moscow, because in his mind it was wasteful to send top-notch diplomats to stable banana republics.[65] "One of the intellectual stars of the American foreign service," Bohlen was instead reassigned to Manila.[66]

A self-made millionaire who prided himself on his elevated social position, Eisenhower's new ambassador to Cuba was hardly the type to remove the stigma of Arthur Gardner's excessive partisanship toward Batista.[67] Throughout his tour of duty, Smith enjoyed repeating what affluent Cuban businessmen had told him upon his arrival in Cuba: that the U.S. ambassador was usually the second most powerful man in Cuba, and often the first.[68] Not only did Smith not speak Spanish, he could not even pronounce the simplest Spanish name. Consequently, he relied entirely upon interpreters.[69]

According to Wayne Smith, Earl Smith created a "poisonous" atmosphere in the U.S. embassy.[70] He distrusted most of its staff because they regarded him as

63. Earl Smith served as the finance chairman of the Florida Republican state committee and as a member of the Republican National Finance Committee from 1954 to 1956. He was a member of the New York Stock Exchange and the founder of the brokerage firm of Paige, Smith and Remick. Personal telephone interview with Earl Smith, March 2, 1989. John Dorschner and Roberto Fabricio, *The Winds of December* (New York, 1980), 49.

64. Personal telephone interview with Earl Smith, March 2, 1989.

65. John Foster Dulles' belief that top diplomats were wasted in stable Latin American republics is particularly evident from a meeting he had with Eisenhower on July 20, 1954, one month after the CIA-sponsored coup in Guatemala. With Guatemala cleansed of communism and controlled by Castillo Armas, a U.S. pawn, Dulles argued that John Peurifoy, the U.S. ambassador to Guatemala who had served through the highly sensitive planning and active stages of the CIA operation, was no longer needed there. As Eisenhower's personal secretary recorded the conversation: "Dulles said we have a good man in Peurifoy, but felt situation in Guatemala didn't call for a man of his great talents." Meeting between Eisenhower and John Foster Dulles, July 20, 1954, Ann C. Whitman Diary, July, 1954 (3) file, box 2, Diary Series, in AWF, EL.

66. Thomas, *Cuba: The Pursuit of Freedom,* 947.

67. Smith spoke frequently about his aristocratic lifestyle in New York and Palm Beach, once admitting to a journalist: "I have lived in two eras. One when the country was run by the classes, and now when it is run by the masses. Something in between is probably best, but I'll be honest: I enjoyed it more when it was run by the classes." Quoted in Dorschner and Fabricio, *Winds of December,* 48–49.

68. *Ibid.,* 49; Earl Smith, *The Fourth Floor: An Account of the Castro Communist Revolution* (New York, 1962), 23.

69. Wayne Smith, *Closest of Enemies,* 33.

70. See note 8.

a dilettante.[71] There was frighteningly little conversation between the ambassador and John Topping, the embassy's chief political officer and the former assistant secretary of state for middle-American affairs. Despite Topping's expertise, Earl Smith prohibited him from sending official correspondences to the State Department without his prior approval.[72] Because Earl Smith often substantially changed Topping's telegrams before forwarding them to Assistant Secretary Rubottom, he and Topping often bickered. When Bill Bowdler, Topping's assistant, tried to mediate their disputes, he only incurred the ambassador's wrath.[73]

Like John Foster Dulles, Earl Smith was a shrewd man, who, out of a perception that the cold war was a zero-sum struggle between good and evil, tended to gloss over the distinction between social democracy and communism. Nonetheless, as Smith revealed soon after arriving in Cuba, he was compassionate toward the Cuban people. When in July, 1957, Batista's troops attacked a group of two hundred women engaged in a peaceful antiregime protest in Santiago, Cuba, Ambassador Smith publicly declared his outrage. John Foster Dulles quickly rebuked him. Though praising Smith's reaction as "a very human thing to do," he explained that it "may not have been perfectly correct."[74]

Dulles' reaction made Smith wary of criticizing Batista again in the future. Indeed, as Castro's strength grew and Smith became convinced that he was a Communist, Smith learned to invoke the principle of noninterventionism as an excuse for refusing to meet with political dissidents—despite recommendations by William Wieland, the director of middle-American affairs, and Daniel Braddock, the deputy chief of mission in Havana, that Smith encourage a broad-based coalition to restore order to Cuba.[75] Moreover, Earl Smith rejected opportunities in March and April, 1958, to help responsible moderates establish a middle ground between Castro's fanaticism and Batista's authoritarianism. That an able diplomat in Smith's place in some way could have changed the course of events in Cuba is quite probable: In the 1950s "the American Embassy was more important to Cuban politics than the Cuban parliament itself."[76]

71. Wayne Smith, *Closest of Enemies,* 33–34.

72. It was widely rumored in the embassy that Earl Smith's wife, a bright woman who lacked training in political analysis, also drafted numerous of the embassy's telegrams to State. Rubottom, oral history, 49.

73. Wayne Smith, *Closest of Enemies,* 34.

74. Earl Smith, *Fourth Floor,* 71. Dulles' belief that Smith's response was highly improper is suggested by the fact that Dulles informed Eisenhower about it, marking one of the few recorded instances in which Dulles spoke with the president about Cuba between the end of the sugar controversy and Castro's triumph on New Year's Day, 1959. Memorandum of Telephone Conversation between Eisenhower and Dulles, August 7, 1957, August 1957 Telephone calls file, box 26, DDE Diary Series, in AWF, EL.

75. See Morley, *Imperial State and Revolution,* 62; Wayne Smith, *Closest of Enemies,* 20.

76. Sergio Lopez-Miró, "Gran señor failed Cuba," Miami *Herald,* February 21, 1991.

Earl Smith's first chance came when Cuban bishops issued a public statement on February 28, 1958, calling for the end to violence and the establishment of a provisional government: "Those who truly love Cuba will know how to accredit themselves before God and before history, not refusing any sacrifice in order to achieve a government of national unity." [77] In response to this call for his resignation, Batista repeated his intention to hold free elections in June, 1958. Castro, who just four days earlier had electrified the Cuban people with his shout of "¡Aquí Radio Rebelde! ¡Transmitiendo desde la Sierra Maestra en el Territorio Libre de Cuba!" (Here, Rebel Radio! Transmitting from the Sierra Maestra in the Free Territory of Cuba!), also responded to the bishops' statement.[78] He lauded the bishops' call for peace, but protested Batista's participation in any such government. Likewise, the leaders of another revolutionary group, the student-run, Havana-based Directorio Revolucionario, emphasized that "there can only be peace if Batista resigns immediately and a provisional government of national unity is formed to return liberty and democracy to the people." [79]

Before the bishops' statement was disseminated throughout the island, Monsignor Luis Centóz, the papal nuncio, had met with Earl Smith. He told the ambassador that the proposed national unity government would include not only the revolutionaries and the political opposition but also Batista, who would preside over the body. Nevertheless, Smith would not give the plan his blessing. In Earl Smith's account of their meeting: "I regretted to say that I was unable to get any commitment from the State Department . . . [which] would not permit me to give any indication of support to the Roman Catholic Church. The position of the State Department was that only if the efforts of the Church were proven successful would the U.S. issue any public statement of endorsement. To do otherwise would be considered intervention." [80]

As Wayne Smith has observed, Ambassador Smith may have sidestepped an even more promising opportunity when the respected Joint Committee on Civic Institutions, an umbrella organization composed of forty-two professional, religious, and fraternal groups, on March 18, 1958, demanded Batista's immediate replacement by a neutral provisional government. Because the Joint Committee was entrenched in the Cuban business community, a civic pool from which Batista garnered considerable strength, the proclamation compounded the blow that the Eisenhower administration had dealt to Batista's legitimacy just four days earlier when it responded to his suspension of constitutional rights on the island by imposing an embargo on arms shipments to the regime.[81]

77. Quoted in Jules Dubois, *Fidel Castro: Rebel-Liberator or Dictator?* (New York, 1959), 216.
78. Quoted *ibid.,* 212.
79. New York *Times,* March 3, 1958, p. 11.
80. Earl Smith, *Fourth Floor,* 69.
81. In the words of then acting secretary of state Christian Herter, "We could not continue

With the failure of Castro's general strike just three weeks earlier, the 26th of July movement, too, was at its weakest moment in months when the Joint Committee demanded Batista's resignation. Because both camps were debilitated, Smith faced a historic opportunity to begin paving a middle way.[82] Had he thown the U.S. government's weight behind the Joint Committee's plan, Castro's *revolución* might never have reached fruition. After all, the Joint Committee's plan satisfied Castro's criteria for a cessation of hostilities.[83] But when the Joint Committee representatives asked for Smith's help, he again asserted that his advising Batista to step down would constitute political intervention.[84]

Why did Ambassador Smith resist entreaties from his colleagues in the embassy, as well from experts in the State Department, to seek out a moderate transitional government? Ambassador Smith perceived Batista as a "rightist dictator," but the lesser of two evils.[85] Under Batista's rule, U.S. investments were sure to thrive, and Castro's communism—Smith claimed to have identified it as early as 1958—was likely to be contained. As Richard Welch notes, Smith saw himself as "the guardian of American influence and American business interests in Cuba."[86] His close friendships with numerous American businessmen in Cuba

---

to supply weapons to a government which was resorting to such repressive measures of internal security as to have alienated some 80 percent of the Cuban people, by all reports, as well as public and official opinion in most of the other American Republics, not to mention important elements of press and congressional opinion in the U.S." Memorandum for the President, Cuba, December 23, 1958, Christian L. Herter (1) file, box 69, Administrative Series, in AWF, EL.

82. Indeed, Castro might have been quite willing to cooperate with the Joint Committee because in December, 1956, José Miró Cardona, one of the leaders of the Joint Committee and the former president of the Cuban Bar Association, had asked Batista's prime minister, Jorgé Garcia Montés, to see that the *fidelista* prisoners captured after Alegría de Pío battle were treated humanely.

83. One of the most important of these criteria for peace—stated by Castro in a November, 1956, interview with a reporter for the Cuban newspaper *Alerta*—were that "Batista ... turn over the presidency to a neutral figure mutually satisfactory to the government, the revolutionary organizations, and the opposition; general elections . . . [and] amnesty for all political and 'social' prisoners." "Interview with Fidel Castro; His Views on Situation," November 23, 1956, 737.00/1–656 file, box 3075, 1956–59 Central Decimal file, in RG 59, NA. It is certainly arguable, however, that by this time in 1958, Castro considered himself to be the only person who should rule Cuba.

84. Earl Smith, *Fourth Floor,* 71.

85. Personal telephone interview with Earl Smith, March 2, 1989. Earl Smith never modified his view that the United States should steadfastly support pro-American anti-Communist dictators. When the Philippine president Ferdinand Marcos feared a Communist coup in 1984, Earl Smith advised President Reagan that Marcos "may be an SOB, but he's our SOB." Quoted in John Dorschner and David Zeman, "Smith Remembered for Role in Cuba," Miami *Herald,* February 17, 1991.

86. Quoted in Earl Smith, *Fourth Floor,* 48.

biased him toward Batista.[87] "The U.S. would never be able to do business with Fidel Castro," he asserted in a Washington press conference on January 16, 1958.[88] Even as late as November 22, 1958, when the State Department became concerned that Castro's triumph would result in anarchy like that of 1933, Smith was preoccupied with the toll taken on American companies.[89] Smith may have sympathized with the women who were attacked by Batista's police when they protested peacefully, but he felt little compassion for Cubans who took matters into their own hands and endangered U.S. multinationals in Cuba.

By April, 1958, the State Department seriously doubted the accuracy of Earl Smith's reports. His assertion that Batista had Castro's rebel army under control clashed with State Department intelligence reports that described the 26th of July Movement as "stronger than it has ever been."[90] Che Guevara and Raúl Castro's new fronts in the central Sierra Maestra and the Sierra Cristal, respectively, created a second "liberation zone" that menaced Batista's forces.[91] The State Department concluded that the 26th of July movement had broadened its ideological base to include "nonrevolutionary segments of the population" and that the rebel army was now "4,000 strong." Morale among the revolutionaries was reported to be "high and currently increasing."[92]

In mid-1958, CIA director Allen Dulles became enraged when Smith prohibited CIA agents and his own political officers from speaking with anti-Batista dissidents in Havana. The ambassador asserted that such contacts "simply encouraged the opposition and generated enemy propaganda."[93] Allen Dulles sent Lyman B. Kirkpatrick, Jr., the CIA inspector-general, to Cuba to tell Smith that intelligence agents had "a duty to listen to all sources of information." Perhaps because the ambassador agreed resentfully, State and CIA officials still distrusted him.[94] They sent Park Wollam, one of Richard Rubottom's aides, to the U.S. consulate in Santiago de Cuba. Wollam was specifically instructed to bypass the ambassador by sending his reports directly to Foggy Bottom.[95]

On November 22, Earl Smith flew to Washington to show "the liberals in the State Department" that they were "blind" to Castro's communism.[96] William

87. Morley, *Imperial State and Revolution*, 56.

88. Quoted in Welch, Jr., *Response to Revolution*, 30.

89. Dorschner and Fabricio, *Winds of December*, 56.

90. "The 26th of July Movement Since the Abortive General Strike of April 9, 1958," Department of State Intelligence Report, No. 7780, ii.

91. Szulc, *Fidel*, 476.

92. "The 26th of July Movement Since the Abortive General Strike of April 9, 1958," ii.

93. Quoted in Dorschner and Fabricio, *Winds of December*, 55.

94. *Ibid.*

95. *Ibid.*

96. Personal telephone interview with Earl Smith, March 2, 1989.

Wieland, who believed that "the ambassador was the reason that the Cuban situation was slipping into disaster and chaos," attended the meeting.[97] Rubottom, too, was there. Secretary Dulles, who was too busy dealing with European and Soviet issues, could not attend.[98] In the meeting, Smith argued that Castro was a Communist because his brother, Raúl, was a member of the Communist Youth, and because Che Guevara, one of Fidel's highest-ranking lieutenants, was a Marxist. Wieland responded, "We know all that, of course. But that doesn't make it a Communist-dominated movement. There are plenty of moderates in it as well. Far more moderates than radicals."[99] Hearing this, Smith became irate. The United States, he said, had no choice but to support either Andrés Rivero Agüero, Batista's hand-picked successor, or Fidel Castro. Wieland retorted angrily, "Sure there are. Go to Miami, and you'll find dozens of moderates who hate Batista and distrust Castro. It's not an either-or situation." "Nonsense," Ambassador Smith retorted.[100]

After this conference, the State Department gave up on Earl Smith. In early December, 1958, William Pawley, an American with investments in Cuba, was sent as an official representative of Dwight D. Eisenhower to urge Batista "to capitulate to a caretaker government unfriendly to him, but satisfactory to us, whom we could immediately recognize and give military assistance to in order that Fidel Castro not come to power."[101] The Cuban leader, however, refused to step down. Two weeks later, Batista's forces reported that 90 percent of Cuba supported Castro's rebel army. In the climactic battle of Santa Clara, numerous civilians joined Che Guevara's column in its defeat of Batista's army. When Batista fled the country on January 1, 1959, the Rebel Army numbered 50,000.[102]

The State Department replaced Earl Smith with Philip Bonsal in mid-January, 1959, to show Castro that the United States was not opposed to Latin American governments that sponsored progressive social programs. Bonsal's appointment was hardly, as Morris Morley describes it, "an index of U.S. mistrust of the Castro leadership."[103] It signaled an intention on the part of the United States to work *with* Castro. As the U.S. ambassador to Bolivia from March, 1957, to December, 1958, Bonsal had maintained cordial relations with a socially democratic government. Despite his appointment of Bonsal to Cuba, however, Eisenhower

97. Quoted in Dorschner and Fabricio, *Winds of December,* 52.
98. *Ibid.*
99. Quoted *ibid.,* 58.
100. Quoted and described *ibid.*
101. Quoted in Pérez, Jr., *Cuba Between Reform and Revolution,* 311.
102. *Ibid.*
103. Morley, *Imperial State and Revolution,* 73.

was less inclined than the new ambassador, acting secretary of state Christian Herter, Richard Rubottom, and Allen Dulles to stomach Castro's anti-American philippics and his decision in February, 1959, to execute 550 of Batista's supporters.[104] When the Cuban premier visited Washington in April on the invitation of the American Society of Newspaper Editors, Eisenhower purposely went golfing in Augusta, Georgia. The president's decision to leave town upset Ambassador Bonsal, who believed that Castro might have been flattered by an invitation to visit the Oval Office and that their meeting might have opened an avenue for improved U.S.-Cuban relations.[105]

Eisenhower did, however, leave Vice-President Nixon and Herter to meet informally with Castro in order to probe his political bent and plans for the new Cuba. Both men wrote reports of their meetings with the rebel leader. Nixon concluded from his meeting that Castro was "either incredibly naive about Communism or under communist discipline."[106] Herter emphasized that Castro did not have the same concept of "law and legality" as Americans and cautioned that "it would be a very serious mistake to underestimate this man. . . . We should await his views on specific matters before assuming a more optimistic view . . . about the possibility of developing a constructive relationship with him."[107] Eisenhower scribbled in the top margin of Herter's report, "File, we will check in a year!!"[108] He seems to have falsely inferred from Herter's memorandum that it was safe to pigeonhole the Cuban problem until Castro either betrayed whether or not he was a Communist or revealed whether or not he would cooperate with the United States.

Castro promptly moved further to the left when he returned to Cuba. First, he promulgated the Agrarian Reform Law of May, 1959. By September, the Cuban government had expropriated over 1,000 acres of American land, without providing prompt and adequate compensation to U.S. owners, as the State Department had demanded.[109] Coupled with Castro's continued slanders against

104. John Foster Dulles was gravely ill by this time. Although concerned by Castro's anti-American diatribes, Herter optimistically reminded himself that Castro had repeatedly expressed his intention to restore the Cuban Constitution of 1940. When Castro executed 550 *batistianos,* Allen Dulles reasoned that "you kill your enemies." Rubottom, too, tried to give Castro the benefit of the doubt. There was, he said, still "potential greatness in the Cuban Revolution." Quoted in Rabe, *Eisenhower and Latin America,* 123.

105. Welch, Jr., *Response to Revolution,* 36.

106. Richard M. Nixon, *Six Crises* (New York 1962), 351–52.

107. "Unofficial Visit of Prime Minister Castro of Cuba to Washington, A Tentative Evaluation," April 20, 1959, Christian A. Herter, April, 1959 (2) file, box 9, Dulles-Herter Series, in AWF, EL.

108. *Ibid.*

109. Memorandum for the President from Herter, "Recommendations of Mr. Robert Kleberg on the Cuban Situation," July 7, 1959, Christian Herter, July, 1959 (2) file, box 9, Diary Series, in AWF, EL.

the "imperialists to the north," Castro's illegal nationalization of American-owned land infuriated Eisenhower. While meeting with advisers about the Cuban situation, he called Castro an "idiot—an utter fool" and compelled the State Department to finally abandon its strategy of appeasing Castro.[110] Indeed, Eisenhower recommended that the United States quarantine Cuba. "If [the Cuban people] are hungry, they will throw Castro out," he predicted.[111] Apparently, Eisenhower did not anticipate at this point that an embargo of the island might invite or force Cuba to align with Russia. In the end, Eisenhower abandoned his thought of blockading Cuban ports when Ambassador Bonsal advised him "not [to] punish the whole Cuban people for the acts of one abnormal man."[112]

III. Conclusion

Eisenhower's actions during the sugar controversy undermine the traditionalist caricature of him as inept and indecisive and buttress the revisionist view of Eisenhower as a president who acted deliberately after informing himself and carefully evaluating his alternatives. His decision to oppose the sugar states' efforts to prematurely amend the Sugar Act shows that a common traditionalist criticism of Eisenhower, that he factored his popularity too much into his decisions, is exaggerated.[113] And his success at forging a compromise between the sugar states and the Cuban government that was favorably received by both sides shows that Ike was in fact a skilled politician.[114]

But Eisenhower cannot be excused for having ignored Cuban affairs once the sugar controversy was settled and for having appointed Arthur Gardner and Earl Smith as ambassadors to the island. He is ultimately responsible for Smith's fail-

110. White House Staff Meeting, December 5, 1959, Staff Notes, November, 1959 (1) file, box 45, DDE, Diary Series, in AWF, EL.

111. Memorandum of Conference with the President, January 26, 1960, Cuba (2) January–April, 1960, file, box 4, International Series, White House Office, Office of Strategic Services, EL.

112. *Ibid.*

113. Piers Brendon, for example, writes that Eisenhower's "entire career can be seen as a selfish effort to do nothing that might jeopardize his popularity." *Ike: His Life and Times* (New York, 1986), 13.

114. A common traditionalist view is that Eisenhower, in Harry Truman's words, knew less "about politics than a pig knows about Sunday." Quoted in Peter Lyon, *Eisenhower: Portrait of the Hero* (Boston, 1974), 472. This view has been dispelled largely by the opening of the Ann Whitman files. See, *e.g., The Cycles of American History* (Boston, 1986), 388, in which Arthur M. Schlesinger, Jr., explains that the declassification of Eisenhower's presidential papers convinced him that Ike, far from being politically naïve, was politically astute.

ure to nudge the Cuban Revolution down a less radical path. Also, Eisenhower allowed his dislike of Castro, whom he regarded as a "little Hitler," to stand in the way of his meeting with the Cuban leader.[115] His avoidance of Castro parallels his earlier neglect of McCarthyism.[116] In both cases, the president's "engagement in personalities" (an indicator of ineffective leadership, according to Fred Greenstein) hamstrung opportunities to negotiate pressing problems.[117]

John Foster Dulles should have interceded in the policy dispute between Earl Smith, his assistants, and advisers in the State Department. Moreover, the secretary of state showed minimal interest in Cuba's turmoil until Batista suspended constitutional rights in March, 1958. By reprimanding Smith for his July, 1957, protest of police brutality in Santiago, Cuba, Dulles registered his intention that Smith adopt a tolerant, *laissez faire* attitude toward Batista's excesses and thereby set the tone for Smith's ambassadorship.

Most lamentable, the Eisenhower administration seems to have learned nothing from Castro's triumph. On February 2, 1959, the administration effectively rejected entreaties from Congress, the New York *Times* editorial board, the Council of Foreign Relations, and the U.S. embassies in Peru, Argentina, Paraguay, and Colombia, to treat Latin American strongmen less favorably.[118] Following Richard Nixon's suggestion, the administration opted for cosmetic changes over a fundamentally new U.S. policy: "[Vice President Nixon believes] that we should adopt a policy of the 'abrazo' [hug] for the democratic governments and the 'correct hand shake' for the dictators. . . . This approach may be desirable; this involves essentially a matter of emphasis rather than a real change in policy . . . [which] is not recommended." [119]

Justifying no shift in U.S. policy toward Latin America required a stretch of the imagination (or some sloppy arithmetic). The "Fourth Floor" of the State Department reasoned that there was no need to reformulate U.S. policy because there were "only two or possibly three" Latin American dictatorships remaining

115. Eisenhower wrote the "Little Hitler" comment beneath the "Notations" section of his personal calendar, July 5–6, 1960, Ann C. Whitman Diary, July, 1960 (2) file, box 11, AW Diary Series, in AWF, EL. He grouped McCarthy, like Castro, with Hitler. See Ambrose, *Eisenhower*, 57.

116. Eisenhower waged only an "indirect assault against [McCarthy], one so indirect as to be scarcely discernible, and one which contributed only indirectly—at best—to McCarthy's downfall." Ambrose, *Eisenhower*, 57.

117. Eisenhower liked to think, however, that he did not engage in personalities. See *ibid.*, 82.

118. "U.S. Policy Toward Latin American Dictatorships," May 28, 1958, and "Dictatorships vs. Democracy," February 27, 1958, 1958-Policy file, box 8 (Operation Pan America to Policy file), RRRR, in RG 59, NA.

119. "Attitude of United States and OAS Toward Dictatorial Governments," February 2, 1959, 1959-Dictatorships file, box 12 (Colombia to Dr. Milton Eisenhower, Mexico Trip file), RRRR, in RG 59, NA.

244 / STEVEN F. GROVER

in the region.[120] Even Milton Eisenhower, the president's brother and an expert on Latin America, held this view. By cooperating with Latin American countries ruled by dictators, he explained, "One may hope that a growing understanding of the strength, glory, and basic morality of democracy will enable the people of a harshly ruled country to achieve and maintain democratic institutions of their own design." [121]

Perhaps the Eisenhower administration would have been less oblivious to growing anti-Americanism in Latin America had the State Department used its embassies more effectively. In May, 1958, several months before Batista's fall, Assistant Secretary Rubottom had been advised to informally poll Latin American ambassadors to either the United States or the OAS as to whether U.S. policies toward Latin American dictators needed modifications. Rubottom had written on the top of the memo containing this suggestion, "Let's try to do this. A very imaginative plan." [122] No one, however, ever followed through.[123]

Considering their desire to keep Cuba in the Western camp, Eisenhower and John Foster Dulles' successor, Christian Herter, overreacted to Castro's unlawful nationalization of American-owned property. By demanding that the Cuban government immediately compensate U.S. investors for its expropriation of land they had owned, the State Department showed little or no understanding that Batista had virtually drained Cuba's treasury before he fled the island.[124] Their antagonism toward Cuba's agrarian reform program confirmed in Castro's mind that America was Cuba's enemy and that a friend and arms supplier was needed if he and Cuba were not going to suffer the same fate as Jacobo Arbenz and Guatemala. As such, Eisenhower inadvertently helped nudge Castro closer to the Soviets.

If there is an explanation for the Eisenhower administration's relatively casual attitude toward the rise of Fidel Castro and belief that no shift in Latin American policy was in order, it lies in the fact that everyone—but especially the president, John Foster Dulles, and Allen Dulles—trusted that the CIA could "turn back the clocks" of any Third World nation that gravitated toward communism. To quote Assistant Secretary Rubottom: "The relative success in dealing with the Communist problem in Guatemala tended to blind a little bit in the eyes of all of us . . . not so much to the fact that [Cuba] was a serious problem, but that maybe the problem, if it became an open sore, could be dealt with in some de-

120. *Ibid.*
121. Report from Milton Eisenhower to the President, December 27, 1958, 37, in RG 59, NA.
122. "U.S. Policy Toward Latin American Dictatorships," May 28,1958, in AWF, EL.
123. Personal telephone interview with Richard R. Rubottom, September 16, 1989.
124. Welch, Jr., *Response to Revolution,* 47.

gree like the Guatemalan problem was dealt with." [125] Indeed, on March 17, 1960, Eisenhower authorized a CIA program to overthrow Cuba's Maximum Leader, full knowing that neither the State Department nor the CIA had proven that Castro's regime was Communist-dominated. [126] Just as the Czechoslovakian arms shipments to Guatemala in May, 1954, convinced the Eisenhower administration that communism had entered America's backyard, Castro's signing of a commercial agreement with the USSR in February, 1960, had signaled to the administration that Cuba had fallen prey to communsim.

Although the declassification of Dwight D. Eisenhower's presidential papers reveals that the traditionalist portrait of him as inept and passive oversteps historical truth, the study of those documents pertaining to Cuba weakens the revisionist view that Eisenhower was a decisive and perspicacious leader, especially with respect to foreign affairs. Most conspicuously, Eisenhower's relations with Cuba from 1953 to 1958 corroborates Stephen Rabe's conclusion that the Eisenhower administration prioritized U.S. security over Latin American democracy and bolsters the critique of his presidency as eight years of "great postponement." [127]

125. Quoted in Immerman, *CIA in Guatemala*, 196–97. According to Kermit Roosevelt, the engineer of the CIA ouster of Muhammad Mussadegh in Iran, "Foster Dulles had been so . . . mesmerized by the success I'd had in Iran that he just figured that I could solve any problem anywhere in the world." Quoted in John Ranelagh, *The Agency: The Rise and Decline of the CIA* (New York, 1987), 264. For the impression that Operation SUCCESS made on Eisenhower, see Walter LaFeber, *Inevitable Revolutions: The United States in Central America* (New York, 1984), 264; Ambrose, *Eisenhower*, 196.

126. This Eisenhower-approved plan to aid the anti-Castro underground in Cuba was the fledgling form of Operation Trinidad, which evolved into Operation Zapata, or the Bay of Pigs invasion. John F. Kennedy inherited the CIA plan from Eisenhower.

In mid-March, 1960, Eisenhower initialed a report from Secretary Herter that stated, "Intelligence reports do not substantiate that the Castro government is under the 'control and domination' of International Communism." See Memorandum for the President from Herter, "Status of Possible OAS Action on Cuba," March 17, 1960, Herter March, 1960 (2) file, box 10, Dulles-Herter Series, in AWF, EL.

127. William V. Shannon quoted in Mary S. McAuliffe, "Commentary/Eisenhower, the President," *Journal of American History*, LXVIII (December, 1981), 625.

STEPHEN E. AMBROSE
EPILOGUE
Eisenhower's Legacy

H is place in history was fixed as night fell on the Normandy beaches on June 6, 1944. Hundreds of thousands, indeed millions, of men and women contributed to the success of Operation Overlord, and 200,000 sailors, soldiers, and airmen participated directly on D-Day itself, but the operation will forever be linked to one man, Dwight David Eisenhower. He was the central figure in the preparation, the planning, the training, the deception, the organization, and the execution of the greatest invasion in history. At the decisive moment, he was the commanding general who, standing alone, weighed all the factors, considered all the alternatives, listened to the conflicting views of his senior subordinates, and then made the decision to go.

Ike would object strongly to being thus singled out. "No man alone could have brought about the victory," he said in his Guildhall address on June 12, 1945. "Had I possessed the military skill of a Marlborough, the wisdom of Solomon, the understanding of Lincoln, I still would have been helpless without the loyalty, vision, and generosity of thousands upon thousands of British and Americans." And he insisted that "humility must always be the portion of any man who receives acclaim earned in the blood of his followers and sacrifices of his friends." [1] He was almost fanatical on the subject of teamwork.

Yet every team must have a leader, and Ike was the Allied leader in World War II. His skillful and courageous command of the invasions of northwest Africa, Sicily, Italy, and France, and his bold generalship in the campaign of northwest Europe, were critical, to the point that we can say without qualification that he was indeed the one indispensable man.

So the first legacy we have from Dwight Eisenhower is our freedom.

He made his contribution by working at understanding the art of leadership, and then exercising it. "The only quality that can be developed by studious reflection and practice is the leadership of men," he told his son John, then a cadet at West Point. [2] It was in his first battle command, in November, 1942, during

1. London *Times*, June 13, 1945.
2. Dwight Eisenhower to John Eisenhower, May 12, 1944, in Eisenhower Library, Abilene, Kansas (hereinafter cited as EL).

the invasion of North Africa, that he "realized how inexorably and inescapably strain and tension wear away at the leader's endurance, his judgment and his confidence. The pressure becomes more acute because of the duty of a staff constantly to present to the commander the worst side of an eventuality. In this situation, the commander has to preserve optimism in himself and in his command. Without confidence, enthusiasm and optimism in the command, victory is scarcely obtainable."

He discovered that "optimism and pessimism are infectious and they spread more rapidly from the head downward than in any other direction." For that reason, "I firmly determined that my mannerisms and speech in public would always reflect the cheerful certainty of victory—that any pessimism and discouragement I might ever feel would be reserved for my pillow."[3] He carried through on this resolve through the darkest days of the war; recall that when the Germans launched their surprise offensive in mid-December, 1944, in the Ardennes, everyone around him was downcast, fearful, pessimistic. Ike met his commanders at a squad room in a barracks in Verdun. "The present situation is to be regarded as one of opportunity for us and not of disaster," he ordered. "There will be only cheerful faces at this conference table."[4]

There was a great deal more that went into Eisenhower's success as a leader of men, of course. As he put it on another occasion, the art of leadership is making the right decisions, then getting men to *want* to carry them out. But the words he wrote about his learning experience during the North African invasion are a classic expression of one of the most critical aspects of leadership, perfectly said by a man who knew more about the subject than almost anyone else.

A second Eisenhower legacy was abhorrence of war. It was not that he was immune to its attractions. "There is a real fervor developed throughout the nation that you can feel everywhere you go when war comes," he said at a news conference on the tenth anniversary of D-Day. "There is practically an exhilaration about the affair." But then he quoted his favorite line from Robert E. Lee: "It is well that war is so terrible; if it were not so, we would grow too fond of it." And he pointed out, "I personally have experienced the job of writing letters of condolence by the hundreds, by the thousands, to bereaved mothers and wives. That is a very sobering experience."[5]

3. From the unpublished first draft of Eisenhower's memoirs, in EL. See also the Greenstein essay in this volume.

4. Omar Bradley, *A Soldier's Story* (New York, 1951), 470; Dwight D. Eisenhower, *Crusade in Europe* (Garden City, N.Y., 1948), 350.

5. *Public Papers of the Presidents of the United States: Dwight D. Eisenhower, 1954* (Washington, D.C., 1960–1961), 1074–77.

Many generals are war lovers. One thinks of George Armstrong Custer, or George S. Patton. Dwight Eisenhower was a war hater. The only thing he hated more than war was the Nazi party.

He gave us victory, and he gave us the advice to never approach war lightly or in a spirit of adventure, but prayerfully.

As a politician and statesman, his place in history is a more relative matter.

William Ewald, in *Eisenhower the President,* concludes that "in the fifties, many terrible things that could have happened, didn't. Dwight Eisenhower's presidency gave America eight good years—I believe the best in memory."[6] There were no wars, no riots, no inflation—just peace and prosperity. Most white middle-class and middle-aged Republicans would heartily agree with Ewald. But a black American could point out that among the things that did not happen were progress in civil rights or school desegregation. People concerned about the cold war and the nuclear arms race could point out that no progress was made in reducing tensions or achieving disarmament. People concerned about the Communist menace could point out that no Communist regimes were eliminated, and that in fact communism expanded into Vietnam and Cuba. On these and every issue, in short, there are at least two legitimate points of view. What did not happen brought joy to one man, gloom to another.

For Eisenhower personally, in his eight years as president, there were many disappointments, domestic and foreign. Eisenhower had wanted to achieve unity within the Republican party, on the basis of bringing the Old Guard into the modern world and the mainstream of American politics. In addition, he wanted to develop within the Republican party some young, dynamic, trustworthy, and popular leaders. He never achieved either goal, as evidenced by the 1964 Republican convention, where the Old Guard took control of the party, nominating a candidate and writing a platform that would have delighted Warren Harding, or even William McKinley. Franklin Roosevelt did a much better job of curbing the left wing of the Democratic party than Eisenhower did of curbing the right wing of the Republican party.

Eisenhower wanted to see Senator McCarthy eliminated from national public life, and he wanted it done without making America's record and image on civil liberties issues worse than it already was. But because Eisenhower would not denounce McCarthy by name, or otherwise stand up to the senator from Wisconsin, McCarthy was able to do much damage to civil liberties, the Republican party, numerous individuals, the U.S. Army, and the executive branch before he finally destroyed himself. Eisenhower's only significant contribution

6. William Bragg Ewald, Jr., *Eisenhower the President* (Englewood Cliffs, N.J., 1981), 1.

to McCarthy's downfall was the purely negative act of denying him access to executive records and personnel. Eisenhower's cautious, hesitant approach—or nonapproach—to the McCarthy issue did the president's reputation no good, and much harm.

But although Eisenhower's record on civil rights and civil liberties is more negative than positive, he did leave us with some valuable legacies. He hated having to send American troops into Little Rock in 1957 to enforce court-ordered desegregation, but he did it, and thereby settled the question of whether or not the segregationists could use force to maintain their system. He did not agree with the Court's ruling in *Brown* v. *Topeka,* but he acted on the basis of a deeply held belief. As he explained to his friend Swede Hazlett, "I hold to the basic purpose. There must be respect for the Constitution—which means the Supreme Court's interpretation of the Constitution—or we shall have chaos. We cannot possibly imagine a successful form of government in which every individual citizen would have the right to interpret the Constitution according to his own convictions, beliefs, and prejudices."[7]

His legacy in dealing with McCarthy was executive privilege. Those words appear nowhere in the Constitution, but when McCarthy demanded that aides to the president come before his committee to testify, Eisenhower boldly set a precedent. "Congress has absolutely no right to ask my aides to testify in any way, shape, or form about the advice that they were giving to me at any time on any subject. It is not in the public interest that any conversations or communications, or any documents or reproductions, concerning such advice be disclosed."[8] This was the most sweeping assertion of executive privilege ever uttered. In view of Nixon and Reagan's use of the doctrine, it was not, perhaps, Ike's happiest legacy.

Speaking of Nixon, there were two other legacies from Ike, one of which he used, the other he rejected. The first came at a cabinet meeting in 1954; Ike advised those present, including Nixon, to tape record their telephone conversations. "You know, boys," the president said, "it's a good thing when you're talking to someone you don't trust to get a record made of it. There are some guys I just don't trust in Washington, and I want to have myself protected so that they can't later report that I said something else." The second bit of advice, also at a cabinet meeting, was: "I learned a long time ago, when you get caught, don't try to be cute or cover up. If you do, you will get so entangled you won't know what you're doing."[9]

7. Eisenhower to Swede Hazlett, July 22, 1957, in EL. See also the Kutler essay in this volume.
8. *Public Papers: Eisenhower, 1954,* 483–84.
9. James Hagerty Diary, June 13, 1953, July 16, 1954, in EL.

Eisenhower's legacy also includes a CIA far more active in carrying out covert activities than Harry Truman, who founded the agency, ever envisioned. Ike elevated the CIA into his principal weapon for fighting the cold war. He did so because of his most basic strategic insight: that in the modern age, limited war is unwinnable and nuclear war is unthinkable. But stalemate was unacceptable. So he turned to the CIA, which he used in Iran, Guatemala, the Congo, Cuba, and elsewhere to overthrow unfriendly governments. He also used the FBI for illegal surveillance of the American Communist party. This last was a dangerous precedent. Ike limited FBI black bag operations to the Communist enemy, but his successors, Kennedy, Johnson, and Nixon, went much further in defining the domestic enemy, and soon they were carrying out black bag operations against their political opponents.

One legacy from Ike his successors ignored was the importance of foreign aid. He believed it was the best possible way for the United States to spend its money abroad, far more important than military aid. He was an early and strong advocate of the Marshall Plan, and he wanted to extend the help to Third World countries as well. In 1947 he wrote in his diary words that could well be applied to our relations with the East European nations today: "I personally believe that the best thing we could now do would be to post 5 billion to the credit of the secretary of state and tell him to use it to support democratic movements wherever our vital interests indicate. Money should be used to promote possibilities of self-sustaining economies, not merely to prevent immediate starvation." [10]

He was also sensitive to the plight of the oppressed. When Nixon returned from Africa in 1957 and told the president that Algeria was not ready for independence, Ike replied, "The United States cannot possibly maintain that freedom—independence—liberty—are necessary to us but not to others." [11]

Although he was ready to spend money to help the cause of democracy in the Third World, he wanted to do so at the expense of defense expenditures, not at the expense of a balanced budget. He was the last of our presidents, unfortunately, to insist on balancing the budget. He refused to lower taxes unless expenditures came down.

Further, he was a good steward. He did not sell off the public lands, or open the National Wilderness Areas or the National Parks to commercial or mineral exploitation. He created the Soil Bank program, designed to protect marginal lands from erosion. And in his farewell address, he declared: "We—you and I, and our government—must avoid plundering, for our own ease and con-

10. Eisenhower Diary, September 9, 1947, in EL.
11. Notes, Legislative Leaders Meeting, May 5, 1959, in EL.

venience, the precious resources of tomorrow. We cannot mortage the material assets of our grandchildren without risking the loss also of their political
and spiritual heritage. We want democracy to survive for all generations to
come." [12]

He spoke to the problems of the nineties in other areas, too. When Secretary
of State Herter told him on the telephone in 1959 that the Christian Democrats
in West Germany were secretly opposed to reunification, for fear that the So-
cialists in West Germany would team up with East Germans to vote the Christian Democrats out of power, Ike gave a reply that is, for all lovers of democracy,
perfect: "If they get a true free unification, then they have to take their chances
on politics." [13]

His policy with regard to Eastern Europe and the Soviet Union was to contain them so long as necessary, and wait for change. In 1959 he told congressional
leaders, "Our most realistic policy is holding the line until the Soviets manage
to educate their people. By doing so, they will sow the seeds of destruction of
Communism." He warned that "this will take a long time," but he was sure that
eventually what Thomas Jefferson called "the disease of liberty" would spread
among an educated people. [14]

His greatest successes came in foreign policy, and the related area of national defense spending. By making peace in Korea, and avoiding war thereafter for the
next seven and one-half years, and by holding down, almost single-handedly, the
pace of the arms race, he achieved his major accomplishments. No one knows
how much money he saved the United States, as he rebuffed Congress and the
Pentagon and the JCS and the AEC and the military industrial complex. And no
one knows how many lives he saved by ending the war in Korea and refusing
to enter any others, despite a half-dozen and more virtually unanimous recommendations that he go to war. He made peace, and he kept the peace. Whether
any other man could have led the country through that decade without going to
war cannot be known. What we do know is that Eisenhower did it. Eisenhower boasted, "The United States never lost a soldier or a foot of ground in my
administration. We kept the peace. People asked how it happened—by God, it
didn't just happen, I'll tell you that." [15]

Indeed, it did not just happen. Five times in 1954 virtually the entire NSC,
JCS, and State Department recommended that he intervene in Asia, even using
atomic bombs against China. First, in April, as the Dien Bien Phu situation grew

12. *Public Papers: Eisenhower, 1960,* 1035–40.
13. Memorandum of Conversation, April 4, 1959, Christian Herter Papers, in EL.
14. Legislative Leaders Meeting, May 15, 1959, in EL.
15. Peter Lyon, *Eisenhower: Portrait of the Hero* (Boston, 1974), 851.

critical. Second, in May, on the eve of the fall of Dien Bien Phu. Third, in late June, when the French began leaving the country. Fourth, in September, when the Chinese began shelling Quemoy and Matsu. Fifth, in November, when the Chinese announced they were sentencing downed American pilots to prison terms as spies.

Five times he said no. When the Joint Chiefs proposed a preventive strike against the Soviet Union, in 1954, when America still had a lead in strategic weapons and could "win," Ike thundered: "I want you to carry this question home with you. Gain such a victory, and what do you do with it? Here would be a great area from the Elbe to Vladivostok torn up and destroyed, without government, without its communications, just an area of starvation and disaster. I ask you what would the civilized world do about it? I repeat there is no victory except through our imaginations." [16] Pressed to intervene in Vietnam, Ike again said no. For one reason, "The jungles of Indochina will swallow up division after division of U.S. troops, who, unaccustomed to this kind of warfare, will sustain heavy casualties. Furthermore, the presence of ever more numbers of white men in uniform probably will aggravate rather than assuage Asiatic resentments." For a third reason, "The standing of the United States as the most powerful of the anti-colonial powers is an asset of incalculable value to the Free World. The moral position of the United States is more to be guarded than the Tonkin Delta, indeed than all of Indochina." [17]

It is in the area of defense spending that Ike's legacy has been most ignored, at great risk and expense. More than any other world leader, he spoke directly and eloquently to the cost of the arms race. In the finest speech of his presidency, in 1953 to the American Society of Newspaper Editors, he declared:

> The worst to be feared and the best to be expected [from a continuing arms race] can be simply stated. The worst is atomic war. The best would be this: a life of perpetual fear and tension; a burden of arms draining the wealth and the labor of all peoples. Every gun that is made, every warship launched, every rocket fired, signifies, in the final sense, a theft from those who hunger and are not fed, those who are cold and are not clothed.
>
> This world in arms is not spending money alone. It is spending the sweat of its laborers, the genius of its scientists, the hopes of its children. We pay for a single fighter plane with a half-million bushels of wheat. We pay for a single destroyer with new homes that could have housed more than eight thousand people.
>
> This is not a way of life at all, in any true sense. Under the cloud of threatening war, it is humanity hanging from a cross of iron. [18]

16. Hagerty Diary, June 19, 1954, in EL.
17. From the first draft of Eisenhower's presidential memoirs, in EL.
18. *Public Papers: Eisenhower, 1953,* 179–88.

He believed that a healthy economy was as critical to national defense as a powerful military. "Let us not forget that the armed services are to defend a way of life, not merely land, property, or lives," he told his friend Swede Hazlett. And he gave a warning: "Some day there is going to be a man sitting in my present chair who has not been raised in the military services and who will have little understanding of where slashes in their estimates can be made with little or no damage. If that should happen while we still have the state of tension that now exists in the world, I shudder to think of what could happen in this country." [19]

He showed what he could do in 1957, in the aftermath of the launching of Sputnik. The country was in a panic. The Ford Foundation, the Rockefeller Brothers Fund, the JCS, the Congress, indeed almost all of what would be called the Establishment, clamored for more defense spending. Ike said no. America's defenses were adequate, he said. In so saying, he stood virtually alone—but he was unassailable, because he was who he was. The demands for fallout shelters, for more bombers, for more research and development of missiles and satellites, was nearly irresistible. But General Ike said no, and General Ike assured the American public that they could not achieve security by building more weapons of destruction. He thereby saved his country untold billions of dollars and no one knows how many war scares. Eisenhower's calm, commonsense, deliberate response to Sputnik may have been his finest gift to the nation, if only because he was the only man who could have given it.

It was Eisenhower's view that seeing a first-strike capability was not only immoral but futile. So was the search for a perfect security. "There is no amount of military force that can possibly give you real security," he told a news conference in 1953, "because you wouldn't have that amount unless you felt that there was almost a similar amount that could threaten you somewhere in the world." [20]

He thought the proper strategy was to be able to threaten the Soviets with retaliation, not total destruction. He once told me, "There is nothing in the world those boys in the Kremlin want so bad that they would risk Red Square to get it." He went on to explain—this was in an interview in his office on the Gettysburg College campus—that there was a fundamental difference between his position in 1944 and 1954. In 1944, he said, if he sent out one hundred bombers on a raid, and ninety came back, he had lost that battle, even if the target was destroyed, because he could not afford such losses. But ten years later, as president, if he sent out one hundred bombers and only one came back, he had won that battle, so long as the one dropped its bomb on Red Square. [21]

19. Eisenhower to Hazlett, August 20, 1956, in EL.
20. *Public Papers: Eisenhower, 1953,* 546.
21. Personal interview with Eisenhower.

Sufficiency, not superiority, was what he sought. But his JCS wanted superiority. He told me that when he became president, the Chiefs assured him that if they could hit seventy targets in the Soviet Union with atomic weapons, they would make it impossible for the Red Army to carry on an aggressive war. When he left the Oval Office, eight years later, the number had gone up to seven hundred. By the late sixties, it was approaching seven thousand. He regarded such numbers as "astronomical." He said, "The patterns of target destruction are fantastic. One of these days we are going to realize how ridiculous we have been and at that time we will try to retrench. We are taking council of our fears when we should indoctrinate ourselves that there is such a thing as common sense." He wanted to know, "How many times do we need to kill each Russian?" [22]

Ike was impatient with the argument that a booming armament industry was essential to America's economic health. "We are now scratching around to get money for such things as school construction and road building," he told a 1960 news conference. "There are all sorts of things to be done in this country. I see no reason why the sums which now are going into these sterile, negative mechanisms that we call war munitions shouldn't go into something positive." [23]

All this led up to one of his most famous statements, in his farewell address: "This conjunction of an immense military establishment and a large arms industry is new in the American experience. In the councils of government, we must guard against the acquisition of unwarranted influence, whether sought or unsought, by the military industrial complex. The potential for the disastrous rise of misplaced power exists and will persist." [24]

He was the general who hated war, the president who promoted peace. As a man, he left us with a legacy of love, for life, for people, and for democracy.

Nixon spoke to this point, on the day Ike died. "Everybody liked Ike," he told speechwriter Ray Price, "but the reverse of that was that Ike liked everybody. Ike didn't hate anybody. He would disagree with people, but he never allowed those arguments to get him emotionally involved, as a personal antagonist. He didn't think of people who disagreed with him as being the 'enemy.' He just thought, 'For some strange reason, they don't agree with me.'" Nixon could scarcely believe it, even though he knew it was true. Nixon told Price that the "normal thing" for politicians was to have "strong hatreds." [25]

Eisenhower was a man who took great pride in his triumphs, but whose

22. Ibid.
23. Public Papers: Eisenhower, 1960, 347.
24. Ibid., 1037.
25. Raymond Price, With Nixon (New York, 1977), 61.

immediate and instinctive reaction to victory was to reach out his hand to the defeated, to help them back on their feet—as with the Germans in 1945, or with Bob Taft after the 1952 struggle for the Republican nomination.

He was a man who was entirely trustworthy. His word was his bond. Montgomery captured this best: "He has but to smile at you," Monty said, "and you trust him at once." [26]

This came about, in largest part, because of the respect he had for others. No matter what a man did—be he a common laborer, or a doctor, or a teacher, or an atomic physicist, or a politician, or a businessman, or a preacher—so long as he did his job to the best of his ability and met his responsibilities, Eisenhower respected him.

He expressed this feeling best in a 1947 letter to Swede: "I believe fanatically in the American form of democracy, a system that recognizes and protects the right of the individual and that ascribes to the individual a dignity accruing to him because of his creation in the image of a supreme being." [27]

A small incident from his West Point days captures this attitude. A plebe, rushing down the hall on some fool errand, ran into him. Ike reacted with a bellow of mock indignation and scornfully demanded to know what the young man had done before coming to the Academy. He added, "You look like a barber."

"I was a barber, sir," the plebe answered.

Ike went red with embarrassment. He turned away, and that night told his roommate, "I'm never going to haze another plebe as long as I live. I've just done something that was stupid and unforgivable. I managed to make a man ashamed of the work he did to earn a living." [28]

Because of this attitude of respect for the individual, and thanks to his ability as a writer, Eisenhower was able to say, in a few words, better than any other leader, what was involved in World War II. In a private letter to a friend training a division back in the States in October, 1942, Ike wrote: "The Allied cause is completely bound up with the rights and welfare of the common man. You must make certain that every GI realizes that the privileged life he has led is under direct threat. His right to speak his own mind, to engage in any profession of his own choosing, to belong to any religious denomination, to live in any locality where he can support himself and his family, and to be sure of fair treat-

---

26. Bernard Law Montgomery, *Memoirs* (Cleveland, Ohio, 1958), 484.

27. Eisenhower to Hazlett, July 4, 1947, in EL.

28. Stephen E. Ambrose, *Eisenhower: Soldier, General of the Army, President-Elect* (New York, 1983), 45.

ment when he might be accused of any crime—all of these would disappear if the Nazis win this war." [29]

So his legacy includes common sense, and caution before setting out on mad-cap adventures, and fiscal integrity, and making certain that we hand on to our grandchildren an intact heritage, and a love of democracy, and a respect for the individual, and freedom, and much more.

That legacy also includes a model of how to live one's life. No one could ever come into contact with Dwight Eisenhower without being impressed by all sorts of things—his vitality, that marvelous grin, his intelligence, his self-confidence, his knowledge and experience and accomplishments, his bearing, his intense curiosity, his sense of humor, among many others—but one attribute stood out above them all. It was the pleasure he took in living.

29. Eisenhower to Leonard Gerow, October 10, 1942, in EL.

SELECTED BIBLIOGRAPHY
Compiled by OLGA IVANOVA

PRIMARY SOURCES

DOCUMENT COLLECTIONS

Boyle, Peter. G., ed. *The Churchill-Eisenhower Correspondence, 1953–1955.* Chapel Hill, N.C., 1990.

Franklin, Noble, ed. *Documents on International Affairs, 1955.* London, 1955.

Galambos, Louis, *et al.,* eds. *The Papers of Dwight D. Eisenhower.* Vols. VI–XIII of 13 vols. Baltimore, Md., 1975–89.

Public Papers of the Presidents of the United States: Dwight David Eisenhower, 1953–1961. 8 vols. Washington, D.C., 1960–1961.

Schilcher, Alfons, ed. *Österreich und die Grossmächte: Dokumente zur Österreichischen Aussenpolitik, 1945–1955.* Vienna, 1980.

U.S. Department of State. *Foreign Relations of the United States, 1951.* Vol. III, *European Security and the German Question.* Washington, D.C., 1981. Hereinafter abbreviated *FRUS.*

———. *FRUS, 1952–1954.* Vol. II, *National Security Affairs.* 1984.

———. *FRUS, 1952–1954.* Vol. V, *Western European Security.* 1983.

———. *FRUS, 1952–1954.* Vol. VII, *Germany and Austria,* parts I and II. 1986.

———. *FRUS, 1952–1954.* Vol. VIII, *Eastern Europe; Soviet Union; Eastern Mediterranean.* 1988.

———. *FRUS, 1952–1954.* Vol. XIV, *China and Japan.* 1985.

———. *FRUS, 1955–1957.* Vol. II, *China.* 1986.

———. *FRUS, 1955–1957.* Vol. III, *China.* 1986.

———. *FRUS, 1955–1957.* Vol. IV, *Western European Security and Integration.* 1986.

———. *FRUS, 1955–1957.* Vol. V, *Austrian State Treaty; Summit and Foreign Ministers Meeting. 1955.* 1988.

MEMOIRS, DIARIES, AND LETTERS

Acheson, Dean. *Present at the Creation: My Years at the State Department.* New York, 1969.

Adenauer, Konrad. *Memoirs, 1945–1953.* Chicago, 1956.

Churchill, W. S. *The Hinge of Fate.* Vol. IV of *History of the Second World War.* 6 vols. Boston, 1951.

Colville, John. *The Fringes of Power: 10 Downing Street Diaries, 1939–1955.* New York, 1985.

Eden, Anthony. *The Memoirs of Anthony Eden: Full Circle.* Boston, 1960.

Eisenhower, Dwight D. *At Ease: Stories I Tell to Friends.* Garden City, N.Y., 1967.

————. *Crusade in Europe.* Garden City, N.Y., 1948.

————. *Mandate for Change, 1953–1956.* Garden City, N.Y., 1963.

————. *The White House Years: Waging Peace.* N.Y., 1965.

Eisenhower, John S. D. *Strictly Personal.* Garden City, N.Y., 1974.

————, ed. *Letters to Mamie.* Garden City, N.Y., 1978.

Eisenhower, Milton S. *The President Is Calling.* Garden City, N.Y., 1974.

Ferrell, Robert H., ed. *The Diary of James C. Hagerty: Eisenhower in Mid-Course, 1954–1955.* Bloomington, Ind., 1983.

————, ed. *The Eisenhower Diaries.* New York, 1981.

Griffith, Robert, ed. *Ike's Letters to a Friend, 1941–1958.* Lawrence, Kans., 1984.

Ismay, Lord. *NATO: The First Five Years, 1949–1954.* The Hague, 1954.

Kreisky, Bruno. *Zwischen den Zeiten: Erinnerungen aus fünf Jahrzehnten.* Berlin, 1986.

Monnet, Jean. *Memoirs.* Garden City, N.Y., 1978.

Montgomery, Bernard Law. *Memoirs.* Cleveland, Ohio, 1958.

Nitze, Paul H. *From Hiroshima to Glasnost: At the Center of Decision, A Memoir.* New York, 1989.

Nixon, Richard. *Memoirs.* New York, 1978.

Price, Raymond. *With Nixon.* New York, 1977.

Truman, Harry S. *Years of Trial and Hope.* Garden City, N.Y., 1956.

Urquhart, Brian. *A Life in Peace and War.* London, 1989.

SECONDARY SOURCES

BOOKS

Alteras, Isaac. *Eisenhower and Israel: U.S.-Israeli Relations, 1953–1960.* Gainesville, Fla., 1993.

Ambrose, Stephen E. *Eisenhower: The President.* New York, 1984.

————. *Eisenhower: Soldier, General of the Army, President-Elect, 1890–1952.* New York, 1983.

————. *Eisenhower: Soldier and President.* New York, 1990.

————. *Ike's Spies: Eisenhower and the Espionage Establishment.* Garden City, N.Y., 1981.

————, ed. *The Wisdom of Eisenhower.* New Orleans, 1990.

Anderson, David L. *Trapped by Success: The Eisenhower Administration and Vietnam, 1953–61.* New York, 1991.

Bacque, James. *Other Losses.* Los Angeles, 1991.

Ball, George W. *Diplomacy in a Crowded World: An American Foreign Policy.* Boston, 1976.

Barrow, Deborah J., and Thomas G. Walker. *A Court Divided: The Fifth Circuit Court of Appeals and the Politics of Judicial Reform.* New Haven, Conn., 1988.

Bass, Jack. *Unlikely Heroes.* New York, 1981.

Beschloss, Michael. *Eisenhower: A Centennial Life.* New York, 1990.

Bickel Alexander M. *The Least Dangerous Branch: The Supreme Court at the Bar of Politics.* New York, 1962.

Billings-Yun, Melanie. *Decision Against War: Eisenhower and Dien Bien Phu, 1954.* New York, 1988.

Bischof, Günter, and Stephen E. Ambrose, eds. *Eisenhower and the German P.O.W.s: Facts Against Falsehood.* Baton Rouge, 1992.

Bischof, Günter, and Josef Leidenfrost, eds. *Die bevormundete Nation: Österreich und die Alliierten, 1945–1949.* Innsbruck, 1988.

Black, George. *The Good Neighbor: How the United States Wrote the History of Central America and the Caribbean.* New York, 1988.

Bland, Douglas L. *The Military Committee of the North Atlantic Alliance: A Study of Structure and Strategy.* New York, 1991.

Blumenson, Martin. *Mark Clark.* London, 1984.

Botti, Timothy J. *The Long Wait: The Forging of the Anglo-American Nuclear Alliance, 1945–1958.* New York, 1987.

Brands, H. W., Jr. *Cold Warriors: Eisenhower's Generation and American Foreign Policy.* New York, 1988.

———. *The Specter of Neutralism: The United States and the Emergence of the Third World, 1947–1960.* New York, 1989.

Bremner, Robert H., and Gary W. Reichard, eds. *Reshaping America: Society and Institutions, 1945–1960.* Columbus, Ohio, 1982.

Brendon, Piers. *Ike: His Life and Times.* New York, 1986.

Broadwater, Jeff. *Eisenhower and the Anti-Communist Crusade.* Chapel Hill, N.C., 1992.

Bundy, McGeorge. *Danger and Survival: Choices About the Bomb in the First Fifty Years.* New York, 1988.

Burke, John P., and Fred I. Greenstein. *How Presidents Test Reality: Decisions on Vietnam, 1954 and 1965.* New York, 1989.

Burke, Robert F. *Dwight D. Eisenhower: Hero and Politician.* Boston, 1986.

———. *The Eisenhower Administration and Black Civil Rights.* Knoxville, Tenn., 1984.

Caraley, Demetrios. *The Politics of Military Unification: A Study of Conflict and the Policy Process.* New York, 1966.

Carlton, David. *Anthony Eden.* London, 1981.

Chang, Gordon H. *Friends and Enemies: The United States, China, and the Soviet Union, 1948–1972.* Stanford, Calif., 1990.

Cobb, James C. *The Selling of the South: The Southern Crusade for Industrial Development, 1936–1980.* Baton Rouge, 1982.

Condit, Doris M. *The Test of War, 1950–1953.* Washington, D.C., 1988. Vol. II of *History of the Office of the Secretary of Defense.* 2 vols.

Cook, Blanche W. *The Declassified Eisenhower: A Divided Legacy.* Garden City, N.Y., 1981.

Cook, Don. *Forging the Alliance: The Birth of the NATO Treaty and the Dramatic Transformation of U.S. Foreign Policy Between 1945 and 1950.* New York, 1989.

Cooney, James, et. al. *The Federal Republic of Germany and the United States.* Boulder, Colo., 1984.

Cronin, Audrey K. *Great Power Politics and the Struggle over Austria, 1945–1955.* Ithaca, N.Y., 1986.

Dais, Kenneth S. *Soldier of Democracy.* New York, 1945.

Diggins, John Patrick. *The Proud Decades: America in War and Peace, 1941–1960*. New York, 1988.

Divine, Robert A. *Eisenhower and the Cold War*. New York, 1981.

Dockrill, Michael, and John W. Young, eds. *British Foreign Policy, 1945–56*. London, 1989.

Dockrill, Saki. *Britain's Policy for West German Rearmament, 1950–1955*. New York, 1991.

Dodds–Parker, Douglas. *Setting Europe Ablaze*. Windlesham, Surrey, 1983.

Donovan, Robert J. *Eisenhower: The Inside Story*. New York, 1956.

Dulles, Foster R. *American Policy Toward Communist China, 1949–1969*. New York, 1972.

Eisenhower, David. *Eisenhower*. New York, 1986.

Enthoven, Alain C., and K. W. Smith. *How Much Is Enough: Shaping the Defense Program, 1961–1969*. New York, 1971.

Ewald, William B., Jr. *Eisenhower the President*. Englewood Cliffs, N.J., 1981.

Facts on File Yearbook, 1956. New York, 1957.

Foerster, Schuyler, and Edward N. Wright, eds. *American Defense Policy*. Baltimore, Md., 1990.

Foot, Rosemary. *A Substitute for Victory: The Politics of Peacemaking at the Korean Armistice Talks*. Ithaca, N.Y., 1990.

Fourcade, Marie-Madeleine. *Noah's Ark*. London, 1973.

Gaddis, John L. *The Long Peace: Inquiries into the History of the Cold War*. New York, 1987.

———. *Strategies of Containment: A Critical Appraisal of Postwar American National Security Policy*. New York, 1982.

George, Alexander, *et al.*, eds. *U.S.-Soviet Security Cooperation: Achievements, Failures, Lessons*. New York, 1988.

Gilbert, Martin. *Never Despair*. Vol. VIII of Randolph S. Churchill and Martin Gilbert, *Winston S. Churchill*. 8 vols. Boston, 1988.

Glad, Betty. *Jimmy Carter: In Search of the Great White House*. New York, 1980.

Goldfield, David R. *Black, White, and Southern: Race Relations and Southern Culture, 1940 to the Present*. Baton Rouge, 1990.

Greenstein, Fred I. *The Hidden-Hand Presidency: Eisenhower as Leader*. New York, 1982.

———, ed. *Leadership in the Modern Presidency*. Cambridge, Mass., 1988.

Halberstam, David. *The Fifties*. New York, 1993.

Hanrieder, Wolfram F. *Germany, America, Europe: Forty Years of German Foreign Policy*. New Haven, Conn., 1989.

Heller, Francis H., and John R. Gillingham, eds. *NATO: The Founding of the Alliance and the Integration of Europe*. New York, 1992.

Hewlett, Sylvia Ann. *A Lesser Life: The Myth of Women's Liberation in America*. New York, 1986.

Hoopes, Townsend, and Douglas Brinkley. *Driven Patriot: The Life and Times of James Forrestal*. New York, 1992.

Horne, Alastair. *Macmillan*. Vol. 1 of 2 vols. London, 1988.

Howard, Michael. *British Intelligence in the Second World War*. Vol. V. London, 1990.

Huck, Arthur. *The Security of China: Chinese Approaches to Problems of War and Strategy*. New York, 1970.

Hunt, Michael H. *Ideology and U.S. Foreign Policy.* New Haven, Conn., 1987.

Immerman, Richard H. *The CIA in Guatemala: The Foreign Policy of Intervention.* Austin, Tex. 1982.

————, ed. *John Foster Dulles and the Diplomacy of the Cold War.* Princeton, N.J., 1990.

Ireland, Timothy P. *Creating the Entangling Alliance: The Origins of the North Atlantic Treaty Organization.* Westport, Conn., 1981.

Isaacs, Harold R. *The New World of Negro Americans.* New York, 1964.

Isaacson, Walter, and Evan Thomas. *The Wise Men: Six Friends and the World They Made, Acheson, Bohlen, Harriman, Kennan, Lovett, McCloy.* New York, 1986.

Jackson, Kenneth T. *Crabgrass Frontier: The Suburbanization of the United States.* New York, 1985.

Jacoway, Elizabeth, and David R. Colburn, eds. *Southern Businessmen and School Desegregation.* Baton Rouge, 1982.

Jordan, Robert S. *Alliance Strategy and Navies: The Evolution and Scope of NATO's Maritime Dimension.* New York, 1991.

————. *Political Leadership in NATO: A Study in Multinational Diplomacy.* Boulder, Colo., 1979.

————, ed. *Generals in International Politics: NATO's Supreme Allied Commander, Europe.* Lexington, Ky., 1987.

Kaplan, Fred. *The Wizards of Armageddon.* New York, 1983.

Kaplan, Lawrence S. *NATO and the United States: The Enduring Alliance.* Boston, 1988.

————. *A Community of Interests: NATO and the Military Assistance Program, 1948–1951.* Washington, D.C., 1980.

————, ed. *American Historians and the Atlantic Alliance.* Kent, Ohio, 1991.

Kaufman, Burton I. *Trade and Aid: Eisenhower's Foreign Economic Policy, 1953–1961.* Baltimore, Md., 1982.

Kennan, George. *Russia, the Atom and the West.* New York, 1957.

Kinnard, Douglas. *President Eisenhower and Strategy Management.* Lexington, Ky., 1977.

Kluger, Richard. *Simple Justice.* New York, 1976.

Krieg, Joan P., ed. *Dwight D. Eisenhower: Soldier, President, Statesman.* Westport, Conn., 1987.

Kunz, Diane B. *The Economic Diplomacy of the Suez Crisis.* Chapel Hill, N.C., 1991.

Kutler, Stanley I. *The Wars of Watergate.* New York, 1990.

Langhorne, Richard, ed. *Diplomacy and Intelligence During the Second World War.* Cambridge, 1985.

Larrabee, Eric F. *Commander in Chief: Franklin Delano Roosevelt, His Lieutenants, and Their War.* New York, 1987.

Larson, Arthur. *A Republican Looks at His Party.* New York, 1956.

Lee, R. Alton. *Eisenhower and Landrum-Griffin: A Study in Labor-Management Politics.* Lexington, Ky., 1990.

————, ed. *Dwight D. Eisenhower: A Bibliography of His Times and Presidency.* Wilmington, Del., 1991.

Leffler, Melvyn P. *A Preponderance of Power: National Security, the Truman Administration, and the Cold War.* Stanford, Calif., 1992.

Legge, J. Michael. *Theatre Nuclear Weapons and the NATO Strategy of Flexible Response* (R-292264-FF) (Santa Monica, Calif.: RAND, April 1983).

Leonhard, Alan T., ed. *Neutrality: Changing Concepts and Practices.* Lanham, Md., 1988.

Light, Margot. *The Soviet Theory of International Relations.* New York, 1988.

Lin, Chong–pin. *China's Nuclear Weapons Strategy: Tradition Within Evolution.* Lexington, Ky., 1988.

Lodge, Henry C. *As It Was: An Inside View of Politics and Power in the '50s and '60s.* New York, 1976.

Lyon, Peter. *Eisenhower: Portrait of the Hero.* Boston, 1974.

Maier, Charles S., and Günter Bischof, eds. *The Marshall Plan and Germany.* New York, 1991.

Mansbridge, Jane J. *Why We Lost the ERA.* Chicago, 1986.

Marks, Frederick W., III. *Power and Peace: The Diplomacy of John Foster Dulles.* Westport, Conn., 1993.

May, Ernest R., ed. *American Cold War Strategy: NSC–68.* Boston, 1993.

McCann, Kevin. *Man from Abilene.* Garden City, N.Y., 1952.

Medhurst, Martin J. *Dwight D. Eisenhower: Strategic Communicator.* Westport, Conn., 1992.

Medvedev, Roy. *All Stalin's Men.* London, 1983.

Melanson, Richard A., and David Mayers, eds. *Reevaluating Eisenhower: American Foreign Policy in the Fifties.* Urbana, Ill., 1987.

Merrill, Dennis. *Bread and the Ballot: The United States and India's Economic Development, 1947–1963.* Chapel Hill, N.C., 1989.

Mosley, Philips E. *The Kremlin and World Politics: Studies in Soviet Policy and Action.* New York, 1960.

Ninkovich, Frank A. *Germany and the United States: The Transformation of the German Question Since 1945.* Boston, 1988.

Nove, Alec. *Stalinism and After: The Road to Gorbachev.* 3rd ed. Boston, 1989.

O'Brien, Terence. *Chasing After Danger.* London, 1990.

O'Neill, William L. *American High: The Years of Confidence, 1945–1960.* New York, 1986.

Osgood, Robert E. *NATO: The Entangling Alliance.* Chicago, 1962.

Pach, Chester J., Jr., *Arming the Free World: The Origins of the United States Military Assistance Program, 1945–1950.* Chapel Hill, N.C., 1991.

Pach, Chester J., Jr., and Elmo Richardson. *The Presidency of Dwight D. Eisenhower.* Lawrence, Kans., 1991.

Paret, Peter, ed. *Makers of Modern Strategy.* Princeton, N.J., 1986.

Parmet, Herbert S. *Eisenhower and the American Crusades.* New York, 1972.

Peltason J. W. *Fifty-eight Lonely Men: Southern Federal Judges and School Desegregation.* New York, 1961.

Pérez, Louis A., Jr. *Cuba Between Reform and Revolution.* New York, 1988.

Perret, Geoffrey. *There's a War to Be Won: The United States Army in World War II.* New York, 1991.

Persico, Joseph E. *Casey.* New York, 1990.

Pogue, Forrest. *George C. Marshall: Organizer of Victory, 1943–1945.* New York, 1973.

Poole, Walter S. *The Joint Chiefs of Staff and National Policy, 1950–1952.* Vol. IV of *The History of the Joint Chiefs of Staff.* 5 vols. Wilmington, Del., 1980.

Prados, John. *Presidents' Secret Wars: CIA and Pentagon Covert Operations Since World War II.* New York, 1986.

Rabe, Stephen G. *Eisenhower and Latin America: The Foreign Policy of Anticommunism.* Chapel Hill, N.C., 1988.

Rauchensteiner, Manfried. *Der Sonderfall: Die Besatzungszeit in Österreich 1945 bis 1955.* Graz, 1979.

Rearden, Steven L. *The Formative Years, 1947–1950.* Washington, D.C., 1984. Vol. I of *History of the Office of the Secretary of Defense.* 2 vols.

Reichard, Gary W. *Politics as Usual: The Age of Truman and Eisenhower.* Arlington Heights, Ill., 1988.

Richardson, James. *Germany and the Atlantic Alliance: The Interaction of Strategy and Politics.* Cambridge, Mass., 1966.

Riesman, David, *et. al. The Lonely Crowd: A Study of the Changing National Character.* New Haven, Conn., 1950.

Riste, Olav, ed. *Western Security: The Formative Years, European and Atlantic Defence, 1947–1953.* New York, 1985.

Rostow, Walt W. *Europe After Stalin: Eisenhower's Three Decisions of March 11, 1953.* Austin, Texas, 1982.

———. *The United States in the World Arena: An Essay in Recent History.* New York, 1960.

Ruddy, Michael. *The Cautious Diplomat: Charles E. Bohlen and the Soviet Union, 1929–1969.* Kent, Ohio, 1986.

Rupieper, Hermann-Josef. *Der besetzte Verbündete: Die amerikanische Deutschlandpolitik, 1949–1955.* Opladen, 1991.

Sagan, Scott D. *Moving Targets: Nuclear Strategy and National Security.* Princeton, N.J., 1989.

Saulnier, Raymond J. *Constructive Years: The U.S. Economy Under Eisenhower.* Lanham, Md., 1991.

Schwartz, David N. *NATO's Nuclear Dilemmas.* Washington, D.C., 1983.

Schwartz, Thomas A. *America's Germany: John J. McCloy and the Federal Republic of Germany.* Cambridge, Mass., 1991.

Seldon, Anthony. *Churchill's Indian Summer: The Conservative Government, 1951–55.* London, 1981.

Shoemaker, Christopher C. *The NSC Staff: Counseling the Council.* Boulder, Colo., 1991.

Sloan, John. *Eisenhower and the Management of Prosperity.* Lawrence, Kans., 1991.

Smith, Arthur L. *Die 'vermisste Million': Zum Schicksal deutscher Kriegsgefangener nach dem Zweiten Weltkrieg.* Munich, 1992.

Smith, Jean Edward. *Lucius D. Clay: An American Life.* New York, 1990.

Smith, Wayne. *The Closest of Enemies: A Personal and Diplomatic Account of U.S.-Cuban Relations Since 1957.* New York, 1987.

Snow, Edgar. *Red Star Over China.* New York, 1968.

Steininger, Rolf, et al., eds. *Die doppelte Eindämmung: Europäische Sicherheit und die Deutsche Frage in den Fünfzigern.* Munich, 1993.

————. *The German Question: The Stalin Note of 1952 and the Problem of Reunification.* New York, 1990.

Stourzh, Gerald. *Geschichte des Staatsvertraages, 1945–1955: Österreichs Weg zur Neutralität.* 3rd ed. Graz, 1985.

Stromseth, Jane E. *The Origins of Flexible Response: NATO's Debate over Strategy in the 1960s.* London, 1988.

Szulc, Tad. *Fidel: A Critical Portrait.* New York, 1987.

Thompson, Kenneth W., ed. *The Eisenhower Presidency: Eleven Intimate Perspectives of Dwight D. Eisenhower.* Lanham, Md., 1984.

Thoss, Bruno, and Hans-Erich Volkmann, eds. *Zwischen Kaltem Krieg und Entspannung: Sicherheits–und Deutschlandpolitik der Bundesrepublik im Mächtesystem der Jahre, 1953–1956.* Boppard am Rhein, 1988.

Trachtenberg, Marc. *History and Strategy.* Princeton, N.J., 1991.

Troy, Thomas F. *Donovan and the CIA: A History of the Establishment of the Central Intelligence Agency.* Frederick, Md., 1981.

Ulam, Adam. *Expansion and Coexistence: The History of Soviet Foreign Policy, 1917–67.* New York, 1968.

Wampler, Robert A. *NATO Strategic Planning and Nuclear Weapons, 1950–1957.* College Park, Md., 1990.

Warshaw, Shirley Anne, ed. *The Eisenhower Presidency.* Westport, Conn., 1992.

Welch, Richard E., Jr. *Response to Revolution: The United States and the Cuban Revolution, 1959–1961.* Chapel Hill, N.C., 1985.

Whitfield, Stephen J. *The Culture of the Cold War.* Baltimore, 1991.

Wilkinson, J. Harvie, III. *From Brown to Bakke: The Supreme Court and School Integration, 1954–1978.* New York, 1979.

Winkler, Allan M. *Modern America: The United States from World War II to the Present.* New York, 1985.

Woloch, Nancy. *Women and the American Experience.* New York, 1984.

ARTICLES

Bischof, Günter. "The Anglo-American Powers and Austrian Neutrality, 1953–1955." *Mitteilungen des Österreichischen Staatsarchivs,* XLII (1992), 368–93.

Blumenson, Martin. "Eisenhower Then and Now: Fireside Reflections." *Parameters,* XXI (Summer, 1991), 22–34.

Brands, H. W. "The Age of Vulnerability: Eisenhower and the National Insecurity State." *American Historical Review,* XCIV (October, 1989), 963–89.

Brinkley, Alan. "A President for Certain Seasons." *Wilson Quarterly,* XIV (1990).

Burke, Robert F. "Dwight D. Eisenhower and Civil Rights: Reflection on a Portrait in Caution." *Kansas History,* XIII (1990), 178–90.

Chang, Gordon H. "To the Nuclear War Brink: Eisenhower, Dulles, and the Quemoy-Matsu Crisis." *International Security,* XII (1988), 96–122.

Divine, Robert A. "Vietnam Reconsidered." *Diplomatic History,* XII (Winter, 1988), 79–93.

Dockrill, Saki. "The Evolution of Britain's Policy Towards a European Army, 1950–1954." *Journal of Strategic Studies,* XII (1989), 38–62.

Duchin, Brian R. "The 'Agonizing Reappraisal': Eisenhower, Dulles, and the European Defense Community." *Diplomatic History,* XVI (Spring, 1992), 201–21.

Duffield, John S. "The Evolution of NATO's Strategy of Flexible Response: A Reinterpretation." *Security Studies,* I (1991), 132–56.

Evangelista, Matthew. "Cooperation Theory and Disarmament Negotiations in the 1950s." *World Politics,* XLII (1990), 502–28.

Fish, Steven. "After Stalin's Death: The Anglo-American Debate Over a New Cold War." *Diplomatic History,* X (1986), 334–36.

Gaddis, John L. "The Emerging Post-Revisionist Synthesis on the Origins of the Cold War." *Diplomatic History,* VII (1983), 171–90.

Greenstein, Fred I. "Eisenhower as an Activist President: A New Look at New Evidence." *Political Science Quarterly,* LXXXIV (1979–80), 575–99.

Griffith, Robert. "Dwight D. Eisenhower and the Corporate Commonwealth." *American Historical Review,* LXXXVII (1982), 87–122.

Hershberg, James G. "German Rearmament and American Diplomacy, 1953–1955." *Diplomatic History,* XVI (Fall, 1992), 511–51.

Holt, Daniel F. "An Unlikely Partnership and Service: Dwight D. Eisenhower, Mark Clark, and the Philippines." *Kansas History,* XIII (1990), 149–65.

Hoxie, R. Gordon. "Dwight David Eisenhower: Bicentennial Considerations." *Presidential Studies Quarterly,* XX (Spring, 1990), 253–64.

Immerman, Richard H. "Confessions of an Eisenhower Revisionist: An Agonizing Reappraisal." *Diplomatic History,* XIV (Summer, 1990), 319–42.

———. "The United States and the Geneva Conference of 1954: A New Look." *Diplomatic History,* XIV (Winter, 1990), 43–66.

Kempton, Murray. "The Underestimation of Dwight D. Eisenhower." *Esquire* (September, 1968), 108–109, 156.

Kingseed, Cole C. "Eisenhower's Prewar Anonymity: Myth or Reality?" *Parameters,* XXI (Autumn, 1991), 87–98.

Larson, Deborah Welch. "Crisis Prevention and the Austrian State Treaty." *International Organization,* XLI (1987), 35–39.

Lukacs, John. "Ike, Winston, and the Russians." *New York Times Book Review,* February 10, 1991, pp. 3, 26–27.

Luxenberg, Alan H. "Did Eisenhower Push Castro into the Arms of the Soviets?" *Journal of Interamerican Studies and World Affairs,* XXX (1988).

Mastny, Vojtech. "Kremlin Politics and the Austrian Settlement." *Problems of Communism*, XXXI (1982), 37–51.

May, Ernest R. "The American Commitment to Germany, 1949–1955." *Diplomatic History*, XIII (Fall, 1989), 431–60.

McMahon, Robert J. "Eisenhower and Third World Nationalism: A Critique of the Revisionists." *Political Science Quarterly*, CI (1986), 453–73.

Metz, Steven. "Eisenhower and the Planning of American Grand Strategy." *Journal of Strategic Studies*, XIV (1991), 49–71.

Moore, William H. "Do We 'Like Ike'?" *Kansas History*, XIII (1991), 190–97.

Nelson, Anna K. "President Truman and the Evolution of the National Security Council." *Journal of American History*, LXXII (September, 1985), 360–78.

———. "The 'Top of Policy Hill': President Eisenhower and the National Security Council." *Diplomatic History*, VII (Fall, 1983), 307–26.

Pruessen, Ronald W. "Beyond the Cold War—Again: 1955 and the 1990s." *Political Science Quarterly*, CVIII (1993), 59–84.

Quester, George H. "Was Eisenhower a Genius?" *International Security*, III (1979), 159–79.

Rabe, Stephen G. "Eisenhower Revisionism: A Decade of Scholarship." *Diplomatic History*, XVII (Winter, 1993), 97–115.

Reichard, Gary. "Seeing Red: Eisenhower, the Republicans, and the Anticommunist Consensus." *Reviews in American History*, XXI (1993), 482–87.

Rosenberg, David A. "The Origins of Overkill: Nuclear Weapons and American Strategy, 1945–1960." *International Security*, VII (Spring, 1983), 3–71.

Spaulding, Robert Mark, Jr. "Eisenhower and Export Control Policy, 1953–1955." *Diplomatic History*, XVII (Spring, 1993), 223–49.

Stourzh, Gerald. "Towards the Settlement of 1955: The Austrian State Treaty Negotiations and the Origins of Austrian Neutrality." *Austrian History Yearbook*, XVII–XVIII (1981–82).

UNPUBLISHED MATERIAL

Bischof, Günter. "Before the Break: The Relationship Between Eisenhower and McCarthy, 1952–1953." M.A. thesis, University of New Orleans, 1980.

———. "Between Responsibility and Rehabilitation: Austria in International Politics, 1940–1950." Ph.D. dissertation, Harvard University, 1989.

Dockrill, Saki. "Eisenhower's New Look: A Maximum Deterrent at a Bearable Cost—A Reappraisal," in *Economic and National Dimensions in Strategy*, ed. Michael Handel (Carlisle Barracks, Pa., forthcoming).

Goldlust, Ellen. "The Civil Rights Wars: The Rise and Fall of Southern Resistance to Desegregation, 1954–1964." M.A. thesis, University of Wisconsin, 1991.

Wampler, Robert A. "Ambiguous Legacy: The United States, Great Britain, and the Foundations of NATO Strategy, 1948–1957." Ph.D. dissertation, Harvard University, 1991.

Yoo, John Choon. "Three Faces of Hegemony: Eisenhower, Kennedy, Johnson, and the Multilateral Force." Senior honors thesis, Harvard University, 1989.

NOTES ON CONTRIBUTORS

Stephen E. Ambrose holds a Ph.D. from the University of Wisconsin, Madison, and is the Boyd Professor of History and the director of the Eisenhower Center at the University of New Orleans, where he has taught since 1960. He has spent a lifetime studying the career of General and President Eisenhower: he served as co-editor of five volumes of his wartime papers and has written *The Supreme Commander* (1970), *Ike's Spies* (1981), *Eisenhower,* a two-volume biography (1983–1985), and co-edited *Eisenhower and the German POWs* (1992). He has also written a three-volume biography of Richard Nixon and has just published *D-Day, June 6, 1944: The Climactic Battle of World War II.*

Günter Bischof holds a Ph.D. from Harvard University and is associate professor of history and the associate director of the Eisenhower Center at the University of New Orleans. He taught as a guest lecturer at the Amerika-Institut of the University of Munich (1992-94). He has co-edited *Die bevormundete Nation* (1988), *The Marshall Plan and Germany* (1989), *Eisenhower and the German POWs* (1992), and *Die doppelte Eindämmung* (1993). He also serves as co-editor of *Contemporary Austrian Studies* and is completing a manuscript entitled "Austria in the First Cold War, 1945–1955."

H. W. Brands, Jr., holds a Ph.D. from the University of Texas, Austin, and is a professor of history at Texas A&M University. He is author of *Cold Warriors: Eisenhower's Generation and American Foreign Policy* (1988), *The Specter of Neutralism: The United States and the Emergence of the Third World, 1947–1960* (1989), *Inside the Cold War: Loy Henderson and the Rise of American Empire* (1991), *Bound to Empire: The United States and the Philippines* (1992), and *The Devil We Knew: Americans and the Cold War* (1993). He has also published articles in all the leading American journals and was chosen Stuart L. Bernath Memorial Lecturer by the Society for Historians of American Foreign Relations.

Gordon Chang holds a Ph.D. in modern Chinese and American history from Stanford University. He was an associate professor of history at the University of California, Irvine, and is now teaching at Stanford, where he is also a fellow at the Center for International Security and Arms Control. He is author of the prize-winning *Friends and Enemies: The United States, China, and the Soviet Union, 1948–1972* (1990), and has also published articles on the diplomacy of the Eisenhower era in the *Journal of American History* and *International Security.* Based on new primary sources from Chinese archives, "The Absence of War in the U.S.-China Confrontation over Quemoy and Matsu in 1954–1955," *American Historical Review* (December, 1993), is Chang's latest article, written with He Di.

M. R. D. Foot studied at Oxford University and was a British army officer from 1939 to 1945, taking part in D-Day planning and serving (far under Eisenhower) in the Special Air Service Brigade in 1944. For six years he was professor of modern history at Manchester University. He is author of *SOE in France* (1966), *Resistance* (1976), and *SOE—An Outline History* (1984), among others. He has been a frequent visiting lecturer at the Eisenhower Center at the University of New Orleans.

Andrew J. Goodpaster, General U.S. Army (Ret.), was staff secretary and liaison officer to President Eisenhower from 1954 until 1961. He was graduated from the United States Military Academy at West Point in 1939. He commanded an Engineer Combat Battalion in North Africa and Italy during World War II, and later served in the Operations Division of the War Department and on the Joint War Plans Committee. In 1950 he graduated with a Ph.D. in international relations from Princeton University. Subsequently, he served in Supreme Headquarters Allied Powers Europe; as commander of a U.S. division in Germany; as assistant chairman, Joint Chiefs of Staff; as director of the Joint Staff; as commander of the National War College; as deputy commander of U.S. forces in Vietnam; as commander-in-chief, United States European Command and supreme Allied commander, Europe. He also served as the 51st superintendent of the U.S. Military Academy (1977–81). He advised President Nixon and Vice-President Rockefeller on foreign policy and international security affairs. He published *For the Common Defense* (1977) and was a senior fellow at the Woodrow Wilson International Center for Scholars, Smithsonian Institution. He currently serves as co-chairman on the Atlantic Council of the United States, and as chairman of the George C. Marshall Foundation.

Fred I. Greenstein holds a Ph.D. from Yale University and is a professor in the Princeton University Department of Politics and director of the Woodrow Wilson School Research Program in Leadership Studies. In 1979 and 1980 he was research professor in the Miller Center of Public Affairs at the University of Virginia. He is author of numerous books and textbooks and co-editor of the eight-volume *Handbook of Political Science* (1975). Among his books dealing with the Eisenhower presidency are *The Hidden-Hand Presidency: Eisenhower as Leader* (1982) and, with John P. Burke, the prize-winning *How Presidents Test Reality: Decisions on Vietnam, 1954 and 1965* (1989).

Steven F. Grover holds an A.B. from Harvard University, a J.D. from the University of Texas, Austin, and an LL.M. from Tulane University. He graduated magna cum laude from Harvard with his thesis on Eisenhower and Cuba (directed by G. Bischof). He has published articles in the *Texas Law Review* and the *Journal of Martime Law and Commerce*. He has traveled to Castro's Cuba twice as a free-lance journalist for the Dallas *Morning News.*

Olga Ivanova, born 1968 in Moscow, graduated with a B.A. from the Moscow State Institute of International Relations. From 1991 to 1993 she studied history as an Eisenhower Center junior fellow at the University of New Orleans and graduated with an M.A. thesis, entitled "Stalin's German Policy and the 'Missed Opportunities' of 1952," directed by G. Bischof and S. E. Ambrose.

Stanley I. Kutler is the E. Gordon Fox Professor of American Institutions and professor of law at the University of Wisconsin, Madison, where he has taught since 1964. He is the founder and editor of *Reviews in American History,* a journal that has been widely praised as the standard for book reviewing. He is the author or editor of more than a dozen books, including *The American Inquisition: Justice and Injustice in the Cold War* (1983) and *The Wars of Watergate: The Last Crisis of Richard Nixon* (1990). He is a winner of the Silver Gavel Award of the American Bar Association for his work on political trials.

Anna Kasten Nelson holds a Ph.D. in history from George Washington University and is an adjunct professor in history at The American University. She has also taught at Tulane University. A specialist on nineteenth-century American diplomatic history, she is also an expert on the early National Security Council under Truman and Eisenhower and has published articles on it in *Diplomatic History, Political Science Quarterly,* and *Reviews in American History,* as well as in *The Illusion of Presidential Government,* edited by Heclo and Salamon.

William L. O'Neill holds a Ph.D. from the University of California, Berkeley, and is a professor of history at Rutgers University, where he has taught since 1971. He has written and edited more than a dozen books. Best known among them are *Feminism in America* (rev. ed., 1989), *Coming Apart: An Informal History of America in the 1960s* (1971), *American High: The Years of Confidence, 1945–1960* (1986), and *A Democracy at War: America's Fight at Home and Abroad in World War II* (1993).

Forrest C. Pogue holds a Ph.D. from Clark University and studied in Paris before World War II. The dean of American military historians, he is the author of the unsurpassed *The Supreme Command* (1954), co-author of *The Meaning of Yalta* (1956), as well as the monumental four-volume official biography of George

C. Marshall. The final volume, *George C. Marshall: Statesman, 1945–1949*, appeared in 1987. For many years he acted as the executive director of the George C. Marshall Research Foundation and was the director of the Dwight D. Eisenhower Institute for Historical Research at the Smithsonian Institution. He has now retired to his native Kentucky.

Thomas A. Schwartz holds a Ph.D. from Harvard University and is an associate professor of history at Vanderbilt University. In 1993 to 1994 he was a fellow at the German Historical Institute in Washington, D.C. He is the author of the prize-winning *America's Germany: John J. McCloy and the Federal Republic of Germany* (1992), which was recently translated into German. He is currently at work on a study of America's alliance with postwar Germany, focusing especially on the Eisenhower years and the early 1960s.

Thomas M. Sisk is currently a Ph.D. candidate in the Strategic Studies Program at Temple University, where he works with David Rosenberg and Richard Immerman. He graduated with distinction from the University of New Orleans with his M.A. thesis "Forging the Weapon: Eisenhower as NATO's Supreme Commander, Europe, 1950–1952," directed by G. Bischof.

Robert A. Wampler holds a Ph.D. from Harvard University and is presently a visiting fellow and director of the U.S.-Japanese Relations Project at the National Security Archives in Washington, D.C. He was also a fellow at the multinational Nuclear History Project. He is completing a book manuscript entitled "NATO and Nuclear Weapons, 1950–1957," and has published several articles on the United States and the origins of NATO strategy. He is presently assisting retired ambassador Gerard C. Smith and former secretary of defense Robert McNamara in the preparation of their memoirs.

INDEX